OLIVIA M. STONE

TE ___IFE
AND ITS SIX SATELLITES

OR

The Canary Islands Past and Present

VOLUME II

Elibron Classics
www.elibron.com

Elibron Classics series.

© 2005 Adamant Media Corporation.

ISBN 1-4021-4510-1 (paperback)
ISBN 1-4212-9379-X (hardcover)

This Elibron Classics Replica Edition is an unabridged facsimile
of the edition published in 1887 by Marcus Ward & Co., Limited,
London.

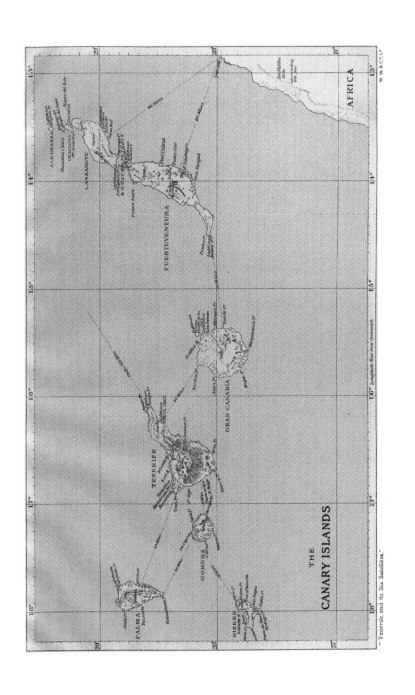

THE
CANARY ISLANDS

AFRICA

"Tenerife and its Six Satellites."

Frontispiece.]   BARRANCO DE LA VIRGEN, GRAN CANARIA.   [*Page* 225.

TENERIFE
AND ITS SIX SATELLITES

OR

The Canary Islands Past and Present

BY

OLIVIA M. STONE

AUTHOR OF "NORWAY IN JUNE"

*WITH MAPS AND ILLUSTRATIONS FROM PHOTOGRAPHS TAKEN BY
J. HARRIS STONE, M.A., F.L.S., F.C.S., BARRISTER-AT-LAW*

HOW WE RODE IN LANZAROTE (*page* 321)

IN TWO VOLUMES

VOL. II.

GRAN CANARIA—LANZAROTE—FUERTEVENTURA

London:
MARCUS WARD & CO., LIMITED
ORIEL HOUSE, FARRINGDON STREET, E.C.
1887

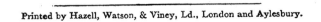
Printed by Hazell, Watson, & Viney, Ld., London and Aylesbury.

CONTENTS.

———◆———

APPENDICES.

LIST OF ILLUSTRATIONS.

MAPS.

ILLUSTRATIONS.

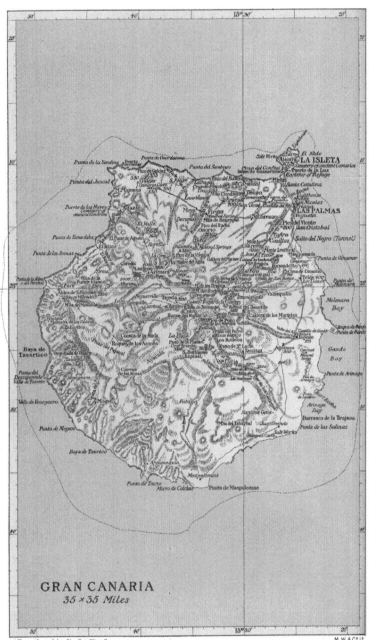

Punta de la Sardina
Punta del Juncal
Puerto de las Nieves
Punta de Toma daba
Punta de la Arenas
Punta de las Nieves

Agaete
El Puente Agüete
El Risco
Tirma
Aldea de S.Nicolas
Mesa del Medio día
Tasartico

Baya de
Tasartico

Punta del
Descansadero
Valle de Tasarte
Valle de Venezuela

Punta de Mogan

Baya de Taurico

Punta de Tauro
Morro de Colchas

Puerto de Guadalume
Punta del Sombrero
Salt Works
LA ISLETA
Faro El Nido
Isleta
Puerto de la Luz
Harbour of Refuge
Santa Catalina
Lighthouse
S. Nicolas
LAS PALMAS
Vegueta
San Cristobal
Salto del Negro (Tunnel)
Punta de Ginamar
Telde
Punta de Guaman

Melenara
Bay
Roque de Baxle
Punta de Gando
Gando
Bay
Punta de Arinaga

Arinaga
Bay
Barranco de la Tirajana
Punta de las Salinas

Salt Works

Maspalomas
Punta de Maspalomas

Firgas
Moya
Teror
Osorio
Pico del Radio
S. Mateo
Tejeda
La Cumbre
Tafira
Valsequillo
Caldera de los Marteles
Arucas
San Lorenzo
Ingenio
Agüimes

GRAN CANARIA
35 × 35 Miles

TENERIFE

AND ITS SIX SATELLITES.

———◆———

CHAPTER I.

GRAN CANARIA—LAS PALMAS—HISTORY OF THE ISLAND.

Many of the houses are built in the Moorish style, round patios, or courts, cooled by fountains, and open to the sky; and as the inhabitants pass much of their time in these courts and on the terraced roofs during the summer season, it follows that many a glance at their domestic life may be obtained by an aerial spectator like myself, who can look down on them from the clouds.—WASHINGTON IRVING.

> Long, long agone there was a day
> When there were giants in the land.
>
> JOAQUIN MILLER.

THE Canary Islands are roughly divisible into two groups, the western and the eastern. The western islands are Tenerife, Palma, Gomera, and Hierro. The eastern are Gran Canaria, Lanzarote, and Fuerteventura. Having visited the western islands, we have still to see Gran Canaria, Lanzarote, and Fuerteventura.

November 6th, Tuesday.—We arrived at Gran Canaria at 5 a.m., but did not go ashore until 6.30. It was with feelings

I

of considerable interest that we looked upon this island, where
so many battles had been fought.   Here we were at anchor
in the very roadstead where Juan Rejon and Pedro de Vera
anchored when they made those successful landings in the
island by which it was finally conquered.

An interpreter from the Fonda Europa, the best hotel in Las
Palmas, came on board and took us under his wing.   We,
however, had to fight our own battles with the boatmen as to
landing fees, the English-speaking interpreter being no doubt
in league with the boatmen.   The same individual was sacked
later by his master, to no one's regret.

We came ashore at the Puerto de la Luz, as the landing
is considered safer there.   When vessels stay a couple of
days, they prefer this anchorage, as there is more shelter.
By this means we saw the commencement of the proposed
Harbour of Refuge, and had a pleasant drive over the isthmus
to the town of Las Palmas.   The Isleta, adjoining Canaria
on the north-east, is a miniature island of Gran Canaria.
The same forces, on a smaller scale, have been at work there,
as in the larger island.   It is formed by craters.   One conical
hill in the shape of a peak, with a small portion of sloping
land around its base, faces us as we lie in the roadstead.
No doubt at one time it was an island, for it is now joined
to Canaria only by an isthmus entirely composed of sand.
On the western side of this isthmus of Guanarteme, there
is at the present moment a bar, some distance from the
isthmus, but running parallel with it, showing that the sand
is still accumulating.   Only small boats can enter there.   It
is somewhat like, though on a small scale, the isthmus at
Auckland, which divides the Hauraki gulf from the Manakau,
the latter corresponding to Confital Bay.   The New Zealand
isthmus is, however, seven miles wide, whilst that of
Guanarteme is but a mile.   From the Isleta to Las Palmas
the coast line makes a grand sweep.   In the centre of the
curve, where it is greatest, the new harbour is being made.
From La Luz the town of Las Palmas looks large and rather

imposing as it lies along the coast, for the most part on almost level ground, gradually ascending behind the town until stopped by a precipitous rock. Nothing apparently grows on the isthmus, which is entirely composed of light, drab-coloured dune sand, except tamarisk bushes, scraggy as usual.

On the western side, next the town, a bluff of basaltic-looking rock, rising abruptly out of the sand, no doubt formerly out of the sea, is good evidence of the formation of the isthmus. Two old forts, those of La Luz and Santa Catalina, one on the Isleta and one on the main island, are only worthy of note on account of their age, for they are very small.

The road is excellent the whole way to the town, a distance of about three miles. As we cross the neck of land, we pass on the left mineral baths, and on the right the land begins to show signs of cultivation; palm groves appear, with a large, well-built house in their midst. Soon each side of the road is lined by houses, these presently forming a continuous street, through which we passed into the town.

Along this street it was curious to note the braziers, not because they are new, but because their surroundings are altered. Instead of old houses and broken pavements, we have here even rows of new houses, a regular, flagged pathway, and a macadamised road. It seems an anomaly to have a little black brazier standing on the edge of the public pavement, and a woman crouching over it fanning the charcoal with a palm fan.

We passed through almost the entire town, and by a bridge crossed over the barranco, in which was a little water, before reaching our destination, the Fonda Europa, kept by Don Ramon Lopez. There was no English hotel * in Las Palmas when we arrived, but before we left one had been started by a Mr. and

---

* I hear lately that on some fifty acres of land near Santa Catalina a hotel and fincas are going to be built.

Mrs. Quiney (English people) in a part of the town near the mole. The Fonda Europa is a large house, in which an English merchant formerly dwelt. It is high, as are most of the houses in Las Palmas. We seem to have left Europe in Tenerife, and reached Africa in Gran Canaria, so different do the houses appear. All are flat-roofed. I could not see a single peaked one in the entire town, and the Moresque appearance is completed by the domes of the cathedral, which are decidedly Moorish. Las Palmas is a finer-looking town than Santa Cruz. The streets are broader, the houses newer and generally larger, but it lacks the picturesqueness that crooked, narrow streets, with overhanging eaves, give to its rival, and, owing to the distance of the background of mountains, has not that bold and majestic scenery in its vicinity that lends a charm to Santa Cruz. Both towns are unfortunate in being placed in barren situations, but both might be much improved could a liberal water supply be secured. Las Palmas, besides being the chief commercial town of the island, is also the residence of the bishop and clergy; it is, in fact, Laguna and Santa Cruz rolled into one. It was owing to this, I suppose, that the moment we left the hotel we were besieged by beggars, who were most persistent and annoying.

After some coffee and bread-and-butter and the usual fight with the men about their charges for luggage, which to us is annoying, but which they look upon as part of the daily business, we sauntered forth. The cathedral, we knew, from seeing its domes, must be in our immediate vicinity. Turning to the left on leaving the hotel, we walked to the end of the street Balcones, where there is a picturesque old fountain, at which the inhabitants obtain water. Some girls had long bamboos, which they placed at the dribble of water at the tap, several feet above their heads, and by these conveyed the attenuated stream into their barrels. Very picturesque they looked in their coloured head kerchiefs, out of which peered sunburnt faces as they leaned in unconscious grace against the grey stones.

The exterior of the cathedral of San Cristobal is very

massive, though the edifice is not finished yet. Two towers, dome-shaped, rise on either side of the main entrance. Between them is the foundation of a tower which is no doubt intended to rise above the others and complete the building, when sufficient money is forthcoming. The church is at one end of the plaza,

FOUNTAIN, BALCONES STREET, LAS PALMAS.

the town-hall and museum at the other; the fine open space shows off the cathedral well. Part of the church is old, dating back to about 1500. Its foundations were laid in the days of Isabella the Catholic by Don Diego Montande, who was the first architect. He was paid for his services the magnificent sum of ninepence a day! It was really erected, however, by

Don Diego Nicolas Eduardo, of Irish descent, who, it is stated, built the roof of so light a stone, that the workmen refused to work, whereupon he sat beneath it to encourage them. The interior, Gothic in style, is lofty, with fluted and well-proportioned pillars. The ceiling is a light stone-work tracery; whitewash in between, covering we know not what, is no improvement. The ceiling reminds one a little of that of Bath Abbey. The chancel is hung all round with crimson and gold cloth, and looks simple and in good taste. A massive silver candelabra, the work of Genoese artists, presented by Cardinal Ximenes in 1690, hangs before the altar, on which are silver candlesticks. A funeral service is going on, a black-and-gold sarcophagus being placed at the foot of the altar. There is a lantern dome, so the church is not very dark. There are aisles at either side, containing many chapels. The grandeur of the interior is, however, spoiled by a heavy piece of masonry in the middle of the nave, in which the organ and choir are placed. There are two holy water fonts, supported by turbaned dwarfs, and two pulpits, one on either side. The windows have small circular, coloured glass panes; the colouring is not good, the effect on one's sense of the artistic being painful. There is yellow at the top, then blue, then magenta, and green at the bottom. We will hope these are only temporary, until some good Churchmen present stained glass windows. We saw the cathedral frequently, and later we were shown the vestments.

It was breakfast-time at the fonda, so we returned there. Having a letter of introduction to Dr. Chil, and finding he lived next door, we sent the letter in to him, which he promptly answered in person, introducing himself to us. Señor Don Gregorio Chil is a fine, hale elderly man, with white hair, and upright as a soldier. He is one of the historians [*] of the island, and is more given to literature than to his profession. He studied medicine in Paris, however, and practises a little;

[*] "Estudios Historicos, Climatologicos, y Patologicos de las Islas Canarias" (1879).

but he is a thorough student. He is the founder and careful, tender nurse of the young museum, not long started, and is interested in everything connected with the past of these islands. His freedom of thought has rendered him obnoxious to the clergy here, and, although, I believe, not exactly excommunicated for holding Darwinian opinions, he is more or less at variance with the Church. He had to be married elsewhere, in France or Spain—I forget which—owing to the feeling against him.

Again setting out, we called on Mr. James Miller, our vice-consul, to whom we had letters of introduction. We then called on Señor Don Agustin Millares, another historian, who is also a novelist. Canaria is rich in writers. Dón Agustin took us into his well-filled library, and kindly gave us two of his works —his " History of the Islands," which is going through the press, and his " History of the Inquisition in the Islands." * For this latter work Don Agustin has been excommunicated ; so I fear what he says on the subject must be true. It must keep the " Holy Catholic Church " out here busy excommunicating all its thoughtful and learned men. Several of those who had been excommunicated told us that the religious sentence passed upon them did not trouble them. After it had been pronounced they found that they were just as well in body, and as for their souls, they considered they were at least just as good Catholics as, if not better than, they were before. Many of the undoubtedly "faithful" told us that they held those excommunicated for holding advanced scientific opinions and liberality of thought in just as high esteem as before they were excommunicated. So we gathered that out here the thunder of the Church of Rome has lost much, if not all, of its ancient power. We had a number of letters of introduction to the people of Las Palmas, and delivered many of them. One was to a gentleman of the mercantile house of Ripoche, Señor Don Nestor de la Torre, who most kindly called on us and accompanied us to several places.

* " Historia de la Inquisicion en las Islas Canarias " (1874).

Dr. Chil took us to see the museum in the town-hall. There is a hall inside this building for municipal purposes, decorated in florid style in pale mauve and white, the floor tiled. The museum is at the top of the building, and is situated in a long, narrow room or gallery. Here is the first printing-press used in the island at the end of the eighteenth century. Bits of iron and balls, found in the old walls of a castle when pulled down, are also here. But to us the Guanche remains were the most interesting. These people, however, were Antiguos Canarios, not Guanches, a name that belonged only to the inhabitants of Tenerife, as I have before mentioned. A jar of butter found in Fuerteventura, and smelling strongly still of goat's milk, is a curious relic. It is not every day one sees butter at least five hundred years old. There are a number of small earthenware, seal-like devices in triangles and squares of various shapes, whose use is unknown. Amongst the mummies was that of a woman, with curly brown hair and rather projecting teeth. The stitching on the skins is as fine as "top-sewing." Whole cases full of skulls occupied one side of the room, while specimens of the pelvis lay together in a heap under the windows, and of the femur in another heap, and of the humerus in another place. One femur shown us was that of a large man, about the size of a big Englishman. Another femur had been fractured, and, being badly set, had shortened. There was also a skull with short reddish hair on the skin. Later we photographed some of the curiosities, but just now we had not time to do so, having to make arrangements for starting into the interior.

It takes much time and many inquiries to learn what is the best mode of seeing this island, as to go round the coast would not by any means be the most satisfactory way. The heart of the island is the part we particularly wish to see. As it is getting late in the year, we think it advisable to take the highest parts first, before the snow comes to render mountain-travelling impossible. We finally decided to make two separate excursions, the first to be by way of Arucas, Guia, Agaete, and

Aldea to Artenara and Tejeda, in the centre of the island, and back to Las Palmas by Teror; on the second to go by San Mateo to the Roque del Saucillo and the Pico de las Nieves, in mid-island, returning by Tirajana, Aguimes, and Telde. By this means we should see the most interesting parts of the island. The southern portion is barren and lava-strewn, like the south of Tenerife; still, if time permitted, we hoped to visit it as well. It was now November 6th, and we wished to get back to England for Christmas, so we reckoned upon giving three weeks to Gran Canaria and a week to Fuerteventura and Lanzarote, going by steamer from the latter island to the coast of Africa and Cadiz, taking a peep at Morocco and Gibraltar and a run home through Spain. How our intentions were frustrated remains to be seen.

November 7th, Wednesday.— There is a patio of course to this fonda, situated at one side of which is the comedor, a long, narrow room, with one table down its length, capable of accommodating about forty people. An open verandah goes round the other three sides, and the comedor is really only the fourth side enclosed. The centre is filled with trees and shrubs, grouped round a fountain, which rarely plays. A plantain droops its long leaves in the middle, and in the corners are a couple of young dragon trees. There are also palms, geraniums, eucalypti, and papyri, while creepers twine round the pillars to the floor above, making the spot green and pleasant to the eye. The rest of the ground floor is divided into bedrooms, chiefly occupied by residents at the hotel. A broad staircase leads to the next floor, upon which are situated the sala and more bedrooms. There are two bedrooms on each side of the sala, opening into it; these are kept, as a rule, for English visitors, and we had the larger one. There is no outlook from the windows, but this matters little in a climate where it is possible to be always in the open air. The bedrooms opening off the verandah which runs round the house, upstairs as well as down, are all dark, having only borrowed light. The doors open on the verandahs, and the bedrooms, having no outer walls, cannot of course have windows. This is not considered a disadvantage by Spaniards, who like darkened rooms; but we English prefer windows. The temperature this morning at eight o'clock in the shade of the patio was 53·6° F. (12° C.). The food here is very good, and the wine supplied with the meals a light, pleasant kind of Burgundy. Although breakfast is served at ten o'clock, and is not our idea of that meal, as it consists of meats only and wine, it is possible to get a comfortable English breakfast, as Don Ramon quite understands the ways of English people. It is always difficult to get good tea, although Don Ramon has it made properly; but we had some of our own, which I used to give to Pedro, the head waiter, to make for us. The butter was very good, and there was always a plentiful supply. As we did not require such a substantial meal as the Spaniards, Don Ramon kindly gave us our breakfast when we liked, and had eggs or fish, ham or omelets, chops or steaks, cooked for us specially. Although we were only a couple of days in Las Palmas at this date, we spent more time here later, when we got into our own ways and hours. Nothing could exceed the courtesy of Don Ramon and his household. It must be remembered, too, that we only paid so much a day, and no extras were charged. We had luncheon too, and when more English stayed in the hotel, dinner was served later for their and our benefit. I had tea always brought to my room after dinner, and although it was my own tea and biscuits, still we frequently had Don Ramon's bread, butter, and honey, not only for ourselves, but for other English people. Considering all things, and even supposing provisions to be cheap, I think the charge of six shillings a day was very moderate and reasonable. The only real fault we had to find was with the attendance. There were but two waiters and two chambermaids, and sometimes only one, Maria, a jolly, fat negress; so when the house was full our bedrooms would be neglected until late in the afternoon.

Las Palmas is divided into two parts by the Barranco Guiniguada. The northern part is called Triana, and the southern Vegueta. The former is the commercial part; in it are situated the large shops, the mole, and the barracks. The other district, where we are, is devoted to the clergy, the magistracy, the prison (which used to be the headquarters of the Inquisition), the college, and melancholy. We seldom meet people in the streets here; what bustle there is goes on at the other end. Las Palmas is not so lively nor full of interest as Santa Cruz, owing to the anchorage for vessels being so far from the town.

There is a curious tradition of the founding of Las Palmas by Juan Rejon * in 1477. He had intended to disembark at Gando, to rebuild the fort, but passing near the Isleta bay of La Luz, he thought the anchorage seemed better, and cast anchor there instead on June 22nd. The troops disembarked, and the Dean Juan Bermudas, who accompanied the expedition, said mass on shore under a tent, on an improvised altar. Immediately after this they commenced their march towards Gando, where they intended to encamp. They had not gone far, however, when a woman in Canarian dress asked them in Spanish "where they were going." Hearing it was to Gando, she advised them not to go so far, and said that the way thither was bad and dangerous, owing to precipices overhanging the road, but that at a short distance from where they then were was a " commodious plain, with a rivulet of good water, plenty of firewood, with palms and fig trees, from whence they might have easy access to all the principal places on the island." After consultation, they agreed to be guided to this place, and the woman conducted them to the spot where now stands Las Palmas. They pitched their tents by the banks of the Guiniguada, and looking for their guide, found she had vanished. Juan Rejon, a devout worshipper of St. Anna, at once concluded it was she who had thus appeared to him. Be this as it may, the place was suitable, and thus was founded Las Palmas.

The history of Gran Canaria is long and complicated, as there were numerous attempts to subjugate the island. In fact, as I

* See vol. i., page 59.

mentioned before,* it took seventy-seven years to conquer the island. It was owing to the "strength, courage, and number" of its inhabitants that Bethencourt named it *Gran*, or great, not grand, as it is erroneously often called now. Bethencourt sailed to Canaria with two ships, and landed his men at Arguine-guin, in the extreme south of the island; he marched a little way into the interior, was furiously attacked by the Canarios, defeated, and driven to the sea-shore, where he re-embarked. He sailed for Palma, but returned again to Canaria, where, however, he found so many people assembled to resist him, that he gave up the attempt and retired to Fuerteventura. He made a second attempt, after having conquered Gomera and Hierro as well as Fuerteventura and Lanzarote, in 1406, when he anchored at Gando. He landed at night, as he thought secretly, but in reality the natives had seen him, as they kept a sharp look-out from their mountains. He was repulsed again, and with so much loss, that it was with difficulty he and his forces made good their retreat. It was after this defeat that Bethencourt decided he must have more men with whom to conquer Canaria, and this made him determine to return to Spain to procure assistance. This he did, and while paying a visit to his family in Normandy died, in 1422. Many attacks were made by various expeditions sent from Spain against the unconquered islands, but all failed until 1444. Diego de Herrera, who had then succeeded to the islands, made several ineffectual attempts on Canaria, and finding it could not be conquered by force, determined it should by stratagem. He went therefore to the Isleta port in 1461, taking with him the Bishop of Rubicon and others. The natives met, prepared, as usual, to repulse the invaders, but the Bishop represented to them that they came in peace to trade. The Spaniards were then allowed to come ashore unarmed, when they were met by the *Guanartemes* (kings) of Telde and Galdar. A libation was poured upon the ground, and Herrera, in the presence of natives and Spaniards, took possession of the island, August 16th, 1461. It is

* Vol. i., page 59.

unnecessary to add that the Canarios of course did not understand what was going on, or they would not have stood by so
calmly and seen their country thus coolly given away. The
following year the Bishop, "moved with an ardent zeal to
gather his scattered sheep of Canaria into the fold of the Romish
Church, went over there." He had, however, three hundred
armed men with him, and they anchored at Gando. The natives
not allowing them to disembark, the Bishop endeavoured by
"fair words and soft speeches" to prevail upon them; but on
no account would they permit armed men to land. If the
Spaniards required anything, they had only to say so, and the
Canarios would bring it to them. So the Spaniards thought
better of converting the natives, returning to Lanzarote, and the
worthy Bishop, who only wanted their souls, could not get them
except at the point of the sword! They made another attempt
under this good bishop in 1464, but finding the whole island in
arms, passed on to Tenerife. Meanwhile Spain and Portugal
had disagreed as to the ownership of the islands, and sent one
Diego de Sylva with armed men and ships to Lanzarote.
Peace, however, was restored between the nations, and also
between Sylva and Herrera, by the former becoming the son-in-
law of the latter. Seeing so many men gathered together,
Herrera, no doubt urged on by the pious Bishop, started once
more for Canaria, and landed at Gando. The Spaniards and
Portuguese were now so numerous, that they marched boldly
into the island, but were attacked and driven to the sea-shore,
where they took refuge in a sort of natural fortress, from which
the natives could not dislodge them. The invaders had sus-
tained so much loss, that Herrera endeavoured to find other
means of subduing the heroic islanders. He therefore sent Sylva
during the night to attack another part of the island. Sylva
landed at Agumastel, near Galdar, and arranged his forces on
land before being discovered. They marched towards a steep
hill, covered with trees and shrubs, which the Canarios perceiving, they let them gain the top of the ascent, when the
natives secured the pass and set fire to the bushes to prevent

their escape. Thereupon Sylva marched on to the plain near Galdar, where he found a large space enclosed by a stone wall, to which they retired for security. The natives, however, surrounded the place so closely, they could not get out, and were two days and nights without food. A woman came to the rescue. She had been a captive in Lanzarote, but was returned in exchange for a European prisoner. She could therefore speak both languages, and told Sylva that they were all going to be killed, and that their only chance lay in surrendering. This they did on condition of having their lives spared. The natives, naturally incensed against their invaders, were unwilling to spare their lives, but the King of Galdar persuaded them to be merciful. The Spaniards and Portuguese gave up their arms, and the king embraced Sylva and conducted him to Galdar, where he lived, very possibly in the cave we saw in that place. All were fed and then escorted to their ships. Here comes one of those episodes of the conquest of the Canary Islands which instance the fine character of their inhabitants. The way to the coast led them along a narrow path by a high precipice. The invaders thought they were betrayed and were going to be thrown down the precipice, and expressed their fears to the Canarios. The natives were much affronted. "The *Guanarteme*, however, made no reply to this accusation, but desired Diego de Sylva to take hold of the skirt of his garment, and he would lead him down ; he likewise ordered his men in the same manner to assist the Europeans ; thus they all descended safe to the bottom." The king complained bitterly of their being suspected of so much baseness, and Sylva, at a loss to express his gratitude and remorse, gave them presents. When Sylva returned to Gando, he told Herrera of his adventures, "at which he was greatly astonished, and could not conceive whence these Barbarians had acquired such noble sentiments of valour and generosity." To show how magnanimous a Christian could be, however, Herrera, accompanied by Sylva, attacked the Canarios again, in which for the first time the islanders were worsted. Many were killed and wounded on both sides, and among the prisoners was a valiant chief, Mananidra, whom Sylva remembered seeing at Galdar. He immediately entreated of Herrera that the chief should be set at liberty, who *unwillingly* granted this boon. The Portuguese objecting to any more fighting, Herrera made peace with the *Guanartemes*, and returned to Lanzarote.

The next expedition to Canaria was one of stratagem, so consequently the worthy Bishop was of the party. It was upon this occasion that a treaty of peace and for trade was made, and the fort of Gando built "as a place of worship" for the traders. The Canarios helped to build the fort, and Pedro Chemida, with a good garrison and provisions, was left in charge by Herrera. "With him he left orders that, notwithstanding the treaty of peace, if a fair opportunity should offer of making himself master of the island he should by no means neglect it, at the same time advising him, if possible, to divide the natives by fomenting quarrels and stirring up jealousies among them, so as to form a party in favour of the Europeans." Glas goes on to say, "After leaving these honest and generous instructions," Herrera and the Bishop, "highly pleased with the success of his project," departed for Lanzarote.

Chemida consequently by various means roused the just ire of the Canarios, until the latter, aggravated beyond endurance, turned on their persecutors, and by a ruse made themselves masters of the fort, taking the Spaniards prisoners. They rased the walls and burned the wood to prevent another fort being erected, "but as to the prisoners, they treated them according to their usual custom, with gentleness and humanity." A fishing barque, seeing the fate of the fort, set sail immediately, and told Herrera of its destruction, at which he was extremely grieved, but Yllescas, the Bishop, "was afflicted beyond measure," for, being old, he feared he should never bring the natives to profess Roman Catholicism. Chemida, however, appears, when prisoner with the Canarios, to have talked to them until he made them believe they were the aggressors, whereupon a new treaty of peace was ratified. Representations had been made to Spain by dis-

satisfied subjects of Herrera concerning his inability to take
Canaria, and he was obliged to sell his right to the three unconquered islands in 1476.   It was then that Juan Rejon, by
order of their Spanish Majesties, came to Canaria, accompanied
by the Dean of Rubicon, and founded Las Palmas.   The natives,
seeing that the invaders were preparing to build, remembered
the trouble the fort of Gando had caused, and gathered together
two thousand men under a celebrated chieftain, Doramas.   The
battle of Guiniguada was fought on the banks of that barranco,
when, after a desperate and long-sustained fight, the Canarios
were obliged to retreat, though in good order, having lost three
hundred men.   They never again ventured a battle on the
plains, but retired within their native mountains, where the
Spaniards continually harassed them.

When Spain and Portugal were at war, the troops of the
latter, having arranged with the Canarios to help them,
attempted to land at the Isleta, but Rejon saw them coming and
placed his men "behind certain hillocks of black earth," the
Guanche cemetery in fact, and as the Portuguese could only
land in detachments, they were surprised and dispersed rapidly.

Meanwhile the camp at Las Palmas was suffering much for
want of provisions; raids were made on the Canarios constantly,
and some procured, but not enough.   The Dean Bermudas, no
doubt not getting sufficient of the fat things of this life, complained to Spain privately of his commanding officer, so that,
after a fruitless expedition to Lanzarote for food, Rejon found
himself superseded on his return by a governor—the first sent
by Spain to these islands—called Pedro de Algava.   Rejon
went to Spain, and having satisfied the court of inquiry there as
to his doings in Canaria, returned, accompanied by the new
Bishop of Rubicon, Juan de Frias.   Algava would not permit
him to land, however, and he had to return to Spain to get a
royal warrant.   He again appeared before Canaria, landed by
stratagem, and finding Algava in the church, rushed in with
his followers, took him prisoner, and threw him in chains into a
dungeon.   Rejon procured false witnesses to swear against

Algava, ordered his beheadal, and became governor in his
stead. He was, however, soon superseded by Pedro de Vera,
sent out from Spain, and Rejon was sent by him home as a
prisoner. The Dean Juan Bermudas died, it is said, just
before this " of mere chagrin and vexation " ! De Vera fought
with the Canarios at Arucas soon after his arrival, and, after
single combat with the celebrated Doramas, who had already
killed one of his officers, the chieftain was vanquished and
surrendered. The natives on seeing this fell upon the
Spaniards, and there was a great fight, ending in the retreat of
the Canarios to their mountain fastnesses. Doramas died of
his wounds, and was buried on the top of the mountain which
still bears his name. A wall of stones round his grave and a
crucifix mark the spot of his baptism and burial.

The plains were now in the hands of de Vera ; but, in order
to reach the mountain passes, he determined to build a fort at
Agaete, where he placed a garrison under Alonso de Lugo. He
then made a second attempt on Tirajana, where he was at first
driven back, but eventually forced the pass. After this the
Canarios made an attack on Las Palmas, which was, howevel
repulsed. Rejon having been killed in a scuffle in Lanzarote,
his widow accused Peraza of murdering him, and the latter was
only forgiven on condition that he should help to subdue
Canaria. He accordingly landed at Agaete, and sent word of
his arrival to the Governor, de Vera. The Governor ordered
him and de Lugo to attack Galdar, while he started from Las
Palmas for the same purpose. The Governor went accordingly to Arucas the first night, while de Lugo went to
Artenara, where he secured some flocks, and then to Galdar,
where de Vera had already taken the Guanarteme and other
prisoners. This chieftain was the means of the final reduction
of the island, for being sent to Spain as a prisoner, he became
overpowered by the wealth of the nation and the magnificence
of the court, and begged to be baptised, whereupon he was
loaded with presents and given the Valley of Guayayedra, in
Gran Canaria, abounding in fig trees and pasture, and sent

back to that island. Troops were also sent at the same time for the further conquest of the island. The Guanarteme Semidan, of Galdar, gathered together his people and their chiefs at that place, and represented to them how useless it would be to fight against the power and wealth of Spain. Some submitted on hearing what he said, but the greater number refused to follow his advice. They begged him to return and be their king, and on his refusing, elected Tasarte, son of the late King of Telde. The people reproached Semidan much, telling him that he could not trust the good faith of the invaders, they had so often proved perfidious. "What confidence," said they, "can we repose in a people who are not ashamed to break their promises and engagements?" Semidan returned to Las Palmas and told de Vera of the non-effect of his interference. All the troops were now combined, and a determined effort was made to subdue the people in their fastnesses. A few were left to garrison Las Palmas, and the rest laid siege to the fortified Pass of Bentayga. They waited for fifteen days, hoping to reduce the natives by famine; but learning that they had provisions for some months, more active measures were adopted. The first attempt was repulsed. Huge stones were tumbled from the precipices upon the Spaniards, as well as showers of stones and darts, so that they were glad to retreat, moving off to Tirajana and Acayro, where they took much cattle. From thence they attempted another natural fortress, that of Titana, which was considered so strong, both naturally and artificially, that the Canarios were careless, and being surprised, killed, and the place taken. De Vera, however, not leaving any garrison there, the natives returned, and taking possession, refortified it. De Vera next proceeded to a stronghold called Aradar, where many Canarios had retired with their wives and children, and where there was a good spring of water. It was forced, however, prisoners and cattle taken, and many killed. Two women, to avoid falling into the hands of the enemy, threw themselves down from a precipice, which has since been called Risco de las Mujeres

(Women's Rock). The invaders next seized Fataga. The interior of Canaria, and especially its centre, is one mass of rocks, precipices, and narrow passes, which form natural fortifications, and could be held by a few men. Tasarte the valiant, feeling his countrymen were deserting him, that the precipices were unavailing in guarding them against the Spaniards, resolved to die rather than submit, so, going to the top of a steep precipice, now called Tisma, near Galdar, he called aloud, " Atirtisma ! Atirtisma ! " (the Canarian invocation to their supreme being), and threw himself down into the sea.

De Vera continued his progress, "hunting the distressed Canarios from their caverns and hiding-places," until he came to Ajodar, where a number were gathered together determined to resist to the last. The attack was to be made from the sea by Miguel de Morisca and the troops levied in Biscay, and was not to be attempted until they received orders to that effect. The troops, however, were desirous of avenging their defeat at Bentayga, and thinking de Vera overcautious, they proceeded to climb the rocks, and finding the first pass undefended, penetrated the defile. The Canarios, however, had seen them, and allowed all to enter. Then suddenly, with a shout, they threw down huge stones upon the enemy from the adjacent heights. The Spaniards, unable to resist and unable to fly—for only one at a time could get down the pass on hands and knees—were nearly annihilated. De Vera coming from the other side, prevented their total destruction, and Semidan persuaded his compatriots to desist. Three hundred Canarios were said to have been at Ajodar. The Spaniards left fifty dead, and numbers of wounded were taken to Galdar, mass being performed where the church now stands. This is said to have been the worst defeat the invaders encountered in their conquest of the island. Resting and refreshing his troops, de Vera gathered them all together again and rearmed them. These and some conquered Canarios made up about a thousand men, with whom he determined to completely subdue Gran Canaria before returning to Las Palmas. Hearing that the entire force of the islanders, some six hundred men and a thousand women and children, was assembled at Ansite, a place thought impregnable, situated between Galdar and Tirajana, he marched thither and pitched his camp at the bottom of the mountain. All the native nobles and the young King of Telde, who was just on the eve of marriage with the King of Galdar's daughter, were at Ansite. The old Guanarteme Semidan, knowing that his countrymen were determined to die rather than surrender, went, with de Vera's consent, to try and persuade them to come to terms. A most affecting meeting was that between Semidan and his former subjects and peers. No one could speak from emotion, and all wept over the past glories of their native land and the future prospects of bowing their free and proud heads to the conqueror. Semidan used all the arts of eloquence to induce them for the sakes of their wives and children to lay down arms, as resistance would only mean their destruction. He promised on behalf of the Spaniards that they would be kindly treated. They at last consented, throwing down their arms with wailing and crying. The Guanarteme of Telde, however, and an old Faycag* could not bear the reverse of fortune, so, going to the brow of a precipice, they embraced each other, called out, "Atirtisma!" and threw themselves down. De Vera was relieved to see the Canarios surrender, for he felt sure that he could not have taken the place without much bloodshed. The Bishop, Frias, sang Te Deum on the occasion, April 29th, 1483, seventy-seven years after the first attempt by Bethencourt upon the island.

What a melancholy history, and all done "to the glory of God." The natives killed in order that they might be made Christians!

Two of Semidan's daughters were married to Spaniards, whose descendants are living at the present day. The extra

---

* The Faycag was a person of great rank, next in dignity to the Guanarteme. He decided differences among the natives, and regulated their religious ceremonies. He appears to have been a sort of priest, and also a judge in civil affairs.

troops were sent back to Spain, and privileges were accorded by the King to those who would settle in the island. Those who did came chiefly from Andalusia. The King also ordered fruit-trees and plants to be sent thither from Madeira. "The Bishop and Governor distributed the children of the Canarians of both sexes amongst the Spaniards, to be instructed in the faith and doctrine of the Church of Rome; and, to avoid scandal, the girls were committed to the charge of the married women, and the boys to the unmarried men."

Arrangements were made for governing the island, and Pope Innocent VIII. a few years later granted the removal of the see from Rubicon, in Lanzarote, to Las Palmas. February 20th, 1487, the island was incorporated into the crown of Castile, and the Pope handed over the bishopric to the King of Spain and his successors. In 1499 laws and charters were framed, and certain regulations *made formerly by the natives* confirmed. Charles V. in 1515 gave Las Palmas the title of "Noble and Royal City of Palmas," it having been only a town before. It is this which causes so much dispute between Las Palmas and Santa Cruz. The former had been made a city first, Gran Canaria being of course conquered before Tenerife, and Las Palmas established before Santa Cruz. If Lanzarote were able, it might dispute the right of either to be the capital, for it was conquered and the bishop's see was established there before any other island was subdued.

CHAPTER II.

Christians have burnt each other, quite persuaded
That all the Apostles would have done as they did.
BYRON.

November 7th, Wednesday.—Mr. James Miller, our vice-consul, kindly sent one of his clerks to show us the various sights in Las Palmas to-day. The first place we visited was the Courts of Justice, or the Law Courts. Here there is a *sala criminal* and *sala civil.* The court rooms are comfortably carpeted, with small tables, a table for the stolen articles, and chairs, neatly upholstered, for the lawyers. There is a room for the witnesses, where an official is always placed to see that they do not speak to each other. The secretary's room contains, in little cardboard boxes, registers of all the cases tried. The articles whereby convictions have been obtained are also kept; these lie on the top of a number of papers, loosely tied in parcels, and consist of such things as stones with blood upon them, knives, and guns. The barristers' room is a pleasant one, from the windows of which it is possible to fish, which no doubt the briefless do. Another room contains the registers of births and deaths, and of marriages, civil marriages only, of course. The deaths are recorded in long black records, an unnecessarily melancholy proceeding. As we went from one part of the courts to another, we passed a respectable elderly, grey-haired man, who walked with head slightly bent and a consciousness of being somebody. Our guide, after he had passed, said, with bated breath, "That is the public executioner." He is held in such horror by the isleños, that, when the common people meet him, they murmur, "Dios me libre de tus manos" ("God deliver me from thy hands"). His salary is a thousand pesos a year (one hundred and fifty pounds), and three pounds at every execution. He has a house provided near the courts, and takes his exercise there, chiefly walking up and down, for to encounter other people would not be too pleasant. Poor man, he looked harmless enough, but no doubt human nature has an antipathy to hands that shed blood, even though it be not "innocent."

. This antipathy to blood-shedding individuals is in the Canaries extended even to butchers, who are looked upon as the lowest class of the community. Even the very criminals object to mix with them in prison, so that, if convicted of misdemeanours worthy of punishment, they are whipped at the Courts of Justice, and not imprisoned. This horror of butchers is of very ancient origin, and is a remnant of the customs of the Antiguos Canarios. Only the dregs of the people would adopt the business of butchers, and so ignominious was it considered, that they were not allowed to enter any of the other people's houses or touch their belongings. Butchers were not permitted to mix with anyone but those of their own trade, and when they wanted anything, they were obliged to stand at some distance and point to what they required. During the wars of the conquest, when some Spaniards were taken prisoners, it was considered a sufficient punishment and degradation to turn them into butchers.

We next visited the archive room, which is surrounded by shelves, in which are square packets of papers, the labels of the places to which they belong hanging from them. We passed up a staircase and out upon the roof, whence there is a fine view. The Isleta always makes a charming picture, lying beyond the blue sea of La Luz. The town lies on level ground close upon the sea. At its back are hills faced by bluffs. Valleys run between the hills, and lead to the interior of the island. The bluffs or promontories are rocky, and are named

San Nicolas and San Bernardo, while between San Lazaro, up which part of the town climbs, and San Roque runs the barranco of Guiniguada. Upon the top of these bluffs is a level platform, on which is a look-out station, where the arrival of the ships is signalled by means of a bell first and then flags. It can be seen from every part of the town. There is also a signal station, or watchtower, on the Isleta, from which the arrival of ships round the north of the island can be signalled. This useful custom is interesting because the Antiguos Canarios did in their way exactly the same. They had watch-places on the summits of their mountains, from which they signalled the arrival of enemies, the circular form of the island rendering this possible. There is one spot in mid-island from which the entire coast line of Canaria can be seen. Southwards we can see as far as the Punta Melenara. The roofs of Las Palmas are quite flat, and as every place is painted white, the glare is awful. A number of flagstaffs rise in the town, chiefly from the consuls' and business houses. The glare is so great, that coming down the stairs we walk by faith, being quite blinded. This we always found to be the case in Las Palmas whenever we ascended the azoteas or roofs. We did not notice it anywhere else, but for that town blue spectacles or goggles would be most useful. Coming down, the gentlemen—for we were now accompanied by many, chiefly, I believe, of the legal profession, whom we had encountered in the courts—held a consultation, and then doubtfully proposed that we should see the garrottes.

Screwing up my courage for a nasty sight, we entered the room. On the floor, surrounded by the *registro de la propiedad*, in little numbered cardboard boxes, was a plain deal, inoffensive-looking box, about a foot in height and two feet long by eighteen inches wide. In it lay the ghastly instruments of death, horrid from their association, but nevertheless skilful mechanical works. They are two in number, an extra one having been made for the double execution to which I have elsewhere referred.* The instruments were of bright steel,

* Vol. i., page 392.

covered with grease to prevent them rusting. One of the barristers took a garrotte out of its resting-place, and by means of his leg explained to us its working. It is two feet in length and six inches wide, and consists of a steel collar, hinged in the middle and locked. A massive, quick-working screw, turned by a powerful lever handle, would rapidly compress the criminal's neck against the post, which also is included within the collar's embrace. A couple of turns and seconds are sufficient to send a soul into eternity.

There are five judges, and when they sit in court, they are dressed in black silk gowns and lace cuffs, with gold chains round their necks, and a medal hanging in front.

Our next visit was to the prison, which being in the old Inquisition, is of double interest. The prisoners were marched out that we might inspect them, a proceeding we did not at all relish. They minded it less than we did, however. My inspection began and ended with a fine young fellow, fair-haired and blue-eyed, who did not look like a gaolbird. His offence, we were told, was trivial, and it seemed wicked that he should be in constant and unrestrained intercourse with regular criminals. It was painful to have a man pointed out to us and audibly mentioned as being the perpetrator of such and such an act. I was told that a woman who brushed past me with a basket of clothes on her head had murdered her uncle. Whatever sense of decency or shame they have left must vanish when interest is thus shown in them, and heroes in a sort of way are made of them. It may be, however, that we were favoured by the officials, in which case I should be sorry to be critical, and that it was not usual to show any or everyone the prisoners. There were not many in the prison. We saw only about a dozen. The floors of the rooms had a number of round holes in them, formerly used by the inquisitors as peep-holes, by which means they could keep a constant watch on their victims at all times. A set of stocks containing thirteen holes is in a room on the ground floor. All the floors of these rooms are of stone. In one a boy was seated, he also in unrestrained communication with the men. The entire place is said to be honeycombed with cells, and there is an underground passage between the Inquisition and the monastery next door, now the hospital.   One cell was shown to us.   Leading out of one small room was another, windowless.   In the floor of this a trap-door was lifted, and we saw down into a deep, dark pit, so utterly devoid of light, that all was blackness.   It was jokingly suggested that we should go down.   No one had ever been in it since the days of the Inquisitors.   But the horrors that might meet us below and the unknown depths of this gruesome chamber had no charms for even our inquisitiveness.   There were no steps into it, so the unfortunate victim of the Inquisitors must have been lowered into its depths.   No sound could have reached him there from the outer world, and not the faintest ray of light pierces the gloom.   The filthy condition of the place must be simply appalling, and it is quite possible one would find the horrible witnesses of past cruelties and ghastly crimes.

An English Roman Catholic captain of a vessel was immured in this prison for two years.   He had been taken prisoner in 1739, and was allowed to remain at large in Tenerife until the Inquisitors one day seized him and conveyed him to Las Palmas. Here he remained in this prison for two years, nine months of which were spent in a dungeon.   He was tortured to make him confess his heinous crime—that of being a Freemason!   His release was at last effected through an interchange of prisoners.

Gladly leaving the prison and its gloomy precincts, we turned in next door to the hospital.   This, formerly a monastery, is now used as a foundling establishment as well as a hospital and a school.   The three departments are kept separate, and there are three chapels.   Sisters of charity conduct the whole. We were told repeatedly that outside the Foundling Hospital in a niche was a cradle on a turnstile into which a woman could place an infant, and turn the cradle inwards, ringing a bell, and so leave it without being seen.   We made many attempts to find this cradle, but never succeeded, though I believe it is really outside some part of the building.   It seems to me that if every convenience be thus made to cover the sinners and to aid them in concealing their transgressions, immorality is only increased, not lessened, thereby. When the children have been two years in the Foundling Hospital, they are offered for adoption to the public. Twenty-seven infants were thus offered one morning, and before evening only two were left. A woman with twelve children, who had lost two or three, took one! The Sisters execute some most beautiful embroidery, which they sell in aid of the funds of the hospital. In the sala is an elaborate piece of needlework, framed and hanging on the wall, of "Our Lady of the Pines," a virgin on the top of a pine tree.

We start in the morning for the interior, driving first by coach to Arucas and thence by horse to Guia. The horses have been ordered in advance, through Mr. Miller's thoughtfulness, as it is said to be difficult to procure animals at that place. In fact, it is not easy to get horses in any part of Gran Canaria, and where obtainable they are generally indifferent.

November 8th, Thursday.—We walked down to a tobacconist's shop, in the commercial part of the town, at 7 a.m., where the coach starts for Arucas, an odd starting-place. It was fortunately open, as a very heavy shower came on, and we were glad of shelter. Presently the coach arrived, a sort of covered waggonette drawn by three horses. We started at 7.15, passed through part of the town, and turned up on the left between San Roque and San Nicolas. On our left, above the ravine in the cliff, are a number of cave dwellings, called *matas* or the Cuevas del Provecho (Prophet's Caves), where the scum of the population are said to reside, those who are too poor to pay rent and, it is also hinted, those who prefer their neighbours' property to their own, in short a kind of Borough neighbourhood. We were told it was hardly safe to visit these troglodytes, but we did so later without meeting with the least inconvenience. I rather fancy the people in the Canaries hardly know what crime means as we understand it in England.

The road ascended rather rapidly between the hills.   Two kilometres from the town, at 7.35 a.m., we were 280 feet above the sea, and at four kilometres 550 feet, fifteen minutes later.   The road was lively with people going to market ; they both rode and carried loads on their heads.   The men wore loose sack coats, called *capotes* or *camisolas*, somewhat like English carters' smock-frocks, but of wool.   The brown faces of the women, with red handkerchiefs tied over, covering them almost to the eyebrows, and light print dresses looked Eastern.   They wear the handkerchiefs much more over the face here than in the western islands, a trifle more Moresque in appearance the nearer we get to Africa.   We saw, for the first time, a curious saddle, or albarda, which used to be very common in the islands, a sort of high chair, with short upright poles or sticks at the corners, these gaily bedizened with coloured wools.   Some of the pack-saddles are of sheepskin, the long wool left on ; others are covered with a sort of sacking, the same as the men's coats, or *camisolas*, are made of.   The barranco in which the people were washing their clothes yesterday has not a drop of water in it to-day.

We reached Tamaraceite at eight o'clock, after crossing a barranco by a bridge, to do which we had first to descend and then ascend the other side.   The seventh kilometre stone was 500 feet up, near Tamaraceite, and from that to Tenoya the road was level.   A post bag was left at Tamaraceite, and we drove onwards.   San Lorenzo lies on our left, in which there is a prominent and ugly church, like one of toy bricks, and a gentleman's residence (*una casa particular*).   A waggonette and a fine pair of horses, driven by a gentleman, met us.   The rich people of Las Palmas generally live a little out of the town, on the many roads which branch into the country.   At a short distance out of bare and barren-looking Las Palmas are lovely little glens and woods, so that charming country houses nestle everywhere, and one comes upon them in most unexpected quarters.   We pass a plantation of aloes ; wherever a hedge is required, it is made of this stiff prickly plant. The plant is also useful in another way, for an industry has lately arisen for making aloe fibre into various articles, such as girths, headstalls, trappings for mules, and such-like articles, where strength is required, and not an absolutely smooth surface. The aloe has therefore become an object for cultivation. The leaves are cut off and buried until they rot, when they are beaten, and the fibre extracted. The road to Teror branches off on the left at the eighth kilometre. The country is undulating here, but further on we pass through a tunnel, about 150 yards long, well built with stone and cement, the ceiling high, two oil lamps shedding their rays on the gloom. At Tenoya a small valley opens out beneath, but as it was pouring rain, and we were closely curtained in on all sides and worried with the *pulgas*, we had not a very clear idea of the scenery. Crossing a broken bridge, and passing along an avenue of eucalyptus, we entered Arucas at 9.15 a.m. It is a small, clean, straggling place, 700 feet above the sea, built round the base of a crater, and with the promise of growing bigger. We delivered our letter of recommendation to Don Pantaleon Quevedo, the largest shopkeeper in the place, and found from him that he had horses ready for us whenever we wished to go further.

We arranged to start again at 1 p.m., and meanwhile we returned for breakfast to the only fonda the place boasts. It was a comical little place. A tiny patio, like a bare yard, was surrounded by rooms with stone floors. The comedor was entirely of stone, and had no entrance door, only a doorway, inside which were a common deal table and forms. The bedrooms, all on the ground floor, the house being single-storied, consisted of two stone recesses, in which were three beds, print curtains hanging across the openings. The place struck cold, and I should not fancy sleeping in those stone recesses. We proceeded after breakfast to the church of San Juan. There is a fine font here, hewn out of one piece of grey stone, four feet in diameter and three feet high. The font-cover is surmounted by an ivory figure of St. John, about ten inches high, which is said to be ninety years old. There were several women in church, draped in black, and a celebration was taking place. Don Pantaleon took us to see a small room fitted up as a theatre for the inhabitants, and then to a part of the town from which we had a view of it and the neighbourhood. But the chief centre of attraction and excitement was a large sugar factory, which was in course of construction. New machinery was on its way from Europe, and some had already come. Forty horses had been required to draw one piece to Arucas from La Luz. Some of the buildings and houses were fine for the size of the town, which in 1883 had 8,000 inhabitants. It is also interesting as being the place where the celebrated chieftain Doramas was killed, and where the Spaniards and natives fought one of their battles.

The great product up to the present, and the chief trade at Arucas, has been in cochineal. As we passed along the streets we saw cochineal everywhere. Large, flat trays full of it were being put into and taken out of ovens, and in one place the insects were being made black. This is done by placing the cochineal along with some black sand in a linen bag several feet long, which two men swing backwards and forwards until the juice exudes, rendering the grey insects black, after which the cochineal is dried in the sun, and again shaken with black sand to give it brilliancy. There are three kinds of cochineal. The first is *Madres*, or mothers, also called grey cochineal, which, being chiefly all colouring matter, is considered the purest. The full-grown young insect is called silver cochineal, and is dried in stones, whilst the *negra*, or black, is produced by the process we saw. More cochineal is exported from Canaria than Tenerife, as it has not yet been supplanted in the former island by other productions. Tenerife is besides the wine-producing island, that commodity being exported from thence in quantity as cochineal is from Canaria.

It appears paradoxical to say that the greatest enemy of the Canary Islands in this century has been chemistry. Yet such is the case, as shown in more than one instance. But though the present generation are bitterly ruing the advances of chemistry in a particular direction, it is likely that future generations will bless the causes which uprooted an inflated industry and placed the agriculture of the country on a firm and reliable basis.

In the height of its prosperity, about twenty years ago, cochineal fetched as much as five shillings a pound. Then everyone hastened to be rich. Crops were pulled up, the ordinary pursuits of agriculture neglected, and everywhere the cactus planted. Land unreclaimed before was cleared of stones and planted with this unsightly crop ; and from the highest to the lowest money in considerable quantities flowed into the islands. A bag of cochineal passed current just the same as money, and was gladly taken in exchange for articles by the shops. One watchmaker in this island told us he used not unfrequently to take a tour in the island and sell watches at forty, fifty, and sixty pounds each, and sometimes in one family he has sold three or four. Those were golden days. The sun of prosperity had arisen on the Canary Islands ; they were indeed Fortunate. Public buildings were advanced ; handsome villas erected ; commodious and imposing warehouses constructed ; large edifices, like the still unfinished opera house in Las Palmas, planned. The wealth which thus flowed in so steadily was not, much to their credit, spent in riotous living,—in champagne, French cooks, gluttonous luxuries or excesses,—but the disease of extravagance took chiefly the form of indulgence in jewellery. Down to the poorest peasant, Spaniards are more or less affected with an inordinate love of display. The French jewellers did a good trade. Even the trumpery but showy Palais Royal jewellery found here a ready market. But other symptoms of the high prices fetched by cochineal were noticeable. The people about Easter-time indulged more than ever in their beloved cock-fights; the stakes were higher ; more money passed from one pocket to another. The Spaniards are born gamblers, and games of cards became frequent. The young man who affected fashion bought a horse with more showy paces than the one he had formerly ridden.

It was in ripples such as these that the wave of prosperity

dispersed itself over the islands. But this was not to last. Chemistry had not been idle. The meetings of the Chemical Society at Burlington House, where only a handful attend, and where the driest of subjects is discussed with the longest of words, though of no interest to anyone but the few chemists who gather there, are frequently fraught with great change to the world's history. The waste product from gas works, for which at one time gas managers had actually to pay to be removed from their premises, was gradually turning out a most fruitful and valuable material, and eventually the aniline dyes were discovered, one of which took the place of cochineal. At the present time cochineal is selling in the islands for from seven-pence to tenpence a pound (although it is given in the Blue Book as one-and-fourpence !), prices which do not pay the cost of production. This is a great come-down from those halcyon days when only one acre of ground planted with the cactus, yielding under favourable circumstances from three hundred pounds to five hundred pounds of cochineal, was worth from seventy-five pounds to one hundred pounds in cash to the grower.

If it be any comfort to them, the Canarios may know that theirs is not the only country which has suffered through chemical discoveries. At first sight no two countries seem more remote than Ireland and Peru. Yet there is a bond of connection between them, which has acted injuriously to the former country. Chemical advances have in Peru been the cause of much distress in Ireland. There all round the coast the poor people employ themselves in gathering seaweed, burning it by the shore, and selling the ashes—kelp, as they are called— from which iodine is extracted. Kelp used to be the great, and about the only, source of iodine, so that gathering the seaweed and burning it was a means of fair sustenance to the poor people. But gradually the price of kelp has been falling and falling, until at the present time the business is barely capable of keeping body and soul together. This falling off in the value of kelp was cited by the Duchess of Marlborough as one of the causes of the late distress in Ireland, but the reason of the reduction in the value of this element is not generally known. In Peru and Bolivia, or more properly, if we accept the result of the last war, which England has not done up to the present, Chili, at certain places there are great beds of nitrate of soda, in which some chemists found enormous quantities of iodine, and in a state in which it could be easily and cheaply extracted. Being very knowing people, though they extracted and stored up tons of iodine, they only sent over and placed it in small quantities upon the English market, so that the price should not fall too low, but they always sell cheaper than any other competitors, and they always manage to keep the market supplied. With this enormous supply of iodine ready and waiting to be put upon the market—we happen to know, for instance, that great quantities are stored at Antofagasta, in Bolivia—and with the unlimited deposits to draw upon, it were much better for the Irish to at once give up kelp-burning and to turn their hands to some other and more profitable industry. Kelp-burning (like cochineal-rearing) is assuredly a thing of the past.

The Canary Islands even from the remotest times seem to have had a great leaning towards the cultivation of dyes. One dye has been grown here for a period only to give place to another. In olden times the ancient Guanches, as I have already mentioned, extracted from the dragon tree a splendid scarlet dye in the form of a gum or resinous exudation, which was designated by the Arabian alchemists "dragon's blood." This was a rare and most difficult dye to collect, for many years must have elapsed before any appreciable quantity of it could have been obtained. The trees, too, are extremely slow in growth, and were never very plentiful on the islands. The "dragon's blood" appears to have been used by the Guanches to preserve their dead, the resinous quality which it possesses being doubtless the main preservative agent, though, at the same time, it is probable that the Guanches regarded the tree with somewhat of reverential feelings. But they were unfortunate with this commodity, for the Spaniards at Gran Canaria exchanged fishing-hooks, old iron, and little knives for it, and the saintly scribes Bontier and Le Verrier go on to say, with great simplicity, " The dragon's blood was well worth two hundred ducats, while what was given in exchange was hardly worth two francs." Poor Guanches! In 1403 they were no match for the Spaniards, who seem to have been fully alive to the means for making the best of a bargain. The style of these transactions is only on a par with the barters between the red and white man in North America, and with those now going on upon the west coast of Africa between the white man and the black.

Don Pantaleon tried to persuade us to mount the crater which overlooks Arucas, but as there was only a view to be gained by the exertion, and time was flying, we thought it better to reserve our strength for the ride to Guia. Arucas was in a state of excitement over a house which had been burned down. Fires are not of very frequent occurrence, owing to the absence of fireplaces, but when they do occur, there is little hope of saving the structures. Even if there were a sufficient supply of water, engines are lacking, and when they are forthcoming, horses to drag them up the hills cannot be found.

We left at 1.15 p.m. on the only horses procurable in the neighbourhood. It was not necessary to ride, as there is a road to Guia, and a coach, by which we sent our luggage, but the new road runs along the hillside some distance above the sea, and is not so pretty by any means as the old, which goes to and along the sea-shore. The latter is also more historical, for it was in the Bañadero that the chieftain's daughter Tenesoya was taken prisoner, and after being married to Maciot Bethencourt, was returned to her native land in exchange for a Spanish prisoner. She had, however, become fond of her Spanish husband, and made her escape from this spot to the vessels of the conquerors, preferring her husband's to her father's house. It is also supposed to have been here that de Sylva landed on his fatal expedition to Galdar. The

Cuesta de la Sylva is just beyond the Bañadero, and is still so called in memory of the event.

Twenty kilometres from Las Palmas we were 300 feet above the sea, and two kilometres further we had descended to its level. The first time we stopped—at the cluster of houses called Bañadero, after the bay beneath—I said that I should prefer walking, for my animal had the most unpleasant motion possible. It had a long step, and was a small horse, so I felt as if it were always stretching its legs too far. John suggested exchanging, which we did, and he preferred my animal. There is a fine coast view after leaving the village. Headlands jut out beyond each other, and at one spot is a little island where the sea has receded, beyond which is a sugarloaf cone, like the Peak. We passed two points, and then an open valley. Before coming to the latter, the road passes under a wall about thirty feet in height, and a curious circular bluff, like an escarped fortress. The carretera is laid out nearly to Agaete, but is not all macadamised. When finished, it will be a very beautiful sea drive, resembling somewhat, though further from the beach, that along the coast of Antrim, without, however, its green glens. Our path took us by the shore almost on the beach, the carretera running higher. A curious rock runs into the sea like a causeway, and the surf rolls thundering in. Some huts close by the sea, made of stones and roofed with mud, might be inhabited by ancient Canarios, so alike to their houses are they. Quantities of cochineal are everywhere around; it will be no loss to the beauty of the scenery when this ugly crop ceases to be cultivated. We were astonished to see in a shed no less than seven milk-cows, so in this part at any rate one should not lack butter. We rode by a steep path up a hill that led us to the carretera, no doubt the very hill that de Sylva and his Portuguese soldiers ascended. Near the top, at 450 feet above the sea, are a number of caves belonging to the ancient Canarios, roughly cut out of the rock, the doorways being square holes. Further up is a large cave, inhabited formerly by a Guanarteme, perhaps the very one to which de Sylva and his men were taken and fed by the humane islanders.   Our arriero, however, neglected to tell us of it, therefore we failed to see it, but it is, I believe, near the new road.   It was 3.45 when we reached the carretera, 700 feet above the sea.   The Peak of Galdar—a magnificent red cone—burst into view, rising out of a plain on which is the town of Galdar, lying at the foot of the mountain.   The country on this side is not pretty, the bright red cone alone giving life to the brown surroundings. The cuttings through which the road passes show a wonderful variety of strata—trachyte, grey pumice, conglomerate, red clay, sand, burnt stone, slate, and mould.   The road itself is only cut, and walking upon it is like going over a ploughed field.

PEAK OF GALDAR.

The Galdar peak reminds one of the Peak of Tenerife as seen from the Cañadas.   There is the same red-and-white colouring that one sees on the Cañadas and Montaña Blanca, surmounted by dark brown, streaks of which run into yellow and red.   Here the similitude ceases, for whereas the Peak of Tenerife rises grand in its solitude, around the foot of the Galdar mountain are dotted white houses, their red roofs lost against the red background, a few palm trees raising their heads above the town, and fields of sugar-cane in the foreground.   To the right in the far distance lies the Punta de Anaga of Tenerife.   The out-lines of that island on each side of the Peak look from here so exactly similar, that it seems as though they were drawn to match.   Suddenly, as we rounded a corner, Guia came into sight.   It and Galdar lie on rising ground, above the surrounding fertile plains. Each has a church with double domes, they are within fifteen minutes' walk of each other, and each contains about 5,000 inhabitants, exactly the same population statistics say within fifty-eight of each other, the inhabitants say within five. I hope the worthy people will forgive my calling them the Cities of the Plain, for anything more similar outwardly to what one imagines Sodom and Gomorrah to have been I cannot conceive. They are at any rate on volcanic soil, and should the neighbouring crater become again active, might possibly meet with the fate that overtook the Biblical cities. I hope not. The plain is entirely surrounded by hills, but its charm lies in the gracefully and beautifully shaped peak, of rich red colour. To it the eye always turns, and upon it the colour assumes shades that give the appearance of clouds flitting between it and the sun, throwing shadows athwart its surface. Frequently we looked upwards to see if there were not really clouds in the sky, or if the marvellous colouring did not come from the setting sun, but the sky and sun were guiltless. It is one of the charms of these islands that in no two does one get similar scenery. It is true that all are volcanic, but Nature seems to have exhausted herself in producing variety of colour and form. Outwardly the seven islands may be classed into three groups of form. Gomera and Canaria are alike in rotundity, but I cannot imagine two more different internally. Both have their highest mountains rising in the centre, but there the similitude ends, the scenery being very different. Palma, Tenerife, and Hierro may be considered as somewhat alike in shape, but anything more distinct than heart-shaped Palma, with its huge crater, Hierro, with its *golfos* and high tableland, and Tenerife, with its world's wonder Peak, cannot be produced. Take again the two eastern islands which are invariably classed together as similar, and we shall see on travelling through them that they are very unlike. The chalk soil of Fuerteventura and its granite gorge have nothing in common with the Burning Mountains of Lanzarote, the Risco and salt-water lake of Januvio. It is needless to say that points of resemblance can be picked out in each

island, but what is the leading feature of one is not that of the
other. Nobody can visit one island and rest content and assured
that he has seen all, that one island is a sufficient picture of the
rest. And the same remarks apply to the inhabitants as to the
physical features. The people in each have distinct, remarkably
distinct, characteristics, differing as did the numerous tribes from
which they have doubtless sprung. Can we wonder at it? Let
us look at home. How long have Great Britain and Ireland
been a kingdom? and are we all welded together so that a
stranger cannot see the difference? Does a Scotchman ever
lose his nationality and his accent any more than an Irishman
forgets to be hospitable? We mix, but we are not one. And
it is better so; it is the very distinctiveness of the nationalities
that has made the greatness of the kingdom. What one nation
cannot supply another produces. The dogged perseverance
and steadiness of the Englishman, the thriftiness of the Scot,
and the delicate tact of the Irishman have all combined to make
England—using the word in its fullest sense—what she is.
That any one of the three could do without the other and yet
remain the greatest nation of the world is an impossibility.
Take an individual as an instance, and endow him with the
virtues of the three nations, and a man as near perfection as
possible is produced.

There is a fair fonda at Guia, at which we arrived at
4.30 p.m. Time in Guia, however, is always thirty-five minutes
in advance of Las Palmas, why no one could say. Dinner
proved good, and after it we went out and paid some visits,
delivering our letters of recommendation. Señor Don Francisco
Martin Bento received us in his office. Most of the houses
have a room on the ground floor close to the entrance door,
which is occupied by the gentleman of the house, and is his
office or library, or both. It is to my mind the most cheerful
room in the house, perhaps from the presence of books, which
give an air of comfort and habitation not to be derived from
wax flowers, crochet chair-backs, and pictures of saints. After
a little conversation, Don Francisco took us to his wife, and

they kindly entertained us, producing wine and biscuits. We were desirous of obtaining information of what was to be seen in the neighbourhood, and especially the cave at Galdar, around which so much history gathers. When Don Francisco heard, however, that we had a letter of introduction to Don Rafael Almeida Mateos, he said, " Don Rafael will be able to give you every information and assistance." We therefore went to Don Rafael, whom we were fortunate in finding at home. He told us he feared it was impossible for us to see the cave, as it had been filled up with earth and rubbish. Seeing how disappointed we appeared, he considered for a moment, and said he would send to his brother and try and have it cleared for us. If we could only delay a day or two, it could easily be done. This, however, was impossible, as we had far to go and much to see. It was only the next morning we learned how energetic Don Rafael and his friends must have been in the night in order to compass our desires.

An amusing episode occurred at Don Rafael's. We complained that our horses were very indifferent, in fact that we could scarcely get them to go, and said that we were desirous of procuring better animals if possible. Don Rafael clapped his hands—a custom which is prevalent everywhere, and has a very Eastern and "Arabian Night" sound—and a servant appeared, whom he desired to bring an arriero, the best to be had. After a few minutes' delay a man came to the doorway, whereupon we saw our *own* arriero! I quickly explained in an undertone to Don Rafael the state of the case, at which he, with us, was much amused. He questioned the man as to his animals, but it was hopeless to think of changing if we already had the best in the neighbourhood. Riding-horses are exceedingly scarce and bad, except of course those of the gentry, but the hacks are the worst in the archipelago. I think we discovered why later. We took leave of Don Rafael, making an appointment for next day. As we returned to the fonda we had to enter a shop to ask our way, which was kindly pointed out, the shopkeeper, who was eating his supper, a plate of puchero,

at once offering us some.   It is usual to invite bystanders or
visitors during a meal to partake of it, but you are not expected
to accept the offer any more than you are intended to appropriate
to yourself a man's house, furniture, books, or horses when they
are placed *à su disposicion de Vd.* (at your disposal).   It is merely
courtesy.   The Irish peasant also asks you to partake of what
is in his house, be it only potatoes, but he is genuine in his
invitation, and is hurt if you refuse.   Many consider these
customs of the isleños as a sign of insincerity, and say hard
things in consequence, forgetting that a form of words means
nothing.   Do we really want anxiously to know how everyone
is in health whom we meet, and ask, " How do you do " ?

CHAPTER III.

> I would court content like a lover lonely,
> I would woo her, win her, and wear her only,
> And never go over this white sea-wall
> For gold, or glory, or for aught at all.
>
> JOAQUIN MILLER.

> Traverse yon spacious burial-ground;
>   Many are sleeping soundly there
> Who passed with mourners standing around,
>   Kindred, and friends, and children fair.
>
> ADAM LINDSAY GORDON.

November 9th, Friday.—We had mosquito-curtains last night, so slept peacefully. It rained during the night, and at eight o'clock in the shade this morning the thermometer stood at 62·6° F. (17° C.), a fresh, pleasant temperature. The fonda is 550 feet above the sea, so Guia would naturally be cooler than Las Palmas. We always seek the azotea, from which a good view can generally be obtained, and in this case we were not disappointed, for the scenery is really magnificent. Looking towards the sea, the view directly in front is limited by the Peak of Galdar, rising solitarily from the plain, and 1,500 feet above the sea. The upper half of it is bathed in sunshine, while this morning clouds really flit across the lower. The Peak of Galdar is the feature of the landscape, and it is difficult even to look at anything else. At its base lie green fields, while the blue sea forms the background. Quite to our left and behind us is

another mountain, a shoulder of which runs towards the sea.
Between us and this shoulder, lying more to westward, about a
mile distant, is Galdar. The plain is well cultivated with the
cochineal cactus, maize, and sugar-cane, and is dotted over with
sentinel-like palms. At our feet lies the well-to-do town of
Guia, just awakening into active life. The two towers of the
church, each with a Moorish-like stone dome on the summit,
are prominent objects, and have their counterpart in the church
of Galdar, in the distance. There is a large dragon tree in a
small walled garden at the back of the fonda, its long leaves
swayed by the wind, which is blowing from the north-west, and
is rather strong.

After breakfast another gentleman, to whom we had an introduction, but on whom we were unable to call last night, owing
to the lateness of the hour, kindly came to see us, as we had
sent our letter to him. Don Pedro Dominguez took us to see
the casino, or town club. It is a good-sized house, with a dancing-
room, in which are two pianos. There are no carpets in the
houses at any time, nor is there in the casino, but when they have
a dance, a carpet is put down. We next visited the church of
Santa Maria. The floor is of white tiles intermixed with a
few black, arranged in the form of Maltese crosses. The *bene-
ficiado*, Don Vicente Matamala, was in the church, and was most
courteous. He has made many reforms since his appointment
to the parish, and has done much in renovating the edifice itself,
including the addition of a set of new chairs, plain with cane
bottoms, and numbered, which we discovered were of English
manufacture. The high altar is painted in white and gold, and
the others are plain white, Don Vicente not liking colour. The
images also are in better taste than usual. There are two side
chapels, with carved ceiling. When going round the church, we
came across a chair big and black, and remarking it, the priest
said that it was for a stout lady, who had " no confidence in
the little chairs " !

It was now 11 a.m., so, mounting, we started for Galdar.
We were accompanied by several gentlemen on horseback, and

as we were all chatting, we did not reach Galdar under half an hour, though it is supposed to be but fifteen minutes' ride. We rode round the base of the Peak, and could see where the lava and cinders had flowed down. Numerous are the cave dwellings, cut in soft stone like sandstone, in which people are now living. Galdar lies lower down than Guia. The pretty Plaza de Santiago, in which we drew rein, is 350 feet above the sea. Our letters to Galdar being delivered, our friends there soon appeared at the church, and those to whom we had introductions were accompanied by all the principal men of the town. As I made a few notes about the church the silence was uninterrupted, and it was really painful to have fifteen or twenty men watching one writing. I besought John to make them talk, but his efforts were unavailing, and they evidently thought he was sadly wanting in consideration for endeavouring to do so. The church of Santiago has two side aisles, divided from the nave by seven irregularly fluted pillars of massive grey stone; the floor is of dirty stone. The church was built in 1778, but its site was previously used by Pedro de Vera for the celebration of mass after his defeat at Ajodar, one of the last places where a stand was made by the Canarios against their invaders, and which was for a time successful. We went on the stone roof, whence there is a fine view of the valley. Guia now appears as if lying on a hill, though it is but on a slight elevation. Below us is the plaza, the black walls of the houses, the green trees, the red and white flowers, and the fountain in their midst forming pleasing contrasts and a pretty picture. The town is clean and well paved, but does not seem so busy or wealthy as Guia. Galdar's *pièce de resistance*, did she but know it, is what we are about to visit.

Before the advent of Bethencourt there lived in Galdar a young and beautiful woman, of noble birth, who was as wise and good as she was beautiful. At that time Canaria was governed by many nobles in different districts of the island, who met together and formed a council for general matters. They had much trouble in keeping peace, and Andamana, by

her sage advice to the people, aided them much.   The nobles
or chieftains were, however, jealous of her influence, and not
liking a woman's interference, they persecuted her and her
followers in Galdar, and persuaded the people not to listen to
her.   This hurt her much, as she had given the best part of her
life to them.   She did not rest satisfied with complaints, but
took to action.   Going to Guimidafe, one of the chieftains, who
was considered the " most valiant and prudent of all the nobles
in Canaria," and who lived in a cave, she told him her
grievances, and proposed an alliance with him.   It is not the
only occasion in the world's history that the women of royal
blood have been obliged to be the suitors.   Guimidafe seems to
have consented readily to espouse both the princess and her
cause.   Accounts differing slightly render it uncertain whether
she fought and conquered the island before marrying Guimidafe,
or whether they married first and fought—their enemies, not
each other—afterwards.   The latter is the more probable.   At
any rate, Andamana and Guimidafe reigned over a united
Canaria.   They had one son, Artemi, famous for his courage
and virtue, who became king, and it was during his reign that
Bethencourt landed at Arguineguin, where he was repulsed
with loss.   The Canarios, however, also lost many, and among
the slain was the valiant King Artemi.   Artemi's two sons
agreed to share the island.   One, Bentagayre, was Guanarteme of
Telde, and the other, Semidan, of Galdar.   Bentagayre's share
was the land east of a line drawn between Tamaraceite and
Arguineguin, Semidan's lying to the west.   The council of the
twelve gayres was to have been held in Galdar, as that had always
been the seat of government, and the King of Telde and his
gayres should have attended there.   Bentagayre was proud,
however, and refused to attend, whereupon war ensued.   The
King of Telde had, it is said, 10,000 men, while the King of
Galdar had only 4,000, but the latter, owing to their mountain
fastnesses and superior valour, were able to hold their own.
It was this Semidan who, being taken prisoner and overcome by the power of Spain, refused to fight any more

against the Spaniards, and aided in the conquest of the island. Before that event, however, and after the rasing of the fort of Gando, Bentagayre died, leaving a son and daughter. One Doramas, a subject of the King of Galdar, and "reckoned the most valiant man in the island," had rebelled against Semidan, and, gathering together the chiefs of Telde, declared himself king of that district. Semidan sent for his nephew and niece, fearing their lives might be endangered, and they resided with him in Galdar. Owing, however, to the Spaniards having effected a settlement at Las Palmas, the Canarios wisely put aside their differences, and all joined to resist the invaders. It was the joint forces under Doramas, Adargoma, and Tasarte that fought the fatal battle of Guiniguada. Later, Doramas was taken prisoner at Arucas, as I have mentioned, and died of his wounds. The defence of the island now depended on Semidan, but the joint forces of de Vera and de Lugo were too much for the valiant Canarios, and Semidan was taken prisoner at Galdar. Later, Tasarte was made the general of the forces, and the son of Bentagayre became king in the room of Semidan, who when he obtained his freedom refused the sovereignty. Tasarte, after various hopeless encounters, and deserted by some of his men, threw himself from a rock. The war was continued, or rather the resistance, by the young King and the nobles, but, as we have seen, the King also threw himself from a precipice, and so ended the struggle of the brave Canarios against their invaders.

It will thus be noticed that much of interest centres round Galdar, and especially the cave of the beautiful Andamana, whose history might well form the basis for a delightful romance. It was this cave that we were so anxious to see, and to which, escorted by all the principal people of the town, we now proceeded. We stopped for a few moments on the way at the alcalde's house, where we had some wine and biscuits, his wife and daughters also accompanying us to the cave. Passing through a little piece of ground belonging to a cottage, we found several men still working at the cave to clear an entrance. It seems that on Don Rafael sending a messenger over to Galdar men were procured, and as soon as it was daylight they proceeded to clear the cave.   The rubbish had been put into it to preserve it, as cattle made use of it, and the paintings on the sides and roof were getting damaged.   Unfortunately, however, it is not improved by the depositing and removing of mould.   It was exceedingly kind of those who took the trouble to have it prepared for our inspection.   Of course there was no time to completely empty it, but a passage below the level of the ground had been opened, not the principal entrance, and the interior cleared so that one could creep in and sit upright.   The entrance way was four feet six inches wide by three feet high, and near it a chair had been thoughtfully placed for me, but I found it better to sit on the ground, for the air near the top of the cave was foul from the number of people congregated inside, and we had to creep round to see the painting.   The principal cave was nearly circular, and was, where we could measure it, eighteen feet in diameter.   It is possible that the walls sloped upwards, and that at the bottom, if it had been clear of rubbish, it would have been larger.   Another cave, to the right of this one, is also painted.   The painting is done in sections, generally running round the cave in widths of ten inches.   The ceiling is in squares, like a chess-board, white lines being drawn across the squares; then come red circles of two rings, the outer being ten inches in diameter; next are triangles, that fit into each other, the base of one being beside the apex of the other; these are painted alternately black and red.   The row beneath is a double-lined zigzag, the points or elbows being at top and bottom.   Between the lines the cave is painted red, but the spaces at the bottom are white. Below these are plain squares divided by white lines; the squares are alternately red and black.   Two more designs we noticed, one in squares bisected at right angles, the upper half being black and the lower red; and on a stone we saw red lines like inverted V's, one above the other.   There are no doubt other designs down to the floor, but we could not of course see them.   The temperature and the foul air at last became so unbearable, that we were forced to beat a retreat to avoid suffocation. We had candles inside to see by, for sufficient daylight could not penetrate. The principal feeling with which I left the cave was one of indignation that there was no one with public spirit enough to preserve this ancient and historical relic for posterity. As we slowly walked back to the plaza for our horses, a long procession, I got hold of the alcalde and asked him to whom the land in which the cave was situated belonged. "Only to a poor man," he said. I told him it was a great pity to allow such a place to be either misused or shut up, that the carretera would soon be finished, and visitors would be coming to the island, who would like to see the cave. I suggested that the town should buy the cave soon, while it could be got cheaply; that then they should clear it completely and put gates outside, which should be locked; that if a small fee were charged, say a real (twopence-halfpenny), the place could be kept in repair, and someone always at hand to act as showman when required. The alcalde listened attentively with bent head while I warmly urged the preservation of the cave and tried to make it so apparently feasible, that it should appeal to the pockets as well as the pride of the inhabitants. When I had finished, the alcalde raised his head, looked at me, and said solemnly, "It shall be done, Señora." I thanked him for his courteous attention, but felt doubtful as to how long after my departure this determination would last. How I wronged him may be told here. A few months later a notice appeared in a Las Palmas newspaper to the effect that the *ayuntamiento* (town council) of Galdar had bought the cave, cleared and enclosed it! I felt that one useful result at any rate had followed my visit to the Canary Islands.

Saying good-bye to our Galdar friends at 1.5 p.m., we mounted and rode out of the town, accompanied by Don Rafael and Don Pedro, also on horseback. The custom of escorting one part of the way when leaving, to "speed the parting guest," is very graceful, and takes the sting from farewells, even though the acquaintanceship be of but few hours' standing.

We rode along until we reached the new carretera, and followed it until we came to where a bridge not yet erected is to stand.   The road being thus interrupted, we had to turn off and down a bank some twenty feet high, which is raised above the adjacent land to make it level with the other side.   Don Rafael and John were some distance in front, owing to my animal absolutely refusing to increase its speed.   Don Rafael rode a fine little grey horse, about the size of what we call a cob in England, but large for an island horse.   Most happily for John, Don Rafael led the way down the bank, at the bottom of which was some red clay, dry and cracked by the sun, over which he proceeded to pass.   No sooner, however, did the horse's feet touch it, than he suddenly sank, almost disappearing ! Luckily the ground on the left side proved to be *terra firma*, and Don Rafael was able to extricate himself and get ashore, still holding the reins to keep up the animal's head.   The poor horse, however, could not regain his footing for some moments, in which we held our breath, lest he should sink deeper.   When he got out, Don Rafael leading the mirth, we could not help laughing heartily at the figure they both presented.   Fortunately Don Rafael was only covered with mud up to his back.   He had not been immersed completely, as had the horse, with the exception of his head.   The gentlemen lent a hand, and succeeded in scraping them pretty free of mud.   Notwithstanding our earnest entreaties to Don Rafael to go home to change, he insisted on coming a little farther with us.   We saw him later at Las Palmas, and were glad to hear from his own lips that neither he nor the horse suffered from their involuntary mud-coating.

We followed the old road, which traverses one side of a barranco, while the new is cut on the other.   The new, however, was presently brought to a standstill by a cave, inhabited by people, who will have to be evicted some day.   In the fields as we passed along we were rather amused to see donkeys ploughing.   The landscape is perfectly bare, nothing but stones and a little soil.   In places the stones are cleared away, and the ground ploughed.   The mountains as we approach them are very fine, and rear themselves grandly. The magnificent pointed headland of Aldea came in sight, and a little later we saw the grey gables of Agaete's almost solitary street. The village (population 3,385) runs at right angles to the sea, and consists, with one only exception, of single-storied and flat-roofed houses. The exception was that at which we dismounted. Passing along the street, we stopped at a large house at the further end, that of Don Antonio Armas. We were received by two of his sisters, who conducted us to the sala, where we waited for some time, in the presence of a life-size image of the Virgin of Dolores, dressed in black. It gave me quite a shock upon entering the doorway to see this figure in front. The room being in semi-darkness aided the effect considerably. It turned out later that the image had been brought from Spain, I think by the wife of Don Antonio, now dead, so that a melancholy interest attaches to it. We went out to see the sights of Agaete, accompanied by Don Antonio and his daughter, a pretty, pleasant maiden of about fourteen. We bend our steps to the barranco which runs through the town, in which there is a small waterfall over a shelf of basalt; water produces vegetation, and the greenery on either side as well as the water itself are pleasant to the eye. The waterfall is, however, the least curious part of the barranco. On the right bank the basalt is twisted and columnar, and caved in underneath. Through this basalt the water is continually dripping, and so fast, that jars can be filled beneath the drips. A number of women had their jars under the shelving cliff, to get them filled with the water. It was curious to note that, while the water in the fall was muddy from the rains, that dropping through the basalt was as clear as if filtered. Don Antonio says that in summer, when there is no water in the barranco, the supply through the basalt never ceases. This might lead one to suppose it came from a spring and had nothing directly to say to the rainfall. Leaving the barranco, Don Antonio took us through his garden, one not adjoining his large house, but lower down in the valley. A heavy shower of rain came on, but the thick foliage of the trees sheltered us completely. Oranges, mangoes, and guavas were dropping off the trees, and we trod upon them as we walked, while bananas, aguacatas, and all kinds of fruits were growing in abundance. The garden was, in fact, a wilderness of luxuriant vegetation. An excellent substitute for tea is used here, a plant (*Sida rhombifolia*) growing wild in the neighbourhood, but introduced into the gardens around.

Returning to the house, we found Paolo, our arriero, waiting to tell us that Don Sebastian Perez, of Aldea, to whom we had letters of recommendation, was in this town, on his way to Las Palmas. We therefore sent our letters to him, and he called to see us. He tells us that the road between this and Aldea is so dangerous, that we cannot possibly go unless we have good horses, but that if we will wait here in Agaete until the day after to-morrow, he will send for horses of his own and take us himself to his house. This kind offer we accept, after much hesitation at imposing so much upon the hospitality of Don Antonio, who courteously wishes us to stay as long as we please.

Don Sebastian is a Spaniard from the Peninsula, and lives at Aldea as agent for some property. We learned later that life was not too pleasant for him. He had been shot at once, so agrarian crimes are not confined to Ireland. We noticed that when he called he was armed as well as equipped for a long ride. As in Ireland, however, it is only the unfortunate agents who are interfered with; travellers go and come unmolested. Besides, it was only in connection with Aldea we ever heard of such trouble, the people there, it was said, being very poor, troublesome, and unruly.

Our next difficulty was with Paolo, who felt considerably aggrieved at not being taken on to Aldea, and requested four and a half dollars (eighteen shillings) instead of nine shillings, his due. We gave him three dollars, paying for a day's work, though it was but a short and easy day indeed of about three hours' work. We had warned him before leaving Guia that if we could procure better horses at Agaete, we should not employ him longer. He was so sure, however, that no better could be had, and that we should be obliged to take him on, that the disappointment was all the greater. His horses were considered "the best in Guia." I am sorry for Guia. One horse had only one eye, and stumbled; the other was broken-winded, and could not or would not go!

By the time this matter was settled it was nearly seven o'clock, and as we had eaten nothing since 9 a.m., we were quite ready to do justice to Don Antonio's substantially and hospitably laden table. The family in this house is large, several brothers and sisters living together; ten in all sat down to table. The party was a pleasant one. Each recorded the events of the day, and we gained much information on various matters.

November 10*th, Saturday.*—Our bedroom was on the ground floor, on one side of the courtyard. The outlook was upon a garden, a perfect wilderness of vegetation, which we were about four feet above. Coffee shrubs, pomegranates with white, bell-shaped flowers in full bloom, peach trees, a large eucalyptus, and hosts of others were what we saw. As we unclosed our shutter—for there was no window; in such a climate it was unnecessary—we beheld this small paradise. At 7.30 a.m. it was 64·4° F. (18° C.) in the shade. When we opened our door in order to go upstairs to the comedor, we found a number of people lounging about in the paved courtyard, or patio. They were chiefly women and children, who, notwithstanding, or perhaps because of, their rags and tatters, looked picturesque; they were good-looking too. The Armas family are bounteously charitable, and give away much to the poor people around, who consequently congregate here for alms. The worst of it is that they leave behind them more than one bargains for, and after walking across that courtyard into my bedroom I picked *twenty-one* off my stockings and threw them out of the window, slaughtering so many being too exhausting.

We had arranged last night to ride to-day to the mineral water situated at the head of El Valle (the Valley), as the upper part of the Valley of Agaete is called. The valley and spring belong to Don Antonio, and at the latter he has erected a few baths for the benefit of those who come for the water, which is said to be good for skin diseases.

After coffee, bread-and-butter, and cakes, we started at 9 a.m. on a horse and mule. I have seldom seen a more lovely little valley. We followed the barranco which flows through it, ascending all the time. The ascent was appreciable, but not until the end did it become stiff. Dark green orange trees, covered with showers of gold, pines, and palms, interspersed with greenery of all kinds, little cottages, or rather huts, poor and picturesque, and wandering in and out the river, only a streamlet now as we ascend higher and higher, form one of the most lovely spots imaginable. The rough path along which we scramble is generally on the right bank of the streamlet, and a little distance above it. Where the cliffs and mountains are bare, the stiff, straight stems of the euphorbia rise from amid the barrenness. The valley is a little like the Caldera in Palma, but on a minute scale. The mountains on either side are not so high, and the valley at the bottom is wider. We passed a woman spinning and a couple of men in blankets just come down from the mountains. It is said that de Lugo marched from Agaete to Galdar by way of Artenara. To do that, he must have come up this very valley, at the head of which, far distant in the mountains, lies Artenara, the cave town, to this day.

I have seen many curious articles used for roofs, but the strangest I saw to-day in the leaves of the aloe, which were arranged like tiles and pegged down. Most of the way the river runs through rocky beds, forming caves and slits, and falling in cascades. The mountains are all around, but not in that awfully frowning way that makes one long to escape from them. El Valle is, in fact, a cheerful, bright, contented, and happy-looking spot, haunted by yellow butterflies, which evidently appreciate its sunny depths.

We saw a man reading and, as usual, wearing spectacles. The eyesight of the lower classes is very bad in Canaria, and they suffer much from affections of the eye. We used often to think when we saw the flies allowed to remain in the corners of the children's eyes, six or eight of them at a time, that they must surely carry infection going from one to the other.

The boy who accompanied us went in search of the man who kept the key of the baths, but could not find him, so we were obliged to go on without it.

The ascent from this point, where a few cottages are clustered, is very steep. We at last reached the top, or rather our destination, which is but half-way up the mountain. Not a creature was here, but we found a little wooden shed, with three doors, like a bathing box. On its further side next the cliff was a sort of long-shaped tank, in which the water bubbles up as if boiling furiously, but it is not, being merely surcharged with carbonic acid gas. The temperature is 77° F. (25° C.). The height above the level of the sea is 1,650 feet. The iron (ferrous carbonate) in the water has made the sides and bottom of the tank quite rusty red.* After passing through the baths this aerated water flows out at the back into the river. The tiny plateau on which the baths stand is surrounded on three sides by rocks. It is curious to note that only a thin wedge of rock divides the fresh water from the mineral. The rock is very hard, like basalt in fact, and is covered immediately above and around with iron oxide. We of course tasted the water, which was as if powerfully aerated, quite taking away from the nauseous flavour so trying generally in chalybeate springs. It was perceptibly tepid. I was anxious to know the depth of the little tank or cutting, which was a foot and a half, so pulled my sleeve up and immersed my hand and arm. It may be remembered that I mentioned before that I suffered much from the sun raising spots on my hands and wrists, which were very irritable. These spots had come again with our riding, and on putting my hand into the water, I felt how soothing it was. So I put in both hands, and held them in the pleasant temperature for a few moments. I scarcely felt the spots again, and

* See Appendix for analysis of this water.

never to the same extent, the irritation ceasing at once. Not
being able to get inside to see the bath-houses, we peeped
through the chinks and keyholes, and saw white tiled baths,
about four feet long by two wide. There was nothing very
remarkable about the sheds. They were primitive, but answered
their purpose and the demand. That they had been built at
all is sufficient proof that they were needed, and that the water
is a powerful healer. It is wonderful how Nature provides her
own medicines. Owing to the dryness of this climate, skin
abrasions are difficult to heal, even in healthy people. Besides
accidental irritation of the skin, skin diseases are prevalent in
the islands, culminating in elephantiasis. The mineral waters
found in such abundance in Gran Canaria, and here and there
in the other islands, are said to cure many of these diseases, and
at any rate to alleviate them, so that the remedy is found alongside of the disease. We came across many of these springs,
but this of El Valle de Agaete had the most powerful mineral
flavour. What an opportunity for opening up the neighbourhood thus presents itself. That the owner is not at all unaware
of the value of the water, the situation and the beauty of the
place, we know. Even in the days of the conquest, this spot
was bestowed upon Alonzo de Lugo because of its productive-
ness and value. I was given a list of the advantages of Agaete,
not by any means intended for publication, but I do not think I
can do better than reproduce it, for it is perfectly truthful.

1. *Bonito valle*	=	Pretty valley.
2. *Buen clima*	=	Good climate.
3. *Muchas frutas*	=	Plenty of fruit.
4. *Mucho y buen pescado*	=	Much and good fish.
5. *Nacimiento de agua con cascada*	=	A spring of water and a waterfall.
6. *Iglesia en construcion*	=	A church being built.
7. *Aguas minerales muy curativas*	=	Mineral water of great cura-tive power.
8. *Un cimenteria de antiguos Canarios*	=	A cemetery of the ancient Canarios.
9. *Buen puerto con su muella*	=	A good port with a mole.
10. *Carretera que se esta concluyendo*	=	A high-road that is nearly finished.

Considering that Agaete is within easy access of Las Palmas, being only forty-nine kilometres, or about thirty-two miles, from that town, there is every probability that it may become a celebrated watering-place.

We brought back some bottles of the mineral water with us, which has been carefully analysed by Mr. Pelham R. Ogle, M.A., F.C.S. His full report will be found in the Appendix. The water is certainly unique in its composition. Though the salts in solution are not large in quantity for a mineral spring, they consist almost wholly of carbonates, one seventh being ferrous carbonate and the remainder alkaline carbonates. The peculiar feature of the water lies in the iron being present in the ferro*us*, and not the ferr*ic*, state, and the astonishing absence of other salts. Like the Spa water of Belgium, the iron and alkaline carbonates are well combined. Perhaps it most nearly resembles the Lower Soda Springs (No. 1), about thirty miles south from Salem, in Oregon, U.S.A., where there is about the same proportion of sodium carbonate to the iron carbonate, but with a considerable amount of the thirst-provoking common salt, of which the Agaete water has but a trace—a remarkable feature, much in its favour. I should think this spring has a great future before it as a tonic and as a valuable drink for anæmic people.

As we turn from the spring and begin the descent, it strikes us how perfectly charming it would be to have a cottage situated on the little plateau, 1,475 feet above the sea, on which we stand to admire the scene. Far down below us lies the sea, at the end of the valley, while to right and left and behind us rise the mountains. The view is enchanting, the silence unbroken, save by the soothing murmur of the rivulet. The women here are pretty, some of them beautiful, a fact not by any means to be despised from an artistic point of view. As long as we are human, we cannot fail to admire beauty, whether in things animate or inanimate; so to my friend's ten advantages of Agaete let me add an eleventh—beautiful women. But our contemplation of the beauties of the scene must end, and we

must wend our way homewards, where we arrive at 12.30 p.m.
I find a note to this effect after crossing the courtyard: "Caught
ten fleas and lost two!" The latter fact is significant, for those
two would probably be picked up later on, perhaps in bed, when
I should not bless them.

There are two peculiarities that we noticed in these islands,
one more in Canaria, but the other all over the archipelago.
The former was a curious way of saying "No" without speaking, by rapidly moving the forefinger in front of the face.
This custom would appear to be of Eastern origin by what Mr.
Ensor says of the habits of the Nubians. He mentions of a
girl in Nubia that " her sudden exclamation was ' La, la, la,
la' ('No, no, no, no'), and she energetically waved her forefinger in front of her face in order to emphasise her negative."
The other peculiarity is the habit the men have of allowing
the finger-nails, particularly those of the little finger, to grow
very long and pointed. I never measured one, but I should think
the nail on the little finger is frequently half an inch beyond
the finger. We were told it was a mere caprice, a fashion, but
at the same time that long nails were useful for playing the
guitar and making cigarettes! It is not a fashion to be
admired. Speaking of cigarettes, their use is productive of yet
another disagreeable sight. The constant smoking of them
stains the tips of the fingers, especially of the forefinger and
thumb, making them appear dirty.

Almuerzo, or what we would call luncheon, over, Don
Antonio and his daughter took us for a pleasant walk to the
sea. Crossing to the left of the valley, we went by a good
path to the port. As we neared the sea we saw an immense
field of black lava, about half a mile long and not quite so
broad, situated in mid-valley, but on the sea-shore. This in
the distance looked like an ordinary lava eruption, and so it is,
but it is also a Guanche cemetery, or, to be absolutely correct,
a cemetery of the Ancient Canarios. As we neared it we also
came from behind the shelter of the cliff at the end of the
valley, and saw on our left the remains of Alonzo de Lugo's

castle, a modern building—only four hundred years old—compared with the burying-ground of the Canarios. Beside it is a little mole, giving a good landing-place for small boats. The fort is very small, but was sufficient no doubt to give shelter to de Lugo's thirty-five warriors. The conflicts between the invaders and the natives were more remarkable for their fierceness than for the numbers engaged. The fighting men of the whole island were said to have been but 14,000; and as many were killed, others taken prisoners and sent to Spain and elsewhere as slaves, the Spaniards soon effected their object in depopulating Canaria. Geologically, the formation of the surface of this island is older than that of Tenerife—that is, there have been no eruptions within historical times—and if the Canarios buried here at the time of the conquest, we may be sure that within memory of their traditions this lava stream had not flowed. As we neared the cemetery we saw that the natural irregularities of the lava were still further increased by art. Every few yards there is a pile of cinder-stones, some round, some oblong, some square, and varying in size from twelve to sixteen feet. They are only a few—two, three, or four—feet in height above the surrounding lava, and are very irregular in shape, the top being nearly as broad as the bottom. So Bory de St. Vincent's exhaustive dissertation on pyramids, by which he strives to make a connection between Egypt and the Canary Islands *without having seen the supposed pyramids* of Canaria, is rather a stretch of imagination. Some of the graves were open, when one could see a space of sufficient length in which to place a body. In some there are bones and skulls, in others nothing but dust. Round the body are placed small stones, and upon these rest large masses of lava, forming a hollow space, and at the same time covering the corpse. These are again covered by stones, or rather pieces of lava, of varied size and shape. Some have red stones upon them, a kind of sandstone found in the neighbourhood, and it may be that these are the graves of chieftains. As we seat ourselves on the lava and look around, we are overcome by a feeling of awe.

Here we are in the vast cemetery of a past race, one whose antecedents are buried in obscurity and whose descendants are lost to futurity. When one thinks of the marvellous virtues displayed by the ancient Guanches, virtues which are supposed to belong only to so-called civilised nations—gentleness, chivalry, honour, purity—of the wise laws and institutions for governing, and, last, though not least, of the mode of embalming, the mind is lost in the mazes of wonderment.

That the Guanches and their language should have so completely been destroyed or absorbed as to all intents and purposes of distinctiveness they have been is a matter of deep regret, though scarcely of wonder when we remember who were their conquerors. I always feel, when speaking of this matter, that the present inhabitants of the islands represent the Guanches, for they are a very different people on the whole from the Spaniards of the Peninsula. Either their insulated position, their partial descent from the Guanches, or their mixing with and preserving many of the customs and habits of that race, any one of these or all together, have produced a completely different race in character and appearance, with which the Peninsular Spaniards will ill bear comparison.

The view towards Aldea is magnificent. A massive headland in the foreground drops perpendicularly into the sea, while next to and beyond it is the Punta de la Aldea, rising high near the land and dropping by degrees until it reaches the sea, the outline torn, jagged, and serrated, one mass of teeth, like the Dent du Midi in Switzerland or Troltinderne in Norway. Close by the black cemetery is a little white church, and by the sea, almost in it, a white windmill—contrasts in colour, religion, and race. It is a matter for posterity to decide as to which nation has proved the better both physically and morally.

Turning from the cemetery, we walked along the beach northwards, and entered some fields, passing through and along them. Maize was the chief crop. Some were in stubble, and the paths were in many instances of grass, quite a relief from the usually hard, unproductive bye-ways. As we neared one farm, before going upon the owner's land, our host had to shout loudly to him to gain his attention, to keep his dogs off. The dogs are half tamed, but fierce, and thorough watchdogs, so that if we had attempted to go on the land which was close to the house without the owner's leave and presence, the probability is that we should have been at least kept at bay by them.

A brother of Don Antonio's and a man from a neighbouring finca through which we pass come to meet us, the latter accom-

PUNTA DE ALDEA.

panied by a white cat, his companion in many a walk, he tells us. The evening air—for it is six o'clock—is cool and pleasant [62·6° F. (17° C.)], unaccompanied by any feeling of chilliness, for no dew falls in these happy isles.

Crossing the river near the source of which we had been this morning in El Valle, and on whose banks grow some tall and stately palms, we ascend a low hill, and half-way stop and turn to look at the scene stretched around.

The setting sun is shining on the mountains and point of

Aldea, bringing them out in clear and beautiful relief.   Over
the sea the sun itself is going down amid an array of attendant
clouds in gorgeous attire, bewildering by their beauty and
distracting as they rapidly robe and disrobe in every colour and
shade imaginable.   Teide rises high in the air like a peaked
cloud, far above the distractions of earth.   Leftwards the moon
is high in the sky over El Valle.   Silence reigns, and at our
feet lie the buried Guanches.   Teide gradually disappears
behind the clouds of night, and the moon alone watches over
the tombs of the sleeping warriors.   And so as we turn
away

" One more day
Drops in the shadowy gulf of bygone things."

CHAPTER IV.

AGAETE—ALDEA—ARTENARA—TEJEDA.

It is better to rein in a willing horse than urge on a stubborn donkey.—*Proverb.*

> Hardly we breathe, although the air be free;
> How massively doth awful Nature pile
> The living rock, like some cathedral aisle,
> Sacred to silence and the solemn sea.
>
> THOMAS DOUBLEDAY.

November 11*th, Sunday.*—We went out at 7 a.m. to take a photograph of the cemetery and the Punta de la Aldea. The flat end of the valley near the sea is well planted with sugar-canes and maize. The weird peak on the Punta looked black and forbidding, but the sun soon penetrated, catching the jagged pinnacles and tipping them with gold, until they seemed even grander under the newly risen than the setting sun. A schooner had arrived during the night, for we could see the upper half of her masts swaying as she rolled in the port, which is not visible from where we stand.

I forgot to mention that the mineral spring of El Valle was only discovered in 1883, by Don Antonio. Some members of his family actually went a few years ago to Hierro, to the waters of Sabinosa, for their health, and were greatly benefited, coming back fat and well, and this much more powerful water at their very door, and belonging to them, all " unbeknownst."

We had to delay our departure for three reasons this morning. A horse required to be shod, it was pouring rain, and we were waiting for Don Sebastian. Eventually Don Sebastian proved unable to come, the horse was shod, and the rain cleared. It still threatened to rain a little, so I put on my waterproof. Our friends were very anxious we should stay with them, and even when in the saddle, Don Antonio besought us to remain. We did not, however, like to trespass longer on their hospitality. It was partly the rain which made them so eager to detain us longer, for they feared the dangers of the road for us, as it is said to be the worst in the archipelago. Every road seems to be described by those in the locality as "the worst," owing no doubt to their only knowing the immediate neighbourhood. We started at last, with great reluctance, leaving our hospitable friends, whose kindness was untold. Don Sebastian had lent me his own white mare, a fine-spirited animal, on whose back it was a pleasure to be mounted. John had a mule, sober and trustworthy, so envied me my mare. The beauty of being a woman is that one gets the best of everything! The mare had a curb, which, however, Don Sebastian requested me not to use, as she would not stand it. He had lent us the two animals most familiar with the road, and he said the mare especially knew every inch of the way. So we started. At the further side of the valley, as we commenced to ascend, we heard some shouting, and looking round, a man called to us to wait for him, as he was going part of the same road. It reminded one of a caravan, this picking up of stray travellers.

We soon reached a narrow road or path cut out of a precipice, immediately above the sea. Perpendicular cliffs towered above, and 465 feet below the sea broke against the rocks. We are walking along a ledge scarcely four feet wide, but the path is so level and firm, that although there is no protection between us and the sea, we do not realise the danger, for to us it seems broad compared with others over which we have ridden. My horse insists, as usual, upon walking near the edge, but I am on the inside this time, therefore safe. It is a fine, nay a magnificent, ride. The rain has disappeared, the sun is shining, the air exhilarating. The good mare feels this as well as I, and dances until I give her rein and let her canter along the ledge. The arriero runs breathlessly after us, and, with terror on his face, begs me not to do it again, so we subside and walk as soberly as possible. I believe the mare knew what the man said; at any rate, she danced no more; perhaps the little stretch satisfied her. The path was continually winding in and out. As the precipices led, it followed. Presently we descended into a steep and narrow barranco, the bottom dedicated to a solitary palm tree, a hawk, a humming-bird moth, and a stream trickling downwards. The back-ground is formed by a magnificent escalade of escarped mountain, El Pinar, some 3,000 or 4,000 feet high. We now came to a wall rock, similar to the one near the Pico del Muchachos, in Palma, but not so perfect. Its summit was 650 feet above the sea, towards which it ran. The road descended once more into another barranco, at the foot of the majestic El Pinar, out of which we ascended by a steep cutting, until 750 feet above the sea. The path now became a little narrower, but we were near its end, and after again descending, we turned a corner, when a valley, more like an enclosure surrounded by an amphitheatre of hills, came in sight. Into this we descended. Two large barrancos and several smaller ones enter the Valley of El Risco. The land quite at the bottom is cultivated by the owners no doubt of the two houses situated there. Beautiful bright yellow flowers, growing in wild profusion, found, we were told, in but few places, tempted us to pluck them. As we entered the valley, we turned away from the sea, and advanced in a south-easterly direction inland up the main barranco. The sides are not very preci-pitous, comparatively speaking, but are completely bare, save for balo and euphorbia intermixed with stones. As we pro-ceeded up the barranco we came to a little green plateau, so fresh and green, that water must be near the surface. We rode up another barranco, leading out of the main, and con-taining six giant boulders. Thence we ascended the face of a rock very steep, and with very insecure footing, for there

was no regular path.   Here we met a man and woman with a
donkey, coming perhaps from a few huts we saw on the hillside.
The tops of the mountains are wooded, chiefly with pines.   As
we got higher we rode upon a ridge, only some twenty feet
in width, along which the path led.   We reached the top
and end of this at 2.15 p.m., and found we were 1,450
feet above the sea and had left the Valley of El Risco
behind.   Small shrubs of camomile abound everywhere, and
there is vegetation cropping up on all sides among the stones.

Our road was now rough, very rough.   Boulders, ridges,
and mountain shoulders were in our way.   The actual path
was narrow, barely wider than a goat-track, so we walked in
single file.   I generally led, as my mare refused to play second
fiddle.   Luckily she knew the path well.   Up and downhill,
over rocks and stones, climbing smooth rocks without the sign
of a foothold, the good little animal pursued her way steadily,
and without a slip or the faintest attempt at a false step.
She was not apparently overcautious either, for her pace was
a quick, proud walk, whether her forehead or her tail was
pointed skywards.   Rough as was the latter part of the road
leading across the mountains to Aldea, it was not so
dangerous as the part preceding it or what was to follow.

We reached the summit, a pile of stones surmounted by a
small cross, at 3.15 p.m., 2,300 feet above the sea, and
overlooking the Valley of Aldea, a flat plain conducted
seawards by ranges of mountains on either side.   Our path
lay down a steep cliff at the upper end of a narrow valley.   I
was pretty well used to bad paths by this time, but when we
began (3.35 p.m.) to descend this, I felt my only chance of
not being precipitated to the bottom lay in the mare.   The
path wandered down the hillside, twisting and turning as
seemed best to it in avoiding the boulders and rocks and stones
that lay scattered around.   The track itself was about one foot
wide, and frequently dropped in uneven steps, varying in depth
from six inches to twenty.   The mare never hesitated, walking
down quickly and boldly, but I must confess I only drew a free

breath at the bottom. No animals unaccustomed to the path could have carried us safely. The cliffs on the north side were entirely covered with euphorbia, while those on the south had none. Opposite, the mountains which terminate in the Punta de la Aldea present striking and magnificent outlines. As we reached the bottom of the ravine, we found some houses nestling under the shelter of its crags. Crossing the barranco of Fure, which was waterless, we rode along a narrow path past a farm built on the very edge of the barranco, its walls seeming dangerously placed upon crumbly soil above the edge of the river-bed. Plenty of cows around, and a big threshing-floor, testify to the well-to-do-ness of the farmer. We continued down the barranco, passing many houses or hovels, with mud roofs, and quantities of breso and euphorbia. It was now getting late, and our guide, a servant of Don Sebastian's, without saying a word, left us, and ascending the south side of the barranco for a short distance, hastened onwards by what we supposed was a short cut. We rather wondered at being thus left, but concluded he would turn up further along. We had now reached the end of the barranco and the mountains which bound it on either side, and beheld in the fast-growing darkness the large barranco of Aldea. The setting sun had flushed the sky over the mountains a rosy pink, while to the eastward the heavens were entirely lit up by the reflection. Meanwhile on tramped the animals, whither we did not know, for no one but ourselves was to be seen in the vast expanse. The barranco, or at any rate the stony ground, extended for some half-mile in width, and without the vestige of a path across its barren surface. I shouted to John—for I was ahead—had the arriero told him anything about the path; but he said, " No. You had better give the mare her head, and I daresay she will lead us home." There was nothing else to do, so we gave the animals their own way. They led us straight across the stony plain, winding in and out among some boulders, to cultivated ground, then took a turn to the left leading towards lights that were apparently issuing from a village ; before reaching it, however, they again turned to the left down a lane, the approach to a solitary house standing in mid-valley. At the door stood the señora, Don Sebastian's wife, who courteously received us, conducting us at once to a bedroom, so that we might have a much-needed wash before dinner, which was awaiting our arrival.

Doña —— is, like her husband, a Spaniard, and feels quite buried alive in such an out-of-the-way and inaccessible spot. There is no inn, of course, in fact no decent house in the neighbourhood save this, so that her hospitality is freely and kindly dispensed. But few travellers, however, penetrate here. Doña —— amused us much by recounting the adventures of three Englishmen who had arrived one night. They actually were travelling without knowing one word of Spanish. We thought of course this must be an exaggeration, but the señora assured us that among them they did not know a solitary word. One can scarcely conceive such individuals journeying in a little-known country without an interpreter. The señora had heard we were English, and it was a relief to her to find that she had not to sit opposite us at table like a mute, dispensing hospitality to guests who could not even thank her. It led them into awkward mistakes, too, for they actually offered her money, as if the house were a fonda.

November 12th, Monday.—When I threw open the window this morning, I was still more delighted with the view than I had been last night under the setting sun. Right and left are mountains. The former are in jagged peaks, crowned in the centre by a high and curiously shaped rock, the Montaña del Cedro. This mountain and the range which stretches southwards to Mógan form the oldest portion of the island, and are of basaltic formation. Immediately in front and around lies a flat plain or valley, the upper part of which is cultivated, but the lower is almost occupied by the barranco, a few scattered shrubs alone rising amid the vast extent of stones. Above all is the blue sky, perfectly blue, without a cloud north, south, east, or west. The climate here feels much warmer than at Agaete, which would be a comparatively cool summer retreat, and we find it is, for at 8 a.m. the thermometer registered 69·8° F. (21° C.), and at 11 a.m. it was 95° F. (35° C.) in the sun, which would account for the number of butterflies flitting around. *La Aldea* means "a little village."

After a cup of coffee our hostess took us out to see the farm, which for the neighbourhood is large, containing a good many animals. Although there are seven goats and a cow, there is not a drop of milk to be had, and the two little children of three and five drink wine and coffee like old men and women. The three donkeys are pretty animals. One is the mother, and the other two her colts of last year and of this. Good donkeys are worth from three to four pounds. There are a great many of them in the island, and especially in this valley, and numbers of them being almost black, I have mistaken them frequently at first sight for mules. The little colt, which is only four months old, follows us about the yard, and pushes his nose into my hand. All the animals are very tame, the señora frequently visiting them. The mare that I rode yesterday searched Doña ——'s pocket with her nose for treats she was accustomed to receive. The stables in these islands are very different from ours, the climate not necessitating so much care in avoiding cold. Here they form a square, and are merely sheds, their exteriors enclosed, but open to the yard. One contains the horses, another the mules, a third the donkeys, while a black mare and the white one I rode yesterday have another to themselves. Turkeys, the only ones in the island, the señora tells us, have a separate establishment, but the geese, ducks, five dogs, and seven cats roam at will. The extraordinary number of dogs, large and fierce to all but those of the household, and the presence of several menservants, were explained by the señora saying "the people were rough here, and her husband much away." This, coupled with what we had already heard of the difficulty of getting any rents in, suggested scenes that have been lately enacted nearer home. The landlord is an absentee, he, or rather his wife—for he is dead—living in Laguna, Tenerife. Out of a population of some 1,300 people, only fifty-six possess land. There is not a baker's shop in the place, nor even a venta.

The land around is under cultivation all the year, it never rests, yet it does not suffer from exhaustion, though three crops are obtained every twelve months. A field near this has just been prepared for barley, which will be reaped three months hence, when beans will be planted, to be gathered twelve weeks later. Such a country ought to be rich, and there must be " something rotten in the state of" Spain that it is not so. We have not far to seek the cause when we examine into the taxation.

Pepi, one of the servants, escorted us to see the village and the church. Both are poor, the latter naturally being affected by the poverty of the former. The houses are single-storied, and excessively poor in their appearance and surroundings. We entered the village church, where the first thing we saw was the ghastly coffin, black cloths, skull, and cross-bones ready to represent the corpse to be buried in the cemetery. The *cura* kindly showed us everything there was to be seen, which was not much naturally in such a poverty-stricken neighbourhood. The roof of the church is of stained wood, and in the chancel the whitewash of the walls is continued a few feet up the sloping roof, greatly to the detriment of the latter.

The isleños are great crochet-workers, so thinking I might buy a little from the poor people here, we went to several houses to see what work they had. It was difficult, however, to obtain any that one could utilise. When making the crochet, they do it all in one piece for pillow-cases, on which it is inserted a few inches from each end. Towels are also heavily encumbered with insertion and fringe, until there is but little towel left for use. The women of all classes sew a great deal, spend their time, in fact, in doing all kinds of needle-work, but chiefly embroidery and crochet. Even sheets are sometimes decorated with the most lovely crochet, many of the patterns being exquisite. It seems a waste of good things to put such work on towels and sheets, and for use it is not at all pleasant. Four or five inches of heavy embroidery and several more inches of heavier crochet at the end of a fine linen towel gives one the impression that the latter is only intended for ornament.

The houses of the poor people that we entered in Aldea consisted generally of only one room, behind one end of which a couple of beds would be curtained off by muslin curtains. The earthen floor was covered by a large palm matting. A few small tables round the walls, perhaps a chest of drawers, and a chest with a padlock would comprise the furniture; and very often in the most unexpected places we saw a sewing-machine. The women here are a great contrast to those in El Valle, being particularly ugly and very brown from the sun.

Don Sebastian's house is a little way from the village, and has a kind of path or lane leading to it from the main track. It faces the sea, but being one-storied, and the ground not rising all the way from the port to some distance behind the house and village, one cannot obtain a view of the ocean without going on the azotea. The house itself is built in the usual way, with a patio, surrounded by a verandah, into which all the rooms, except the two to the right and left of the entrance door, open. These are Don Sebastian's library and office and the guest-chamber, a bedroom which we occupy. The hall-door always stands open, and outside it are stone seats. These are occupied at intervals during the day by the servants, farm-servants, their mistress, and ourselves. There is a constant going and coming, and a continual demand for the "señora," over nothing apparently. To-day, however, there has been a little extra fuss, owing to the difficulty of finding a man and mule to carry our small quantity of luggage. The difficulty lies in the fact that we are strangers, that we must have our luggage carried, and that we won't give way to extortion. One man came and calmly asked two pesos and a toston (seven shillings) for a bag and two small cameras. We offered him one peso (three shillings), and he took a dollar (four shillings), and no doubt even now considers himself well paid.　But all day this matter has been hanging in the balance.　Continually Pepi has been coming to me as I sit writing in Don Sebastian's room, each time with a fresh proposition.　It would have been much easier to have given what was asked at once than to have haggled over it; but, learning that the sum was extortionate, it did not seem right, in the interests of future travellers, to "spoil the market."　The people themselves expect you to dispute what they ask.　Bargaining is a great amusement and occupation to them, and they would be immensely surprised if you gave them their demands.　It simply becomes a matter of how much they can be beaten down, and one is pretty safe in offering exactly half of the sum first asked.　All this is eminently uncomfortable; it is a worry, in fact, that I don't appreciate; and it is difficult to take it philosophically and look upon it as being as much part of the day's routine as getting up in the morning.　The two principal islands are decidedly the worst in this matter, and between them Canaria carries off the palm, for in out-of-the-way places, where the foot of a stranger has never been before, extortion is attempted.

Not having had Sunday's rest, we took it to-day instead, remaining quietly in our hospitable quarters, imitating the Spaniards in that we wandered in and out, but took no walk nor exerted ourselves in English fashion.　We went on the azotea towards evening, when the heat and glare had moderated. Seeing a seat on the edge, we sat down to look at the view.　A strong smell of dinner, however, assailed us, which at first we did not notice much, but when it became stronger, I jumped up and exclaimed, "I believe we are sitting on the chimney!"　It was quite true.　Charcoal and dry wood are used for the fires, so there is very little smoke from them.　The chimney is on a level with the wall round the azotea, and is covered on the top, so what smoke there is escapes out of the sides.

We looked, as usual, for our Guardian, the Beacon of the Isles, and after some time I found him, rising above the clouds.　I never can get accustomed to looking high enough for the Peak.

I suppose, because there is nothing to be seen but the summit, it is difficult to gauge whereabouts in the clouds one ought to look for it. The view we see is of the same side as that we saw from Chasna. The guardian of the valley here, the " Cedro," is a very fine, bisected-looking mountain. A number of valleys seem to converge towards Aldea, and there are a quantity of palm trees, the only trees to be seen, in our rear.

While sitting on the stone seats by the hall-door after dinner, a chicken of fair size jumped upon my knee, and calmly settled itself down to roost upon my hand. I was sorry to disturb the tame little thing, but *I* could not roost there all night. At 6 p.m. it was 66·2° F. (19° C.). We had arranged to start next morning for Tejeda. We should have liked to have passed up the centre of the barranco, as Fritsch did, but were told it was impossible, the boulders were too large, and there was water in it. As we were dependent upon our hosts for horses, we felt we could not do otherwise than go what road they chose. It was decided therefore that we should go over the mountains to the north of the barranco, and descend by Artenara to Tejeda.

November 13*th, Tuesday.*—We started this morning at 6.30, and crossing the barranco at the back of the house, began immediately to ascend on its northern side. John was mounted on the same reddish brown mule that he rode from Agaete to Aldea, while I had a bay horse, not the spirited white mare. A donkey carried the baggage, and, like most donkeys, he was of a bumptious disposition, and insisted upon leading. He had no bridle on him, but we did not fear his running away. The ground was very rough, loose stones of various sizes giving insecure footing. Intermixed with the stones was a good deal of the little thorny plant called " Christ's thorn," supposed, as I have before mentioned, to be the same as the thorn used for the Crucifixion crown. It has long spikes or thorns of about one to two inches in length, and an inch apart, on the sides of a pliant stem, which can be very easily twisted into any shape.

The colour is a dull grey-green. We found a shrub (_Teline congesta_) also growing in great abundance.

The morning was lovely, and the mountains stood out majestically against the sky. As we reached a solitary pine some 1,150 feet upwards, we turned to look behind us, and gained a magnificent view of the Peak, higher and grander than ever. We reached the top of the ridge at 8 a.m., 2,400 feet above the sea, from whence was a fine view over ridged hills and gorges, and into the barranco beneath. We followed an undulation on the mountain-top, on the side of which some men were busily working. Their trousers were short to the knee, and so loose, that they looked like petticoats. The shirts had a number of pleats in the sleeves. The women were working too, hoeing the ground, while a couple of donkeys were feeding near a spring of water. Bushes were being burned recklessly around. Reaching the top (2,859 feet) of the ridge, we had a splendid view of the sea, and were near the road we passed along from Agaete. Beneath, a point of land runs out, while to the left, behind, and nearer to us, is a precipice. Above the distant clouds and everything earthly is a small triangular brown patch, striped with white—the Peak.

Just as we were thinking of a halt and breakfast, we reached a kind of plateau at 9.35 a.m. (3,400 feet). As we and the men prepared to breakfast, we saw no arrangements being made for the poor animals that were so patiently carrying us along, and on whose surefootedness our safety and even our lives depended. We questioned the men about their food, but they only smiled benignly at us. We even tried to raise their pride by trading upon the rivalry between the two islands, telling them that in Tenerife the horses always had a feed when we did, but our endeavours were vain ; the horses got nothing to eat. We now understood why the beasts of burden here go so indifferently and are so poor. After leaving our halting-place, the path wound along dangerously on the edge of a steep slope, wooded with young pines. We climbed rocks on horseback that one would have to attempt with the aid of one's hands if walking.

The view all the time is splendid, extensive, and grand. Artenara is pointed out to us on our left, and we wind round the mountain side to get to it. As we were traversing, most fortunately, a tolerably level and broad path, John's mule stumbled and fell, throwing him violently to the ground on his arm. At the first moment we thought his arm was broken, but were thankful to find our fears were groundless. As soon as he found his bones were whole, John seized the solitary feed reserved for the horses at night, and opening it, gave it to the animals, telling the men his mule would have regained her footing had she been fed. It had put its foot into a hole, but was such a surefooted beast, that its fall was very astonishing. The men looked rather aghast at the provender being demolished, but entered a vain protest. We had a most hazardous journey still before us, and we could feel for some time past that the animals were going heavily, as if not up to the work. When they had eaten and rested for a little, we started again, walking for a time. John's arm was very painful, but how he would have got to Tejeda if it had been broken, I know not. The fatigue of walking would have been too great, and the jolting over the bad path would have been agony, and when we had arrived at Tejeda, there would not have been a doctor nearer than Las Palmas. So a stiff arm, not a broken one, was a fortunate escape.

The road over the ridges was awful. Whole slabs of smooth rock we rode up without a foothold for the horses. Then would come a step a foot or two high, when, our horses having planted their fore-feet, we would clutch their manes and move forward on the saddle, so that, the weight taken off their backs, they might draw up their hind-legs. It was useless to attempt walking to ease them, for this kind of road continued for a long distance, and was too fatiguing to be traversed on foot. Our arrieros said it was a track "not fit even for goats, only for eagles," and they were right. It and the path across the cumbres by the Pico del Muchachos, in Palma, we consider, are the two worst in the archipelago. I think on the whole, however, that

this is the worse of the two, as the bad part continued over
a longer stretch of country.   We met a number of men, women,
cows, goats, and donkeys going along the ridges, so the track is
an acknowledged one.   Beneath, to the north, wandered a rivulet,
and above it a cluster of white houses, named Corona.   The
ground is bare everywhere, yet there is quite sufficient soil for
trees or cultivation.

Clouds hover above, and when we are on the north side of
the ridge, on the edge of the crater in which Tejeda is situated,
and unprotected from the wind, it is decidedly chilly.   For some
time we had been on a tolerably level mountain-top, or rather
ridge, but presently we began to ascend once more.   A little
pool of water, formed by a trickle down a rock (3,900 feet),
was refreshing to man and beast.   We ascended by a *vuelta*,
or corkscrew path, up the face of a ridge or saddle that rose
higher than the surrounding hills, until we reached an altitude
of 4,000 feet, where we noticed some cave dwellings, so concluded we were nearing Artenara.   They are square holes in the
rocks, evidently artificial.   Two animals precede us carrying
codeso bushes, in which they are so enveloped that we
cannot ascertain if they be horses, mules, or donkeys.   Any
day one might see the woods of Birnam walking to and fro
in this neighbourhood, for firewood having failed in the vicinity
of the caves and Tejeda, it has to be brought from the mountains
on the backs of animals.   The opposite hillside is being
ploughed by five yoke of some—it is difficult to distinguish
what—animals at this distance.   There is plenty of what looks
like grazing common ; and there are green dips in the hills, very
refreshing to the eye.   A little cemetery, enclosed by four walls
of loose stones, betrays our proximity to a village of considerable
size.   The burying ground is entirely covered with grass, and
contains only two or three crosses of sticks.   A weather-beaten
church, its glass windows broken, the corners and buttresses
of red stones cemented and the rest built of loose stones, the
tower broken, and only the bells and belfry left, stands with three
houses on a little plateau, from which there is a splendid view of

the valley (3,850 feet). We are at Artenara, but the habitations of the population are nowhere to be seen. It is 1.30 p.m. We hear a loud and confused murmur of voices proceeding from a cave on our right, so, dismounting, we walk towards it, and looking in, find we are at the village school. The walls are some five or six feet in thickness, and inside is a fair-sized room. It is very odd to see the children sitting at desks in a cave. One feels as though they must be playing at school, but they seem serious enough, though we do not. Next to the school is a cave occupied by the cura, and another which is a venta. Turning aside further down the valley, we find the lower part of the cliff is entirely honeycombed with caves. Here and there they are evenly in terraces, but more frequently they are excavated irregularly. It was the inhabitants of Artenara that were despoiled of their flocks, which doubtless fed in the adjacent mountain valleys, by Alonzo de Lugo when he marched to meet de Vera at Galdar, taking Artenara on his way. Their route was a much shorter and more direct one than ours, as we came round by Aldea.

The people of the caves were pleased to see us, and invited us to enter and view their dwellings. We took some photographs of the exteriors. Caves of all sorts, sizes, and shapes abound everywhere; only just sufficient room has been left between to render the walls thick and roofs secure. Out of one cave comes a goat; in another stands a cow. Nearly all the dwelling-caves have doors of some kind, the rocks being cut square to fit them. If the mouths are too wide, however, they are built up with stones until they reach the required measure, a custom, as I have mentioned, noticed in the Atlas mountains. The rock out of which these caves are hewn is soft yellow-brown volcanic tufa, like the surrounding soil. Above, below, and around, little path-ways and steps lead to the caves. Some caves are over others, and some have low stone walls built in front of them. The sloping ground in their vicinity is cultivated, chiefly with pota-toes. Seeing the cura visiting his flock, we spoke to him, and elicited much information. We asked him if the people would mind our seeing the interiors of any of their caves, whereupon he told a woman standing near our request, and she gave us a cordial invitation to enter. This dwelling was formed of a square sitting-room, behind which were three smaller rooms or recesses, with beds in them, and clean white curtains in front. It was curious, but ought not to have been unexpected, to find the innermost caves, the bedrooms, entirely destitute of light unless artificial. The floor was tolerably even, also the ceiling, but both contained the marks of stones that are in the tufa. Shelves are cut in the inner walls, and cupboards formed. There are few, if any, chairs, only some boxes or chests. Palm mats cover the floor, on which the people sit or recline at their meals. They tell us the caves are always dry, and that they are cool in summer and warm in winter. No doubt the Guanches, or rather the ancient Canarios, to be correct, occupied these identical dwellings. They preferred living in caves, and it was, as a rule, only the poorest who dwelt in houses made of stones and mud. The cura tells us there are two hundred and thirty-seven caves, and allowing five people to each would give 1,185 inhabitants, a number not far wrong, as I found later, the official population in 1883 being 1,101. From the doors of the caves is a fine view over the Valley of Tejeda, the Roque de Bentayga, of ancient notoriety, standing out in mid-valley. Near it, apparently at this distance, is another gigantic monolith, the Roque de Nublo, from here needle-shaped. It is some 5,500 feet above the sea, and stands above the mountain on which it rests, overlooking the entire neighbourhood.

The cura, Don José Quintana Henriqulen, next took us to a chapel carved out of red sandstone by a hermit, Enriquo. The hermit did the work entirely with his own hands. The sandstone is not, however, so dry as the conglomerate, and the damp comes through a little above the stone altar. This as well as the chancel, a confessional, holy water font, pulpit, seats round the sides, and at the left of the entrance a sort of cell above the level of the chapel, containing a stone bed and reached by a few steps, are all hewn out of the solid rock, the cave being cut away from them, not they cut out and placed in the cave. There is also a solitary chair. The door is of stone, and there are seats outside of stone also. A garrulous old woman is the keeper of the chapel, and she begged for a donation towards it. There is a fiesta held here, but no regular services. Much to our amusement, she told the priest to his face that if they did not get enough money to pay him he would not come and hold service for them, so she was anxious to get what she could from us! The priest did not deny the accusation, but he is hardly to blame, as his salary depends so much on the services he performs, and among such poor people they cannot be remunerative.

This troglodyte village, the highest in the island, is situated on a steep, almost perpendicular hillside, with such a view lying in front of the doorways as the inhabitants of many a stone-built mansion might envy. Looking at the caves from a little distance, we could see that the entire hillside was excavated and looked really more like a gigantic piece of honeycomb than anything else. The land is cultivated where one can scarcely stand, it is so steep, but every corner is turned to account. We spent a pleasant hour and a half among the caves and their kindly troglodytes, being escorted round them by Don José.

It was 2.35 p.m. when we again started. The path, after leaving the caves behind us, was still cut out of the mountain side, which continued along on our left. It was a narrow pathway about three feet wide, and of firmly trodden soil, pleasant to walk upon. The afternoon was lovely, the temperature like a fresh June evening in England, so we went on foot for some distance. Some water trickling down the hillside, guided over an aloe-leaf as pipe, was fresh and cool. Potatoes are planted here in great quantities, and our men have orders to take some back; they find, however, on inquiry that they are very dear. Whenever they see anyone about the fields, they shout to him to ask if he have potatoes, and how much they are. Three pesos (nine shillings) is asked for one quintal, while in Aldea two quintales are sold for one peso (three shillings), rather a difference, and only a mountain ridge between. But communication is rare. As we approach Tejeda we find the land more cultivated. Looking at the maps, one has an idea that Tejeda is in the bottom of the valley. Such, however, is not the case. It is very high up, near the summit of a ridge which lies in mid-island, and across which one can pass to the gentler slopes of the north-eastern side. Presently we came to a little barranco, which crossing, we found ourselves among houses ; and leaving these, we descended into another barranco, in which was also water, after which the road led again along the hillside and among boulders, until we came to a valley, or rather hill, of rocks. The mixture of terms is confusing, yet fitting. Tejeda is a sloping hillside, intersected and cut up by innumerable barrancos, which all converge towards a lower and narrower part, where in a precipitous gorge they join, and form one large watercourse, which runs westward until it emerges at Aldea. Surrounding this valley of barrancos are high mountains, especially on the south, so that, although lying high, Tejeda is indeed a valley,

> · "A giant valley strewn
> With giant rocks; asleep, and vast, and still,
> And far away."

The shoulders or saddles which lie between the numerous barrancos look like hills, and are formed of rocks interspersed by grass and codeso bushes, with here and there houses. Crowning all this, in its midst rises the Roque de Bentayga, looking like a huge castle, with just now the sun setting behind it, throwing it into relief and lighting the surrounding panorama. Beyond and around are mountains, which dovetail into one another, and stretch further and further as far as the eye can reach. Jagged edges, serrated outlines, are their characteristic. The centre of Gran Canaria is a compressed mass of mountains. There is nothing soft or peaceful in their forms, but even the very rocks and mountains would seem to be a part of, and bear evidence to, the heart-rending struggles they witnessed between their gentle owners and ruthless invaders. Much of the scene around is historic. From Bentayga to the pitiless rocks below many threw themselves rather than fall into the hands of the conquerors, while in the neighbouring fastnesses occurred those heroic struggles made by patriots for their country.

Our road still winds along the upper and eastern end of the valley. Above us is a sloping hillside, and beneath the abrupt descents of barrancos and spurs. Several cisterns are formed in the upper part, where the land lies above the water supply of the barrancos.

We had two letters of introduction, and the first, to Don Marcial Rodriguez, we proceeded to deliver. Our men did not, however, know his house, and we were nearly at the village of Tejeda before we ascertained that we had passed half a mile beyond where he lived. So we were obliged to return, and going down a small barranco, arrived at the house. The arriero unpacked his donkey at once, without waiting to see if Don Marcial were at home, which, alas! he was not. We knocked at all the doors and windows in the place, but without avail, until a labourer living near, going home from work, told us that Don Marcial was from home, and not expected back until late that night. The house was a pretty little summer residence, and his family consequently were not here, only Don Marcial himself having come up for a few days on business. We had therefore to repack and start afresh to seek Don Antonio Hernandez, the owner of our other letter. Daylight was fading fast, so we were obliged to hurry. Close to the church we found Don Antonio's house, a large general shop, or village store. The owner was not there, unfortunately, but his wife, a fine-looking young woman, came out on receiving our letter, and, not very hospitably, bade us enter. The shop was filled with customers, who had an extra excitement, which they much enjoyed, in seeing us. Passing behind the counter, we entered a good-sized room, the windows of which overlooked the valley. It was built in the usual style, with rooms opening out of it at either end. After some delay, during which we starved in silence, our hostess asked us what we should like to eat, to which we replied whatever they could give us. Coffee, eggs, bread, and honey were finally set before us in a little room opening out of the sala, at a bare and dirty table. The supply was limited, but staved off immediate dissolution. There was a roof near this, so we went out to see Tejeda by moonlight, for a glorious moon was shining upon the jagged mountains. It was, however, so cold, that, notwithstanding our wraps and the beauty of the scene, we were forced to re-enter the house. At 9 p.m. it was 51·8° F. (11° C.), but at the altitude of 3,250 feet, and in the middle of November, one could not expect it to be warmer. While in the sala several men came in, and one, who had a newspaper—*El Liberal*—which had just arrived, pointed out a paragraph in it which stated that we were visiting Guia and Galdar and were then going on into the interior. The fact of our names being in print made the worthy people gaze at us with even more curiosity and astonishment.

John's arm had become very stiff, so I asked for a little brandy—a cheap commodity here, cheap enough to burn in a spirit-lamp—with which I rubbed it, very much to the interest of those around. One lives in public here. The brandy proved efficacious, and he was able to sleep during the night, and arose next morning with his arm much better. We rather wondered where we were going to sleep. However, a small stretcher-bed was presently brought in and placed near the wall. Our visitors cleared out, and our hostess and another woman retired into the bedroom opening off the sala. This was entered by a glass door, which, I was much relieved to see, was covered up by a curtain. I never slept in a more public bedroom before or since. There was a door in each wall, and none of them could be fastened from the inside. A basin was put on a chair, and a little ewer of water and a towel supplied. Soap was also there, but we always had our own, as the French soaps in general use are very burning and disagreeable.

CHAPTER V.

*TEROR—OSORIO—PRESENT INHABITANTS—
EDUCATION.*

'Tis pleasant, I ween, with a leafy screen
  O'er the weary head, to lie
On the mossy carpet of emerald green,
  'Neath the vault of the azure sky.
Adam Lindsay Gordon.

Harmonious nature, too, looked smiling on ;
Clear shone the skies, cooled with eternal gales
And balmy spirit all ; the youthful Sun
Shot his best rays ; and still the gracious clouds
Dropped fatness down ; as o'er the swelling mead
The herds and flocks commixing played secure.
J. Thomson.

November 14th, Wednesday.—The temperature at 8 a.m. was
50° F. (10° C.), decidedly cool, but bright, fresh mountain air
is always delicious. The church was open for matins, so we
entered. Near the door was a small figure of a female child
crowned, beside which lay offerings of maize and wheat. As
each person who entered presented his offering, he said, " Ave
Maria Santissima !" The interior of the church was plain, the
pillars grey, the roof of wood, with carved beams. The floor
was of uneven stone, and the windows small and square. The
tower had fallen on the outside, and only the little flat, open
belfry remained, as at Artenara. No doubt the wind, straight
from the Atlantic, works havoc in these mountain heights. The
exterior is whitewashed, except the corners, which are of red
sandstone. The worshippers consisted of five women, four

being in white mantillas and one in black.   When taking a
photograph of the scenery, we showed the men the view upon
the ground glass.   Some could not see it at all, but others were
able to make out the reversed landscape.   The views are
magnificent in this valley.   Tejeda is really a crater or cauldron,
somewhat like the Caldera of Palma, but more extended and
open, and its sides not so precipitous.   The saddle-backs
which run down into the centre, and, in fact, fill it, are all

ROQUE DEL NUBLO.

cultivated, while little barrancos, like gigantic cracks in the
ground, divide each shoulder from the other.   Surrounding
these is a circle of steep declivities, which on the left, or south-
west, rise in two abrupt points.   One of these is perfectly
sharp, a pinnacle, pointed like a needle.   If the eye travel
along the ridge from amid which it rises, it is arrested by yet
another rock, like a grand Norman castle towering on the
heights.   The former is the Roque del Nublo, the latter that of
Bentayga.   On the summit of the Nublo there is said to be
a spring of water.   This weird-looking pinnacle is situated at

6,000 feet above the sea, and is formed of trachytic agglo-
merate. Most of the houses in Tejeda are tiled, toning therefore with the landscape more harmoniously than the glaring
flat roofs common in the lowlands. Stones are placed on them
to hold them down, as there is much wind every night, as well
as storms. Where there ought to be a view of the sea to the
north-west, it is shut out by a range of mountains which run
transversely. A little nearer us than this range, and lying to
our right, is a reddish-looking cliff, which, if one scans it closely
with shaded eyes, will be seen to contain holes—the troglodyte
village of Artenara.

Having again, with some difficulty, procured animals, we
prepared to start for Teror. Our hostess sent her servant to
demand, somewhat peremptorily, payment for the night's
sojourn. We were rather astonished first at being asked at all
for money, as before leaving Las Palmas we had ascertained
where and where not we should have to pay, and secondly at
the smallness of the sum asked,—two dollars! We had only
been given eggs, no meat, bread, coffee, and honey, at breakfast. We felt convinced that the good woman was endeavouring
to provide herself with a little pocket-money which her husband
would never know anything about, and that he would be very
much annoyed that his guests should be charged at all. Still
we gave her the money, and she seemed quite happy and
satisfied.

Starting at 9.25 a.m., we wound up the hill at the back of the
house. The day was lovely, the sky blue, against which the
jagged mountains rose gloriously, and above and beyond them
the triangular summit of the Peak became gradually larger as
we mounted higher. The Peak really becomes in our eyes
almost endowed with life, seeing it as we do wherever we go.
It is the omnipresent genius of the islands. As we wound
along the hillside we saw two men riding towards us. One of
these when within a few yards shouted out to me, " Are you
the English writer who is going through the island ? "
Replying in the affirmative, he asked me how I liked Tejeda

and Bentayga, had I seen Artenara, and altogether proved
loquacious. We were much amused, and answered all his
queries to his satisfaction, as we were able most honestly to
praise the magnificent scenery of Tejeda. We found after
leaving him that he was Don Rafael Hernandez, and his
brother, who rode beside him, but did not speak, was Don
Antonio. With "adios" we proceeded on our way, still
climbing higher.

The view increases in beauty and extent over the mountains
westward as we rise, range after range dovetailing into one
another, until the eye gets lost amid their rugged tops and jagged
summits, lit by the morning sun. The Peak seems to rise as
we do, as if it would not be overtopped by any other pile. Here
and there a few pine trees can be seen against the blue sky as
the eye follows the outline of a hill, but they are the sole signs
of vegetation on those wild mountain summits. We now cross
by a dip in the hills surrounding the caldera of Tejeda on its
eastern side, and before losing sight of it turn once more to
see the view. Perhaps from here the weird pillar and needle
rocks that guard the valley look finest. The view to eastward is totally different, as is the character of the soil. Sheep
browse on close, short, sweet grassy slopes, and there is a pastoral air over the green valleys, undulating hills, and wandering
streamlets that is characteristic only of this particular district.
The height above the sea precludes all appearance of tropical
vegetation, and one could readily imagine one's self in an
English grazing county. When we meet the inhabitants,
however, they seem an anachronism. The men in Canaria,
and particularly in Aldea, are thick-set. The women are
comely on the whole, wearing red petticoats, affecting bright
colours in their head handkerchiefs, and throwing round their
shoulders scarves of yellow, green, and blue. We crossed
a streamlet (4,650 feet) surrounded by vivid greensward,
while huge boulders rested in the little valley. No better
camping ground could be wished for than this valley of boulders and greensward, while the stream murmuring down-

wards supplies the only necessity for a good camp. The sides
of the glen are filled with codeso and grass, plenty of both
being scattered around. It is only when one sees the bare
trees and the leaves lying on the ground that one realises that
it is autumn. The blue sky, hot sunshine, and bright verdure
suggest summer, while here there is just sufficient freshness in
the air to hint of June. And it is November, that month of
damp and fogs, the very name of which suggests more to an
Englishman than any amount of epithets.

> " No warmth, no cheerfulness, no healthful ease,
>   No comfortable feel in any member;
>   No shade, no shine, no butterflies, no bees,
>   No fruit, no flowers, no leaves, no birds.
>   November ! "

The antithesis of the above is the exact state of our feelings
and surroundings, and it is the fourteenth of November. But
we are in the Elysian fields, not in England.

An exceedingly lovely bit of giant rocks and greensward
meets us as we round a curve, still further intoxicating us with
the joy of existence. A little ridge we cross next, and beneath
lies another valley, through which a stream wanders, the green
hillsides being covered with sheep-tracks. We are reminded of
bits of Derbyshire. Flocks of sheep and whole hillsides of sweet,
short grass are to right and left; as we cross one mound or
hillock we descend into a valley, out of which we again pass
into another, and so on, until, getting further and further from
the mountains, we gradually get nearer and nearer to the sea.
We come to a basin of green hills, where we meet a flock of
sheep, in charge of a shepherd and dog. The bottom is
ploughed land, the first we have come to, with a house and a
few trees in its midst. The scene might have been English,
save that the front of the house was hung, and the ground
around covered, with rich golden maize. Bracken, too, helped
the delusion, but an eagle soaring overhead, not so common an
object at home as it is here, dispels the illusion. We make the
altitude of this house 3,900 feet. Very shortly after, 300

feet lower down, we came upon Valleseco, a valley surrounded by hills, well cultivated and thickly dotted with
tiled houses. We passed the village a little on our left, and
rode round it to La Madre del Agua, still in the same district,
where two springs unite to form the Barranco de la Virgen.
There are plenty of trees. As our road leads us along the top
of the low hill between the valleys, we look down into both.
These valleys are not deep, but are more like undulations, with
hills on either side proportionately low. The path left the hill,
and descended again into Valleseco, near the cemetery, which
is planted with poplars. The church, a plain stone, whitewashed edifice (3,150 feet), we reached at 12.15 p.m. As we
entered Valleseco, we became enveloped in mist, which
depressed us at once. The effect of these mists is marvellous.
Quantities of the graceful fern *Polypodium vulgare* abound.
The mist was not wide-spread, and we soon escaped from it, and
found ourselves once more in the sunshine of the pleasant
valley. We again ascended a hill. The sides of the road were
lined with aloes, and the top was crowned by a grove of
Spanish chestnuts. A valley opens out on our right, but a
thick mist hides it from sight. Passing round and over a hill
of red earth and green codeso bushes, we descend into a valley
beneath, where lies Teror. This town is situated in the middle
of the valley, which is green and cultivated, and scattered on
both sides of it are houses, white and with tiled roofs, a well-
to-do look being generally observable about the neighbourhood.
The path all the way from Tejeda has been of soil pleasant to
ride upon. Near here, however, we strike the new carretera,
along which we ride for a time, until it abruptly ends in a hole.
Alongside the road runs a deep, wide ditch, filled with caves.
As we descend we get beneath the clouds, and see that Teror
is surrounded by lofty hills on all sides, but particularly on the
south. The valley is wide, much larger than Valleseco ; the
soil is deep and good ; and there are numbers of chestnut and
other trees.

We had a letter to Don Carlos Yanes at Teror, but unfortunately he was not there. His son, however, showed us every kindness, and took us to his sister's house, where we left our luggage.

Teror is one of the larger towns of the island, containing over four thousand inhabitants. It has two objects of interest, one of which is likely to make it a still larger place in the future. The church of the Virgin of the Pines, which we visited immediately upon our arrival, has a massive but ugly exterior. The interior, however, belies the external promise. The stone pillars are painted grey, and the arches between the nave and side aisles are well proportioned. The altars are all gilt. The entrance doors are of handsomely carved stone, the floor is stone, and there is marble round the high altar. There is a dome, and lantern windows, spoiled by the same round, ugly coloured glass as in the cathedral at Las Palmas. The altar rails are of *caoba* (mahogany). Two figures, one of Joseph Nicodemus with a hammer in his left hand and the other of Joseph of Arimathæa with pincers in his left hand, adorn side altars. The silver is rich and heavy. Massive candelabra, splendidly wrought, artificial flowers, stiffly arranged and an extensive assortment of robes show that in the past if not now, the church was richly endowed. The doors which are old and carved, excited our greatest admiration. The floor of the church was once a cemetery. "Promises" are hung up beneath a picture of the Virgen del Pino, framed in silver. It is to this that Teror owes its notoriety. Formerly a pine forest stood here, and one night the Virgin is said to have appeared under a large pine, still shown, near the church, whereupon immediately a healing spring sprang up. A church was erected and dedicated to the Virgin of the Pine, and the pious come here, leaving tokens of "promises" that they make at her shrine. Thus Teror is now famous among the islanders for her church. But it is from a more practical point of view —its possession of a mineral spring—that one would predict a future for Teror. Leaving the church, Don Juan Yanes escorted us to the Baños Minerales. The mineral waters of

Teror are all situated on the right bank of the barranco, close to the bed of the river. Several springs issue from the rocky bank. Some are stronger than others, but all are pleasant to the taste.

On leaving the barranco we walked up behind a camel carrying three blocks of heavy hewn stone. The donkeys and horses that it met got hurriedly out of its way, giving it a clear berth. It seems that camels are considered very dangerous. This, as we found later, is only the case in this island, where all animals seem to be curiously misunderstood and terribly ill-treated. The men in Teror are very handsome, but the women are ordinary-looking.

By the time we returned our dinner was ready in a sort of venta. The inn really consisted of only one room, in which there were two beds, curtained off by white muslin. A woman, Señora Carmen, owned the place, had a little shop, and cooked for any strangers who might come. Grass matting was on the floor, and the windows were high above our heads. A girl came in frequently and disappeared mysteriously behind the curtains, whence she issued with various articles necessary for our consumption and use. During the evening we sat in Don Juan's sister's house, and had quite a *tertulla*, a reception of all the principal men of the town. Among them was the doctor, Don Manuel Bazo y Lamana. It is most difficult to gain information, as people do not realise what we want; but, by much practice in judicious pumping, we are becoming quite adepts in extracting the facts we require. Women rarely appear at these *tertullas*, though Don Juan's sister was present; but the men seem to enjoy conversation with others whose lives do not run in their grooves, and are much interested in our accounts of other parts of their island, of which they are as totally ignorant as if we were speaking of a far-distant country.

Beds had been kindly provided for us in Don Carlo's house, at present closed and uninhabited. We shared our room with piles of nuts of all kinds that had been placed there to dry.

Don Juan locked us in, as there was but one key, so that he could send us coffee in the morning, and left us to a comfortable night's rest.

November 15*th, Thursday.*—We took a photograph of the church this morning, and were stared at by a number of boys going to school, each carrying pencil or pen-cases, made of cane, with a cane stopper at the top. Behind the church is the plaza, bounded by the Palacio, where the Bishop resides when not in Las Palmas. Teror being only about ten or eleven kilometres (seven miles) from Las Palmas, many of those who are obliged to be frequently in the capital have houses here, which they can readily reach, this being a much cooler situation in summer. This morning it was only 59° F. (15° C.) in the shade at eight o'clock quite three or four degrees cooler than Las Palmas.

The Palacio is a long, one-storied building, facing the plaza. There is only glass in the upper part of the windows, the lower being closed by green shutters. The building is whitewashed, save at the corners and round the windows, where there is red stone. The roof is tiled. A curious arch, leading to nowhere, is at the top of a flight of steps; no doubt it was once open, but has been filled in recently. We sat down in the plaza on one of the usual stone seats, of which there are four. Grass grows between the stones, and the ground is strewn with the autumnal leaves of the fine trees which adorn the esplanadè. They are chiefly sycamores, while rose trees and geraniums grow luxuriantly around. In front of the Palacio and plaza is a fountain, with its back to the palace, but facing the main street of the town. The plaza lies on higher ground, above the principal street. As we sit here we can see the outside of the dome of the church, which is white, with bands of plain black stone. A winding stone staircase runs outside up to the circular balcony which surrounds the cupola, and in which are the windows, a cross of course surmounting the whole.

A convent is in the course of construction, the nuns at present living in an old building unsuitable for their purposes. They are eighteen in number, the rich paying about six hundred dollars (one hundred and twenty pounds) on entering and a peseta (tenpence) a day afterwards, while those who are poor pay nothing. They make artificial flowers for their sustenance. The new convent is built in very gloomy fashion, the world, so far as its beauty and sunshine are concerned, being indeed shut out. It stands on high ground, and might have a lovely view, being quite above the tiled, lichen-covered roofs.

We returned to Señora Carmen and breakfasted, that worthy woman demanding two and a half dollars (ten shillings) for our dinner and breakfast. It does not seem a great deal to English people, but it is a very high price in these islands. However, she cooked well, and the food was good and plentiful of its kind.

We started after breakfast on two horses, accompanied by several of the inhabitants as an escort, for Osorio, a wooded peak near Teror, famous in the past history of the islands, and now used as a picnic resort. After leaving the town, we ascended for some fifteen minutes, when we came to a chestnut wood, through which we followed a road until we reached a grove, where there were stone seats, a table in the centre formed of the trunk of an old tree, and a fountain of delicious water. Most unfortunately as we ascended higher it began to rain, and with the rain a thick mist came on. We struggled upwards for some time, but the rain became heavier, and the ground too slippery for the horses. John dismounted and reached the summit on foot, with one gentleman whose horse managed to get there, and found the height 2,750 feet. After sheltering under the trees for a little until the rain passed over, we returned to Teror. There are a few eucalyptus trees about Teror, and if only they were plentifully planted, they would help to drain the clayey tufa foundation on which the town is built, and which causes cracks in the walls of the church and houses.

We left at 12.40 for Las Palmas, riding as far as Tamaraceite, where we expected to catch the coach from Arucas to the town. Our way led through a pretty gorge, and over a long and old bridge. The new road, the carretera, is not yet completed, but will be shortly, as it is being worked at now. Our arriero was a very talkative individual. He began by paying me a compliment, telling me I " got on horseback like a bird " ! This was because in order to mount a chair was brought out, which I of course scorned, John helping me up in the usual English fashion. So few ladies ride, that no doubt he had never seen anyone mount properly before ! He tells us there has been already more rain this winter than for the past thirty or forty years. I questioned—feeling a return compliment was due—if he could remember so far back, as he looked too young, whereupon he informed me he was forty-two. We met ten men with mules carrying stones for building. A little more rain came on again, but we had wraps, and it did not last long. There must have been a good deal on the cumbres, as the barranco has water in it. We came upon another valley, opening out to the sea. The road is very good here, the ground being suitable for its formation. The sides of the valley are partly cultivated and partly covered by rocks and grass, upon which sheep graze. Potatoes planted on the slopes are nearly ready for digging. We met a woman carrying on her head a table, the legs turned upwards, with a drawer in it, on which were placed a basket and a bundle. It is marvellous how much and what awkward loads they can thus carry. The walls along the road were twenty feet high, and covered with moss, hare's-foot, and polypodium ferns. For the first time we saw cows grazing. Some caves are cut in the sides of the sloping hillside for animals, and further on are more caves for human beings, which are cut with eaves to throw off the rain. We met three more women, with baskets on their heads, and another carrying a shawl rather than nothing. They gave us the usual " adios," or as they pronounce it " adió." Our path now led along rising ground, and on the top, away from all habitations save one, we came upon the church of San José el Alanio. It is now desecrated, being used for fowls by the owners of the neighbouring house. The date upon it is 1676. The beams and a wooden pulpit still stand, the edifice

itself being of grey stone. The house beside it is of ecclesiastical
structure, and is surmounted by a cross; doubtless it was an
old convent or monastery.   Near San José a turn in the road
reveals to us six large reservoirs, lying like white sheets below.
John's mule has its fore-feet shod, but not the hind.   The ground
is much softer on the north-western slopes of the island than
elsewhere, so does not knock out the horses' feet.   Some more
women, carrying various articles on their heads, looked comical
with umbrellas held above all.   We had now reached the high-
road, along which a coach was passing.   The driver hailed us,
and asked if we wished to go to Las Palmas.   On answering in
the affirmative, he kindly offered to take us there for two pesos
(six shillings).   As the proper coach was due shortly, and its
fare for each of us was a toston (one shilling), we did not see any
object in paying more for his indifferent vehicle.   We walked
on to a venta close by, where we paid and dismissed our
arrieros and their horses.   It took us an hour and a half walking
leisurely to ride from Teror to the carretera, a short distance
above Tamaraceite.   Don Diego —— passed, driving in a carriage, and offered us seats, but as we had a little luggage and our
saddles, we refused his kind offer.   While waiting two coaches
went down and three passed up, so there must be a good deal
of traffic.   The mail-coach came at last at 4.20 p.m., and we
took our seats.   While delaying at Tamaraceite for a few moments
some beggars asked for money, saying, "Un pobre por Dios!"
Those in the coach answered, "Perdone por Dios," whereupon
they desisted from their importunities.   It is six kilometres
from Tamaraceite to Las Palmas.

Our travelling companions were much interested in seeing me
write while we were driving along, and commenting thereupon,
we got into conversation.   My note-book acted like a badge,
and when I was using it, everyone knew who I was, there being
no other woman making notes in the archipelago but myself.

The conversation turned upon longevity, and our two companions told us the ages of their respective grandparents.
One had a grandfather ninety-six and a grandmother eighty-

four, and the other a grandfather ninety-eight and a grand-mother who died at eighty-one. These are long figures, but coming as they did from two casual natives, they may fairly be taken as not exceptional. But it is no wonder that people live here to great ages. Everything seems placid, quiet, even, and conducive to longevity. The seasons change, certainly, but they glide so imperceptibly into each other, that they never jar upon the system. Now it is well established that in northern climates it is the change of season which is so dangerous to health. The hottest time of summer, the depth of winter, are more or less innoxious to the mass of persons ; but the trying times are when summer is departing, when winter has not yet arrived, and when spring is only budding. The greatest cold of winter out here only equals that of one of our warm spring days. The heat of midsummer is always endurable, owing to the delicious, cooling sea breezes. On Christmas Day a beautiful nosegay of roses may be gathered in the open garden, and young potatoes may be eaten in any month for which one likes to arrange. The people, like their seasons, do not move rapidly. Life is taken easily. They are deliberate in their actions, in fact far too much so if gauged by our northern standards, and when they do think, they take time to formulate their thoughts. They would dream the whole summer through—and their year is one long summer—eating about as much as a butterfly, whose life in many respects theirs resembles. They live, in short, in the Happy Islands, which they will tell you are indeed the Islands of the Blest. They, are content to do the minimum amount of work and to live upon little more than the God-sent fruits which abound so plentifully. Agriculture has always been of the non-laborious kind, elementary in character, as is generally the case in countries where vegetables and fruits are lavishly bestowed by nature: But the energetic eye of the Viking-bred or the commercial acumen of the Saxon, seeing the enormous capa-bilities of these islands, regrets the apathy everywhere apparent. Under British rule, and with British brains and capital, they would soon be the wealthiest islands for their size in the world.

But to return to the subject of our coach conversation, it does not require much scientific knowledge to see that were the climate not peculiarly dry and deodorising longevity would not be the rule, mortality must be great.   As it is, these islands—at least, the towns—are not at all prepared to fight any epidemic which might visit them.   There is a total lack of sanitary science, no drains, water scarce, and only laid on to a few houses.   It is terrible to think of the havoc which would follow an invasion of typhus or cholera.   But still the islands are wonderfully healthy.   Illnesses of the ordinary kinds, which are frequently fatal in the north, here lose their sting ; when they do come, it is in milder forms.   The climate is moderate, and it seems capable of spreading that desirable quality over the ills that flesh is heir to.   It may therefore be judged that the medical is not a lucrative profession.   The poor people are all herbalists, having their simples for every evil under the sun.   A doctor in a country part near Las Palmas told us that the peasants there considered a toston (one shilling) sufficient payment for setting a broken arm.   We inform our fellow-travellers, however, that Englishmen too have long-lived grandparents, and that modern science does for England much what nature does for the Fortunate Islands.

But though we might enlarge to almost any extent upon the want of enterprise and energy shown here in everything, a wrong impression would be conveyed by leaving the matter thus.   Applied to the great bulk of the peasants and the majority of the richer classes, what we have been saying about the apathy holds good, and is incontrovertible ; but scattered through the population of each island are individuals who are acting as most vivifying leaven.   We have met many such, men who have been on the continent of Europe or in Cuba, or who, being Freemasons, have read a good deal and know the state of progress of other nations.   Indeed, all the educated classes know that Spain is behind the nations in civilisation, but while deploring it, seem unable to resist the past influences and habits which still surround them.

We were glad to come back to comparative civilisation in the Fonda Europa, where we found some Englishmen belonging to the Cable Company had arrived to lay the cable and start it working.

November 16th, Friday.—We set out this morning soon after breakfast to deliver the remainder of our letters of introduction that we had been unable to present when last in the town. We could of course have remained in Las Palmas until we had seen all our friends, but finding that in order to see the island thoroughly we should have to return every few days to this town and make a fresh start, we thought it advisable to do our sight-seeing and pay our visits by degrees, thus resting before each new journey. Unfortunately, however, by so doing we missed one or two people whose country houses we had passed, and who would have entertained and given us much information in the interior.

The beggars in Las Palmas are terrible. They are allowed to congregate at the door of the fonda and advance even into the patio itself, to the great annoyance of everyone. They thrust under one's eyes, whether one will or no, all sorts of horrible diseases and sores, disgusting to see.

Mr. and Mrs. Thomas Miller kindly invited us to tea this evening. As Mr. Miller is now an old man and has lived all his life in Canaria, he was able to give us much and accurate information.

The agricultural peasants are most conservative in their habits. They use a large-sized hoe for digging the ground, a very inferior instrument to the spade, besides having the great disadvantage of the turned-up earth being at once trodden upon by the worker as he progresses. Several intelligent Spaniards and Englishmen have tried to introduce the spade, showing the people its manifest advantages—that it goes deeper, turns the earth more thoroughly, and that the workman goes backward, not treading upon the broken soil—

but all to no avail. As their fathers did, so will they do. The only hope is that the education of the children will be raised in standard, so that intelligence and enlightenment may eventually spread over the islands. The peasants are universally gentle, kind to one another, and soft in manner and speech, all of which excellent qualities make it the greater pity that they are so blind to their own advancement and the real progress of their country. The plough used throughout the islands consists of a piece of wood, which is pulled through the earth, at a depth of three or four inches, by a yoke of oxen. It is merely tickling the soil, for the earth is not regularly turned over. If they want to go deeper, the same ground is gone over again for another three or four inches, and so on. Relays of four, five, or six teams of oxen are kept waiting to continue this laborious work. A gentleman we know obtained from England a plough and a harrow, and did his best to induce his labourers to use them; but since the day when he himself used them with a pair of horses, twenty years ago, these implements have been lying neglected in a shed.

When a cow has a calf which dies, the latter is invariably skinned, stuffed with straw, and placed beside the mother in the byre, because, the peasants say, the cow will not continue to give milk unless she sees the calf. They refuse to milk goats or cows more than once a day—in the morning —giving as a reason the fact that it has never been the custom so to do in these islands. Now it is a well-known physiological fact that if these animals be milked twice a day —morning and evening—and thoroughly on each occasion, they will give more milk. Until the rudiments of physiology are known here it seems hopeless to attempt to alter these absurd and old-womanish conceptions. The Government, if anxious for the real advancement of Spain, and that she may once more attain a creditable place among the nations of the world, must at once see to education being compulsory, to the teachers themselves being taught, and the general standard raised much higher. A labourer, asked to mend a hole in the road which was dangerous for animals, replied that that same hole had been there during his lifetime and that of his father, and what was good enough for his ancestors was good enough for him !

There is quite a disproportionate abundance of copper coins, owing in part to an enormous quantity having been bought in the Peninsula, as there was a small profit on the sale here. The coinage is of very little value, a large-sized coin the size of a half-penny being only worth about a farthing and called a quarto. It is a very usual occurrence for a man to pay a bill of several hundred dollars in quartos. Copper is not a legal tender, but he will tell his creditor that unless he takes it he can give no other. The trouble to the shopkeepers is consequently something incredible. A large store has to keep two or more clerks simply to be counting up all day the quartos, the fiscas, the tostones, the pesetas, the half-pesetas, the reales, without taking into account the dollars and the weighing and marking of the onzas (a gold coin of about £3 value). It seems ridiculous, but it is nevertheless true, that the first payment by the Government to the contractor here of the Harbour of Refuge, consisting of £1,000, was made entirely in copper coins, stored in boxes. The contractors were told that there was no other medium then available, and unless they took the amount in this bulky fashion they must go without their money. There are no banks here, so that the merchants and others have to store large sums of money in bulky boxes containing paltry coins. The difficulties in the way of transmitting money and generally doing business are therefore very great, and to a London business-man would be insuperable.

The thermometer registered 60·8° F. (16° C.) this morning at eight o'clock, and last night at eight it was 59° F. (15° C.), a change from Tejeda, yet chilly, comparatively speaking. It rained during the afternoon, and it sounded as if floods were coming down from the heavens, owing to the water from the azotea running through rude gargoyles and falling upon the paved streets beneath.

When in the interior, we carry a few eatables with us, and these had been lying in our rooms since last night. The consequence was, we found, ants had attacked them, as they did in Orotava. There, however, they were red. Here they were tiny black ones, with white abdomens, and were more easily killed than the red. We rapidly got rid of them by removing the causes of their presence. The rooms are very lofty. Our bedroom is some twenty feet high, which makes it cool. The boards are bare, a strip of carpet only being beside the bed. Some coloured prints adorn the walls. A series comprising the life of Esther, scenes from the lives of Jacob and Joseph and Alcibiades, is bearable, though agonising artistically, but one of purgatory, hung at the foot of the bed and the first thing one's eyes rest upon in the morning, is too horrible. The idea of the Virgin standing and placidly and contentedly looking down upon unfortunates who are surrounded by fire, and whose faces are contorted with frightful agonies as they vainly stretch their hands to her for aid, is repulsive and revolting to one's ordinary ideas of a woman's nature.

The serenos are here as well as at Santa Cruz, and I had leisure to listen to them during the night as I lay awake, suffering from neuralgia and bothered by mosquitos. There were not many of these insects, but one or two had got inside the curtains, and I could not find them. I would adjure the buzzing insect,

> " With thread-like legs spread out,
> And blood-extracting bill, and filmy wing,"

to avoid us poor thinned-down travellers as not being worth "powder and shot," and to

> " Try some plump alderman, and suck the blood
>   Enriched by generous wine and costly meat;
> On well-filled skins, sleek as thy native mud,
>   Fix thy light pump, and press thy freckled feet :
> Go to the men for whom, in ocean's halls,
>   The oyster breeds and the green turtle sprawls,'

for,
> " Alas! the little blood I have is dear,
>   And thin will be the banquet drawn from me." *

* William Cullen Bryant.

November 17*th, Saturday.*—We started again this morning to see more of the town. Most of the sights are on this (the southern) side, but a few are in Triana. The casino, or club, we visited first. It is situated near the Plaza de Cairasco. The casinos are not in the least like English clubs. Anyone can belong to them by merely paying a subscription and intimating to the president his wish to become a member. The subscription is twelve dollars a year, paid monthly. It was

STREET, LAS PALMAS, OLD THEATRE AND CASINO IN THE DISTANCE.

10.30 a.m. when we entered the casino, which, however, we found tenanted only by two members. A small room, containing a table filled with newspapers and two cases of books, is designated the library. A long-shaped room, with stuffed seats round the wall and a few plain chairs, is the smoking-room, where conversation is allowed. Beyond it are a card-room and a few more used for various purposes, such as dances. All the rooms are *en suite*, so form a pleasant promenade on ball-nights. A printed list of the dances, as the same order is always preserved, hangs in one of the smaller rooms, where there is a Collard piano. Here for strangers a dress coat is not indispensable, travellers being excused, as the inhabitants know that dress clothes are not always carried when travelling. In Tenerife the aristocratic, however, a dress coat is a *sine quâ non*. The same roof covers the casino and the old theatre, the latter fronting the three-cornered Plaza de Cairasco, forming its base. A garden fills the centre, and in its midst is a statue of the poet Cairasco.

Cairasco chiefly eulogised in poetry the climate and air of his native land, but he also wrote on some of the events of the conquest. His accounts are so poetical, that they are not trustworthy. He was born in 1540, of noble parents, in Canaria, and while yet young was made a canon of the cathedral, which post he held for forty years, when he was made prior, or rector, of the same church. He was foremost in the negotiations with Drake in 1595 and the Dutch in 1598, when they invaded the island. He lived in the house appropriated to the canon, and which is now the convent of Santa Clara. He died on October 12th, 1610, and is buried in the chapel at Santa Catalina. Perhaps the best tribute to his memory is that Cervantes eulogised him in his *Galatea*.

Meanwhile we enter the old theatre. It is very small. The stage is more like that of a drawing-room than of a public theatre. We could not, however, see the place very well, as it still contained the platform and other erections necessary for the banquet which was given to the Cable Company. The new theatre, a fine building in course of erection, is on the banks of the barranco, near the sea.

We next visited the barracks, which are in an old monastery. There is only one company here of a hundred men, Santa Cruz being the chief depôt. The soldiers of these islands are more like militia, as they only report themselves on the first of each month, the remainder of the time being spent at home. The standing army is consequently very small, though every islander is a soldier. We passed unchallenged into the barracks. Spacious corridors and large patios, with not a soldier to be seen, looked dismal and unguarded indeed. Seeing no one, we wandered for some time along swept and garnished passages until we came across a civilian, to whom we addressed ourselves. He kindly conducted us to headquarters, to the presence of the colonel, who most courteously took us over the house, not even sparing his own quarters. There was plenty of accommodation for soldiers, endless rooms and wide passages, which before had only been "swept by many a long, dark stole." Few, however, were in the place, only a handful of men.

Leaving the deserted corridors, we passed to a more lively and stirring scene. The Colegio de San Agustin is a large school for the sons of the wealthier classes. It is in the same building in which the Jesuits had their college, abandoned since the year 1767, when they were expelled by Don Carlos III. The present seminary was founded in 1777 by the Bishop, Don Juan Bautista Servera, and the building has been enlarged at various times, and now accommodates three classes of students and boys. We asked for the rector, Don Juan Hidalgo, who kindly gave us permission to inspect the school. We came later in the day to see the Seminario, or theological college, as the students were in class when we first called. The boys of the Colegio sat in classrooms on seats round the walls, except in the writing-room, where there were desks. The books are badly printed and antiquated, of the hodge-podge description. When passing one of the class-rooms, the boys all rose instantaneously, and remained so standing until we requested them to be seated. It was odd to see many of the masters smoking. The dormitories were airy, and the beds of iron, some feet apart. Between each bed was a washstand. Downstairs, in a room for the purpose, were a number of tiny wardrobes, each about six feet high and one and a half feet wide, for the boys' clothes. Besides this room there was another, formed of separate cells or closets, for washing; here there were baths and basins. The dormitories and every place looked very clean, but, as usual in these islands, the sanitary arrangements were bad and particularly offensive. The boys walk out on Thursdays and Sundays, but do not seem to have sufficient exercise.*

It was in this school that Leon y Castillo was educated, who has since become a "minister of the Crown."

In the present course thirty-six students have matriculated in the Faculty, in the secondary there are one hundred and fifty-four matriculated students, and in the Seminario—those who are going to be priests—there are five resident and twenty-six non-resident students.

Leaving the Colegio, we went down the sloping streets to the sea by the barranco. Here, in an open situation, stands the new theatre. It is a fine building, and is opposite the market, the river lying between. Workmen are still engaged on the interior. It holds 1,600 people, and is well arranged, as from every seat the stage is easily visible; the pillars are small, and do not interfere with the view. There does not seem to be enough space for scene-shifting on the stage, nor do the exits appear sufficiently easy of access in case of fire. Las Palmas is very proud of having such a fine theatre, and one which outstrips Santa Cruz in point of size. It is questionable, however, if it will ever be filled. It is fit for one of the capitals of Europe, whereas the whole population, from the mountains to the sea, of Gran Canaria is not 90,000 souls.

There are very few advertisement placards on the walls of the town, and those which are there relate chiefly to the sailings of emigration vessels to Cuba.

Perhaps what strikes one as most remarkable from a commercial point of view is that the trade here, and in Tenerife to a less extent, is chiefly in the hands of English people. There is still an export trade done from Las Palmas in cochineal, which is far greater than that from Tenerife. The latter is the wine-growing island, however, and will gradually, it is hoped,

* The terms are seventy-eight dollars (fifteen guineas) for eight months. There are at present one hundred and five boarders and ninety-two day-boys.

now that the cochineal fever is over, resume its export of wines. Santa Cruz at present is chiefly dependent for its trade upon its being a coaling station, daily increasing, and which, when the cable is laid, will no doubt increase enormously, to the detriment of Madeira. Messrs. Blandy Brothers, of the latter place, have, however, wisely for their own sakes, started a coaling depôt at Las Palmas.

There is a quaint and pretty little church, called San Teophilo, in an out-of-the-way corner of Las Palmas. It has a painted dome that must be two centuries old at least, and a carved altar, to the right of the main altar, in well-executed, florid style. A large picture behind the altar is also said to be of ancient date.

CHAPTER VI.

SANTA BRIGIDA—SAN MATEO—POZO DE LAS NIEVES—TIRAJANA.

Let others repine at the lack of turnpike-roads and sumptuous hotels, and all the elaborate comforts of a country cultivated into tameness and commonplace; but give me the rude mountain scramble, the roving, haphazard, wayfaring, the frank, hospitable, though half wild manners, that impart such a true game flavour to romantic Spain!—WASHINGTON IRVING.

> These are Thy glorious works, Parent of good,
> Almighty! Thine this universal frame,
> Thus wondrous fair. Thyself how wondrous then!
> > MILTON.

November 19*th, Monday.*—There has been a heavy swell for some days, and as the sea is just at the end of this street, we can hear it very distinctly at night as the waves break upon the shore. It is one of the disadvantages of Las Palmas that nowhere in the town can one get upon the sea-shore—the real beach. It is even impossible to see the break of the waves as they dash on the land without going a long distance out of the town.

The temperature this morning at eight o'clock was 68° F. (20° C.), so was pleasant for our projected journey. We propose this time driving to San Mateo by Tafira, and thence riding across the highest mountain, the Pozo de las Nieves, to Tirajana, from which, if time permit, to Maspalomas and Juan Grande, returning by Aguimes and Telde to Las Palmas. We have, however, not too much time to spare if we would be back in England by Christmas.

Owing to some misunderstanding, the carriage did not arrive until 11 a.m. instead of ten o'clock, so it was 11.15 before we started. When twenty minutes on our way, we suddenly remembered we had forgotten the saddles, so had to turn back for them, greatly to the disgust of the coachman, who declared we could get saddles in San Mateo. This we knew to be a fable. So our second start was made at 11.50.

We drove up by a dip in the hills at the back of the town, on the right bank of the barranco. Palms grow luxuriantly here, and by the roadside we saw a set of four curiously springing from the same root, and a little further three growing in the same way from a solitary root. The road led up by the Guiniguada, a valley between low hills, rugged and bare. Three kilometres from the town the ascent becomes more rapid, and we leave the valley, ascending the brown hillside by a vuelta. Numerous pack-horses, mules, and donkeys were leaving the town after the morning's marketing, and where the road wound up the hill they took the shorter and older way, readily keeping pace with our more rapid motion on the new road. A good many of the breechbands used with the pack-saddles have the wool left on the hide; one black mule looked particularly handsome, with the white, soft wool against his flanks. The more I see them, the more I marvel at the way the women carry everything on their heads, regardless of weight or form. A woman passed just now with a pair of boots slung across her head by the laces.

A small peaked hill by the side of the road, called the Pico del Viento, is 800 feet above the sea. These little peaked cones are pretty, and give a peculiar appearance to the landscape everywhere. We began to enter Tafira—the elder—at 12.25. This portion of the village is a long, straggling, sleepy-looking street of one or two-storied houses, which continues straight up the hill, but the new road diverges to the right, bringing into sight a fine view of the Isleta. In the foreground are some of the numerous villas of the inhabitants of Las Palmas, for this is the summer resort. Mounds and hills, green and cultivated, assist the landscape, which is almost pastoral, the nearest approach to the pastoral at least that one sees in these islands. Upper and modern Tafira (1,200 feet) has a larger street, full of houses, and looks down upon a well-cultivated valley, with pretty homesteads, surrounded by gardens. The valley is almost flat below, with steep hillsides, and always beyond lies the Isleta, making a picturesque background. Don Agustin Bravo's house is 1,350 feet above the sea, and close by the road we pass Mr. Swanston's, buried in trees, the height and short distance from Las Palmas making this a very suitable as well as pretty summer retreat.

Alongside of the road runs a narrow watercourse, at which all the neighbourhood seem to be washing, a few yards of short turf on either side and aloe hedges affording drying ground. Many of the women who were washing had cooking utensils with them, and made fires, so that they need not return home for meals. We met two waggonettes, with fine grey and cream-coloured horses, seeming almost out of place in these primitive islands, but this isle at least is becoming rapidly civilised under the influence of the carreteras. The mixture of civilisation and primitiveness struck us forcibly as we at the same time noted that the roads were weeded and our driver offered John a cigarette! It was done of course with the air and grace of a marquis. The road leads past gentle, sloping ground, not terraced, and at present with an artistic, yellowy brown look, given by the withering vines. The vines here creep along the ground, sometimes only a foot or two above it and again quite upon it, so that they give colour without destroying the contour of the hills. It is like an English county but for the peaked hills and the cacti. The new carretera has spoiled the privacy of many of the houses which formerly lay at some distance from the old road ; we could have stepped from our carriage on to many of the azoteas of houses lying below our level. A large cistern that we pass suggests a swimming bath. The road towards Santa Brigida descends, crossing over a hill from one valley to another, and as we enter this village we pass the thirteenth kilometre stone, at a height of 1,550 feet, at five minutes past one o'clock.

There is a tobacco manufactory in Santa Brigida, belonging to the same owners as those in Orotava and Adeje. Having a letter to the manager, we present it, and are shown over the building. This is almost square, being fifty-five metres long by forty-four wide. Thirty-five women and seven men are employed in the manufacture of cigars. Outside the doors grow tobacco and canes, ready to hand. The latter are used to make cages, in which the leaves are placed to ferment, or as lines upon which they are hung to dry. Long passages or avenues of these hang beneath a large shed, in five tiers, and some three feet apart. The tobacco leaves do not grow here suitably for making the *capa*, or outside covering of cigars, but have to be imported from Adeje, where they are finer. We were shown some tobacco seed, which is very like snuff, but not so fine.

We started again at 1.45 p.m., passing the Santa Brigida church, a plain white edifice, save for its brown stone tower, with bells at the top.

Our poor horses are very indifferent animals. One of them is really suffering from some illness, and ought to be in his stable. Both are broken-winded, and entirely unfit for driving. Frequently we had to stop them in order to let the poor beasts get their wind. One of these stopping-places was near Los Peris (1,900 feet), by a huge mulberry tree. The ground rises more abruptly now, so our road winds up the hill, enabling us to look back on Santa Brigida. What a contrast these broken-winded beasts are to the little grass-fed Norwegian horses, that eat and drink as they please all day, whereas these poor animals are only fed at night! They are brutally whipped. What can be expected from such a bad system? It is impossible to get good work out of badly fed animals. The driver changed the horses from one side to the other to try and make them go, but it was perfectly useless; the poor things *could* not. It was an agonising drive. If we had not had luggage, I should have preferred walking, which indeed we often did as it was. A gigantic chestnut tree attracted our attention as it stood near the side of the road quite by itself in a field, so we got down to look at it, and found it was a magnificent specimen. Having no tree near it, it has grown evenly, and is indeed a spreading chestnut tree. It is not so large as the one in Orotava, but is still in the height of its glory. It has a girth of twenty-five feet at four feet from the ground, and branches at five feet. There are three main branches, subdivided near their junction with the trunk into many other large boughs. Only one branch has been cut off. Its interest lies, however, more perhaps in its beauty and symmetry of form than in its size. It is the property of Don Francisco Manriquez. It is on higher ground than the one at the Villa de Orotava, being 2,250 feet above the sea, and is some eighteen or nineteen kilometres (about twelve miles) from Las Palmas.

A few kilometres further, and twenty-one from Las Palmas, we reach San Mateo, a fresh little town nestling in a valley amid the mountains, containing over 3,800 inhabitants in its district, though the town has only five hundred and sixty-four people. Here, a warning having been sent that we were coming, we found we were expected by the schoolmistress, the only person who could give us food and beds. As the afternoon was yet early, we delivered our letters of introduction, and were conducted about San Mateo by two most intelligent men, one of whom was the village shopkeeper, Don José N. Gil, and Don T. Socorro. The Valley of San Mateo is a lovely spot. Water trickles from the mountains down the various valleys surrounding it, forming cascades and rivulets, producing glens of exquisite beauty. A pretty little natural fountain is the Fuente de la Cersa. Further on is a charming miniature cascade, and beside it a spring, which, issuing from a rock overhung with ferns and moss, might belong to fairyland. Another and a bitter spring, Charco de la Higuera, 2,600 feet above the sea, creeps out from under a stone near a side waterfall. A charming cascade, about thirty feet high, framed in green, overhung with polypodium and other ferns and brambles, lies behind two paths, with rocks between, looking like cave entrances, covered with greenery. Two streams flow here, and to the left, under the rock, is a deep pool, which is never empty. There is water and a small waterfall in it even in summer, and a watercourse is cut out of the rock to convey the water elsewhere. The whole place teems with water, and is verdant in consequence. We had a very delightful walk up a little barranco surrounded by grass where there were only a few fig trees, but the verdure was great. The water in this barranco does not come from the mountains at the back, as one might suppose, but through a cave on the left, which has been made in order to bring it from the Charco del Naranjo. Further up the barranco there is a fine wood, called El Calero. To these charming springs, waterfalls, and woods the people of Las Palmas make excursions and have picnics in summer, though there is not then of course so much water as there is now.

The chief product of San Mateo is chestnuts, as much as twelve or fourteen thousand dollars being received from Habana for them in a year. Meat is dear, as it has to be brought from a distance. It is tenpence a pound, and pork is a shilling. A quintal (one hundred and four pounds) of potatoes in July is three shillings and three-halfpence, and in November four shillings and ninepence, the latter crop being considered the best. Apples are six shillings and threepence a quintal.

Our hostess and her daughters, one of whom was exceedingly handsome, of the Jewish type, gave us a good dinner, the meat for which had to be brought from Las Palmas, so it is always well to let her know of the advent of visitors, or there may be nothing solid to eat. We did not sleep in her house, but were conducted by the light of a lantern to one which was untenanted. Here in the sala, a large room with several windows, we found two canvas-bottomed stretchers. There were no mattresses, which in general is a cause of rejoicing, as it makes the bed much cooler. To-night, however, the air was cold, being 46·4° F. (8° C.) at nine o'clock. We put our rugs under us, for, no matter how much is piled on top, one never feels warm unless the air be prevented getting at the body from beneath. Experience in roughing it soon teaches this. When the light of the candle was out, we could see why we felt so very cold : the roof was not either air or water-tight, and as we could see the stars of heaven peeping through, though not immediately over our heads fortunately, we could only hope it would not rain during the night.

November 20*th, Tuesday.*—A most lovely morning greeted us as we opened our shutters. It was fresh at eight o'clock [41° F. (5° C.)], with the cold, crisp feeling of a fine English autumnal morning. The view of the mountains around from our bedroom window, culminating in the gigantic Saucillo, standing against the clear blue sky, was fine and inspiriting. Around, the valleys and slopes were green and fairly wooded. The Roque de Saucillo rises on the left, and on its right is the Montaña del Rodeo, and the saddle-back to the right again of it is the Montaña de Chigi-nique.

A good many people attended matins this morning ; there were thirty women, three men, and one boy. The women wore white mantillas, only a few black being visible. One knelt with a bundle beside her, and all seemed very poor. They knelt on the uneven stone floor of the one aisle while the priest mumbled the prayers at a side altar. The walls are white, and the roof of wood. The chancel walls are covered with red paper and curtains.

The view from the azotea of the fonda is very inspiriting, the bright sun pouring its rays upon the green hills and mountains. Those behind the grey bell-tower of the church are well wooded, and beyond them the mountains lying at their rear look purple in the bright light. Near the centre of the town is a little black volcanic cinder hill, but even this has been made productive, and, wherever the slope allows of it, is culti-

vated. The roofs of the houses are tiled and lichen-covered.
Red maize lightens the dull brown appearance of the village, as
it hangs from nearly every wall, in front of the doors, and on
the balconies and pillars of the verandahs, as if solely for deco-
rative purposes. There is a little terracing along the sides of
the hills, but not much, the cultivation following the undulations
of the ground. Three bells and a single wall form the belfry of the
church, a type very common in these islands. The two barrancos
are small, but pretty, and do not give one the feeling that they
are all barranco, with nothing but stones to be seen. The
women are fair-faced and fresh-coloured. Altogether I could
imagine San Mateo being a most delightful summer retreat,
much more charming than Teror, for here one could be buried
amid the mountains, and it would be a good centre from which
to make excursions on foot among the neighbouring cumbres.
It is quite possible to ride of course if you have your own
horses, but those animals are few and far between in San Mateo.
We, with all our endeavours, could only get a terribly poor
scratch team, consisting of two, one a big white horse, all
angles, for the luggage, and the other a little black horse, for
riding; a third was not to be had for love or money. Both
these had bad sores.

We started at 9.30 a.m. to cross the cumbres. The view
as we ascend out of the town is very pretty. The cinder hill
lies at its back, and beyond are the hills of Tafira, forming a
distant background. The foreground is filled with green fields,
trees and hills being on either side. The mountains, as far as
the eye can see, are perfectly clear and distinct, save for an
occasional gossamer cloud which floats between us and the
Saucillo. Our road leads upwards, above the right barranco
of the two which enter San Mateo. Presently we pass through
a chestnut wood. The path is good. The wall on one side is
covered by polypodium, maiden-hair ferns, and moss. Beneath
the chestnuts is grass, and jonquils are in abundance, while
withered leaves testify to the season. The soil appears to
be chiefly red. We presently reach some houses, which are

Lachuza. Most beautiful looks the little mountain hamlet, with its brown-tiled roofs, its outhouses roofed with aloes held down by stones, while along the banisters and rails of its balconies and verandahs and upon the pillars hangs the golden-red maize; even the bare fig trees are maize-laden. The colouring is heightened by red petticoats drying on the walls of the houses. There is not so much whitewash as usual, the stones being left plain. Leaving Lachuza behind, we crossed a hill and came down into Lechucilla and the Barranco de Iguerra. We are now 3,100 feet up. There is a cinder hill here, as at San Mateo, but this is almost entirely covered by a few feet of mould. We crossed the barranco, at the bottom of which was a little water, the path winding in and out among odd houses. Poles stuck in the ground are covered with maize drying in the sun. Nestling among the stones, at a height of 3,200 feet, we found some lovely, sweet-scented violets, larger than our ordinary wild ones, and more open.

We now climbed a steep and rocky path past El Roque de Lechucilla. The view as we rise higher is magnificent. We look down into the valleys, low hills lessening into mere undulations as we pass above them. The thickly populated Valley of Guiniguada, in which lie Tafira, Santa Brigida, and San Mateo, is at our feet, while beyond rises the barren Isleta, surrounded by a fringe of white foam, which extends round the coast as far as we can see. Immediately around are huge blocks of stone, monoliths, which, if standing separately in a grassy valley, would be "El Roque" of the valley *par excellence*. A few of these have here fallen in the form of a Druid's altar. The tinkle of the sheep and goat-bells warns us of the proximity of these active little animals, and presently we meet them on the hillside, jumping from crag to crag, and herded by a shepherd in a long coat. The path is very rough, and scarcely appears artificial. Nature at any rate has had the largest hand in its construction. Rocks, immense and immovable, lie so close together, that often there is but a foot or a foot and a half of space between them for a path.

These spaces were possibly once filled with mould, since carried away by the rain. A little further up, and we came to a great road, washed bare by the rain of a few days past, where we met a woman and two little boys bringing down dry brushwood from the mountains. The arriero got on the horse which carried the luggage. This would not have been too great a load for an ordinary animal, but the white horse was too old for work, and soon the poor brute fell on both knees. The man got off and urged him to rise, but instead he lay down and rolled over on his side ! We groaned for fear the cameras would be smashed, and hastily unloaded the animal. He was lying lengthways across the hill, and, much to our amusement, on his refusing to move, the arriero took him by his legs, which were lying uphill, and rolled him over until they pointed downwards. But even then, although almost put on his feet, the horse refused to move. Whipping was next resorted to, but also failed. Finally the man shoved the horse downhill, when, perhaps thinking he was going over a precipice, he consented to get on his feet. The spectacle was ludicrous. It was pitiable, however, to bring so poor and old a horse on such a frightful journey, even though his load were light. We were nearly at the top of the Saucillo, and very steep was the ascent, so steep, that I got off my horse and sent him on in front, for the path was irregular, and the foothold uneven. We reached the foot of the Saucillo at 11.30, and found by our aneroid that the altitude was 5,000 feet, which measurement is almost identical with Von Buch's. The rock itself is said to be 350 feet high. As we rounded a rock near the foot of this huge crag and turned in upon a little plateau to rest, a large eagle rose from a few yards distant, a handsome bird, with white on its wings and a brown tail. The Saucillo is a mass of yellowy rock, perforated by small holes and caves. On its further side is a tiny stream of water, coming perhaps from a spring on the summit, like that on the Nublo. The ground below and around the Saucillo is bare, consisting of sloping rocks and loose, hard stones and boulders. It would seem as though the softer rock had been washed away and only the hard left, for it crops up under one's feet at irregular intervals. The neighbouring hillocks have retama bushes, closely allied to the codeso, and more like it than the retama of Tenerife. This shrub is, however, locally called retama, which leads to the mistake of supposing that the real retama is found here. The view on the eastern side is very extensive and fine. We can see from Arucas to the Punta de Gando. The entire district looks as if consisting of low, sharp-pointed hills, surmounted by peaks, valleys, and little plains lying between, dotted with houses. The island-like Isleta, with the white bar of surf on the northern side of its isthmus, stands out, as usual, a unique feature in the archipelago. The entire surface of the ground looks uneven and broken. From this place or the summit of the Saucillo may have looked the ancient Canarios. It would take but a short time for messengers to reach the valleys from these heights, and so warn their inhabitants of strangers having landed on their shores. There is one spot on Canaria from which the entire coast line can be seen without interruption, and it is said to have been the look-out station of the Canarios. Valleys run from the central heights of the island to near its shores, often commencing in cauldrons near the centre. The eagles alone now survey the island from these heights, as they shelter in the caves of the Saucillo. Gomera is of similar structure, but there the separating ridges are narrower and often broken down, while here they are broad.

We moved on at 11.55 a.m. across the cumbres. Suddenly on our right eastwards we saw the Peak of Tenerife and most of the upper part of the island itself, snow-clad. We next crossed a level plateau (5,400 feet), called by our arriero Lojono. As this is local pronunciation, the name may not be quite correct. It consists of a little herbage, and bracken cropping up among loose stones, and a white, velvety-looking plant like sage, or rather more like edelweiss, also with a small yellow flower (*Teline congesta*), and a great deal of the Canarian retama. At the further side we came upon a purling stream, flowing from the Siente Fuentes (Seven Springs). Cultivation is actually carried on up here, and lentils are sown in almost stone furrows. When out of the north-east wind, it is pleasantly warm. A few women are about, and we presently come to a house on the top of a hill, erected to shelter those who come for the snow in the snow-wells. The first well we came to was a deep circular hole at 5,850 feet of altitude. Not having an ice cave, as in Tenerife, the people of Canaria are obliged to use snow, and, in order to preserve it for use in summer, throw blocks of it into deep holes made for the purpose, which they cover over with straw, and sometimes render still more secure from the sun by erecting sheds over them. This was the case in El Roque del Ajugerade, at the foot of which, and carved out of it, was another *pozo de las nieves* (snow-well). It is from these wells the highest peak in Canaria receives its name. Our aneroid registered 5,900 feet at this well. Von Buch gives the height at 1,898 metres, Arlett at 1,951, and Fritsch 1,910 metres, by which it will be seen that we agree most nearly with Von Buch, the couple of hundred feet of difference being sufficient to cover the rise of the slightly higher ground a little further south. The well, about sixteen feet in diameter and about thirty feet in depth, has a wall, slightly plastered, built round it, and at the bottom are a few blocks of snow, covered by straw, to which a ladder at one side affords access. A roof of tiles supported on beams covers in the well, and a door at either end of the shed admits of its being locked. One door was open, however, by which we entered. Getting on the sheltered side, away from the wind and in the sun, we sat down and ate our luncheon of eggs and bread. We can see from here into the Valley of Tirajana, lying beneath.

Just as we leave the wells and ascend a low hill, a truly magnificent prospect bursts into sight. Clear against the sky stands out the Nublo, behind it are hazy clouds, and above and beyond, like an island in cloudland, is the upper part of Tenerife, with its snow-covered Peak. Below the Nublo and north of it is the Roque de Bentayga, and beneath these two is the Valley of Tejeda, which we visited a short time ago. We are,

roughly speaking, on a plateau in mid-island, whose outer heights
are guarded by sentinel rocks, chief among which are the Nublo,
Bentayga, and Saucillo.   All around are jagged ranges, their
seamed and scarred sides standing out clearly in shadow and
sunlight.   The heights of Pinar on our left and south-west are
thickly wooded, while to the right the mountains beyond and
above Artenara are bare and rugged.   The extent, variety,
and grandeur of the view are simply wonderful.   The immediate foreground is filled with Canarian retama and the white
velvety plant already mentioned.

Our horses had gone round the hill, and we were alone,
admiring the scene spread around us, when a boy, with long
leaping-pole and a dog, came up to us and thoughtfully asked
us were we "lost."   This was because we were not on the
track.   I suppose it was difficult for him to conceive one
wishing to be anywhere but on the trodden paths.   That we
had deliberately gone out of our way just to look at the mountains that he saw from day to day with careless and indifferent
eye was beyond his comprehension.   So, thanking him, we
merely said we were not lost, and he passed on his way with
a puzzled look.   There is no path just about here once the
well-trodden one to the " Wells " is left.

Returning to our horses, we remount—or rather one of us
does; having only one horse between us, we share it—and leave
at 1.15 p.m. for the descent.   As the horses tread upon and
break the white edelweiss (*leucophäe*), it emits a strong and
pungent odour.

The mountain side down which we now descended was
covered by sharp stones.   It was not difficult, however, to
walk, as we had thick boots and strong ankles.   Gradually the
slope narrowed into a ravine, from which, however, we turned
aside ; and crossing the stream we had encountered higher up,
we descended down the face of a rock in which a winding road,
the Paso de la Plata, has been built.   The stones are loose, and
the road is very bad indeed for horses.   Half-way down it
becomes tolerably level for a little, winding round a precipice,

the mountains above being wooded. Below is a solitary house, called La Plata. We again descend by a badly made road, which leads us to a rocky ridge, not more than six feet wide, overlooking to the right and west the Valley of Ayacata and to the left and east that of Tirajana. Paths lead into both down each side of the ridge, that into Tirajana being tolerably safe and about three or four feet wide.

When coming down these bad paths from the cumbres, the unfortunate white horse, whose name, we find, is Paloma (Pigeon)—a mockery in its old age—continually fell on its knees, owing to the rolling stones, and they being sharp, the poor brute's legs were streaming with blood. The arriero, with disgusting cruelty, used to whip it to make it go fast, and then when it stumbled laughed with enjoyment. We appealed to his humanity in vain; we protested and ordered equally in vain. He only said the horse was not his. At last in desperation we said, " If any of the luggage is injured by these continual falls, we shall not pay you one centimo on reaching Tirajana." The appeal to his pocket sobered him, and at last poor Paloma was allowed to proceed unmolested. Near an empty cave dwelling is erected a cross to mark the summit of the rocky bridge between the valleys, which we reached at 3.35 p.m. It is 3,800 feet above the sea. The path winds along the mountain side, and is a very rough road. Before we had proceeded far along it, we were joined by a most remarkable-looking woman and her mule. She was very tall, about six feet high, wore stout shoes, a man's hat on her head, had a whip in her hand and a cigarette in her mouth. A black skirt, worn over a white petticoat, a short jacket once black, and a shawl, twisted into a muffler in thick folds round her throat, completed a costume as extraordinary as its wearer. She had a bright expression, and her dark brown eyes twinkled with amusement and observation. She greeted us, and then passed on to the arriero, beside whom she walked and upon whom she looked down. She seemed to have some secret enjoyment which amused her much, and looking at the bent head, the morose, if not fearful, aspect of the man, and his reluctant answers to her voluble utterances and questions, it struck us that he was decidedly uncomfortable, to say the least, at her attentions. Her dress and free, swinging walk conveyed the idea that she was a native of some village on the mountains, and her bronzed skin denoted an out-of-door life. She accompanied us as far as San Bartolomé, and on leaving we could not get the arriero to tell us anything about her. She seemed well aware of his repugnance in speaking to her, and appeared to enjoy his confusion.

There is a curious community living near Tirajana, about which I have had some difficulty in obtaining exact information. It is a small colony of free blacks, negroes. They are the remains of a large number who were brought from the neighbouring coast of Africa by the Spaniards, after their conquest of the island, to cultivate it, they having depopulated the country. Some people in Canaria have never heard of their existence; others say they are copper-coloured, others that they are *negros oriundos* (descended from negroes); others, who have never seen them, give long and graphic accounts of them. Out of a tissue of assertions not to be depended upon I extract this much that may be taken as pretty correct. They are very few in number, and they live in houses far from the beaten track. They are very dark, and those who have seen a few in Las Palmas call them " negroes," but do not define if they mean the black, curly-headed, pure African negro. They only appear in Las Palmas at the time of the nut and almond crops, once or twice in the year, when they disappear once more into their solitudes. Most unfortunately, we did not hear of the existence of these people until after our visit to Tirajana, so that we were unable to make inquiries on the spot. The Tirajana district is large, and the mountain recesses numerous, so it would be easy for a small community to hide from the world and be seldom seen and rarely heard of, especially as the isleños would look upon them with great contempt if " touched with the tar-brush."

Meanwhile we are descending by a very rough road along

the mountain side, euphorbia the only living thing. Just before reaching the cemetery, which is invariably some distance from the towns, we come upon a tolerably flat piece of cultivated ground, lying like a basin surrounded by small hills. The cemetery wall is built of loose grey stones, a style of building in which the former inhabitants were particularly skilful, and which skill seems to have descended upon the present isleños. Close to the town, a pair of hawks flew out as we rounded a corner. It was 4.35 p.m. when we arrived and delivered our letter of introduction to Don Antonio Yanes, the largest shopkeeper in San Bartolomé. I cannot find out that this place is ever known by the name of Tunte, which von Fritsch calls it on his map ; no such place is mentioned in Olive's valuable "Diccionario Estadistica." It may be the district name, as Chasna is that of Villa Flor, which Olive does not mention either. Unfortunately this valuable and exhaustive work is frequently incorrect, not having been properly edited, so that one cannot place absolute reliance upon the information therein contained.

Don Antonio conducted us to his azotea, from whence there is a view of the Valley of Tirajana, one of the most fertile districts in the island. Two crops of maize and one of potatoes are here obtained out of the same piece of land. The potatoes are planted in March, the maize in June and November. The first crop of maize takes three months to come to perfection, the second three and a half months. Both crops are eaten by the people, but they say the first is the better.

As we expressed a wish to see the Guanche house which we had heard still existed here, Don Antonio took us to the owner, Maria Sarmiento. It was, however, too dark to go inside, so we arranged for a visit next morning. It is situated on the side of a hill overlooking the valley, and is almost in the present town, which lies on a slope, with a rocky hill behind. The plaza lies between Don Antonio's and the church, which latter is 2,650 feet above the sea.

Dinner proved a failure in matter of quantity. It is difficult for those who do not move from their own firesides to realise how hungry riding and walking across the cumbres make one. After dinner we adjourned to a room with a stone floor, in which there was a bed. Here we found seven or eight men, among them the priest and the doctor, seated around a large palm mat, which covered the middle of the floor. They were evidently awaiting our arrival, so, though hungry and tired, we had to talk and relate our experiences. A child of three rolled herself in a shawl and lay down on the mat, going to sleep, while her mother, with a baby of six months, just awakened, sat among the men, to keep me in countenance, I suppose. The doctor told us that diseases of the stomach are very frequent, and he attributes them to the use of gofio. As the gofio eaten in this island is maize or Indian corn, one can well believe that living upon it is unwholesome, none of the people in the other islands, where it is made of wheat, rye, and barley, suffering inconvenience from this food. As we were tired, we received with thankfulness our host's proposal to retire, and were in bed before 7.30 p.m.! The tertulla broke up when we left, so apparently the hour was not an unusual one for retiring. Our room was a sala, adjoining another, and to which we were conducted through a yard and up steps. Some brackets on the walls were adorned with splendid specimens of bearded wheat. Just as we were going to sleep, a dog, that from its movements and voice seemed a large animal, came to our door and growled very viciously. He evidently knew there were strangers in the room, and resented it. Presently he began to paw the door, which shook and rattled in a manner that suggested he might effect an entrance. The good people of the house seemed all asleep, so we barricaded the door, not desiring a night attack. After a while a voice called to the animal to desist, otherwise the faithful beast would have guarded his master's possessions all night, I believe, to the loss of our repose. An erratic clock that was in our room insisted upon striking each hour twice, so altogether it was broken slumbers we enjoyed. At 8 p.m. the temperature was 53·6° F. (12° C.).

CHAPTER VII.

SAN BARTOLOMÉ—GUANCHE HOUSE—SANTA LUCIA —CANARIO CUSTOMS—AGUIMES—INGENIO—CIMA DE GINAMAR.

> Alas! the strong, the wise, the brave,
>   That boast themselves the sons of men!
> Once they go down into the grave—
>   Alas! the strong, the wise, the brave—
>   They perish, and have none to save,
>   They are sown, and are not raised again;
> Alas! the strong, the wise, the brave,
>   That boast themselves the sons of men!
>
> ANDREW LANG.

November 21st, Wednesday.—It was decidedly cold at 7.30 this morning, being 42·8° F. (6° C.). We visited the Guanche house commonly so called, but of course an Antiguo Canario dwelling. It is in good preservation, but it seems a careless way of keeping such a priceless relic to let it be at the mercy of a peasant. The Government would do well to acquire possession of the house, and keep it as a national show-place. Maria Sarmiento's descendants may not be so careful of it as she is, and the place may be lost to posterity. Houses of the present inhabitants are opposite it, but at its back is a hillock. The walls of the house are composed of stones and mud, and the roof on the outside is of mud too. The entrance door is set back a little, a seat being on either side of it. The house is circular. We measured, and found it fifteen feet six inches from the door to the opposite wall, and exactly the same distance from

the opposite corners of the recesses in the interior. The wall
on the left is three feet thick at the bottom, and seven feet six
inches high to the beams. The entrance is five feet three
inches wide by six feet two inches high. The interior is
circular, save for two recesses, the corners of which are formed
of upright stones ; that on the right is three feet ten and a half

ANCIENT GUANCHE HOUSE, SAN BARTOLOME.

inches high by nine and a half inches thick, and three feet six
inches deep, being a flat stone ; the other is an angular upright of
basalt, four feet two inches high. The height to the top of the
roof inside is eleven feet. The floor is of earth ; from the spring
of the wall the roof slopes upwards. The gables, as it were, are
formed of two large pine trunks, and the roofs of the recesses
are of pine trunks laid across. The door is of the same,

the spaces being filled with stones. The lower part of the walls is formed of very large stones, the middle of smaller, and the top again of large. The roof is entirely of small pieces of trees, evidently split, but the rest of the wood is used whole. There are two layers of wood forming the roof, above which is earth, that which is there now having been recently put; but we are assured it is identical with that found there after the occupation of the ancient Canarios. The stones on the outside of the walls are tolerably flat, put in horizontally, and, not being filled in with mud, remain rough. The beams have been blackened and some of the interior wall plastered by later inhabitants, it having been lived in occasionally. The stones forming seats outside the entrance are roofed with pine trunks. From these identical seats how often must the noble and persecuted Canarios have looked down upon the smiling valley beneath. How bitterly they must have hated their invaders, coming to force them from their quiet retreats and teach them vices that they knew not of, for the old inhabitants were pure compared with their Christian and civilised conquerors. This spot was no doubt well populated with the ancient inhabitants, and

> "Murmured with their toils,
> Till twilight blushed, and lovers walked and wooed
> In a forgotten language, and old tunes,
> From instruments of unremembered form,
> Gave the soft winds a voice."

We cannot help wishing we knew more of the Guanches—of their habits, customs, and manners—as we inspect one of their habitations. Alas! we fear this knowledge, like their language, is irretrievably forgotten.

Three soldiers, forming the garrison of San Bartolomé, and a woman looked on while we made our measurements. The latter wore a pair of shoes with the black hair on the outside, the soles protruding much beyond the uppers. As we ascended the rocky crags above the ancient cottage we could see the roof. A short but steep scramble brought us to the summit of the crag

overlooking the town and valley. It is 150 feet higher than the
church, so was quite at a sufficient height from which to throw
down stones upon the Spaniards as they toiled up the hill below,

> " Fit spot to make invaders rue
> The many fallen before the few."

The expedition under Cabron, who, having only lately arrived
from Spain, was inexperienced in the valour of the Canarios,
landed at the barranco of Tirajana,* and marched into the
interior. A Christianised native who accompanied the invaders
warned Cabron not to proceed into the interior, but, with the
contempt born of ignorance, Cabron answered that he was not
afraid of naked people. They accordingly proceeded inland,
plundering the villages as they went, and collecting a quantity
of sheep, barley, and dried figs, which they sent to their ships
—so Tirajana was always a productive district. The natives,
however, awaited their return by a steep rock by which the
Spaniards must pass, where they fell upon and routed them,
taking eighty prisoners, killing twenty-six, and wounding
about a hundred. This event, so disastrous to the invaders,
was called the St. Bartholomew of the conquest, because it
was undertaken on that day. Hence the name of the village
which has since arisen beneath the brows of the cliff that saw
the defeat. Later, Pedro de Vera sent troops to attack Tirajana,
but they were driven back with loss. De Vera, however,
coming up, renewed the assault, when the natives, not being
prepared for a fresh attack so soon after their victory, were
overcome and driven further into the mountains. Altogether
Tirajana has seen troublous times, and was one of the most
remarkable of the battle-fields of the conquest.

The barranco which we look down upon in its course from
the mountains passes through precipitous places, while at
others it widens out, where the ground lies flatter. It is on one

---

* Viera says at Arguineguin, but the physical features of the country
favour Glas's version, as the troops would then march direct by the bed
of the barranco into the valley.

of these more level expansions that San Bartolomé is situated. A rock, like a steep step, cuts the town in two, however. The lower flat, level opening, though a poorer part of the town, is also occupied by houses, the surrounding land being green and cultivated. Beyond, and lower in the valley, lie other green spots and cultivated places—Santa Lucia is one of these—affording striking contrasts to the brown mountains around and on either side. The opposite hillside is perforated with caves, some two hundred in number, the residences of the old Canarios, whence they poured down their warriors to defend their homes. Behind us lie the splendid mountains over which we passed yesterday. The ranges on either side which continue from them to the sea get lower as they reach the coast, until they cease altogether and are lost in the littoral plains. The barranco winds in and out, surrounded at its upper end by cultivation, but towards the sea becoming gradually more and more barren, until it and the hills on either side appear but a mass of brown plains and heights. The scenery around the cauldron-like upper valley is magnificent. It is impossible to convey an idea of scenery which is all sublime. The compressed body of mountains in the centre of the island affords one view after another, each surpassing the other in magnificence, so that words utterly fail in giving a correct idea of the wild, weird mountain-tops, the sterile grandeur of the gorges, the grim and awful craters, the romantic, boulder-strewn passes. Each scene has its own individuality, each its characteristic beauty. The great variety of the sublime pictures in the centre of Gran Canaria,

> " Where savage grandeur wakes
> An awful thrill that softens into sighs,"

is not the island's least charm.

Leaving the noble Canarios of the past, we descend and note the occupations of the Canarios of the present. Not that they differ very materially. Much as one would like to see these islands progress in the world's civilisation, it is with regret one would lose the primitive life and customs of their inhabitants, derived as they are from an interesting ancient race. The natural difficulties of access to the most beautiful scenes of the interior will, it is to be hoped, long preserve these happy hunting grounds to the real lover of nature, animate and inanimate, the promiscuous nineteenth century tourist confining himself to the more comfortable towns and more get-at-able scenery near the coast.

The cooking is always done in the open air, and generally with charcoal, but as we descended into the town we passed a man sitting outside his house making gofio over a fire of almond shells. He was stirring the maize with an instrument like a drumstick in a large flat red earthenware pan, about two feet in diameter. We stood a few moments watching the process, while the man, with a conscious and pleased smile at our interest in his cooking, strove to continue his stirring as if no one unusual were present. The continued indifferent look vanishes, however, as soon as we move away, while the eyes follow us with eager curiosity, to be dropped once more on the task in hand when their owner perceives he is noticed.

The church, which we entered, has centre and side aisles, separated by arches and pillars, the latter painted to imitate green marble. The roof is of split canes, except over the chancel and side altar, where it is of wood. The floor, windows, copings, and mullions are of the same kind of stone. The windows are of coloured glass. A hollow pillar like a six-sided box contains a green-and-red figure of St. Bartholomew, carrying a knife in his hand.

This town is said to have 3,500 inhabitants, but it is difficult to ascertain the real population of any of the towns and villages, for numerous smaller and outlying hamlets are contained in the number given as the population of a single place, it being really a municipal district. There are, for instance, in this district thirty-six or so of these hamlets and villages.

Breakfast of eggs, bread, water, and nuts over, we prepared to leave, but had some trouble with the arrieros. Finally we settled on two animals, our quantity of luggage being so very small, that John could ride on top of the albarda. We told our arriero that we wished to go through Santa Lucia by Temisas to Aguimes. How we failed to accomplish this will be seen.

As we rode down (10.50 a.m.) a steep descent into the lower part of the town, we came upon six or eight men, dressed in their best clothes, sitting upon the roadside, and on a wall, which was part of the gable of a house, was a long box without a lid. All unconsciously we passed on, and it was with a shock I learned the contents. My horse went along that side of the road next the wall, which was just on a level with our shoulders, and I peered into the box in passing. Seeing a very brown hand, I thought it was a figure being carried to the church, especially as it was dressed in a veil and dress and boots, the toes of which slightly protruded from the box. Following rapidly with my eye the figure as my horse passed on, I reached the face, when judge of my horror on seeing it was that of a corpse! The shock was in proportion to the revulsion of feeling, for the idea of its being a dead body had not occurred to me. I was looking at it lightly and unthinkingly. One hand was laid across the breast and the other along the side of the woman, who was old, haggard, and very brown with years and exposure to the sun. Mummies are found in the islands with the hands placed in this identical position.

The road was winding, and passed down through the poor houses we had seen from the cliff above. We reached the bottom of the valley, the sides of which are steep and clothed with a goodly amount of shrubs and palm trees. The path winds along the right bank some distance above the river. A hill on the left bank is perfectly honeycombed by old Canario caves, of which there are some three or four hundred; and the doors of many are cut out evenly, in the same way as those of Artenara. As we ride under the shade of the trees, the water purling below and the canary birds singing, the sun shining down with only a pleasant heat and dancing in shadows across our path, we feel it was no wonder the Canarios fought and died for their pleasant land. A woman by a house near the river is making palm matting, platting the strips together, while the golden maize lies in front of the door drying in the sunshine. How perfect it all seems, and how content falls on one at beholding it. Yet, difficult though it may be to credit it, human passions are the same under the palm groves as in the crowded lanes of the world's metropolis.

A narrative by Boccaccio, written in 1341, gives the earliest account we have of the habits of the ancient Canarios. An expedition went in search of the islands, and the pilot, Nicoloso de Ricco, says of the islanders on Canaria that they were nearly naked. Some, however, wore goats' skins, dyed yellow and red. On the north of the island the sailors landed, and found houses built of loose stones, and "covered with large and handsome pieces of wood," and very clean. Four men who swam to the ship were taken on board and carried away. They were young and handsome, with beardless faces, and wore aprons of cord. "Their long, light hair veiled their bodies down to the waist, and they went barefooted. . . . They did not exceed their captors in stature, but they were robust of limb, courageous, and very intelligent." The apron of one, who appeared a chief, and to whom the others showed marks of deference, was of palm leaves, the others wearing reeds painted red and yellow. They sang sweetly and danced well, were gay and merry, and "much more civilised than many Spaniards." Money and gold and silver ornaments were unappreciated by them. "They showed remarkable faithfulness and honesty, for if one of them received anything good to eat, before tasting it he divided it into portions, which he shared with the rest." This is a custom, as we have noted, prevalent in the islands to-day. "Marriage was observed among them, and the married women wore aprons like the men, but the maidens went quite naked, without consciousness of shame." Azurara says that "the Great Canary was ruled by two kings and a duke who were elected, but the real governors of the island were an assembly of knights, who were not to be less than one hundred and ninety, nor so many as two hundred, and whose numbers were filled up by election from the sons of their own class. The people were intelligent, but little worthy of trust. They were very active and powerful. Their only weapons were a short club and the stones with which their country abounded, and which supplied them also with building materials. Most of them went entirely naked, but some wore petticoats of palm leaves. . . . They had abundance of sheep, pigs, and goats, and their infants were generally suckled by the latter. They had wheat, but had not the skill to make bread, and ate the meal with meat and butter. They had plenty of figs, dragon's blood, and dates, but not of a good quality, and some useful herbs. They held it an abomination to kill animals, and employed Christian captives as butchers when they could get them. They kindled fire by rubbing one stick against another. They believed in a God who would reward and punish, and some of them called themselves Christians." These must have been the followers of the two priests who were on the island prior to the advent of Azurara.

In the MS of Bethencourt's conquest it is stated, with great *naiveté* and unconscious self-condemnation, by the priests that when the Canarios came to trade with Gadifer on his first expedition to Canaria " the dragon's blood was well worth two hundred ducats, while what was given in exchange was hardly worth two francs " ! They further state that the country was well wooded. The inhabitants were tall, and looked upon themselves as noble. They were great fishermen, fishing by torchlight and by poisoning the water with euphorbia juice. A similar custom of poisoning the water prevails in Kerry. " Most of them print devices on their bodies, according to their various tastes, and wear their hair tied behind in the fashion of tresses. They are a handsome and well-formed people. Their women are very beautiful," and they had plenty of animals, and a " kind of wild dog like a

wolf, but small." Glas's MS adds a valuable sequel to all this
information from different quarters. It states that when
Bethencourt landed the natives annoyed them "with stones and
darts, which they threw by hand with amazing dexterity, and
with such velocity as to exceed the motion of those thrown
from slings or bows." Glas's MS further states that the
natives of Gran Canaria were of dark complexion, "well
proportioned, and of a good stature, active, warlike, chearful,
good-natured, and strictly faithful to their promises, insomuch
that they considered a lye as the greatest of crimes. They
were very fond of hazardous enterprises, such as climbing to
the top of steep precipices to pitch poles of so great a weight,
that one of them was a sufficient burden for a man of common
strength to carry on level ground. The Spaniards affirm that
the devil assisted them in placing these poles, that others,
attempting the like, might fall down headlong and be destroyed." In like manner later the Spaniards believed that
the devil assisted the English out of the bay of Santa Cruz.
In those days it was so easy to attribute one's own impotence
to the supernatural, and when an enemy was in question to his
being aided by the Spirit of Evil. The worthy friar, Galineo,
who wrote the MS in 1632, evidently believed in the person-
ality of Satan, for he says he "believes this to be true; and
that the devil appeared to them in the shape of an animal
resembling a shock dog, and sometimes in other figures, which
the natives called Tibicenas."

Hereditary nobility was not sufficient to entitle a man to be
called noble among the Canarios, but each man had to stand or
fall by his own merits. If a man applied to be ennobled,
inquiries were made by the Faycag, a person next in rank to
the king, in the place where the man lived, as to whether he
had ever dressed food for himself or milked or killed sheep
or goats, if he had ever stolen, or if he were ever "discourteous,
ill-tongued, or guilty of any indecent behaviour, especially
to women. If to these questions they all answered in the
negative, then the Faycag cut the youth's hair in a round form,

and so short as not to hang beneath his ears, then, giving into his hand a staff or pole, called *Magade*, declared him noble." If, however, the candidate was found guilty of any of the above misdemeanours, his head was shaved—it must have been a painful process, with stones for razors—and he was sent away in disgrace, remaining ever after a plebeian.

What could be more civilised than their conduct in war, when they held it as base and mean to molest or injure the women and children of the enemy, considering them as weak and helpless, therefore improper objects of their resentment? neither did they throw down or damage the houses of worship.

They had specially appointed places where duels were fought, first with stones and afterwards with flints and clubs. The friends and relations of the combatants were always present, and the combat was continued until the *Gayres* called out, "Gama! Gama!" when they stopped, and "ever after remained good friends." The noble spirit of this people may further be gathered from this fact: that "if during the time of the combat one of the parties happened to break his cudgel, then the other immediately desisted from striking, and so the dispute ended, and the parties were reconciled, neither of them being declared victor."

Galineo confidently affirms that the men had only one wife, and the women but one husband. Before marriage a girl was set apart for thirty days, during which time she was fattened, a custom also formerly prevalent in Lanzarote. They punished their children when necessary. A very curious custom was the pointing out of two youths as examples of virtue and vice, with whom the evil and the well-doing were compared. It is said that in Canaria a number of religious women, called *magadas*, lived together in houses, which were held sacred and regarded as "sanctuary" by criminals. The *magadas* wore long white garments that swept the ground, and they were daily sprinkled with goat's milk, set apart for that purpose. These *magadas* have been erroneously called nuns by some, but they appear to have been more like vestal virgins, or even the priestesses on the banks of the Nile in their purer days.

Two rocks—that of Tirmac, near Galdar, and that of Vinicaya, in Telde—were looked upon as sacred. Certain rocks seem to have been regarded as sacred throughout the archipelago. To these there were processions in times of public calamity, in which the *magadas* joined, carrying branches of palm trees and vessels filled with milk and butter for libations, and round these rocks they danced and sang.

The Canarios administered justice strictly. For murder the criminal was executed by a large stone being dropped upon his head when he was stretched upon the ground, and for other crimes the *lex talionis* was enforced.

They seem to have known the art of irrigation, and broke up the ground with hoes of goat's horns. Altogether they appear to have been a marvellous nation, cut off from communication with the world and yet considerably advanced in civilisation. It is not their manner of living or dress that fill one with astonishment, but their internal laws, the integrity and morality of their lives, their belief in a supreme Being, to whom they prayed, but of whom they had no outward symbol. Not an idol or image of any sort was found in the archipelago, save that of Candelaria in Tenerife and those of the two saints erected in Canaria by the shipwrecked Majorcans, of which more later.

But we are on the way to Santa Lucia. The road now crosses the river, and winds in and out, up and down, among houses and farms. A goat, with a tiny kid, seems happy beneath the olive and orange trees which adorn our path, while above are the golden bunches of dates, the palm leaves cut off to allow the fruit to ripen in the sun. We are glad of the shelter of the trees, for the sun is hot on this side of the valley. The ruddy gold dates, surmounted by a few green plumes, look like coronets crowning the tall and stately palm trees. We ascend a small hill, and leave the bottom of the valley behind. A better idea of the cauldron, or crater-like formation, of Tirajana is obtained by the view looking backward from farther along the valley towards the sea. The mountains at the top of the valley are particularly precipitous, though all on both sides are more or less so. Everywhere jagged and peaked outlines meet the eye. The range on the south side is still high as it nears the sea, while that on the north becomes much lower.

A pathway of a rough sort leads up and through a mass of piled stones to Santa Lucia. The usual walled cemetery was the first object to greet us, and next the single wall of the church bell-tower. We reached the latter at 12.10 p.m. (2,100 feet). The cemetery, the church, plaza, and a couple of houses stand on a little plateau by themselves. Descending, we cross a barranco, in which there is now only a tiny rivulet, and ascending upon the other side through olive, fig, and palm trees, reach the village. Here we presented a letter at Don Vicente ——'s house, and were told he was not at home. For this we were sorry, as we thought we might have obtained information concerning a spot where an inscription stone was found in the neighbourhood. It was not until looking up archives at the British Museum, upon our return to England, that I discovered the facts concerning this stone, and of how much value it may be in elucidating the origin of the former inhabitants of this island. M. Verneau, the discoverer of these stones—for there are parts of two others—has begun in the finding what it is to be hoped other learned men will finish by translating these unknown characters. As mentioned previously, it is thought some of the characters are Phœnician, while the first stone, which is bilingual, being graven in the same characters as the Tougga stone, with a translation in Punic letters, fixes the date as not later than the second century B.C.

Asking and getting a drink of water without dismounting at Don Vicente's, we rode on through the village streets, which are paved and narrow. Santa Lucia is the most charmingly shaded town we have seen in the archipelago ; it is literally embosomed in trees, nevertheless it is not so pretty as San Bartolomé. A boy as we rode along brought me an orange, offering it shyly and without speaking. As we left the town, another boy ran after us to say that Don Vicente was now at home. No doubt, having deciphered the letter of introduction, he had discovered what illustrious visitors he had refused to see! We, however, decided not to return, but to pursue our way to Aguimes. Olives grow very plentifully here, and we passed through quite a plantation of them. A large bird, entirely white, except the tips of its wings, which were black, and the head and beak, which were yellow, attracted our attention. We could not see, however, if its beak were hooked or not. The road after leaving Santa Lucia is almost level, uninteresting, brown, and stony. A pleasant breeze tempered the heat. The euphorbia, with twisted, gnarled, and dragon-like stems, grows plentifully. The land is divided by stone walls, on which gourds, the same as those at Guia, in Tenerife, spread and flourish.

At one o'clock we left the road, which continued to Sardina Geire, and ascended by a precipitous ravine to the summit of the range on the right bank of the barranco. Nothing grows on either side of the gorge but euphorbia and Palma Christi. There are numbers of birds the same as the one I have already attempted to describe, and a few small caves, fit eyries for them, are in the sides of the cliffs. The ravine is very rocky and stony, with a small barranco at the bottom. We cross to the eastern side at a natural level, which must form a waterfall when there is water, and ascend the other side. Neither of our mules have shoes, and the pack-mule, unhappy animal, has only one ear! The arriero is a youth of, it might be, eighteen. He has little to say for himself, and it is impossible to extract any information from him. I suspect he possesses none. I have again a rope halter, the cruel iron bit, and a headstall of undressed leather.

Beautiful white clouds and blue sky form a soft and pleasing contrast to the brown rocks. Nature often combines colours fantastically, and frequently presents startling contrasts. The pass is rather fine and wild, destitute as it is of vegetation.

Opposite, on the other side of the Valley of Tirajana, rise brown and rugged mountains. Our road now is cut through solid rock until we reach an altitude of 2,000 feet, after which we descend a little way into what one might call a higher level ravine. Here a few olive trees, figs, aloes, and cacti grow, and we meet a little girl carrying a small sack and a lump of wood on her head. Ascending by the left side of the ravine, we come upon some angular, basaltic-like formation. As we double back the view of the rocks behind is rather grand. Presently we reach a sort of plateau. The ridge at the further side of the barranco continues further, until it falls abruptly to a lower level. At the foot of this lies a little red house, surrounded by brilliant green vegetation, and with numbers of caves just in front of it. The ridge finally ends in a huge pillar, more massive than high.

As we kept on eastward we asked our arriero whither he was leading us. He said, " To Aguimes." " Yes, but where is Temisas ? " we questioned. " Oh, over there," he said, pointing to the north-west. " And why did you not take us there ? We must go now," we said. According to him, we ought to have gone by another road from Santa Lucia, and it would be necessary to return to the barranco we had just passed in order to get to Temisas. As it was getting late, we reluctantly gave the order to proceed. It is said that the view from Temisas is very fine, and worth climbing to see. No doubt it is a worse road; hence our being brought another way. The maps of the island that we had with us were not sufficiently good for us to know in time where we were going.

Descending a little into a barranco, we ascended again, and crossed another plateau, from which we looked down upon Sardina. The ridge we are crossing is 1,800 feet in height, and below lies what looks to be almost a level plain to the sea. The road winds along under a cliff, while precipitous slopes lie below us, until we at last descend into a barranco. There is an extensive view from the path on the

cliff over the country, the only green spot to be seen being
Sardina, consisting of a handful of scattered houses. A few
brown hills and browny-grey plains lie between us and Aguimes,
which place comes in sight—a city of the plain—the dome of
its new church rising from out of the surrounding monotony.
One incident alone varied our dreary tramp over the stony
bed of the barranco. Before we left the foot of the precipitous
hills round whose base we walked, we saw a man far above,
standing upon a crag. We excited his curiosity apparently,
for upon seeing us he whistled to his dog, and, lancia in hand,
rapidly leaped or vaulted down what to an ordinary mortal
would have been impossible crags. A few seconds really
sufficed to bring him to the bottom. Placing his pole below
him, he would jump down to it, his hands sliding down the
stick. Similarly no doubt the old inhabitants sprang from
crag to crag. This method of progression is more like the
bounding of a chamois than that of a man, and one who was
not accustomed to such a mode of descending mountains would
be utterly unable to keep pace with, much less overtake, a
Canario. These poles, varying in length, are used in all the
islands by the isleños.

We finally reached the bottom, and proceeded along in a dry
barranco, formed of masses of red pumice rock, such as we
rode over in the Cañadas. Flocks of the little green canary
birds fly hither and thither, whistling and singing to one
another in a delightful fashion. I had walked a long way,
being tired of my steed, but soon found myself left some
distance behind in these solitudes. It is not easy to keep pace
on foot with the mules or horses, for they walk fast, so I was
obliged at last to remount. Tramping over the rough stones
under a warm sun, and looking upon the barren landscape, one
is inclined to take a melancholy view of life, and one is
impressed with the fact that after all England is the best
country for everything except climate, and that unfortunately
expatriates many of her children.

We followed the bed of the barranco for several miles, until, leaving it on the northern side, we passed over a perfect desert. That vegetation is possible we could tell from two places that were under cultivation. This was soon explained, for we came upon a watercourse which irrigated these two oases. A lovely white and sky-blue butterfly flitted past us, having spots and a sort of down on the tips of its wings; and in the distance was a grey eagle. These were the only signs of life. It was 4 p.m. when we left the watercourse and climbed a rock-hill, at the top of which was a cave. The summit was a cultivated plateau (500 feet), which we crossed, and descended at the further side to another watercourse. Ascending again a hill of stones and euphorbia, we arrived at a "Calvary" on the top, whence there is a view of Aguimes and the sea-shore, which here is quite flat. We met two horses on our way up carrying leaves of green maize, of which there is a great quantity just now.

Aguimes is like an Eastern city, with its mosque and palms. It lies on a gentle slope, higher hills rising behind it. We reached the church of the town at 5 p.m., 850 feet above the sea. We had a letter of introduction to the owner of a house facing the church. This we delivered, but finding that the man was out, we sent our two other letters. No one arrived, but as on inquiring we learned there was no fonda, we were obliged to await the advent of one of these three individuals. After waiting in the plaza and wandering from one house to another in quest of a hospitable inhabitant, Don Francesco Melian turned up, and asked us to wait for a few minutes until he got the key of a house—his own, I think—which was closed. Meanwhile a number of people stood by looking at us, men, women, and children, amounting to sixty-eight all told! When the vesper bell rang out, the men raised their hats for a few seconds, and the women reluctantly disappeared into the church for a short space of time, being more concerned with the Ingleses. Finally, after half an hour, Don Francesco returned without the key, and conducting us down a narrow street, brought us to a poor one-storied house inside a yard, which he called a fonda. He and his companion seemed much relieved at having got rid of and deposited us safely somewhere, and hurriedly bowed themselves out. The woman of the house asked us in, so we entered a room which comprised the house. It was a good-sized place, the roof of wood, and a palm mat partially covering the earthen floor. A row of chairs was placed against the wall, and at one end two large beds were curtained off from the room by lilac cotton print hung on cord. A small plain table and another bed occupied the other end. Two cradles almost completed the furniture, except for a little crockery, which, with the food, was kept under the table and beds. The place was not inviting. We had a welcome, however, and that is the principal thing. An old man came up to us, and placed in the usual formulæ " the house at our disposal," adding, " It is poor, but I hope you won't want for anything." Our food—some fried eggs, bread, and coffee—was put on the solitary table of the establishment, at which we were seated with our faces to the wall. This is a universal custom, and almost everywhere we found the table placed against a wall, at which we were to look, whilst very often at our backs was some magnificent scenery. It must not be supposed that the above coffee was a luxuriant supply, with good milk and sugar. It was only a small cupful, brought to us after we had eaten, guiltless of milk, and with sugar that was not overclean, being mixed with straw and dust of various kinds. The eggs were fried in oil. The bread, the one redeeming feature of the food everywhere, was very good. As we had not had too much to eat since leaving San Mateo, we were very hungry, but could not gain much alimentary satisfaction out of eggs and bread after a long day's journey. The cooking was performed outside in the yard.

We were consumed with fears as to what the night might bring forth, and wondered much where we were to sleep. How we wished we had brought our tent, where cleanliness at least would have been an assured fact. When we had finished our meal, the household came in for theirs. A piece of sacking, as table-cloth, was spread in the middle of the floor, and a tin can placed on it. Then two tin basins, one of them containing gofio, were put down, and a saucepan, taken off the charcoal fire outside the door, was brought in. Out of it were taken a little salt fish, potatoes, and a piece of maize, and the water in which these were boiled was poured over the gofio and mixed with it. All now sat down on the floor, and a few spoons were passed round. At one side reclined the old man, an old woman, his wife, sitting cross-legged beside him, rocking with one hand a cradle and eating with the other. The mother of the children sat at the other end, and the five children, one a big girl, sat round, all cross-legged. Just as they were seated a big black cat walked in, fat and handsome, the best-cared-for cat I have seen in the islands. There was no loitering over the meal, which was sharply and silently despatched. When they had finished, they still retained their places, when the old man repeated some prayer, in which the others joined, after which the girl, about twelve years old, presented herself to me with folded arms. As she stood before me meekly and shyly, waiting for me to do something, I gazed at her blankly, quite unaware of my part of the performance. Seeing this, the mother called her to go to her first, saying I did not understand. She stood in front of her mother in the same way, and the mother laying her hand on the folded arms, the girl carried it to her lips and kissed it, after which she came to me, and then to each of the adults in turn. As one child after the other came, and so said good-night, the performance struck me as pleasing and patriarchal in the simplicity and reverential attitude of the children to their seniors. I have never heard or read of this custom elsewhere. Is it of Spanish, Moorish, or Guanche origin?

We had been given our choice of sleeping in this room, in any of the three beds, or in another room opening off the yard, in one of two big beds there. We wondered much who else would occupy the room with us. Divining our thoughts, the woman said, "You can take whichever room you like, and we shall have the other." So we took the smaller one, thinking it would inconvenience the family less. Before retiring the old man again placed the house *à su disposicion*. We were the only English

they had ever seen or heard of in Aguimes.   Our bedroom had
two immense beds in it against the wall, and behind curtains.
I had asked the woman if there were any chinches in it, and was
relieved when she shook her head.   I then asked were there any
minor nocturnal evils.   About this she was doubtful, and appealed
to the elder woman, who was also uncertain on the subject;
they " thought not," however!   Evidently pulgas don't worry
them as they do strangers.   There was a grass matting on the
floor of our bedroom, and heads of maize lying about; these
the woman put into sacks.   A chest of drawers stood against
the wall, and there was a crucifix in the corner.   Two doors
opened from the room, one into the street, the other into the
yard.   There were no windows.   The beds were very high, and
there not being room to take a running leap into them, we had
to mount by chairs.   Four or five could readily have slept in
one without touching, they were so wide, and not at all uncomfortable.   The bedsteads were really made of wood, built into
the walls like shelves.   We were awakened at 3 a.m. by the
young woman's husband coming into the room for something.
He worked at a distance from Aguimes.   He returned home
after we were in bed, and had to start again at three o'clock in
the morning.   That the door was guiltless of a fastening we
had noticed previously.

November 22nd, Thursday.—Being awake at 6 a.m., we got
up, but had to dress in semi-darkness, as if we had opened the
door ever so little for light, we knew we should have the good
people in upon us.   The street was perfectly empty when we
set out, but in a few minutes there were quite a couple of
hundred watching us, our advent having evidently been noised
abroad.   The dresses are light in colour here, pink, green, and
mauve being the favourites.   We walked through the plaza to
the old, wooden-roofed church, which is going to be pulled down
when the new building is finished, and took a photograph of
the old church, with the dome of the new beyond it.   There is a
curious and quaint old balcony at a corner house in the plaza,

though perhaps it would not be considered an architectural success. The streets are narrow, with high walls, the doors opening into yards, or patios. Very Eastern-looking are both the town and the new church. The latter is a massive building. Square pillars are outside the grey stone cupola, while surmounting the dome is a still smaller one, with a cross at the top. The upper dome has glass in it, and inside the cupola are white stars. Fine grey stone pillars support a not very good stone roof, which looks, I fear, as if it were going to be painted. Scaffold-

AGUIMES.

ing just now surrounds the church, and the building is at a standstill, for want of money. The dome is the only one of its kind in the island, and is considered architecturally a success. The town is quaintly picturesque, requiring no effort of the imagination to conjure up the most romantic features of mediæval Spanish life. Had we met Don Quixote himself issuing from one of the Moorish portals, attended by Sancho Panza, we should not have expressed surprise. The gallant knight engaged in his chivalrous enterprises would only be in keeping with the character of the place at the present day.

It is much warmer here than in our resting-places during the

past few days.   At 6.30 a.m. it was 68° F. (20° C.), and during
the night a sheet was quite sufficient covering.   Breakfast over,
we sent for the animals, when one of our friends of the previous
night came, bade us farewell, and looked relieved at our departure.   We started at 8.55 upon two good mules, and shook the
inhospitable dust of Aguimes off our, or rather the mules', feet.

We wished to see a mineral spring which is near Carrisal, so
rode first down the Barranco Ecoha, according to our arriero.
He was, however, so utterly unintelligible, that it is quite
possible I have got the name wrong.   Riding along the stony
bed of the barranco, we arrived at some canes, and dismounting
walked through them to the right bank, where was a little
indentation or glen.   A few palms waved their stately heads
over a split cane stuck in the side of the hill or bank near the
bottom, out of which a small stream of mineral water was
flowing.   It is not strong, and there is very little of it.   It
was scarcely worth turning aside to see.   A little mauve
flower in the barranco our arriero called *alabiate* (*Cavandula
spica*), which native name must also be taken with reservations.
I never came across a more unintelligible individual in our
wanderings among the seven islands.   At first when questioned
he only shook his head.   He took for granted, without listening
I think, that we were speaking English to him—not compli-
mentary to our Castilian !—and when he found it was Spanish,
he never ceased asking us question after question, the half of
which it was impossible to interpret, he spoke in such a *patois*.
We have seen a number of people carrying bundles of " Christ's
thorn," which they bring down from the mountains for burning.

It was ten o'clock when we left the spring and the barranco
and passed up the hill, through divisionless fields and by
watercourses for irrigation, to the likewise Moorish-looking
town of Ingenio.   We reached the church at 11 a.m., and
found that it lies a trifle higher than Aguimes, being 975 feet
above the sea.   The church has a high, square tower like a
pepper-box, with a small stone cupola at the top.   Having
a letter of introduction here, we delivered it, and found ourselves

heartily welcomed by apparently the schoolmaster. He pressed
us to stay with him, and seemed really disappointed at our
refusal. If we had known what a short distance Ingenio lay
from Aguimes and what a different welcome awaited us, we
should have come on last night, tired as we were. However,
we got a glimpse of peasant life at Aguimes which was most
interesting, and well repaid us. Finding we were determined to
move on, as there was nothing particular to be seen at Ingenio,
the worthy pedagogue left his school, and, with a friend of
his—the alcalde, I think—accompanied us through the town.
Crossing a quaint little bridge over a small and steep barranco,
we walked on foot over fields towards a valley. A really
charming and quite unexpected scene burst upon us, and one
that we little anticipated in this bare district. The Valle de
Algodones is wide and surrounded by low hills that slope away
towards the sea. This slight shelter and depression has caused
a luxuriance amid the desolation around. A few scattered and
well-to-do houses, farmsteads, lie surrounded by trees, especially
orange trees. Just now the oranges are ripening, and the
brilliant golden balls lie embosomed in the thick dark shiny
green foliage in a manner at once tempting to the eye and
palate. Near our path was a cottage, and a young girl looking
out at us, our friends asked her to pull a few of the ripest
oranges. She ran down the hill, and presently returned with a
dozen or so, large, ripe beauties, one of which would have made
at least two or three of those we ordinarily get in England.
Conducting us a little further, until we reached the carretera, our
friends piled the oranges upon us and our luggage, and bidding
them good-bye, we rode along the uninteresting highway. Our
recollections of Ingenio and Aguimes are slightly different.

We are close to historic ground as we ride onwards. Below
on our right is the Punta de Gando, so famous in the history
of the conquest. Here Bethencourt made his second attempt to
land on the island, and was repulsed with great loss; here
Herrera, coming also from Lanzarote, landed, and was likewise
obliged to retreat to the shelter of the rocks on the sea-shore;

and here later the same Herrera contrived through stratagem and deceit to build a fort, which was afterwards rased by the Canarios. Gando sinks into obscurity after this, more suitable landing-places having been found for the invasion. It is coming into prominence again, however, in more ways than one. Unfortunately the Punta runs a long way into the sea, and has rocks lying beyond it which mariners are too fond of trying to shave as they steer round the island. Consequently wrecks are not unknown. A Spanish mail steamer, *Alfonso XII.*, sank there not long ago, and having gold as part of her cargo, an endeavour was made to reach it, which succeeded a year later. The people were taken ashore to Las Palmas and hospitably treated, though it is said those in the neighbourhood of Gando were very heartless in their attentions. There is about to be built also at Gando, on the south side, a lazaretto or quarantine station, in this same port where the old fort was built.

We are riding along the carretera, a straight, uninteresting road through a stretch of country entirely devoid of trees or even cultivation. At present only nineteen kilometres of road is finished, but leave and money have been obtained, it is said, to continue the road to San Bartolemé, a distance of twenty-seven kilometres.

There are three classes of carretera, called first, second, and third class. I believe there are none of the first in the archipelago, certainly not in Gran Canaria. The distinction is in the width, those of the second class being ten metres in width and those of the third eight metres. The roads to Agaete and the Puerto de la Luz from Las Palmas are of the second class, while the one we are upon and those to San Mateo and Teror are third-class. It is curious to traverse these roads and only meet a few, very few, people, either on foot or horseback. Carriages, except near Las Palmas, one rarely sees, and carts are unknown. The boon of roads has been so recent, that the people have yet to be educated up to them and their uses, pack-horses still tramping laden to market.

Meanwhile we near Los Llanos and Telde, really one and the

same town, the former being the upper part and the latter the lower. Leaving our luggage at the coach office—for there is a coach from here to Las Palmas—and engaging two seats, we pay and dismiss our arriero, and proceed to deliver our two letters of introduction, as it is only 2 p.m. Our first is to Don José Padrón, who takes us into the church of San Gregorio, where we find the cura, Don —— Yanes, to whom we have also a letter of introduction. This church lies 500 feet above the sea, and at the bottom of a steep street leading from it lies another church, just 100 feet lower. The former is in Los Llanos, the latter in Telde. There is a kind of market under the shadow of the former church in an open space, where two roads branch. A number of women stand or crouch beside fruit and nuts piled on palm mats and tripods of sticks, from which are suspended sets of scales. The regular market is held on Sunday in this same spot. The streets are wide, and the houses flat-roofed. It is a cheerful-looking town, well intermixed with trees of various kinds, including a good many palms. There is a dome with small cupola of coloured glass on the church of San Gregorio. There is also coloured glass in the west window, of plain colours, red, yellow, and blue, but not in the circular form we have seen so often. The floor is of stone, and four grey stone pillars support the roof, the arches between which are in well-proportioned curves. The high altar is painted white and gold, and there are four side altars, but the church is poor and bare. The pulpit is of wood, painted white, with yellow heading. The nave gives one the idea of being too short in proportion to the chancel. The friendly priest kindly conducted us into his own house, adjoining the church, where he gave us cake, wine, and information. He is a fine-looking man, with the pleasant, jovial appearance that denotes more feasting than fasting, in short one's ideal of a popular parish priest. Our friend Don Gregorio Chil's father was formerly priest at Telde, a man nearly as remarkable as his son, being highly educated and extensively read.

Finding that we were returning to Las Palmas by the

afternoon coach, our friends made us promise to return and
see Telde properly another day, as there are many fine houses
here, the country residences of the aristocracy. This we did
one day later, much later than we dreamed we should be in the
archipelago. Don José saw us into the coach at the bottom of
the town, and we started at 3.45 p.m. Don —— Yanes, in
common with many other priests in these islands, does not
seem to object to the noise or confusion consequent upon having
children in his house. I suppose it is not always easy to get
housekeepers "free from encumbrances," and the children have
to be put up with. The officially given population of Telde
and its environs is over 9,000, a thousand more than Orotava.

We left Telde by a road leading across a long bridge of seven
arches over a barranco. Our coach was well packed, with eight
inside and four outside. A short time after leaving Telde we
came to a wide valley, with a distinctly marked lava-flow
running down its centre like a river. A most odd-looking
sight was it to see a high rock rising from mid-valley with a
house perched on the summit. The rock was in a perfectly
isolated position. We stopped for a few minutes at the new
village of Ginamar, merely the church with an open space in
front and a venta (200 feet), the old village straggling up behind
and off the new road. Actually we saw carts here, but the
pack-horse is not given up, for two donkeys with baskets on
either side walked soberly along.

There is a curious bit of history and tradition connected with
the mountain, or Cima de Ginamar, lying on the left of the
road. It may be remembered that Luis de la Cerda was made
Prince of Fortune, and given possession of these islands—if he
could take them—in 1345. He never reached the archipelago,
dying before his ships sailed. Some of these vessels, or others
from Majorca, or a chance vessel, some say, came at this time to
the islands, and anchored at Gando, others say at Guiniguada.
No natives appearing, they concluded the island was uninhabited, and advanced inland, when they were suddenly surprised by overwhelming numbers and made prisoners. The

Canarios dispersed their captives all over the island, and, according to their custom, treated them well, "for the Canarians excelled perhaps all other people in greatness of spirit and generosity to those whom they vanquished." The Majorcans in return behaved well, and gained the friendship of the islanders. Some of the captives were said to have been good artificers, and built houses and showed the natives how to paint them in colours extracted from herbs and flowers. Among those taken prisoners were two priests, who were much respected. They built two hermitages of stone, without cement; one they called St. Catherine's, in which three images were placed, and the other St. Nicholas's, near Agaete, in which was put an image of that saint. Some years later there was a long and severe famine in Canaria, when the natives secretly decided upon killing all the strangers to save their maintenance. This apparently treacherous design would seem, however, to be well excused, for the strangers had been guilty of revolting crimes and immoralities. Every one therefore was killed except the two priests, who were carried to the top of a mountain and thrown into a deep cavern. This cave was so deep, that no one knew where it ended, but some days later part of the dress of the priests being found on the sea-shore, the natives concluded it must have communication with the sea. The mountain is the Cima de Ginamar. Bethencourt's chaplains relate how that when they spoke with the people of Canaria on their first visit, one of barter, a young man brought to them a piece of parchment given to him by the murdered Majorcans twelve years previously, and in which they related that the Canarios were treacherous, and that no one, notwithstanding their fair exterior, should trust them. What has become of this MS?

Fritsch says of the Cima de Ginamar that it shows the remains of an old crater within a half-open new one, and that if a stone be thrown in it will be heard rebounding from side to side for a long time before it reaches the bottom. Its height is about 750 feet.

The road to Las Palmas after leaving Ginamar runs near the

sea, and has been cut straight through some loose conglomerate rock.   There is a little beach on the sea-shore, and the cliffs, beneath which lies the road, are not very steep.   Just before reaching a tunnel the carretera runs along very close to the sea, and, with cliffs upon the other side, reminds one much of part of the coast of Antrim, between Larne and Cushendall, the similarity being also increased by the fact that tunnels are also to be seen there.   This one is longer, however, than any of the Antrim tunnels, and is a very fine piece of cutting.   As we drive through it we get a view of Las Palmas, framed in the opening.   A man is just lighting a lamp suspended from the roof, as it is now getting late.   The cliffs are in places honey-combed with holes, and the strata are broken, contorted, and cracked as by fire.   A brown mule covered by a grey-green matting of palm leaves, upon which is seated a woman in a white mantilla, forms a pretty picture beneath the dark cliffs. We next pass a curious old castle, like a box, on a little point, the fort of San Cristobal, and before long reach Las Palmas and the Fonda Europa, at 5.15 p.m.   Here we found so many people staying, that we were obliged to put up with the worst room in the house until a better was vacant.

CHAPTER VIII.

> Thus was this place
> A happy rural seat of various view:
> Groves whose rich trees wept odorous gums and balm;
> Others whose fruit, burnished with golden rind,
> Hung amiable—Hesperian fables true,
> If true, here only—and of delicious taste.
>
> MILTON.

> Have goodwill
> To all that lives, letting unkindness die,
> And greed and wrath, so that your lives be made
> Like soft airs passing by.
>
> EDWIN ARNOLD.

November 23rd, Friday.—There were many small matters to attend to this morning, and indeed we did not feel inclined for any great undertaking, being rather tired after our journey in the interior. It is considerably warmer in Las Palmas, being 69·8° F. (21° C.). The apartment we have at present is small, leading into a bath-room. The proximity of water seems to attract both mosquitos and cockroaches, neither of which are very pleasant night companions. I prefer mosquitos, however, for the cockroaches, if harmless, are so exceedingly hideous and disgusting, that nothing will ever reconcile me to their inability to hurt. These rest-disturbers are brown in colour, and some are two to two and a half inches long. They do not run very fast, but they can fly; hence one is powerless, for no amount of tucking

up of feet can avoid them, and if in bed, unless behind mosquito
curtains, one of these horrors may creep over the pillow or fly
in one's face.   Just as I was getting into bed last night, a cockroach alighted on the iron rail at the foot.   It was impossible
of course to sleep, knowing it was in the neighbourhood—
" where ignorance is bliss, 'tis folly to be wise "—but to get into
bed with that *thing* on the rail was beyond my equanimity.   So
I had to hunt him until I killed him.   This is a very objection-
able operation, for when killed cockroaches emit a disagreeable
odour.   They are also difficult to kill.   When I first tried to
murder one, I crushed half of his body away, and when, some
minutes later, I was near the same place in the room and
cautiously avoiding the, as I thought, dead cockroach, I could
not find the other half of him anywhere.   A streak of moisture
along the floor showed the beginning of his retreat, but the half
had vanished.

Some of the English residents called upon us to-day, and we
returned Don Gregorio Chil's visit.   In the evening he came in,
and kindly brought me a copy of his "History of the Canary
Islands."

Not only are there some English people staying here, but
there are also a number of people waiting for the Spanish
steamer which comes from Cadiz and goes to Santa Cruz.
They naturally, and rightly, go by it, as it is less than half the
fare on the English vessels.   The price charged by the English
companies between the islands helps to retard the communication,
and is absurdly high.   The joint Liverpool companies, the British
and African Steam Navigation Company and the African Steamship Company, charge two pounds, without any food, from Santa
Cruz to Las Palmas, which is only some five or six hours' steam.

November 24th, Saturday.—We had made arrangements last
night with two of the gentlemen belonging to the Cable Company and an English resident to go to the Bandama Caldera.
So at 9.20 this morning we started.   Two of the gentlemen
rode.   We drove up the middle road—leading to San Mateo—

of the three carreteras which lead out of the town, only following it, however, to-day to a little beyond Tafira. About half-way between that place and Santa Brigida, leaving the carriage, we descended by a steep path to a small glen of laurels. This is a favourite picnic resort for the inhabitants of Las Palmas. Just now it is looking very pretty, there being a little grass, which there is not in summer. The laurel trees—not bushes—about fifty or sixty feet high, shade us from the sun, which to-day is shining strong and hot. The glen is a miniature one, being only a couple of hundred yards in length by perhaps seventy or eighty across the centre. The bottom is perfectly flat and smooth, sparsely covered by grass and a few withered leaves. On one side a small streamlet, a couple of feet wide and an inch or two deep, curves round the foot of the hill on the opposite side of the glen, and a few butterflies wander hither and thither across its rippling waters. The bank at one side is also covered by laurel trees, from the bottom of each of which are suckers, straight enough to make walking-sticks for giants or Guanches. This glen, the Monte * Laureles, 1,150 feet above the sea, and a couple of hundred feet beneath the carretera, is famous, and deservedly so, for its laurels. One can scarcely believe, when looking at those immense trees, that they are the same laurel shrub we are accustomed to in England.

We reach the road again about eleven o'clock. The banks on either side are lined by aloes, which, although making good hedges, are not grown entirely for that purpose. A strong, tough fibre can be extracted from the leaves. The so-called leaves are hard, thick, fibrous substances, long, narrow, and pointed, and frequently grow to three feet in length. When mature, the leaves are cut and threshed until soft enough for the fibre to be readily extracted. Whip-lashes, halters, and the breechbands used on mules and donkeys to keep on the pack-saddles are made of aloe thread. The fibre is tough and lasting, and the manufacture of these articles from it is rapidly

* *Monte* means wood as well as mountain.

becoming an industry. Everywhere one sees bare and useless patches of ground planted with aloes. It is a curious feature of these islands, and one difficult to realise the value of, that anything put into the ground will grow. It is only necessary to choose land suitable for a plant, and it can be safely left to its own devices. It was but the other day that I was eating some Tangerine oranges given to me, and the servant in the hotel asked me to let her have the pips, as she wished to plant them. This kind of orange is rather rare in the islands, why it is difficult to say, as it has only to be planted in order to be grown. But there is a general indolence among the peasants, added to a certain amount of stupidity, which prevents any innovations. A great deal of the stupidity must of course be attributed to an entire want of education.

We now drove back a little on the road to Las Palmas, but soon turned off on the right, and followed a good path in a sort of lane for a little distance, until it became too steep and narrow for our carriage, when we dismounted and walked. A few minutes brought us to a house built near Bandama, and passing by it, we suddenly stood on the edge of the Caldera. One's first feeling is intense surprise and admiration that Nature could have formed anything so faultless, that in such a mad freak as a volcanic eruption always is she should have taken care to make a circle perfect enough to be attributable to the hand of man. When the feeling of wonder, which at first is all-overpowering, has subsided, the quiet beauty of the scene steals across one's senses. We are standing on the edge of the crater at its least precipitous part, and that is so steep, that the path beneath winds backwards and forwards in innumerable lashes. The rim is tolerably level all round, rising here and sinking there more or less, but giving the idea from where we stand of a general similarity of height. The altitude here on the path is 1,200 feet above the sea, but the north-west side is 1,450 feet. The sides are perfectly perpendicular, descending into the Caldera some 600 or 700 feet. So abrupt indeed are the wall-like sides, that one feels as though looking into a gigantic dry well. Just near the bottom there is a slight slope, where the rock-crumblings have become overlaid with earth and grass. The bottom of the cauldron is entirely green. At the foot of the path is a solitary house, and in its vicinity we can distinguish cultivated ground. To the right and near the bottom we can see a few orange trees, and the intense green of the herbage near them shows that the once boiling crater now contains a spring of water. Above us, to our left as we stand, is the Pico, a peaked hill or cone, which forms a part

FARM AT BOTTOM OF BANDAMA CRATER.

of the wall, so to speak, of the crater. It is the only place where the uniform edge is altered. The side of the Pico next the Caldera is formed entirely of black cinders, and it is in these cinders that the vuelta, or winding path, to the bottom is made.

The day was very hot, but having rested on a bank under the shade of a tree, we determined to make the descent. The going down, we knew, would be easy, but, with wise forethought, we calculated the difficulties of the ascent. Two of our friends were on horseback, so they were all right.

Although M. Ogier doubts the practicability of descending into this crater upon horseback, I can vouch for its having been done. Ten minutes took us down the 690 feet. It was a rapid but uncomfortable descent. Unfortunately it had not occurred to me that we should have any rough walking to-day, so I wore shoes instead of boots, and as one sinks to the ankle at every step, I was soon nearly lame from the stones, or rather cinders, which got inside them. Shoes, in fact, are almost useless for walking here, except in the towns, and those who are accustomed to wear them would do well to discard them in favour of boots in the interiors of these islands.

Arrived at the bottom, we felt such thorough trespassers in the confined space, that we at once made our way to the house to apologise to the owner. Here we were not only welcomed, but hospitably treated, for the good man brought us almonds and dried figs, both excellent and grown in the crater, and he and his daughter cracked almonds for us until we could eat no more.

The view from the house, outside which we sat enjoying our figs, was circumscribed, but, to make up for that, full of interest. The crater walls are of hard rock until within a short distance of the top, when there is a horizontal layer of black lava. This lava seems to lie along the edge in waves, as though following the outline of the rock beneath.

We had expected to find the heat unbearable below, but there was instead a pleasant breeze, which our host says they always have—surely a curious natural phenomenon. The whole bottom of the Caldera is one finca, or farm, containing one hundred and ninety-six fanegadas (about nine acres). The living souls buried in this cauldron are the *medionero* —a sort of tenant farmer—his wife, and six children. His farm is 760 feet above the sea level. We noticed growing around rhamus, brambles, manzanilla (camomile), branching euphorbia, palms, maize, vines, olives, and orange trees. The pasturage is good; in fact, most of the farm is in grass, as is evidenced by there being eight cows and nine goats. A yoke

of oxen are ploughing in part of the bottom. A good many
big boulders are scattered about. An immense one appears
to have stopped short just in time, for it is within a few feet
of the house, though of course the house was built after its
appearance. The farmer says no boulders have fallen in his
time, and he has been there five years.

Meanwhile the horses had been quietly feeding, and when
Mr. W—— went to look after his, he found as the result that
the girth had broken ! Our host sewed it together very firmly,
but it unfortunately gave way again, and no inducements would
make that girth hold together. Luckily the other saddle had
two, so one could be spared. This little incident showed us
what might have happened to us any day, and perhaps in a
dangerous place, had we not brought our own saddles and
hide girths.

We walked up to the spring, which is on the western side,
on leaving the house. It is situated on higher ground, at the
foot of a cliff 875 feet above the sea. The water comes from
an inaccessible spot further up, and trickles down the rock.
Three small cisterns have been made to catch the supply, for
every drop is precious in a thirsty land. The farmer says there
is only just enough water for the use of the house and a little
to irrigate the part of the farm near the spring. The polypodium fern grows luxuriantly on the rocks around, and there
are several orange trees near the cisterns, off which our host
broke whole branches laden with oranges, and gave them to us.
One only knows the value of oranges in a hot climate. Nature
generally provides compensation for her own defects. We
had a very hot walk up over the cinders, and were only too
glad to sit down and enjoy a few oranges at the top. On our
way up, as we toiled slowly over the loose cinders, we saw,
under a rock beside the path, a number of small circular pits
an inch or three quarters of an inch in diameter, like miniature
craters, in some very fine earth. At the bottom of each of
these is an insect ready to devour other insects that may fall
into the trap so neatly prepared. Aloes and vines are planted

on the steep, cindery hillside, partly to keep the path up. It was 1.45 p.m. when we left the spring, and 2.8 p.m. when we reached the top, those on horseback of course arriving sooner.

After a discussion upon the advisability of climbing to the summit of the Peak, we all except John ended in declaring the day to be too hot. He, however, with his usual energy determining to go, mounted on Mr. T——'s horse, although two boys, who watched our proceedings with interest, said it was impossible to ride up. We are, however, accustomed now to the "impossibilities" of the natives, and are never deterred by the supposed difficulties. He found there was no path leading to the summit. The horse, however, being strong and plucky, and the ground soft turf, with a few bushes here and there, he put the animal straight at it, and in seventeen minutes was at the top, looking down into the crater. The height, he found, was 1,800 feet, which makes the total depth to the bottom of the crater 1,040 feet—a considerable depth to look down into. From the top is a grand panoramic view. To the north lies the Isleta, looking like an island, for the exceedingly narrow isthmus dwindles to nothing at this distance, and a little in front Las Palmas shines in the sun; north-west is Arucas, distinctly visible as a cluster of white houses, nestling against its characteristic little mountain; while to the south Telde, of orange fame, seems quite near at hand. All round the north and east coast line and the sea beyond to the horizon were visible, while the centre of the island, just then slightly covered with clouds, was seen as a confused mass of compressed mountains. Several butterflies seemed to regard the flat, smooth top as a special playing ground. Coming down was more difficult than going up, and part of the way John found it necessary to dismount and lead the horse.

We started for Atalaya upon his return. A good path up one hill and down another brought into sight the cave-village.

There are several cave-villages in Gran Canaria, but perhaps one may pick out three as the principal, each of which is perfectly distinct in character and in the manner of life of the inhabitants. Near the town of Las Palmas there are cave dwellings close to the carretera leading to San Mateo. The inhabitants of these consist of the very scum of the town, those who cannot or will not pay house-rent. Not only do the poorest live there, but also the worst characters. Next we may mention Artenara. The caves there are tenanted by respectable tillers of the soil, people quite as good socially and morally as their neighbours. As I have already mentioned, the interiors of their dwellings are tidy and comfortable. No doubt poverty makes them live in caves, poverty of soil, which here means money. Poverty, however, is not a crime.

The third village of caves is Atalaya. Here lives a race of potters. All the earthenware pottery for the country is manufactured in these caves. The people have lived here from generation to generation ; they are very poor and ignorant, and perhaps a trifle rough. They have also one bad habit, of which we received timely warning, fortunately. They are given to thieving, and will steal almost under the eyes of the owner.

Atalaya is prettily situated on the side of a round-shaped hill, which from the top half-way down is closely honeycombed by caves. The other side of the hill is green pasture land, and the part beneath the caves is terraced and cultivated. Just now the terraces contain potatoes. Beneath lies a valley, and around are hills, all green and fresh after the recent rains, while in the background are the mountains rising in the centre of the island. Close to the village, and before we enter it, we pass a canteria quarry. The men were cutting out the stones in square, well-shaped pieces. This stone is a sort of smooth grey granite, exceedingly hard. It is used for building, makes excellent rollers, and is being employed in the construction of the new Harbour of Refuge.

As we near the village, ragged, very ragged, boys pass us. The solitary white cotton garment they possess seems scarcely capable of holding together. What the vanguard was, so were the rest of the inhabitants, all in rags. The situation, however of the caves could hardly be surpassed for quiet beauty.   The valley beneath a barranco leading to Ginamar has two mounds rising in its midst, cultivated and green ; a little further, and the hills on either side nearly close together, leaving just sufficient space for a glorious view of the sea.   Las Palmas, though so near, lies hidden 1,700 feet below.   Nothing is around save green-clad hills and undulating valleys, and these curious rabbit-warren dwellings, with their wild, almost uncouth inhabitants.

The pottery-making is very simple and primitive.   We entered

CAVE-VILLAGE OF ATALAYA.

by invitation a cave.   The only light was from the open door. On our left was a pig, surrounded by a very low wall of stones, and at the back, in a corner, was a heap of greyish earth. Seated on the ground cross-legged, in the middle of the cave, was an elderly woman.   A flat stone, about a foot and a half square, was in front of her, at one side a lump of grey earth, and at the other an earthenware basin of water.   The regular shape of the various jars, braziers, and other pottery articles had led us to suppose, though erroneously, that they were formed on a wheel.   The woman was finishing a water jar, and we asked her kindly to begin another, that we might see the whole process, to which she readily consented. Taking a lump of clay and damping it, she rapidly rolled it in her hands into a ball, then, placing it on the stone, pressed it out into a basin shape, moving it round and round to preserve the circular form. She then took a small lump of clay, and making it oblong, rolled it out along the edge of the basin, thus increasing its height. This process was repeated continually until the jar was large enough, the left hand always being inside to move it round; and feeling the thickness, where it was insufficient she added some clay. A piece bent outwards at the top gradually assumed the form of the mouth. This part of the pottery-making, though the most difficult apparently, is the quickest. She could scarcely have taken ten minutes to make it, and wonderfully regular it was, without mould or pattern of any sort. Before beginning she sent a boy to bring me a chair. I was seated in close proximity to the pig. A host of children accompanied us, and they all gazed at the jar being made, as if they had never seen anything similar before. Doubtless seeing our intent faces made them imagine there must be something new and wonderful in what was to them an old and well-known process. The grey jar thus completed is put in the sun to dry. When sufficiently firm, lines are drawn on the outside with a smooth, oblong stone. The stones for this purpose are picked up on the sea-shore. These lines add greatly to the trouble and but little to the beauty. It is, however, curious to note that lines exactly similar are found upon the jars of the Guanches, who no doubt made their pottery in like manner.

We next saw the firing process. The ovens are circular, built of stone, filled in with mud, much the same, only larger, as the bread ovens used all over the islands. All kinds of sticks, twigs, and brushwood are burnt, and we met numbers of boys and men carrying the fuel from all points of the compass towards Atalaya. Large round stones are placed in the oven, on which to raise one side of the pans and various articles, so as to allow the heat to reach the whole surface at the same time. The heat from these ovens is very great

and one cannot go within a yard or so of the mouths without
being scorched. When therefore the pottery requires to be
moved, two long pine poles are used to roll the hot stones
from one part of the oven to another and to support the
jars. Water is damped over the charred points of the poles
each time they are taken out of the oven. We took a photograph of a man in the act of moving some pottery. Close to

POTTERY OVEN, ATALAYA, GRAN CANARIA.

the oven, under a projecting ledge of rock, were placed jars
fired and those awaiting the process. The grey of the latter
and the red of the others contrasted pleasingly, and one only
wished that the Quaker grey of the unbaked clay could be preserved. The earth is brought from some distance up the valley.

When the pottery is ready for sale, the women carry on their
heads large baskets of water jars, braziers, and pans for roasting
gofio and coffee down to Las Palmas, about five miles distant. The

price of a water jar such as we saw made is *one penny.* It is no wonder that the inhabitants of Atalaya, notwithstanding that they pay no rent, are among the poorest in the islands.

When we first came in sight of the caves, the troglodytes turned out *en masse,* and a distinct buzz was audible. Children swarmed like ants on an ant-hill, above, below, and around, wild, ragged, and sometimes naked little urchins, uncouth and untaught. Outside most of the caves pottery was standing in various states of progress. The business of the population is pottery-making, and it pervades the whole atmosphere, the very children imitating their elders for amusement. Strange to say, although living so much in the air and under a strong sun, the people are on the whole much fairer than many in the islands. The children for the most part have light hair, and many of them blue eyes. Very seldom, indeed never, I may say, have we seen grey eyes. If not brown, they are blue.

Picking our way along paths in front, behind, and over caves, clambering up and down clay steps, worn by use between the dwellings, we left the pottery-makers, guided, protected, and followed, as at our advent, by the barefooted, bareheaded, and sharp-faced juvenile population.

Ten minutes' walking brought us to a *bodega* (wine-shop) where wine is made and sold wholesale, the house having a name for good wines. A pottery bowl, with a handle and spout, half full of a crimson liquor, the colour of claret, but richer-looking, was brought out. This wine is called by the natives the "blood of Christ," and all pronounced it excellent, the only wine that we considered excelled it being that at San Juan de la Rambla, near Orotava, where the celebrated malmsey used to be made.

Our carriage was waiting for us here. Part of the unmade road was heavy soil, and our coachman stood up the better to urge on the animals. As the three horses galloped along abreast, with flowing manes and tails, it was easy to imagine we were in a chariot of olden days, with the charioteer standing

in front.   It required of course a little imagination to overlook
the vehicle.

Although getting late, we went to the house of Don Felipe
Massieu, whom we had promised to visit.   There is a fine view
over the Valley of Angustina from his grounds, 1,600 feet above
the sea.   He kindly kept us for tea, and we drove home about
six o'clock.   Unfortunately, however, not thinking we should be
out so late, I brought no wraps, and besides was not clothed
in my usual flannel dress, but in cotton material.   I mention
this as a warning, for I suffered severely in consequence.   The
gentlemen wisely smoked vigorously all the way, but not being
a Spaniard, I was unhappily not up to the necessary manipulation
of either cigar or cigarette !   Although not really cold, the air
was fresh, and we found the carriage seats wet with dew.
In Las Palmas at 9.30 p.m. the thermometer was 66·2° F.
(19° C.).

November 25th, Sunday.—The morning broke clear and
beautiful, a bright blue sky overhead and fresh air imparting
healthful feelings.   To think of the fogs of London or the
damp, dispiriting days just now in the country at home makes
this climate still more enjoyable.   Not that it requires any such
comparisons, but unless one now and again remembers what
other places are like at this time of year, one is apt to take for
granted the clear sky, the balmy air, and the moderate temperature we here enjoy, without giving them their just and due
meed of appreciation.   The air is so dry, that biscuits lying
loose about the table retain their crispness.   At 8 a.m. the
temperature is 68° F. (20° C.), while at 1 p.m., about the hottest
time, it did not rise higher than 78·8° F.(26° C.), both observations in the shade.

As usual, the talk at the breakfast-table is all about the cable.
In fact, the whole conversation of the town may be said to
concentrate upon or gyrate round that single topic.   The
news has arrived this morning that the cable is actually laid
between Palma and Garachico on Tenerife.   This is an earnest.

But the great excitement is as to whether or not the main line to Cadiz will start from Santa Cruz or one of the other islands. The amount of the jealousy between Santa Cruz and Las Palmas is impossible to be conveyed in writing. It is bitter; it is intense; it is lasting; it enters into the household and separates families; it divides friends; it restricts commerce; it retards the advancement of the archipelago. That it is foolish, puerile, and simply suicidal to the general good of the two places is here admitted by all thinking Spaniards, but still the one town snarls and growls at the other, and this conduct is returned by vituperation and Billingsgate. The journals pursue the topic, and appear to devote their brains to studiously picking holes in the affairs of the neighbouring island. Credit for good intentions is never given, motives are imputed where none exist, satire is employed to crush what honesty will not relate, and ridicule is heaped upon everything. It may be natural that the press, for its own existence, should thus reflect the feelings of the people, but it is to be regretted that there does not arise an organ of influence and independence, with a strong hand and an energetic pen, to be continually pointing out the paralysing effect of all this childish behaviour, and to be continually reiterating the motto that union is strength, and that the *only* chance for the advancement of these singularly beautiful and singularly neglected islands lies in their being at perfect harmony with each other, and working together in all that they do. It surprised us much to find that in each island a good many of the English residents—not all, I am glad to say—affect these degrading sentiments and are even more ready than the Spaniards to see badness in the neighbouring island. Both Santa Cruz and Las Palmas are tarred with the same brush, and one place is just as bad as the other. Spirited, good-natured rivalry is exhilarating and ·healthy, and competition in trade and agriculture is most beneficial to all concerned, but the feelings existing between these two islands embrace none of these qualities, but express themselves simply in spiteful, snarling jealousy. To have said less than I have upon this unpleasant topic would have been to have left upon my readers' minds a very erroneous impression of the truth.

Much honour is due to a Spaniard for shaking off the national lethargy as Señor Dr. Don Gregorio Chil y Naranjo has done. He has displayed marvellous energy, not only in forming a museum, but in writing, besides other literary efforts, a voluminous history of the Canary Islands, and at the same time practising his profession. Where all is enervating around in customs and society, this must be taken as a sign of great mental and physical energy. Don Gregorio called for us this morning, and took us to the Museum, which has been got up entirely by his unceasing exertions, and is full of antiquarian interest from the relics of the Guanches deposited therein. The Museum is situated at the top of a large building—the town hall—opposite the cathedral. We entered by a back door, and passing some big, sleepy-looking men—the serenos, veritable owls—went upstairs.

Among the Guanche articles of interest is a shelf full of seals so called for want of a better name. Their purpose has, as yet, not been discovered. They look perhaps more like modern prints for butter than seals; they are made of pottery and deeply marked in various patterns. Some are circular, others square and triangular. They vary in size from one inch to four, and are all in nearly perfect condition.[*]

The much-disputed point as to whether it be possible to make fire by rubbing one piece of wood against another would seem to be satisfactorily answered by another Guanche relic, unearthed in Guayadeque. This is an oblong piece of wood, about eight or nine inches in length, scooped out apparently by friction, with which was also found a pointed stick.

The mummies, of which numbers have been discovered, are conclusive evidence as to the appearance of the ancient

---

[*] A few of them I measured accurately, of which these are the sizes : $3\frac{7}{8} \times 1\frac{5}{8}$ inches (No. 3); $3\frac{1}{8} \times 3\frac{1}{8}$ (No. 1); $1\frac{3}{4} \times 1\frac{3}{4}$ (No 4); $2\frac{1}{8} \times 2\frac{1}{8}$ (No. 5); circular ones in diameter, $1\frac{3}{4} \times \frac{3}{4}$ in. (Nos. 6 and 8).

inhabitants. Those found on this island have not in a single instance black hair. Much of the hair is fairish red and reddish brown, besides being dark brown. The black hair which so predominates here in the towns is without doubt the Spanish element introduced later. There are, however, many persons, as I have frequently noticed, particularly in the country, with fair and red hair, and in some districts these colours and brown predominate. Numberless are the customs still preserved which point to a Guanche origin. There can be little

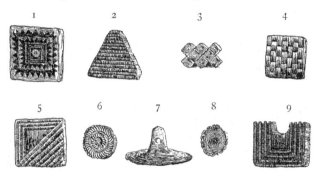

GUANCHE SEALS (?), MUSEUM, LAS PALMAS.

doubt in the mind of any observant person who has travelled extensively over these islands that there was more intermarrying between the ancient Canarios and their Spanish conquerors than the latter are willing to acknowledge. This is evident in many ways. The isleños are a finer race in appearance and a more amiable people than the Spaniards of the Peninsula, more staid in their manners, and more independent. Customs innumerable remain. That of laying one hand across the body of a corpse while the other lies straight by the side is exactly after the manner of the mummies. Gofio, the Guanche food, is eaten throughout the archipelago, and those travelling still carry and prepare it for use in bags of kid skins. Long jumping poles are used in the mountainous regions by the goatherds. The pottery is almost identical in form and decoration, and absolutely so in colour. Many of the present inhabitants live in caves; butchers are still looked down upon and shunned; and shoes are yet made with the hair upon the hide. Who can say, in the face of such evidence and much more that cannot now be mentioned, that the Guanches were completely exterminated? The conquest of each island, whether by war or treachery, except perhaps in the case of Canaria, took a comparatively short time, much too short to allow of customs of this sort being learned and adopted by a foreign and hostile people.

Jars of all shapes and sizes have been found, some with lips. One that was unearthed in Fuerteventura has a curious broad spout, and is marked with lines.* Some of these

lines are black, and some grey, and many of the patterns are similar to those in the cave at Galdar. The earthenware made by the ancient inhabitants is said to stand heat much better than that of to-day. There is also a vessel just like a teapot, exactly the shape of ours nowadays. What it was

LIPPED EARTHENWARE MAJO JAR.

used for is of course a problem. There is, however, a plant growing wild, which I have mentioned before, the water extracted from the dried leaves of which is very similar to tea, and is used now by the natives instead of tea. Numerous lids of all sizes are in the Museum, with two handles, in which are holes, no doubt for cord. Great lengths of cord, made of twisted fibre, for fishing lines, are also preserved. One large jar contains a quantity of goat's butter. Think of butter four hundred years old! It smells now like strong goat's cheese. The Guanches kept rancid butter, burying it in the ground, for rubbing on wounds, as they considered it very curative. Stone hatchets and stones for making the pottery marks, such as we

* Thirteen and a half inches from point of spout to opposite side and six and three-quarter inches deep.

saw at Atalaya yesterday, are also on the shelves of the Museum.

I had not been feeling well all morning, and had gradually become so cold, that my fingers were blue and numb, so that I could not feel the pencil when making notes. When I reached the hotel, I had a violent shivering fit. A dreadful headache, accompanied by feverishness, ensued, and by four o'clock my pulse was one hundred and fifty. Thinking it was ordinary ague, I did not send for a doctor until next morning (November 26th, Monday), when, finding the fever still unabated, John went for one of the leading doctors here, Don —— Rosa, whose son took the message, as the doctor was out, we waiting patiently for his arrival. This was at 8 a.m. About noon a servant from the hotel went to see if he were coming, and later on yet another messenger was sent. At 4 p.m. Dr. Rosa sent a message to say "he would come in the morning"! We subsequently found he had treated two other people in a similar way. It is a rather dangerous experiment to repeat often, as some day the unfortunate patient may die meanwhile. John then went next door for Dr. Gregorio Chil, who came *at once*. We did not send for Dr. Chil in the first instance, thinking he did not practise much, being more devoted to literature than to medicine. Thanks to his indefatigable care and attention, I got quite over my illness, not, however, until I had been sixteen days in bed. Although the illness was doubtless brought to a point by the drive of the night before, it would not have been so severe but for the great fatigue I had undergone previously without sufficient nourishing food. The poorer people did not intentionally underfeed us, but they did not understand how exceedingly hungry we could be after ten or fourteen hours of fresh mountain air, with the exertion of riding or walking. A little piece of overcooked meat or a couple of fried eggs at seven o'clock in the evening, after having had nothing since early morning, was not enough for hungry mortals, for, although in the Happy Isles, we did not feel at all like departed spirits! If again travelling in

Canaria, we would provide ourselves with wheat gofio.   There
is of course plenty of maize gofio procurable, but whenever
we asked for it we were told "it was not good to ride after
eating gofio."   Besides, maize is not at all so satisfying or so
wholesome as wheat.   We had made arrangements to sail in
the correo leaving for Fuerteventura on Tuesday, an engage-
ment, it is unnecessary to say, we could not keep, and it was
with great reluctance we also saw all chance of our reaching
England by Christmas vanish.

November 26th, Monday, to December 12th, Wednesday.—My
note-book is a blank between these dates.   Illness is disagreeable to everybody, and not at all pleasant to read about, but as
I was ill in a country where customs are different from those in
England, a few points may be interesting to record.   First,
although so feverish, a hot-water bottle was kept at my feet,
while my forehead was bound by a wreath of eucalyptus leaves,
gathered in the hotel patio, to allay the headache.   I was also
given eucalyptus tea to drink.   My husband was naturally my
chief nurse, but Don Ramon's wife, the señora, as she was
always called, and a big, fat, kind, and good-natured negress,
Maria, were most attentive.   Don Gregorio was of course the
presiding genius, and he invariably visited me three times a
day, the first visit being paid about 7 a.m.   Don Gregorio is a
tall, fine-looking man, of commanding presence.   His white hair
and moustache suggest more years than do his energy and
upright bearing.   As he tapped at my door every morning in
spotless raiment, with his gold-headed cane and hat in hand,
and bowing low, asked, in slow and sonorous accents, "how the
señora was this morning," he looked the very embodiment of
the old school of the Dr. Johnson type.   I may be excused
giving a detailed account of one who is such a well-known
figure in Las Palmas, and who proved to me such a valuable
friend and clever physician.

A few days after the commencement of my illness—to which,
by the way, no one would give a name; some called it bilious

fever, others whispered typhoid—feeling able to raise my head off the pillow, I innocently asked the señora for some warm water and my brush and comb. I little knew the storm I was bringing down upon myself. "You must not wash; it will kill you; and it is very bad to do your hair." "But," I said, "it is warm water I want. I am not going to use cold." "Hot or cold, there is nothing so bad as water." I explained that we always used it in England in our hospitals as well as in private houses for those who were ill. No, nothing would induce the señora to give me water. "Supposing one were in bed a month," I said, "do you mean to say one should not wash or use a brush?" to which the señora replied, "Certainly not!" I felt that further argument was useless, and gave in for the moment, merely saying, "If my hair were untouched for a month, I then might go to the barber and have it cut off!" An hour later Maria came in, and I made John ask her for hot water, which she brought in all good faith, thinking it was for him. When, however, returning again a few minutes later, she found me at my toilet, her grief and consternation, though evidently genuine, were to me comic. I learned long after that she had gone to the señora and, with despair in voice and gesture, said, "The Señora Inglesa will die. She has washed!" Poor soul! I did not die, however. The only drink I was allowed was warm orangeade, which was brought in fresh every day in a tumbler covered over with a stiff round crochet mat, a little knob, made also of crochet, in the centre for a handle. *Caldo* was prescribed as my food. Now *caldo* is the Spanish equivalent for beef-tea, but as like English beef-tea as chalk is like cheese. It is made by putting a piece of meat into a quantity of water and letting it boil for some hours. A greasy, watery, insipid fluid is then served as the result. I took it and starved upon it for a day or two because I was obliged to do so. Fortunately, however, for my chances of recovery, Mrs. James Miller, the vice-consul's wife, heard of my illness, and knowing the stuff *caldo* is, like a veritable good Samaritan, sent me a large jugful of really good beef-tea every day. I attribute my recovery as

much to that beef-tea as to anything. Her kindness and that
of Mrs. Miller in sending me food that I could eat until out of my
sick-room and in many other ways is beyond all thanks. Some
jelly Mrs. James Miller made would not set owing to the heat,
and no ice or snow was procurable. An English vessel calling,
however, at Las Palmas while I was ill, a little ice was begged
and kindly given. Another kind act was a supply of soft
pillows, those in use here generally being long in shape and
very hard. The tall manservant, dressed in white, who used
to arrive at my door with a tray covered with a napkin, underneath which was everything thoughtful kindness could suggest,
from English cooked and cut meat to the latest papers from
England, was a welcome visitor. When I was able to eat meat,
I was sent up a piece of beef in the hotel cut quite an inch thick,
"because English people liked their meat cut thick"! So I
thoroughly appreciated, in a way those in England cannot
understand, a dinner served in English manner. Seeing the
puddings Mrs. Miller sent me, the Señora Ramon asked how
they were made. I told her how to make a number of puddings,
which were practised upon by sending small ones up to me in
my room first before attempting them for dinner in the comedor!
When it got near Christmas, I suggested that they should learn
to make a plum-pudding, and gave very exact directions. The
result, however, was not satisfactory. It had been boiled in a
shape and turned out on a glass dish half cold, and was very
pale in colour. The señora went over all the items carefully
and the manner of boiling. Everything seemed correct. Where
had been the mistake? At last I thought of asking of the
manner of mixing, and found the suet and eggs had been mixed
first and the other ingredients added afterwards!

A Spanish gentleman staying in the hotel, Don Nicolas
Sala, of Santa Cruz, on coming to inquire for me at my door
one morning, noticed that the window was open an inch, and
most kindly offered to close it. It was no easy matter to do this,
for there were no weights, and the windows were very high and
heavy. A couple of nails supported them, and these had to be

taken out and put in higher. Mrs. Goetz, an Englishwoman, staying in the hotel during part of my illness, supplied us with many odds and ends, luxuries not procurable in the islands. It was really almost worth while being ill to find out how kind everyone could be.

Don Gregorio had ordered a blister for my chest, and when the time came for it to be dressed, the *barber* was sent for. Doctors never do anything of a surgical nature; it is considered derogatory. So my barber came twice a day, and dressed the part blistered with a cabbage leaf and lard. He was very deft and gentle, but it seemed extremely odd for a barber to do such work. There are two classes of barbers, one of them being styled surgeon-barbers, who are qualified to do many things of this sort. John has paid two visits to a barber to have his hair cut, but the sights he saw were sufficient to deter him from again repeating the experiment.

The barbers in this town rank next in number to the shoe-makers. Their shops are a little like those of old-fashioned barbers in England—that race which is fast becoming extinct, and only now to be found in villages and out-of-the-way country towns. A few chairs placed round the single room, which communicates directly with the street by folding doors; a cane settee on one side against the wall, where the friend, guitar in hand, waits his turn; one small looking-glass, of distorting qualities, in a gilt frame; a good many spittoons on the floor, which are more for ornament apparently than use; a small four-legged table, upon which are ranged the instruments of the craft; one small basin and a jug of water—such are the usual accompaniments of the man of scissors. Such you may see fifty times over as you take a short walk through the town of Las Palmas, for the barbers' doors are always open, as if to invite the attention of the casual passers-by. No gaudy red-and-yellow pole adorns the outside; no tempting array of hair-restorers, pomades, and cosmetiques attracts the eye, for there are no shop-windows. The greatest amount of ostentation is when the simple word "Barberia" is inscribed in big capitals above the door. For shaving, a basin of a half-moon shape is placed under the chin.   The barbers mostly combine bleeding, blistering, and tooth-drawing with the more harmless occupations of shaving and hair-cutting.   This combination of barbering and surgery is not agreeable.   On John's first visit to a barber's here he saw a man's boil dressed, and on the second a wound in a man's head washed, and the hair generally picked over by the barber's fingers for lice.   The machinery for brushing the hair with circular brushes very naturally has not yet penetrated to this out-of-the-world spot.   Shampooing is unknown, its place being taken by a kind of dry wash after the hair is cut.

The charges to natives for hair-cutting and shaving are exceedingly small, but when an Englishman asks what he has to pay, the unsatisfactory rejoinder is always made of "leaving it to you."   This cabman-like way of treating foreigners, due to the likelihood of thereby obtaining more than the legitimate amount, is not confined to the hairdressers.   Englishmen are all considered by the natives to be made of money—a want of discrimination which is most unpleasant to those of small or only moderate means.   Hotel-keepers, arrieros, servants, boatmen, and native shopmen by no means unfrequently adopt the same process of extortion as that used by the barbers.   The sooner the inhabitants of these islands learn the honest method of asking only one price for an article or service, be the buyer native or foreign, the sooner will the English and English money flow in their direction.   Of all things an Englishman hates, by no means the least is the idea that he is being "done," and I am sorry to record that this is a very dominant feeling of the traveller in these islands.

There is this peculiarity about the barbers' shops, the shoemakers' shops, the chemists', and even the ordinary stores in Las Palmas and the other towns of these islands : they all appear equal in merit or importance.   There is no barber who enjoys a municipal reputation of being more proficient than his fellows, no shoemaker is said to cobble in a style superior to the general run, and they say you get as well and carefully drugged in one chemist's shop as in another.

The chemists in this island seem to be gregarious, all their shops being collected in a cluster within a stone's-throw of the casino. Why they should not spread themselves over the town, as would seem to be the more useful method, I cannot tell. They evidently like each other's society. One thing I know about them : that, as in England, their prices for the making up of the same prescription vary much. A prescription at one shop cost me three pesetas, at another two, and at another one and a half. So that in this respect they partake of the peculiarity common to the genus elsewhere. Their shops are the great gossiping places of the town, each providing a room where those who have nothing to do—and such are a majority here just now—may meet and exchange ideas upon politics, the weather, the state of trade, or social scandal. The Spaniards are great talkers. If they did more and said less, there would be more chance for the speedy advancement of the islands. The chemists', the barbers', and the lobby of the casino are the places where this surcharge of verbal steam is daily blown off.

Besides avoiding surgical functions, a doctor will not, as a rule, set a bone. An English friend living here broke a small bone in her foot, and sent for her doctor to set it. He did so, but as she has been slightly lame ever since, her servants say to her, " Ah ! if you had sent for the carpenter, you would not be lame, as you are now. What does the doctor know about setting bones ?" For, curiously enough, in this town the great bone-setter among the lower classes is a carpenter !

When I was allowed to get up after my illness, the señora made a kindly fuss about it. First she wanted to dress me, saying I should be so weak, I should not be able to walk across the room. I thought differently, and proved it later, much to her astonishment. Then my clothes must be aired. There are of course no fireplaces in the houses, so I

wondered much how the airing would be done.   Presently
the señora carried into my room a tiny red earthenware
brazier, in which a charcoal fire was burning.   This she put
in the middle of the floor, and placed over it a wicker basket,
like a tall waste-paper basket turned upside down.   The
wickerwork was very open, and the basket was about two
and a half feet high, narrow at the top and wide at the
bottom.   She then threw my clothes over the basket.   Charcoal, as everyone knows, emits a glow of heat, but no smoke
or flame, so there is no danger of one's clothes being burnt.
There is likewise but little chance of airing, for my things
were hardly warmed through !

As, however, morning after morning at 9 a.m. John used to
come in saying, " The thermometer still registers 66° F." (19°
C.), one does not require fireplaces, and there is no damp in the
atmosphere to eliminate from one's clothing.   It really seemed
as if the mercury were glued at 66°, and we hailed a change
on either side as a relief from the monotony.   Whilst we are
revelling in blue skies and perpetual sunshine, it is well to be
reminded of the weather friends are enjoying (?) at home.
We read in the *Times* that for the first week in December
London had twelve and a half hours of clear sunshine, while
the north of Ireland had seven wet days in the week (*sic*) !
and three hours of sunshine.   It is unnecessary to add that
that week London enjoyed more than its usual average of
sunshine, as three hours out of seven days is often registered.
We were also interested in reading that on December 3rd
" a brilliant appearance of the sky at the time of sunrise
and sunset has again been general."   We had noticed this
phenomenon in the archipelago, but particularly when crossing
to Palma.   Not knowing that it was abnormal, however, we
attributed it to the latitude.

CHAPTER IX.

> What matters the sand or the whitening chalk,
>   The blighted herbage, the black'ning log,
> The crooked beak of the eagle-hawk,
>   Or the hot, red tongue of the native dog ?
> That couch was rugged, those sextons rude,
>   Yet, in spite of a leaden shroud, we know
> That the bravest and fairest are earthworms' food
>   When once they've gone where we all must go.
>
> ADAM LINDSAY GORDON.

November 26th, Monday, to December 12th, Wednesday (continued).
—Whilst I was ill in bed, John took several walks, of which he
has given me the following accounts :—

"To-day I started with Mr. Béchervaise to ramble over the
Isleta and to find, if we could, a Guanche cemetery of which
we had heard. The Isleta is only twenty minutes' drive from
Las Palmas, and it might be thought that all interesting details
about it would be known to the townsmen. But this is not so.
Ignorance about the Isleta is almost universal, and reliable
information is difficult to obtain. The Spaniards who drive
there never leave the road which takes them to the mole ; they
care nothing about Guanches, scenes of past volcanic eruptions,
or curious vegetation ; and I suspect in their eyes to take an
interest in such things seems somewhat akin to imbecility of
character.

I paid many visits to the Isleta before leaving Canaria, each of which only served to whet my appetite for further investigations.   Even looked at on the map, this spot excites curiosity. Rudely breaking the rotundity of Gran Canaria, the Isleta juts out abruptly into the sea, being connected to the island by a most slender, unsubstantial-looking neck.   Viewed from a distance, from one of the many high points on the north coast of the island, the Isleta always charms.   It may be when the sky is clear, of a brilliant blue, and then the five or more peaks composing the Isleta stand out proudly against the northern sky, the soft line of white edging the shore breaking, as with a harmonious necklace, the sere browns of the island and the purplish blues of the sea.   Under such conditions the scene is that of quiet beauty, subject of course to the slightly creepy feeling which a view of volcanic peaks always produces.   But when the mists blow in from the sea, and the Isleta, catching the fleecy billows, is alternately veiled and exposed, the wildness of the outline and the rugged contour of the mountains against a murky sky make the picture sternly sublime.

The dune sand of the narrow isthmus is dazzling white, and is just now steadily drifting towards the main island.   This neck of sand is more remarkable as there is no sand on the Isleta where it joins the head, the land there being composed of volcanic cinders and scoriæ, totally devoid of soil of any kind ; nor is there any at that part of the island whence it starts.   The sand is disposed in hills, valleys, small tablelands, and plateaus, over which when one begins to walk their extent seems to be much greater than would be supposed from a distant view.

The only houses on the Isleta are a few grouped together at the south-east, and forming chiefly a single street leading towards and terminating at the mole.   When the Harbour of Refuge is finished, this mole, which is now short, will run out a very considerable distance.   The summit of one of the volcanic peaks on the north is crowned with the white walls and tower of the lighthouse.   More towards the south on another peak is located the Look-out and signal-station for ships—a small white house and flagstaff.

We pass a quarry on the left, whence, beneath the lava, hard granite is being hewn for the harbour works. Dismissing our vehicle at the land end of the mole, we continue straight on, and at once find ourselves beyond the last house and on the commencement of a perfectly barren tract. There is no fresh water on the Isleta, every drop for drinking and washing having to be brought from the mainland. The labour of this is enormous, and it is astonishing, nay almost incredible, that a pipe conveying fresh water has not years ago been laid on here. But the fact remains that women and children have daily to trudge along the dusty road of the Isleta with earthenware pots on their heads, and return by the same weary way heavily laden. Those who can afford it have a donkey-carriage and barrels for the water. The waste of time, the fatigue, and the premium put upon dirtiness, and therefore disease, by this terribly tedious method of obtaining the first necessary of life, are fearful to contemplate. Before lighting her streets with incandescent lights, before indulging in a Harbour of Refuge, a grand opera house, and a European cable, one would have thought the well-built and grandly edificed town of Las Palmas would have provided her suburb with the first essential of health and sanitation. It will always be a disgrace to Canaria that she left the Isleta so long devoid of water, but I trust it will not be long ere this important omission is repaired. There can be no excuse that water is unobtainable. From the town an easy descent would take the water out to the Isleta, or if this be deemed not desirable, there is plenty of water, as we have ourselves seen, in the Barranco Guanarteme, which is quite close to the island end of the isthmus. It shows a certain amount of apathy on the part of those owning houses or land on the Isleta that they have not taken the matter into their own hands, and themselves constructed an aqueduct from the island. In the fetching of water, in the wear and tear of man and beast, far more has been expended in energy and money than would have brought water to their doors.

But to return to our walk. A step, as it were, takes us from the end of the street on to the wild, bare country, and the ground is as savage and chaotic as ground can well be. There is no soil, the surface being one mass of broken-up lava pieces, light, spongy stones of all sizes, and entirely covered with rough, jagged excrescences, which cut the boots and tear in the rudest manner any clothing drawn against them. Walking is very difficult and tiring. It consists in a tedious picking of the way, balancing the body on the top of a shaky piece one moment and then springing on to another, at all hazards avoiding putting the foot between the blocks. The ground is full of small caves— bubbles in the lava, where part of the roof has fallen in—of from one to several feet in size.

What a magnificent sight it must have been to have seen the eruption which caused this !—to have seen the peak pouring out its contents like thick treacle, to have watched this flowing down to the sea, spitting, bubbling, and throwing up short pillars at intervals, now represented by short, jagged eminences of lava blocks, eight, ten, or twenty feet in height, and then to have remained to see the stream-like mass cool, and to watch it contracting and splitting up with a deafening, crackling noise into myriads of separate light cinder stones. Even up to this time the state of tension of some of the bubbles has not been released, for the recent rain we have had has evidently caused fresh bubbles to split up and fall in. We saw fresh cracks and fresh caves, with stones delicately poised on the roof, ready for the slightest touch to cause to tumble.

Vegetation, in the sense of a clothing, the land has none. In the hollows, the little valleys where moisture can linger longer, the lava stones are partially covered with lichen, and here and there are individuals of the square-stemmed, columnar euphorbia (*E. Canariensis*), the dragon tree euphorbia (*Kleinia meriifolia*), and the graceful, feathery *Plocama pendula*. The

roots of these shrubs must go down a long way below the
lava stones in order to find soil. At a few places in some of
the little valleys, and nearer to the bases of the peaks, we found
little forests of these singular plants. But even then each was
quite distinct and separated by an interval from its neighbour,
so that one could walk round it. Though peculiar at first sight,
when one becomes accustomed to their odd shapes these shrubs
are not destitute of beauty. The light, weeping, graceful form of
the feathery *Plocama*, with its lively green colour, contrasts not
unpleasingly with the gouty, branching stem of the *Kleinia*,
resembling a miniature dragon tree, surmounted with its grey-
green foliage; these two plants again serve to set off the stiff
square vegetable columns of the monstrous-looking *Euphorbia*.
Certainly when seen together they blend harmoniously with the
chaotic disorder of the blocks of lava, and mingle their soft
shades of green with the browns of the ground.

The heat is great, so we sit down to rest a while in the midst
of one of these queer forests, though we get no protection from
the sun, none of the plants being higher than four feet. We
throw some pieces of the jagged stones into a clump of the
Euphorbia Canariensis, and watch how the thick, milky, almost
creamy, fluid runs or squirts out. The plant seems charged
with this poisonous fluid, and ready to pour it out at the
slightest abrasion. When dried, this sap forms the drug
euphorbium of the pharmacopœia. A thick, poisonous, milky
juice also exudes from the *kleinia*, the deadly nature of which
I proved there and then upon some ants, a large black
species, which were the only representatives of animal life we
could discover in the place. These three plants are shunned
by every beast that passes by, and I never found any signs of
caterpillars or other leaf-eating insect or animal upon either,
though I have often looked. In such an arid soil as that in
which they delight to grow, it is a matter of wonderment to find
plants so brimming with sap. One also vainly speculates as to
the part they play in the biological economy of these islands.
They are useless for food, fodder, or firewood, injurious to man

and beast, and even not serviceable as a binder of loose soil. They appear, in short, to possess all negative, no positive, economical properties. Yet Glas makes a suggestion, for the uselessness of these plants had not escaped the notice of that observant mariner; he says, " I cannot imagine the reason why the natives do not extract the juice, and use it for the bottoms of their boats and vessels, instead of pitch; I am persuaded it would answer better, and be an effectual preservative against the worms."

The plants are the most characteristic feature of the shores and littoral mountains of the Canary Islands. Even the passing traveller, as the steamer takes him near the coast, cannot fail being struck by the round pale green bushes or clumps of the stiff, leafless, ill-favoured *Euphorbia Canariensis*, dotted over the cliffs in such a manner as to produce a most curious spotty effect upon the landscape. A nearer view of the uncouth physiognomy of this strange and grotesque plant would even more excite his surprise.

All this time as we skirted the shore of the Isleta, a few hundred yards inland, in a north-easterly direction, we kept a sharp look-out for the Guanche cemetery, but nothing could I see at all answering to what I had been led to expect from my knowledge of that at Agaete. We stopped and examined several of the many small caves in the ground, but they were indisputably natural. At last we came upon a solitary narrow trench lined with a layer of flat lava stones, evidently the familiar six narrow feet, having at the bottom a little yellow, dust-like earth. If the grave—for such it was—had ever been surmounted by a pile of stones, such had long ago been removed. As there were no loose stones near this spot, it is probable that this Guanche was buried without the usual monument. The bones had either been removed, or had crumbled ages ago into the dust lining the bottom. No other graves were near. Who then was this solitary individual thus singularly ostracised in death? Did outraged society refuse him a place with the rest of the race? We cannot tell. There lies the lonely violated tomb by the sobbing sound of the sea, and romance can weave around the lava-enclosed narrow space any explanation it pleases. The spot is wild, the ground rough, the scene sublime; everything invites the imagination. A poet has yet to arise who will sing the pathetic history of the persecuted, long-enduring, though noble and gentle Guanches.

Continuing our walk, we now strike a bee-line for the Look-out, and ascending a rapid and difficult incline, at 400 feet elevation, find ourselves standing upon the lower brim of a parasitic crater. The suddenness with which we came upon this extinct volcano very much surprised us, for from below there was nothing to indicate that such a feature existed two-thirds up the peak. We measured the crater, and found it to be about ninety feet deep from the edge nearest the sea—the other side being continuous with the hill—and one hundred and fifty yards in diameter, the sides sloping gradually and almost meeting in a point at the bottom, covered with the same sort of lava stones we had met on the way up. The stones lining the west side were sprinkled over with grey and orange lichens, and here and there grew individuals of the *Euphorbia Canariensis*, *Kleinia*, and *Plocama*. It was noticeable that the east side of this crater was totally bare, not a single lichen, not a single plant, enlivening the monotonous browns and greys of the lava stones. On a small scale this crater and the conical mountain in the background are just the same in formation and mutual relation as those of Bandama. We now walked round the edge of the crater to the mountain side, which we ascended until we reached a shoulder, and then, happening to turn round, saw a little distance off to the north another, and still more perfect and 'volcanic-looking,' crater. It rose isolated from the level ground some fifty or sixty feet, and was perfectly round, but with the edges at the top much crumbled away. Toothlike projections stood up here and there round the circle. It reminded me exactly of the terminal crater of Tenerife, lacking of course the smoke or steam which is always there present. We could not resist the temptation to inspect closely this new wonder, so, starting off at a sharp run down the shoulder of the mountain, in five minutes were standing on the brim, looking into the centre. The brim is 450 feet above the sea level, and the centre only some twenty or thirty feet lower, so much had the sides fallen in. We now partially retraced our steps, and climbed up to the top of the mountain, where the Look-out and signal station is placed. This point we found to be 625 feet high. The signalman had seen us coming up, and though past his time for descending—it was now getting late in the evening—had waited till we arrived. A stone shanty and a flag-post, whence the signals can be seen in Las Palmas, complete the erections. Turning towards the main island, the view from this point is truly sublime. The sun was setting, and his westering rays were fully concentrated upon a mixed mass of rough and wild mountains in the centre of the island. The solitary Roque del Nublo, looking like a stern, upright giant, was distinctly seen. On the left the island appeared to end in the sea in a long, extenuated point, the Punta de Gando, while on the right the striking Peak of Galdar, rising separately from the main mountains of the island, guarded the land end of a blunt promontory. At our feet—so close it seemed—lay the isthmus, narrowed by this bird's-eye view to a mere silver streak, while beyond, on a flat, low-lying tongue of land jutting out into the sea, the white houses of Las Palmas and the two dark towers of the cathedral formed the only spot suggestive of active life in a dreamy, satisfying picture.

Though we could have stayed here some time without tiring of the beauties of the marvellous panorama before us, we were forced to descend, for night was coming on apace, and the friendly signalman was doubtless anxious to return to his family. On our way into the port, we passed five men, accompanied by as many dogs, of a mongrel breed, but containing more of the greyhound than of anything else. They were returning from rabbiting on the Isleta. Each carried, slung over the shoulder, a small wooden barrel, in which was a ferret. Each had also a stick with an iron spike at the end. In spite of all this paraphernalia, they had not a single rabbit among them. The rabbits on the Isleta are certainly shy, but the look-out man informed us that they abounded in great numbers.

Being Sunday evening, the women were sitting outside their doors as we returned to Las Palmas. They were not idle. 'Capital' game seems to abound on Sundays in the 'capillary' forests of Las Palmas, and to-night we saw them busily and industriously engaged in the chase in each other's heads, occasionally cracking the captured spoil between their teeth. Certainly there is no accounting for tastes!

November 30*th, Friday.*—The discovery upon Sunday last of one undoubted Guanche grave and the failure to find anything that could by any possibility be imagined to represent a regular cemetery had ever since made me eager to try again. True, we had seen upon Sunday mounds of lava blocks and even small caves all of which at a distance might be imagined to be graves of the bygone race, but a nearer inspection always dispelled the illusion. I had even begun to doubt whether there did exist a cemetery upon the Isleta, for though one or two, in reply to my interrogations, said that there was something of the sort, by far the majority, including *mirabile dictu* the owner of the land, insisted upon the story being entirely fabricated, and that no Guanche remains were there to be found. Taking a car by the old mole, Mr. Béchervaise and I drove to the Puerto and stopped there by the first houses. Here we dismissed the conveyance, and signalling to two boys who were engaged in placidly sitting on the sand, asked them if they knew where the cemetery was. They at once replied that they did, and that it lay on the other side of Las Palmas. At last, however, we got them to understand that it was not a modern, but an ancient, burying-place of which we were in search, and as they said they could guide us to the spot, we let them lead the way.

There is at this part of the Puerto only one row of poor one-storied, whitewashed houses, passing behind which we found ourselves immediately upon rough, volcanic ground. It was

surprising how swiftly the two little brown urchins, with their
bare feet, ran over the rough cinders. The ground is entirely
composed of these cinders, quite bare of vegetation. Boots
on these children, however desirable, would certainly have been
out of keeping with the remainder of their clothing, which was
only of the strictly necessary kind. Curiously enough, one boy
had dark brown eyes, a typical young Spaniard, while the
other, with his blue eyes and light hair, was a living proof that
Guanche blood has not yet died out. Thus, personally conducted, as it were, by representatives of the old and the new,
we reached a gentle slope of the cinder-covered ground, and I
at once saw that we were indeed standing in the midst of a

GUANCHE CEMETERY, ISLETA.

Guanche cemetery. All around were mounds made of light
cinder stones, some quite perfect and inviolate, but by far the
majority in various stages of dilapidation. The hand of the
spoiler was everywhere apparent, and if the desecration proceeds at the present rate, a few years will suffice to wipe out
this interesting record of an extinct race. Here we find a
mound with the stones half pulled down, having apparently
been left for another more inviting; here a narrow trench about
two feet wide and six feet long, lined along the sides with flat
lava stones, shows that the mound has been removed and the
bones taken; here a small opening has been made in the side of
a mound, and looking in, we can see the white skeleton of a
Guanche, lying in all its grim length, but lacking the skull;

here again is a mound with one end pulled down, the bones lying scattered around showing that pure mischief has been the only motive for the spoliation.

As at Agaete, in each case the body had been laid in a narrow trench, slightly below the level of the ground, encased with large pieces of flat, slab-like lava, over which a carefully built mound of lava stones has been raised. In none of the mounds were there any red stones, so that in this respect the Isleta cemetery differs from that at Agaete. It would be interesting to know who were the persons dignified by having red stones in their funeral piles, and why in regard to this custom the Canarios of the north differed from those of the west. The mounds are of various sizes and shapes, and have apparently been made after no particular pattern, the only uniformity being that the sides for a height of about four feet are wall-like, composed of large cinder stones, whose more or less flat surfaces are carefully ranged upon the exterior. The top of each mound is formed by smaller stones thrown on and allowed to settle in any order, but naturally assuming more or less of a flattish, pyramidal shape.

The stones immediately enclosing the body were carefully selected for their large flat surface. A very large one shows that they are in reality curved. One surface is rough and spongy in appearance, the other more compact in structure, smooth, and slightly concave. They were obtained from bubbles in the lava-flow, many of which are still visible on the Isleta. These small caves generally have an opening, where pieces of the roof, having cracked up, have fallen in. Looking into such a natural cavity in the ground, one sees the roof entirely made up of smooth-surfaced lava, cracked in all directions. To detach and carry off the component pieces would not be difficult. These lava stones are much lighter than their appearance would warrant ; and an immense, solid-looking piece can be carried which it would seem at first sight impossible to lift.

I measured two graves which I could get at, owing to the

piles having been partially dismantled. One I chose for its unimportant appearance, and the other because it was one of the, if not the, largest on the ground. The former was fifteen inches wide and just one foot below the level of the ground, the topping stones which covered in the body resting their ends on the ground on either side. Its length was six feet six inches, and it was rudely squared at the ends. The other grave had been covered by a large, circular mound, and lay due north and south. The stones had been pulled down at the north end, exposing the grave, from which the skull had been, as usual, taken, though there remained the ribs, vertebræ, femurs, and a few small bones, all of which, from their great size and very marked eminences for the attachment of the muscles, showed that the man had been tall, well built, and very powerful, probably a mighty warrior, perhaps a king. I could get into the grave, and found a chamber lined with immense pieces of flat lava stones and roofed with others of a concave shape. The grave was therefore dome-shaped, but seven feet long and rounded off at the ends, not squared, as in the smaller grave. The height from the flat floor to the highest point of the roof was three feet nine inches, and in width the grave was twenty-two inches.

I noticed the direction in which the bodies had been laid in the ground, and had expected to find that the Guanches buried east and west, but this, I found, was not the case, for the first narrow trench I saw ran due north and south. The next lay north-east and south-west, and others I examined were directed to all points of the compass. There were, of the fifty or sixty * graves which I examined, more lying north and south than in any other direction. It must have been from mere cursory examination or hearsay evidence that Captain Glas in 1764 asserted that the Canarios buried their dead with their heads towards the north, and that later Messrs. Berthelot and Webb said

---

* The close examination of so many graves was of course not completed in one afternoon. I spent here many hours on several occasions for the purpose of determining the direction of the graves.

that they buried east and west. Together these assertions are correct; singly undoubtedly they are incorrect. If the Guanches intended to bury in any particular direction, they were most careless in the manner they did it. The inspection of the cemeteries of Agaete and the Isleta, the disposition of the mounds, and a close examination of the opened graves forced the conviction upon me that no particular direction was followed. Here, as at Agaete, the marked difference in the size of the mounds was most noticeable. The largest were quite six times as big as the smallest. Some of the large ones, instead of following the usual oblong shape, were circular. To get an idea of the number, I counted the piles that could be seen from one spot taken at random. Sixty were visible. Altogether in this cemetery there must have been several hundred mounds.

So many of the mounds had been mutilated—I should think not a score of perfect ones remain—that had I not seen the intact specimens of Agaete, the details of their external structure would not have been so easily made out. The ground, situation, and stones are similar in character to the Agaete cemetery.

The Guanches must have liked to be buried close to the sea, so close, that in a storm the spray would blow over their funeral mounds. The choice of this unpromising-looking ground, composed entirely of the roughest of rough stones found in a volcanic country, might perhaps be due to the singularity of the spot, to the great difference existing between it and the neighbouring country. These curious little outbursts of a past volcanic fury very probably assumed in the eyes of the Guanches religious importance. It might be that they did not regard these freaks of nature with dread, but as having something specially to do with the great Giver of all good, into Whose safe keeping they hesitated not to entrust all that was mortal of their dead brothers and sisters. For that they believed in a future state is evident from the care with which they buried their dead, from the mummified corpses which have been found in caves, and from the many utensils and food found with the remains and in the cave sepulchres.

Of course it may also be suggested that, owing to the over-population of the island, land that could be used for pasture was too valuable for burial purposes, or further that, instruments for digging being unknown, this lava-block-covered land afforded an easy means of sepulture.

As we sit upon the ruined mound which once had held all that was earthly of a Guanche we can see from the slightly rising ground the narrow neck of the Isleta isthmus, with the sea foaming on either side. The sand looks dazzling white at this distance as it glares in the heat of the noonday sun. Beyond a monochromatic landscape—for we look not towards where the glaring white town of Las Palmas lies—of lofty mountains, brown and sere. Very rough and wild are those outlines against the sky, a compressed mass of crags, jagged edges, and toothlike eminences. The calm blue sky above, the deep blue sea around, and the infinite silence brooding over all form a fitting and soothing setting for the savageness of the scene. As this picture is to-day, so it was when the funeral trains wound their way up from the main island across the sandy track of the isthmus or descended from the loftily situated caves of the Isleta. A thoughtful person cannot be here unmoved. Around us in all directions lie scattered the mounds —reminders of a race which once inhabited the island, and which has entirely passed away from the face of the earth. It is a curious sensation to be gazing upon the cemetery, ay upon the actual bones of a people that are no more.

> ' How many a bleeding heart hath found its home
> Under these hillocks which the sea-mews sweep ! '

To see a skull in a museum, to notice a piled-up heap of arm-bones of an extinct race, is simply fatiguing to eye and brain ; but to see the remnants of a nation in their natural positions as left by the people themselves, with all the surroundings of scene and climate, is to have one's curiosity aroused, one's sympathy enlisted. We ask ourselves what rites have here been performed at the numerous interments which have taken place within these few hundred yards ;

what ceremonies; who followed the corpse to the grave; did priests attend the burials; how were the mourners clad; did sad strains of wailing wake the echoes of the mountains, causing the passing bird to swerve from its course; whose loving hands piled up those stones which now mutely stand eloquent with hidden meaning? We can reply to none of these questions, and in all probability many of them will for ever remain unanswered.

> 'All is gone—
> All—save the piles of earth that hold their bones.'

There is no Guanche literature, a few scratches upon a few stones being its only representative; and the records of the Spanish conquerors are most egotistical and one-sided, though here and there we are able to read between the lines. But we do know that tears have here been shed, that here grief too deep for words has been over and over again experienced, for it is incontestable that the Guanches were a loving and a lovable race. We feel the ground is as sacred as any land over which a bishop has walked, for it must have witnessed much human suffering; and will any dare say that hope might not also have been there to allay the pangs which death had inflicted?

However, in the midst of death we are in life, for, rising and turning round, we observe that during our reverie the two mischievous urchins we had brought with us have been busily employed in pounding to powder between two stones the skull and cross-bones of a Guanche, which they had unceremoniously, for their amusement, extracted from one of the opened mounds. The bones have quite lost their hard character, and either crumble when touched, or are of the consistency of damp gingerbread. To reprove the boys for their sacrilegious occupation, absolutely ignorant as they are of everything concerning the past history of the island—even if they know anything else, which I doubt—would simply be waste of time, so peremptorily telling them to drop the pounding process, we start to see the caves of which we had heard.

We strike for the west coast of the Isleta by the shortest route, and in ten minutes are down by the shore. Here there is a fairly good path, and we soon can see, high up on the cliffs, the mouths of the caves of which we have come in search. Arriving beneath, we climb up, not without some difficulty, for the cliff is very steep. We notice bits of old pottery and quantities of old limpet and other shells on the way. The caves are 260 feet above the sea, and consist of two main and a number of smaller ones. We measured one of the larger. It was twenty-two feet long by sixteen broad, and nine feet high, with a squarish opening. A small recess had been made near the opening in the right side, on a level with the floor, which was perhaps used as a sleeping place. We found here in flower, just an inch in height, a specimen of the plant *Heliotropium Europæum.*

Leaving these Guanche habitations, we climbed over the top of the cliff, and found the land sloping gradually, forming one side of a small valley. A path at the bottom soon conducts us to the edge of a steep descent, and looking down, we see a flat plateau of considerable size, encircled on the land side by precipitous cliffs, and with the sea for its western boundary.

The ground on this side of the Isleta is much smoother than on the eastern, where the lava streams from the many eruption craters have flowed down. The plain at our feet is bare, save for the salt works of Don Pedro Bravo, which occupy a small area, and look like a number of cucumber frames placed side by side, but lacking the glass on the tops. Descending by a zigzag path, we find Don Pedro himself, superintending the planting of some trees, for he intends to make this arid spot blossom and bloom, and eventually to build a dwelling-house here. We have already alluded at length to the absence of fresh water on the Isleta. Don Pedro has endeavoured to supply this want to some extent at this spot by building a stout wall across the end of a narrow though deep barranco, abutting on the plain. The reservoir thus formed will collect and hold rainwater, but as it only rains in the winter, and in some years even then not much, this is a very precarious source upon which to depend. Until fresh water is regularly laid on in pipes or aqueducts, we fear the trees planted here will stand a poor chance of surviving.

He courteously showed us over his domain. A small windmill pumps up the sea-water to the level of the evaporating pans—the cucumber frames we had just now looked down upon—which are made of a reddish earth found on the spot, beaten well together. The pans are four metres square, and about a foot deep. There are three hundred in operation, though the works are intended to be extended over more of the little plain. The works have been established five years. Don Pedro volunteered the information that in the first year the yield of salt was sixteen fanegas, in the second one hundred and fifty fanegas, the third three hundred, the fourth seven hundred, and last year twelve hundred fanegas. The yield of the last year sold for one hundred and eighty pounds. In a wooden storehouse close by we saw some of the salt. It is sold just as it comes from the evaporating pans, without any process of purification or recrystallisation. In look it is like crystallised sugar of a common kind, the crystals being small, rough, and dirty. Though containing chiefly chloride of sodium, this residue of the sea-water must also contain other salts. We were interested chiefly in the simplicity of the whole process. There is positively no expense in the way of working power. The wind pumps up the water, and the sun may be said to make the salt. The hottest part of summer is of course the time when the salt is produced in the greatest quantities. The very sun and wind conspire to make these islands Fortunate. The largest salt works on this island, on exactly the same principle to the one described, are in the extreme south, at Juan Grande."

CHAPTER X.

*HABITS AND CUSTOMS IN LAS PALMAS—WINTER—
CONFITAL BAY— SUPERSTITIONS.*

> I am so delighted with this world,
> That suddenly has grown, being new-washed,
> To such a smiling, clean, and thankful world,
> And with a tender face shining through tears,
> Looks up into the sometime lowering sky,
> That has been angry, but is reconciled,
> And just forgiving her, that I—that I—
> Oh, I forget myself : what matters how?
>
> JEAN INGELOW.
>
> And o'er the rocks and up the bay
> The long sea-rollers surge and sound.
>
> ANDREW LANG.

November 26th, Monday, to December 12th, Wednesday (continued).
—Don Gregorio, as well as many of the English residents,
strove to beguile my imprisonment during my illness by spending
many a half-hour in chatting with me upon various subjects. In
El Liberal of December 4th, there was a paragraph upon
my being ill and a long notice about the cave at Galdar, which
it says was discovered twenty years ago by the owner, who, on
opening an irrigation channel, found several skeletons, jars,
and other objects, which fell into the hands of private persons.

The best newspapers in the islands are *El Memorandum* in
Tenerife and *El Liberal* in Canaria. The other journals are
very indifferent in every respect, and carelessly edited. What
would the sages of Fleet Street think of the name of the
journal at the top of the second page not corresponding

with that at the top of the first—of *The Times* one morning arriving with *A Times* printed above the leaders? Yet such careless readings or composings are by no means unknown in the journals here. We ourselves have noticed many. Incorrect spelling, misplaced letters, words divided at the end of lines in the oddest and most grotesque fashion— sometimes we have seen even short proper names split into two discordant pieces—and a general vagueness about the art of spacing are prevalent. Carelessness and want of exactness are rampant in the Canary Islands journalistic world. Then, too, every paper you take up either in Santa Cruz or Las Palmas contains a tirade, a sneer, or a scarcely veiled innuendo concerning the other town. Santa Cruz will laugh at Las Palmas, and Las Palmas will retort in what purports to be bitter invective or withering sarcasm. To the unbiassed visitor this paltry wordy warfare is puerile, abject, disgusting. I am glad to say, however, that this opinion is also shared by many of the better-educated and travelled Spaniards of the islands. A patriotic journal which would resolutely ignore this strange rivalry and devote its energies to the general advancement of the archipelago is wanted.

The first cablegram was received here on December 5th, and on December 7th news arrived that Santa Cruz was in connection with Cadiz. There is a most amusing report, scarcely to be understood by English people, that Mr. Gray, the head of the cable-laying company, and also the Governor of Santa Cruz have been bribed to keep back the royal decree ordering the connection to be at Lanzarote, not Santa Cruz, and that the Governor let Mr. Gray sail without knowing the orders!

On December 9th (Sunday) the barranco, which had been perfectly dry the day before, was quite full at 10 a.m. A number of trees were in the river, which surged rapidly seawards like a flood, showing that the rain in the mountains must have been severe.

Those who dwell in less precipitous countries than this

find the barranco perhaps one of the most interesting features. Although the river-bed when perfectly dry in summer is called the barranco, yet when it is filled with water after rain in winter people say, "The barranco has come down." The idea of a continuously flowing river is as difficult for a Canario to imagine as the sudden flood of water, with its as sudden cessation, is to us. After a severe storm of wind and rain, the river-bed will be filled from bank to bank and be five or six feet deep with water. The next morning there will be only a small stream down one side of the bed, and in some districts it will be perfectly dry. One can tell by the colour of the water if the rain have been only near the town or in the cumbres.

The large shops are shut up on Sunday, but the small are open. The men do not work, but take a holiday, and the day is of course like a Continental Sunday, great cockfights and many of the dances taking place.

There are an immense number of canary birds in cages hanging around the small shops and houses. They abound everywhere in cages, in patios, shops, and private houses, which they make lively with their songs. The captives often attract the wild birds of their species, which are thus frequently caught and imprisoned. They were first introduced into Europe at the commencement of the sixteenth century. The vessel which was conveying them to Italy was wrecked, and the birds took refuge in Elba. They are bred extensively in these islands and sent to Habana and Cuba for sale. The chief breeder is a shoemaker, a fact which bears out Dr. Smiles's observations upon the members of that craft, who, he remarks, " are usually very fond of pets, and especially of pet birds. Many of the craft have singing-birds about them, and some are known to be highly skilled and excellent bird-fanciers." Thus what applies to the inhabitants of our islands would seem also to apply to the Canarian Archipelago. It is curious to note how even when bred in their native land the canary birds always turn yellow in captivity, and their voices become harsher,

It was slightly colder on the evening of the 9th. Some black clouds covered the sky, and the wind rose, which brought rain during the night, and a rough sea, and lowered the temperature on the 10th to 62·6° F. (17° C.) at 8 a.m., accompanied by a shady sky. The next day the temperature was also low, being 63·5° F. (17·5° C.) at 9 a.m. John went on the azotea early to see if the homeward mail were in from the west coast, so that we might close our letters. It had not arrived, but did so later, and left without waiting for the mails !

There is a curious use here made of the stone in the alligator pear, or aguacate, which is a species of laurel. We were told that linen can be marked with it by pressing it tightly upon the stone and scratching the linen with a pin. Heat must then be applied to the linen. The stone will also throw out shoots if put in water, a long stem and leaves growing, which look pretty in a room.

December 12*th, Wednesday, to December* 18*th, Tuesday.*—There was an increase of heat on the 12th, it being at 9 a.m. 65·3° F. (18·50° C.), after which it resumed its normal temperature of 66° F. (19° C.), and remained there steadily until the 18th. There has been quite an unusual amount of wind and rain this winter. The " oldest inhabitants" and residents of fifty years' standing tell us they never remember so much rain. The houses are not made for such weather, and the consequent discomfort when it does occur, happily at rare intervals, is great. Water oozes through every window, and in my room not only did it creep through, but it actually rained in— pattered on paper and table and floor. Spaniards sit in great-coats and hats, and the ladies, in thick shawls, shiver on the sofas. We do not feel it cold at all, but for the look of the thing should not be sorry to see a bright, cosy fire some-where. The sight of these poor sun-warmed people sitting in rooms clothed as if in the open air makes one feel very uncomfortable. Fortunately all this outward discomfort—for after all, it does not affect one much—only lasts a day or two at most, and then this beautiful climate, refreshed and invigorated, returns to its normal condition of cloudless skies and bright sunshine.

Maria tells me she has never seen the barranco, and it is not five minutes' walk from the hotel! She also says she has never been once out of the house for the five years she has been servant here! Sunday and Monday she works all the same, from half-past five in the morning until twelve, one, or two at night. For this she receives the royal sum of nine shillings a month! Could any slavery be worse? Her husband, who is assistant cook, has likewise never been out for five years. Wages in these islands are very low. The head waiter here gets twelve shillings a month. He is an Herreño, and it is said the best servants come from Hierro. Certain it is that most of the service is performed by the isleños from Hierro and Gomera, perhaps because those two islands are poorer than the others, and their inhabitants obliged to seek work elsewhere. When labour is so cheap, there is no excuse for not having enough of it. The bad attendance is the great drawback in most of the hotels. Here the bedrooms, as I have said, are not arranged until late in the afternoon, and boots only cleaned at nine or ten o'clock. For three weeks past I have been asking constantly and persistently for mosquito curtains for John's bed, and at last got them to-day. There are no bells, and if after a search of some minutes along the passages, clapping one's hands at intervals, a servant at last appear, one likely has to wait any time from ten minutes to an hour before being served. Everybody is most willing and anxious to please, but there is no method of any sort, besides a scarcity of servants. And yet this is at present the best hote in the islands. The small refinements of arranging the bed-rooms for the night, dusting, and, in fact, all minor attentions are not to be expected. We may dream of thoroughly good hotels here in the future. Faint glimmerings of their advent appear even now. We hear an English hotel is being opened in Puerto de Orotava, and one will be opened here at the end of this month. A gentleman who arrived a few days ago tells us that the Madeira hotel-keepers, doctors, and natives generally are "quaking in their shoes" at the advent of the cable to these islands. They know the climate is much better, being drier and with less variation than that of Madeira, and that good hotels are all that is necessary to make this archipelago much frequented.

One can scarcely conceive any place more suited to invalids. Besides the advantages of a dry and healthy climate, there is great variety. All the islands enjoy much the same climate and temperature. One town may be a degree warmer than another, according to its situation, but nowhere, unless one climb the mountains, is there a perceptible difference. Thus anyone obliged to stay abroad for six or seven months of the year, instead of going to the well-worn and expensive Riviera, or being confined to board ship on the equally expensive Nile, or liable to the sudden lowering of the temperature at Nice and Cannes, or imprisoned in Madeira, may wander here from island to island. Orotava and Santa Cruz in Tenerife are so different in every way, that the variety of going from one to the other is equal to a change of island. It is a feature of these islands that is scarcely to be met with elsewhere that each offers an entirely novel experience to the traveller. Although all are volcanic, nature has apparently made seven different experiments. This to anyone who has travelled over all is of immense interest. Not only is this individuality in the natural features of the islands, but it also extends to the people, their habits and customs. The language is certainly Spanish, but I defy anyone to understand easily the ordinary peasant of Hierro or Gomera, so different is the *patois* of those islands. Even the food differs. This causes the diseases to be to a certain extent peculiar to each. Whether the physical features of the country have effected these variations, or whether they are an inheritance from the various Guanche tribes who, also distinct, inhabited the islands, is a matter for thought and investigation.

December 19th, Wednesday.—The serenos in this town begin their night watch at 11 p.m. and end it at 5 a.m. Throughout the night they cry the hour and half-hour, at the same time informing the waking inhabitants of the state of the weather. We were anxious to procure a photograph of these night-birds,

so one of them came this morning, with cloak, lantern, and spear, for the purpose. He was an exceedingly fine-looking man, tall and straight, with a handsome and powerful face, a little spoiled perhaps by the great depth of the lines on each side of the mouth, which denote one who is a loud and frequent speaker. The morning was fine and bright, although cold for here. At 8 a.m. the thermometer registered 53·6° F. (12° C.), and was never higher than 59° F. (15° C.) all day. The cumbres were entirely covered with snow, causing this fall of temperature, which reached a lower altitude than the before-mentioned "oldest inhabitant" ever remembered. Very beautiful were the jagged peaks in their garb of white, their ruggednesses covered by the robe of purity. Early in the morning a slight mist wandered amid the peaks, stippling off the edges of the white snow into the matchless blue of the sky.

A SERENO.

December 20th, Thursday.—To-day is much warmer than yesterday. At 8 a.m. it was 59° F. (15° C.), and at 10 a.m. 68° F. (20° C.). I was delighted to breathe fresh air once more.

One feels as if life were worth living after being in the house
for four weeks.

> "Blest power of sunshine! Genial Day,
> What balm, what life, is in thy ray!
> To feel thee is such real bliss,
> That had the world no joy but this,
> To sit in sunshine calm and sweet,—
> It were a world too exquisite
> For man to leave it for the gloom,
> The deep, cold shadow of the tomb!"

There is a very joy in the sunshine, the roll of the breakers
on the shore, and the snow-covered mountains, that lifts the
heart and spirit in a perfect ecstasy of gladness and thankfulness. This is one of those rare moments when the mind is
so saturated by the joy of existence, that perfect happiness is
attained. A minute later we recognise that we are happy, and
in that instant felicity vanishes, and we grope bewildered,
wondering are we less grateful this moment than we were in
the previous one.

One of the great drawbacks to Las Palmas is the want of
a good promenade. The town has been utterly spoiled by the
sea-shore having been entirely taken up by houses. Instead
of building one row of houses facing the sea, with a good road
between them and it, houses have been built with their backs to
the shore, thus effectually excluding it from sight. This is the
more to be regretted as the view of the port of La Luz and the
ships lying under the shelter of the mountains of the Isleta is
exceedingly pretty. The disadvantage to those who, although
able to walk a mile, cannot manage three or four, is very great.
Streets have always to be traversed in order to approach the
sea, and it is not pleasant, to say the least, to have to walk a
mile and a half towards the Isleta before a place can be reached
from which to catch a glimpse of the ocean. Towards Telde it
is equally difficult to reach the coast, for to do so one has to
mount up by the back of the town through a poor district.
There is one walk, however, which when finished will be
better; it is a road which has been begun near the Cuevas

del Provecho, on the Arucas road. A little public spirit on the part of the citizens would buy the shore and make a promenade of it, planting trees and placing seats, at the same time constructing a carriage drive. Considering what a small town Las Palmas is comparatively, it is wonderfully difficult to get out of it.

December 21st, Friday.—There is a good deal of steam communication here. Those which concern us most are an English

VIEW FROM ROOF OF THE MUSEUM, LAS PALMAS.

boat calling once a week homeward bound, and another outward bound, besides a monthly French and a fortnightly Spanish boat. The latter is the mail with Cadiz, and is really the only one of them all which is regular. Letters posted by it—for it returns direct to Cadiz—reach London in about eight days. This vessel came in to-day, so we got our letters ready for England, as it always anchors for a night. The cable at present is not open to the public, but anyone may send messages which do not partake of a business character. The Spaniards took advantage of the permission, and wrote long

letters of eighty-nine, ninety-four, and ninety-six words to their
friends! These it was simply impossible to send.

Although I consider myself quite a convalescent, my friends
here continue spoiling me, and almost every day flowers, mandarin oranges, jellies, or books arrive from some of the kind-
hearted English residents.

December 22nd, Saturday.—This morning I did not order my
breakfast until 9 a.m., as I rose first. It was ten, however,
before it arrived! It turned out that there was only one teapot
in the hotel, and someone else was using it, so I had to wait.
This said teapot is not at any rate English-made, for, having
no hole in the lid, we have to open it every time we pour out
a cup of tea.

It is rather chilly to-day, the thermometer at 9 a.m. being
62·6° F. (17° C.), owing no doubt to the heavy rain we had
last night. It came down in sheets, and during the afternoon
it rained again, the temperature at 4.30 p.m. being 60·8° F.
(16° C.).

At the other side of the town, near the mole, a number of
hackney carriages stand in the street. These are rough, old,
lightly made wooden waggonettes and vans, with or without
paint, having remained just as they were when first turned
out of the workshop. One, two, or three wretched-looking
horses or mules, used indiscriminately, draw them. The
harness seems scarcely able to hold together, and one feels
doubtful, but for the anything but runaway look of the horses,
of trusting one's self to its tender mercies. There are four
slight upright iron rods at either end of each vehicle, on which
is stretched canvas, with rolls of the same material, which can
be let down at both sides and front and back. These are used
for either sun or rain, and cause a thorough draught. Half a
peseta (fivepence) is the fare to the port in one of these
vehicles, which are public at that price, so can take other
passengers.

As the isthmus is the only place where one can go for fresh

air from what is, to me at any rate, the enervating Las Palmas, we generally go out there for several hours. Though at first sight the isthmus of Guanarteme is apparently uninteresting, a little closer observation will show to the contrary. Soon after passing the fourth kilometre there is a long stone bridge over a depression in the sand, through which the sea washes at high tide. Close by this bridge the telegraph poles have been erected to connect the cable from Santa Cruz with the town. An iron hut for the shore end of the cable is put up close to the sea strand in Confital Bay, that is on the west side of the isthmus.

Taking a "coach," we drive as far as the telegraph poles, where, dismounting, we walk across the sand hills to the cable hut. We loiter on the way, picking up shells and examining the vegetation. At first sight, looking at this stretch of dune, nothing appears but sand and a few stunted tamarisk bushes. Seeing, however, that goats are browsing, we know there must be something green. A close investigation shows several small plants two or three inches high growing at intervals. So irregular and sparse are they, that the general effect of the surface is·yellow sand, not green herbage. White patches at places as we walk along betray the presence of shells which are in immense quantities, though in only some four or five varieties. Raising our eyes skyward from the sand as we begin to descend the slope towards the sea, we see Teide, only the extreme summit. Beneath is his bodyguard of clouds, that steady, almost motionless belt that perpetually surrounds him. Later on they spread their forces lower, and completely enveloped the island, leaving the cone floating on a sea of white waves. The effect to the eye of all lower earth being invisible is to raise the Peak itself to what appears an almost impossible height. It is then that one gazes awestruck at this world's wonder, a stillness comes o'er the spirit, and we are wafted heavenwards in thought. Surely earthly elevations elevate the mind. They certainly stimulate imagination. Inhabitants of mountainous regions will generally be found more imaginative and poetical, retaining old stories and superstitions more pertinaciously, with less of matter-of-fact hard work about them, than those of champaign countries.

Reaching the hut, we invade Mr. Béchervaise in his solitude, and being supplied with the solitary chair the place possesses, or indeed for which there is room, I sit outside and admire the view.

The view from Confital Bay as we sat on the sand, braced, refreshed, and strengthened by the breeze, was one of quiet beauty, on our left the snow-covered mountains of the interior, on the right the peaks of the Isleta, their bases encircled by white houses. The blue sea lies in front, bound to southward by a rugged shore, which ends in the Peak of Galdar, while beyond it, like its reflection in the air, so similar is it in shape, is the cone of Teide. At our feet is the shining yellow strand, the rocks, and pools, beyond them the ships at anchor undulating gently on the Atlantic swell.

As we drove back to Las Palmas, we saw, for the first time, the two rounded hills of Fuerteventura. In the evening we had an engineer and electrician belonging to the Cable Company for tea. Tea is not an institution in this hotel, but we have it in our own room every night. They do provide the article tea, but it is not the best, and we prefer using our own. Having it in our room is also much more sociable when joined by our fellow-countrymen than being in a public room. It is quite *comme il faut* here, too. Private sitting-rooms, as in most Continental countries, are considered quite unnecessary, every Spaniard receiving in his bedroom. In the private houses of the middle classes the sala is frequently also the guest-chamber, the bed being often a permanent fixture.

December 23rd, Sunday.—The temperature at 8.30 a.m. was 59° F. (15° C.), which by ten o'clock had warmed into 66·2° F. (19° C.).

It is a pity that, with so many English residents here, at Santa Cruz, and at Orotava, there could not be, for the winter

months at any rate, a Church of England chaplain.   The
residents are not wealthy enough to supply one entirely, unless
subsidised by a society.   There must be many clergymen in
England in delicate health who would be only too glad to winter
in such a magnificent climate.   As the presence of a chaplain
would be an inducement to many strangers to winter in the
islands, one would think that some of the many lines of
steamers running between England and the archipelago would
take one out at a reduced fare.   No doubt it would not be
possible for the visitors of any one of the principal towns to
subsidise the income sufficiently, but by dividing his labours
during the winter among these three localities, each thereby
benefiting, a sufficient income might be raised.   It is unnecessary to add that a man of immense tact is required, owing not
only to the already strained relations between the islands and
to the fact that many of the old residents are Scotch Presby-
terians, but also to the number of mixed marriages between
English Protestants and Roman Catholic isleños.

Don Sebastian Perez and his wife arrived here yesterday
from their out-of-the-way home, and paid us a visit to-day.   It
was like a whiff of mountain air.

A steamer was signalled this morning about 8.30, which,
owing to the clearness of the atmosphere, was seen many hours
before arriving.   No wonder the old Canarios were always
prepared for their invaders !

We drove out once more to the Isleta, this time visiting the
cemetery of the Antiguos Canarios, to which I was yet a
stranger.   The view from the rising ground of the cemetery,
as it lies on the slopes of the Isleta, facing southwards, is very
fine.   A strip of sea on our right forms a kind of bay between
the Isleta and the main island.   Behind the bay of Confital, the

> " Mountains on whose barren breast
> The labouring clouds do often rest "

pile upwards and inland, each ridge and group higher than the
other, until a grand climax is reached in that solitary, weird,

gigantic rock the Nublo. The east of the isthmus has another bay, that of La Luz, which is larger, not so confined, but what it gains in sweep it loses in beauty. It is formed by the Isleta itself on the north and a slight outward curve of the coast line culminating in the promontory—if it can be so called—on which Las Palmas is built. These two bays are divided by a narrow strip of yellow dune, productive of little but tamarisk bushes, which have been ·planted to try and bind the sand. A heavy surf usually breaks on the western side of the isthmus of Guanarteme, on a bar of rocks and sand, which lies perhaps half a mile from the beach, and inside which is a smooth lagoon. This precludes the idea of this bay being used as an anchorage,

VIEW OF THE ISTHMUS OF GUANARTEME FROM THE GUANCHE CEMETERY ON THE ISLETA.

although occasionally, when a strong south-east wind is blowing, some ships run round the Isleta and seek refuge outside the rocks. It is on the eastern side, however, that the best anchorage can be had, and there that the new harbour or port of refuge is being constructed. To-day both bays, with their sandy beaches, look tempting bathing places. May they never be desecrated by bathing machines. During the summer the residents in Las Palmas drive out here; some have cottages, where they remain for a time for bathing. Tents are generally used by the bathers instead of those abominable and inartistic boxes which would ruin even the most ordinary scenery in the world. How is it the architecture of bathing-boxes has remained so long at such a low artistic ebb?

Las Palmas looks better from here than from any other point
of view. It appears as a mass of white relieved only by the
dark towers of the cathedral. The curve of the bay between
this and the town is twice broken by points, thus forming two
smaller bays, on one of which is the fort of Santa Catalina, a
small, insignificant, and useless building. Beyond Las Palmas
jut out the points on the eastern side of the island. A number
of schooners lie in the offing, but conspicuous by their absence
are the small sailing and rowing boats that would be scattered
over a similar English bay. It is winter, of course, for a little
boating and fishing is done in summer. Far to the right rises
the magnificent Peak of Galdar, magnificent, not from its
height, but from its beautiful proportions. Its shape is somewhat like that of the pile of sand which accumulates in an hour-
glass as it runs out.

At our feet and around us are masses of brown-black cinders,
piled into heaps at intervals. It was behind these heaps the
Spaniards hid to await the landing of the Portuguese. Little
did the conquerors know what lay unseen at their feet, not
even did their chronicler know, nor yet so late as Glas had any
a suspicion that the rough, cindery masses piled apparently
without order were the last resting-places of a bygone and now
almost forgotten race. Later still, at the moment when we
stood there, it will scarcely be credited that the owner of the
soil—or, to be more correct, the lava—was ignorant likewise of
this venerable possession. A few knew of it, among them Don
Gregorio Chil, and the graves had been rifled by boys to secure
skulls and bones for the Museum. Sloping towards the isthmus,
the lava-flow ceases abruptly as it reaches the sand. Perhaps
when it flowed it was into the sea it entered, and the sand of
the isthmus may have since accumulated. Where the lava
ceases a few houses have been built, chiefly those of the
residents of Las Palmas. No sound breaks the repose of the
Canario braves save the roar on the rocks to westward and the
gentler swish of the waves on the eastern beach. Behind,
the brown lava stretches upwards in a gentle slope until

terminated abruptly in the rounded cone of the "Look-out" hill, over 600 feet high.

During tea this evening those who were present concerted a murder! Owing to there having been so many meals in my room of late, the mice had become very bold. They used to run over our beds at night, and if I shook the coverlet, I could hear them drop on the floor, and one used actually to appear at tea-time and pick the crumbs off a travelling trunk, which acted the part of dumb waiter. Our table was so very small, that the teapot usually occupied a chair, wrapped in a woollen shawl for cosy. If we had many visitors, other chairs, or the floor, or the sofa had to be impressed. In fact, we had a general feeling of being perpetually picnicking. We eyed that mouse frequently, but how to catch him was the problem. "Necessity is the mother of invention," and I recommend the latest patent in mousetraps to anyone similarly inconvenienced. A saucer was placed upon a plate and raised at one side upon an upright match, and in the plate was put some honey. A black thread a couple of yards long was tied round the match and the other end held in the hand as we sat at table. The mouse, all unsuspecting, attacked the honey, when with a slight jerk he was secured, all but the tip of his tail! The next difficulty was to dispose of him. We finally decided to convict him, with "extenuating circumstances," and not to kill him, but to drop him out of the window, in order that, with the whole world before him, he might start his career over again elsewhere.

December 24th, Monday.—We are very near Christmas now, but it is difficult to realise it, with the thermometer at 68° F. (20° C.) at 10 a.m., and at 4.30 this afternoon it was 64·4° F. (18° C), with a north-easterly wind.

Two English vessels fired their guns early this morning as they dropped anchor in the offing, and a few of their passengers came ashore to this hotel for breakfast. We paid some visits, and then, after sitting in the Plaza de los Ingleses waiting for a coach, drove out again to the Isleta, or rather to Confital Bay, to enjoy the quiet and sea-breezes. A man in the coach, or rather van—coach is much too big a name for the "shandrydhans" here—whom I did not know, kindly asked me if I were better. We had brought luncheon with us in the shape of biscuits and oranges, and we bought some sweets from women sitting in the streets, to see what they were like. They were round in shape, like wheels, and made of gofio, honey, and almonds, and were not at all bad. The sea was lovely, and we enjoyed sitting on the sand and wandering upon the rocks. We found three plants in bloom in the sand of the Isleta, interesting to us as Christmas blossoms.* When returning home, we had to wait some time on the road for a "coach," and whether that or the hanging about on the rocks was foolish I know not, but I got what the people here call an *ayre*, a slight chill, so during the night had recourse to mustard leaves. Next day I was feverish, and had to stay in bed, my pulse being high, although I did not feel very ill.

Christmas Day.—Mr. and Mrs. Miller had most kindly asked us to dine with them to-day, and as we could not, Mrs. James Miller sent us a huge plum-pudding. Meanwhile the Ramons had succeeded in making also a good pudding from the "Hero" receipt, so we were well provided. Most of the English staying here ate their Christmas dinner with friends, so there were only ourselves, Mr. Béchervaise, and a German gentleman for the dinner Ramon took such pains to prepare. I unfortunately was in bed, so could not join the festivities. Dinner was served in a room upstairs for the English alone. A turkey and apples cooked whole, two bottles of sherry, and one of champagne, were all spontaneously and hospitably provided by Ramon.

The Spaniards played cards and had music last night in the sala until nearly midnight, and as only high, thin white folding

---

* *Heliotropium Europæum, Helianthemum Canariense,* and *Ononis variegata.*

doors separate our bedroom from that apartment, it was impossible to sleep. They adjourned to the churches towards twelve o'clock, and we breathed a sigh of relief, thinking we should now sleep. But they soon came back, and made the most awful row until four o'clock, more like what overgrown schoolboys would do. Some of course had indulged in too much wine. Morning dawned before we were permitted to sleep, for after leaving the hotel they adjourned to the street. Imagine a sober English hotel proprietor allowing such a disturbance! I am told, however, that this always goes on. It is part of the Christmas festivities here.

There is a south wind blowing, the "Tiempo de Abajo" (climate from below!), as it is called in Tenerife, to-day, which always makes one feel languid. Added to this, a wakeful night has not made us feel very brilliant, but rather headachy, on Christmas Day. The temperatures for to-day may be interesting: at 7.30 a.m. 58° F. (14·5° C.), at 8.30 a.m. 59·5° F. (15·5° C.), at noon 68° F. (20° C.) in the shade and 77° F. (25° C.) in the sun, and at 6.30 p.m. 60·8° F. (16° C.). John and Mr. Béchervaise walked out to the Isleta during the afternoon, and took photographs of the old Canario cemetery. The sky was a clear blue, a few fleecy clouds floating about.

December 26th, Wednesday.—As my feverishness and consequent headache still continued, I remained in bed. Don Sebastian's wife kindly came to see me. She tells me she feels the cold much and has four pairs of blankets over her at night, while I think I have too much with a single one. Those who live here all the year round feel the cold much more than we do. It was still cold this morning at 9 a.m., being 62·6° F. (17° C.).

Invitations were issued for a public ball last night, to which only five ladies responded, I am told, by their presence.

December 27th, Thursday.—A lady who lives here, the wife

of one of the officers, most kindly sent me up some sweetstuff which had been sent her by friends in Spain for Christmas. The manservant brought it into the room when I was in bed. I got up to-day, my pulse having become normal.

I have been endeavouring all day to get a little hartshorn, but have been brought the wrong stuff several times.

There is occasionally music at funerals here, but it has to be paid for, and the march which I got in Palma is quite unknown.   Since I have been ill, a child in the house opposite died of diphtheria, and another one is ill and, it is feared, dying. I could see from my bed the room in which the corpse was laid upon a table. I only wonder diphtheria and typhoid are not more frequent in the towns. It is only the dryness of the climate that prevents their being scourges.   As a fact, however, they are much less frequent and severe here than in most Continental towns, the sanitary arrangements of the places most patronised by English visitors on the Continent being very faulty indeed.

In Las Palmas the rent of houses is higher than in the suburbs. All houses are let in these islands by the month, and in Las Palmas the rent of a house for a family varies from about sixteen dollars (three pounds four shillings) to thirty dollars (six pounds) a month. The tenant can leave on any day without giving notice, provided he pays his rent up to that day. At any moment he can bring the key to the landlord and give up possession. On the other hand, the landlord is obliged to give three separate notices of a month each should he wish the tenant to quit, unless the rent has become due and has not been paid, when he can oust the occupier at once. The first notice of a month is for the purpose of allowing time for the tenant to get another house, but if at the end of that period another month be required, the landlord has to grant it, this process being repeated thrice. An eight-roomed house, exclusive of offices, would cost about sixteen dollars to twenty dollars (three pounds four shillings to four pounds), a month. Furniture is cheap and good, being brought chiefly from Habana. Nearly all the labourers here own their houses and bits of land, and leases are perpetual.

An Englishman, an old resident in this island, told us of some peculiar superstitions which are very prevalent, even in the towns. He possesses a goat, and a butcher happening to visit his place a day or two ago, saw the animal, praised its good qualities, and congratulated our friend upon having one so fine, but asked, with evident concern, whether it had been rendered proof against the evil eye (*mal de ojo*). Our friend replied in the negative. The butcher then told him to obtain from Atalaya an earthenware pot which had never been used, to place some sulphur at the bottom and ignite it, and then pass this extempore brazier through the goat's fore-legs, bringing it out between the hind, and when this was done to pass it beneath the body between the two pairs of legs, and then to break up the pot immediately, so that it could never be used again. It will be noticed at once that the two lines over which the pot was to be passed would form a cross, and this fact perhaps affords some clue to the strange ceremony. To emphasise what he had been saying, and as proof positive of the success of his plan, the butcher related that he was now in possession of a very fine calf, which he had insured against the evil eye by the process we have just related. Shortly after he had performed the ceremony, an old woman called to see him, and looked at the calf, and after gazing steadily at it, went away quite angry because she had no power over it. In the face of such evidence, given with the fullest belief in its truth, our friend said he felt it useless to reason. Now this is not a solitary and therefore remarkable instance of the current ignorance and superstition, but merely one which happened to a friend of ours, and within a day or so of when I write.

How much deplorable ignorance there must be here it can scarcely be imagined. In a town about to be connected by electric cable with Europe, in a town where a contract has already been signed to have it lighted by electricity, possessing two theatres, a museum, and many other signs of advanced civilisation, it is certainly startling to be pulled up by doings which smack so strongly of the grossest superstitions of the darkest times of the middle ages. I might relate many other instances.

If a person is to have a dose of Epsom salts, it is considered ineffectual unless the vessel containing the medicine has been placed in the open all night for the dew to fall upon it. The medicine after this is then taken in the morning. A similar process is always gone through with a purgative for children, composed of manna, Epsom salts, lemon juice, etc. A sweet, too, made of the strings from the interior of the calabash or pumpkin ("angels' hair"), prepared with sugar, is never considered wholesome unless it has been out all night to catch the dew. These superstitions are not confined to the lowest or even the lower classes. A goldsmith's child was very ill, and the mother, when doctors seemed to do no good, insisted that one of these wise women should be called in. The husband laughed at the request, having no faith in the process, but, because of his wife's importunity, allowed one of these old women to exercise her charms over the child. Strange to say, in this instance the child recovered after the visit. Whether the old crone administered herbs, as was most likely the case— for the islanders are all great herbalists—or not, I was unable to ascertain. At any rate, she would not confess to having cured by any such remedies.

A touch, too, of superstition, at least a belief in the efficacy of odd numbers, still hangs about the medical men. I would exempt from this charge those eminent men who have been educated at Paris or some other medical school besides that of Madrid. When prescribing a series of baths for patients at some of the mineral springs of the island, they tell them to take seven, nine, eleven, thirteen, and so on. An isleño always considers it necessary to take sea-baths in a series of odd numbers. He also will not take a single bath. He will not bathe on Monday unless he can bathe each day for a week.

One bath in the sea he considers bad, and likely to be productive of boils or some such evil.

But while it is necessary to speak of these superstitions—a true idea of these islands could not be given without alluding to them—we must not be thought to be laughing at the islanders, as if we were so very much superior. How many persons, even well-educated people, barristers, clergymen, and Girton girls, in England still turn their money at the new moon, consider it unlucky to see the new moon through glass for the first time, always pick a pin up when they see it, never walk under a ladder, and never cut their nails on a Sunday, because "better never born than Sunday shorn." It is not a century ago since a woman was burnt as a witch, and we are inclined to believe that even at the present day in a few out-of-the-way country places in Wales, Devonshire, and parts of Ireland, the power of the evil eye is half believed in.

December 28th, Friday.—It began to blow during the night, and we heard the pleasing variety of " Nublado !" (" Cloudy !") called by the sereno. The wind was due south, and brought torrents of rain, which fell almost in sheets. The temperature was 62·6° F. (17° C.) at 9 a.m., notwithstanding the rain. Everybody declares it is the worst rain there has been for years. It does not last long, however, so it is only for a day one is melancholy and obliged to remain in the house.

I have frequently mentioned how one cannot buy the most ordinary article without haggling over its price. Foreigners rather than haggle pay. The isleños, however, delight in making a bargain. No countrywoman buying a yard of calico in a shop ever thinks of giving the price that is asked. The result is bad, for the shopmen have to price their goods higher than they would do otherwise, and—a much more serious evil of the system—a direct temptation to fraud is put in the way of the assistants. It is easy for an assistant to say that only so-and-so was obtained for an article which was perhaps sold for a higher sum. This rotten system of haggling also prevents the storekeepers balancing their books; they can tell what they gave for articles, but they cannot estimate the amount they will realise when sold or the value of their goods at stock-taking. Altogether, for the sake of the buyer as well as the seller, it is much to be desired that a spirit of trust should be diffused throughout the islands, that prices should be so adjusted as to yield only fair and legitimate profits, and that the execrable spirit of "Do, or you'll be done," should be abolished. Until, however, Spaniards alter their national character, these desirable results can scarcely be expected.

Rottenness to the core is present in the highest Government offices, and descends, as might be expected, through all the grades of public servants. To cheat the Government is considered by Spaniards fair game. The man who does not cheat is regarded as worse than a fool. When dishonesty—for it is no use mincing matters when speaking of a great national evil —is present in the army, in the navy, in the civil service, among those who pay taxes and those who collect them, how can it be expected that strict probity is to be found among the humbler occupations of servant and master, buyer and seller? As an Englishman, in a large way of business for these islands, expressed it to me, a large premium is put here upon immorality; it is impossible for a man to be honest in the full English meaning of that word. "If," he continued, "I made the *correct* return of what I bought and what I sold, the amount I should have to pay in taxes would not only absorb *every farthing* of my profits, but I should even have to expend capital to satisfy the exorbitant demands of the Government. I therefore do as every Spaniard does, and as I am *expected to do* by the tax-collector himself—I make returns of about half of everything which is taxable." So recognised is this method of procedure, that the Government might just as well at once lower all the taxes, abolish the many vexatious impositions upon trade, and thereby encourage the nation to be honest by strictly insisting upon exact returns being made.

From a monetary point of view undoubtedly the Government would be richer, while the moral gain to the national character would be quite inestimable. The masses of the nation are sadly ignorant; multitudes are still grossly superstitious; comparatively few children attend school, and when they do attend, the teachers are as a class very inefficient. All this must be remedied before Spain can ever hope to be anything like what she once was. Reforms must really come from the people, or all the endeavours of the most paternal Government will be in vain. By mixing as little as possible in external politics and concentrating her attention and energies on these far more important internal reforms, Spain, with the good wishes of nearly the whole of Europe, will steadily advance. Her capabilities are enormous, and it is sincerely to be hoped that the nation, putting aside ancient customs of a retarding kind and clogging party and caste considerations, will devote itself seriously to intestine improvement. Nowhere will reforms be more heartily welcomed than in the Canary Islands, for the Spaniards there are already in many things much in advance of those of the Peninsula. The advantage these islands possess in having free ports is fully appreciated, and this one judicious step on the part of the Government, it is hoped out here, is only the precursor of many others. As it is, the ignorance that has been shown in the past by Spain is not only lamentable, but also is simply ludicrous,* and even at the present time the nation as a whole does not know where these islands are situated, and the Government department knows little of their productions, peculiarities, and capabilities.

December 29th, Saturday.—A fine blue, cloudless sky greets us this morning after yesterday's storm [62·6° F. (17° C.) 9 a.m.], but we also have, which is not so pleasant, the south-east wind. Verily it comes from "below," for, like our

---

* When the ports were declared free in 1852, the official paper to that effect issued by the governmental Home Office declared, amongst others, *Laguna* to be a free port!

east wind, it makes everyone cross, even the sweet-tempered folk being irritable.

There is a German gentleman staying here. He has been in the island a few months. Having been a great sufferer from rheumatism, he travelled to all the watering-places of Germany and Italy and finally Madeira, without finding relief until he came here. He attributes his recovery to the waters of Firgas, which he regularly drinks. The water is bottled by a woman in old champagne or wine-bottles, which she carries in a basket on her head from Firgas to Las Palmas once a week and sells to Ramon for a trifle. We all drink the water, which is sparkling and pleasant to the taste when fresh, though of course it becomes flat after being opened for a day or two.*

It is curious that during all the time we were in Las Palmas we never had soles to eat or saw them used. It was by accident that, after living at the Puerto de la Luz for some time, an English gentleman discovered them. He says he has trodden upon them as they came ashore, so numerous are they. Fishermen, although perhaps the most poverty-stricken inhabitants of the islands, hold their heads high, for they consider that their occupation, being that of St. Peter, is therefore ennobled, and look down with disdain upon the richer but lowlier occupation of butcher.

December 30th, Sunday.—It was raining a little at 9 a.m. [62·6° F. (17° C.)], but soon cleared. We went for a walk to the mole, but could not reach the end, though it is but a short pier, the sea was dashing over it in such a rough manner. The sight was magnificent, the huge rollers running in and breaking upon the iron-bound coast. The clear blueness and the majestic swell of the Atlantic cannot be compared for one moment with the dull, muddy waters and chafing fret of the short waves in the channel which divides England from France. As the huge rollers break on a rocky shore, the spray shoots up to immense heights, and for many a yard around, the

* For analysis see Appendix.

sea is one boiling mass of white foam ; or, they roll in long swells, moving majestically, without fret and flurry, but lazily, with the laziness of conscious strength, which one always sees in big people or things, be it a man or an elephant, until they break on the hard, shining strand with a roar that can be heard a mile inland.

Standing on the mole, we can see behind the main street. The backs of the houses are towards the shore, but behind them are a number of wooden sheds, used as dwellings, some of them no bigger than bathing-boxes. As we return to the hotel we encounter some of the señoras and señoritas of the town, who all stop until we pass and have a good stare at us. No doubt they are those who do not live in the main streets, and therefore are not accustomed to the sight of foreigners. There are strangers in the town, too, for we had thirty-two at dinner to-night, all the table would hold, and half a dozen who dined later. Poor Pedro and Juan, our two waiters, had a busy time attending upon so many. The piano in the sala, to which we adjourned, would not be a bad instrument were it only tuned. As, however, this costs four dollars (sixteen shillings), it is but seldom done.

December 31*st, Monday.*—Raining again a little this morning, and the temperature exactly the same as yesterday.

There is something the matter with the clocks. The cathedral, which is close at hand, has a clock of English make, which, unfortunately, is notoriously an ill time-keeper ; consequently it was dark this evening at 5.30 p.m., whereas it was light at 5 p.m. a week ago ! Owing to the rain, the barranco this morning has a terra-cotta colour, showing that much soil, which the island can ill afford to lose, is being carried into the sea.

CHAPTER XI.

FIRGAS—BARRANCO OF THE VIRGIN—COCKFIGHTING.

The rivulet,
Wanton and wild, through many a green ravine
Beneath the forest flowed.   Sometimes it fell
Among the moss with hollow harmony,
Dark and profound.   Now on the polished stones
It danced, like childhood, laughing as it went,
Then through the plain in tranquil wanderings crept,
Reflecting every herb and drooping bud
That overhung its quietness.

SHELLEY.

A gamecock clipped and armed for fight
Doth the rising sun affright.

WILLIAM BLAKE.

January 1st, Tuesday.—Maria, to my astonishment, was arranging my room at the unusually early hour of 10 o'clock this morning. So unusual was it, I demanded the reason, and found that, it being the custom to receive visitors on New Year's Day, Maria thought it well to prepare my room for mine.   It seems this custom, so prevalent in many places, of receiving on January 1st, is in vogue here, but I, being only a bird of passage, am exempt from the habits of the residents.   The mail from England has been expected all day, and came at last late, bringing with it a new addition to the hotel in the shape of an unannounced and "uncredentialled" Church of England clergyman.

We were very anxious to visit Doramas and Firgas, but as I did not feel up to such a long ride yet, it was arranged that

John, most kindly accompanied by Mr. Newman Tremearne, an Anglo-Canario who knew the district, should ride there to-day. Mr. Tremearne proved a valuable ally, and indeed on occasions too numerous to mention gave his services, and procured information for our use. They started at six. John has given me an account of their expedition.

" The ocean-going traveller who stays at Las Palmas for an hour or two only in the course of his journey, while his steamer coals or takes the mails on board, is very apt to go away with quite a mistaken opinion of the island. He sees the town lying, white, ugly, and hot, on a low tongue of land, backed by some of the most arid and uninteresting hills that imagination can picture, and the impression he forms of the island is naturally anything but favourable. And yet a few hours' ride from Las Palmas would reveal spots of delicate beauty, of stony ruggedness, or of sublime immensity, according to the direction he takes from the city, and for ever dispel the notion of only associating Gran Canaria with dryness, heat, barrenness, and the commonplace. The journey I took to-day illustrates this. At 6 a.m. I was in the saddle, trotting through the silent streets. The oil lamps were extinguished, and a faint glimmer of white light illumined the darkness. The town was hardly awake, for to-day is a general holiday, and a little extra sleep one of its incidents. In the Calle Leon y Castillon I find Mr. Tremearne, booted and spurred, sitting motionless on his fine black horse by the door of his house. As I approach the equestrian statue moves, we exchange greetings, and canter briskly along the Arucas road.

As we mount higher and higher, so does the sun, for the eastern sky is becoming glorious in purple hues, and a fleecy mass of clouds lying low down on the horizon is blazing into magnificent splendour. The air at this hour is fresh and bracing, which our horses seem to feel, for they enter into the exhilaration of the moment as much as we do ourselves. They are eager for the journey, and we let them go, for we have a

long day before us. At 8 a.m. we catch sight of the town of
Arucas, looking wonderfully near and distinct, each house
standing out in bold relief, for the sun, as yet not hot enough
for blurring the effect, is slantingly directed full upon it.

We gallop up the avenue of trees, and pull rein at the other
end of the town, at the house to which I had previously sent on
my small camera. The road from Arucas to Firgas is not as
yet constructed for carriages, being only a rough track, which
at places degenerates into most breakneck-looking spots.
To-day, owing to the quantity of rain which has recently fallen,
particularly yesterday and during the night, the path is even
more dangerous than usual. Fortunately it is all uphill, and
though very steep at places, this is better than a downhill path
under such conditions. As the day turned out fine and warm,
when we returned in the evening a good many of the slippery,
muddy places had dried up, and therefore the road was much
safer than when we set out in the morning. The sun is
pouring down hotly on our backs as we ascend to the uplands,
but the bracing and cool air prevents it giving us any trouble.
Everything looks wonderfully fresh and green. Grass is growing by the roadside. Vividly green ferns—hart's-tongue,
maiden-hair, polypody, etc.—peep out at us from every cranny
and recess in the walls, and luxuriate in giant clumps under the
hedges. To-day is a magnificent opening for the year, as fine
as a day can be imagined, longed for, or dreamt of. We pass
several flocks of sheep, led by shepherds along the roadside
to crop the young herbage. Many little lambs are among the
sheep, some only a day or two old, a noticeable sight in my
eyes for New Year's Day, but then in these Happy Isles the
seasons are as you make them. In the middle of the summer,
when pasturage is scarce, and cattle have to be fed in the
stall on grain or hay, the shepherds frequently cannot afford
to keep all their sheep, and they are glad to sell them, in
some dry years as little as two shillings each being taken for
them. My companion, who knows the island well—for he has
resided here for many years—informs me he saw a flock sold

for one shilling and twopence a head last June. The female sheep are not considered good for mutton, but are kept for their wool and milk, a very excellent cheese being made in the island from sheep's milk, either alone or mixed with that of the goat. In fact, sheep's cheese or sheep and goat's are those commonly eaten all over the island. A tax of no less than five shillings is levied for each sheep killed for food. This and many similar vexatious imposts upon the necessaries of life are certainly contributories to the slowness with which Spain—and these islands one of her provinces—advances in prosperity. These internal impositions on inter-rural and civic interchange of commodities and local taxes cause the natives to be dissatisfied with the existing form of government, and, as that at present is a monarchy, to think that under a republic these burdens and oppressions would be removed.

We arrive at Firgas at 9 a.m., and tying our horses up under a cave by the side of a field, proceed at once to the fonda to order breakfast.

Firgas is a small, clean village, of the usual white, one-storied houses, situated on the hills overlooking the lower land lying towards the sea, of which and of the Isleta there is a fine view. Firgas is enjoyable at this time of the year, but in the summer it would be a most delicious place at which to stay. It requires, however, a hotel, for the little house we are in affords only the roughest accommodation. The simple room in which we breakfast is a guest's bedchamber as well, for it contains two old-fashioned wooden bedsteads. The cool, healthy, fresh air up here and the fine view from the windows make us content, however, with anything in the way of creature comforts.

With its bracing climate, its sparkling mineral water, than which I have never drunk a more pleasant, and the exquisitely beautiful barranco close at hand, surely a prosperous day is in store for this much-favoured upland spot. The baths and water are particularly efficacious in rheumatic disorders and in skin diseases. I heard, and on unimpeachable authority, of some really wonderful cures effected here. In taste the water is similar to that of Agaete, but weaker, its carbonic acid briskness making it particularly agreeable to the palate. Like the water of Agaete, it is slightly warm.

The village proper consists of two streets, arranged at right angles to each other, in a T shape. While our breakfast is preparing we follow the white mantilla-clad women, and enter the church, a simple structure like a long barn. Mass is being celebrated, and, to my surprise, the little edifice is full, the day being a festival. The women are kneeling by themselves close to the high altar, and the men by themselves are standing at the lower end by the door. The proportion of men present was much larger than I had seen in any of the town churches in the islands, but this is generally the case in every country. The general impression one gets in these islands is that the whole outward observances of religion are performed by the women. To-day both sexes are clad in their best. The women without an exception are wearing the becoming white mantilla, and the men wide white short trousers and black soft broad-brimmed felt hats.

Breakfast over, we are again in the saddle, on our way to the Barranco of the Virgin. The path is rough, even dangerous in places, but the glimpses of the loveliness of the barranco revealed by each turn of the road fully compensate for the fatigue of the travelling. Speaking broadly, the barranco consists of a long valley, more or less straight, leading up from the sea, and then of two branches, or fork-valleys, which wind about in a serpentine fashion. Everywhere the valley is wide and deep. The higher slopes are gradual and cultivated; the lower depths are precipitous and wild. The actual bottom, just now occupied by a deep, rushing torrent, is at places enclosed on both sides by straight walls of sheer rock, over which are clustering masses of green foliage and festoons of beautiful trailing plants. Looking down the barranco towards the north from the upper part, the eye revels along a delightful fairy vista of prodigal luxuri-

ance, till it rests upon the placid greys and smiling blues of the
sea beyond.

Descending by a tortuous path, our horses at first refuse to
enter the swiftly rushing, muddy torrent, for they are unaccustomed to such a sight, and when at last we overcome their

WATERFALL IN THE BARRANCO OF THE VIRGIN, GRAN CANARIA.

reluctance, the water rises as high as their shoulders, so that
we have to hold our legs up to prevent getting wet. From the
other side on looking up we see a long, attenuated waterfall,
entirely surrounded by the most vividly green vegetation that
can be imagined. A more careful inspection reveals the fact
that the fall takes two leaps, a green interval interposing between
the two plunges, and at this distance the pieces look like two

bars of undimmed, highly polished silver set in wrappers of soft
green moss.   The fall pours its water below the Pico del Radio.

Periwinkles (*Vinca major*), violets, and exquisite ferns grow
all over the barranco in royal profusion.   The windings which
the barranco makes at its upper end considerably contribute to
its beautiful character.   Unexpected avenues of loveliness are
frequently occurring: a turn, and a sublime blending of stern
rocks and gentle foliage; a turn, and a sheer precipice with the
torrent below.   The presiding genius of the scene is the Pico del
Radio, a mountain not unlike Bandama, with an obvious crater
upon its side.

We again ascend, and descend this time into the other fork
of the barranco, and after riding up it for some miles, arrive at
a clump of magnificent laurel trees.   Here the bottom of the
gorge is broad, gently inclining on either side from the stream
for a considerable distance, which meanders, with countless
windings, over its rocky bed, amongst the gigantic stems of
the trees fringing its banks.   Delicate ferns and bright green
grass form a soft and rest-suggesting carpet.   Around this
fairy spot at some distance the steep sides of the barranco
are clothed with a perfect tapestry of vegetation.

Add to the Dargle immense trees and a greater breadth, take
away from it the good path and the tourists, and some idea is
obtained of this paradise in the Barranco of the Virgin.   'The
rills that water these shady groves, the whispering of the breeze
among the trees, and the melody of the canary-birds form a
most delightful concert.   When a person is in one of these
enchanting solitudes, he cannot fail of calling to remembrance
the fine things the ancients have written of the Fortunate
Islands.' *   The shade under the olive-green laurel trees is cool
and in delicious contrast to the glare of the bright sun shining
outside ; the sunlight glints here and there through the vegetation, and dances merrily on the lullaby water as it, with a
constant bubbling, soothing sound, goes steadily onwards ; the
sward is soft and pleasant; all nature invites a siesta.   Mr.

* Captain George Glas.

Tremearne and myself yield to the inclination and to the suggestion of the spot. We lie down at full length in the shade, and doze.

But hark! what is that? A merry peal of laughter! Surely we have not involved the contempt of the nymphs of the stream? Apparently we have, for as we rise on our elbows to look at the place whence the merriment proceeds, some fifty maidens trip into the glen from the shade of the laurels, and are even now wending their way up the path at the farther end of the sward. All are clad in pure white mantillas, which only serve to set off the brightness of their black eyes and the shapely contours of their graceful forms. With the light green at their feet, the dark leaves of the laurels as a background, the brown rocks and the rippling stream as a foreground, a sweet picture of simplicity and loveliness is formed. The scene admirably suits the figures, and these in turn lend life and interest to the picturesque surroundings. It will take long before that picture fades away in my memory. They gaze on us, when we disturb their merry conversation, in silence, and gather a little closer together, like fawns timid in the presence of an unlooked-for intruder. We ask them, beg them, to stay and let us take a group of them, but they are shy, and only crowd still closer together as they slowly back away from us, then, having recovered from their surprise, once more take up the merry, laughing conversation which our untoward presence had interrupted, and trip on lightly towards their country homes. They were returning from mass, for it is a great church-going day. To-night they will foot it briskly and lightly to the sound of the guitar and tambourine, and some of those lovely faces will cause much disquietude if the swains here are as they are elsewhere. Now, shame to relate, my small camera happening to be up, and having an unused dry plate, I hastily focussed and took a shot at them as they departed, but not without several qualms of conscience.

We watched them passing under the trees, and when the

last gleam of a mantilla has faded into indistinctness, we hastily pack up, mount, and depart, for we feel for the first time that the spot is lonesome.*

We take another path back to Firgas, where we arrive at 4.30 p.m., and hurriedly eating our dinner, set off for Arucas at 5 p.m., not wishing to have to travel on that fearful road in the dark. We enter Arucas as darkness falls. The recent rains have caused many pools of water to lie about in the fields and by the roadside, from all of which deafening, hoarse croakings of thousands of frogs are heard. A reptilian concert on a beautiful night like this is well worth hearing, but not frequently. The musicians seem endeavouring to excel each other. There is a sad lack of time about the performance. Each performer is desirous of rapidly quickening and getting above his neighbours. The result is the most remarkable noise imaginable. When the vocalists seem to have all attained the highest notes of which their throats are capable, apparently by mutual consent, at some signal understood among themselves, they pause for an instant, making the stillness of the night intense by the contrast. But the interval is short. The whole start off again at a gallop, and the strange concert is thus spasmodically kept going. Naturalists say that these sudden terminations are due to the approach of owls or of some birds or beasts of prey.

It is too dark to see far in advance, and as I do not know the road well, to canter would be dangerous. A stray beam of light falls aslant the road from the opened door of nearly every cottage we pass, and within we can see men and maidens footing it bravely at the dance. The sound of

'Light laughter round their restless feet'

and the strains of the accompanying guitar and tambourine are cheery and merry, making us push on in order to get to our homes as soon as possible. We walk our horses at a quick step into Las Palmas, where we arrive in the darkness at 9 p.m.,

* See Frontispiece.

tired certainly, for we have been in the saddle nearly all day, and that day a long one.

Looking back, however, upon the New Year's Day spent in the Canary Islands will always evoke pleasant memories."

January 2nd, Wednesday.—We have returned, after some changeable weather, to the 66° F. (19° C.), at 9 a.m., of our early stay here. It is a very pleasant temperature for walking, so to-day we wandered out on the southern side of the town, keeping below the carretera and nearer the sea. As we passed through small and mean houses and streets, and came near the outlets of the town, a loud and unmusical sound met our ears, which gradually resolved itself into crowing. We soon came to the place whence the sounds issued, and found ourselves among a number of cocks ranged in cages round the sides of a room opening direct upon the street. A few men were loitering about, and we were shown the prize cocks. There are two establishments for training cocks for cockfighting in Las Palmas, and this that we had stumbled upon was one. Here there were sixty-eight cocks to supply amusement (*sic*) to the populace. The other cock-pit, being longer established, had a greater number of cocks. We learned more about cockfighting later, when John, to see how it was conducted, attended one of their fights.

Turning from the cocks and their deafening voices, we passed onwards, completely leaving houses behind us. Presently we came to a good road, leading to a large walled enclosure, which we guessed would be the cemetery, and on coming to it found we were correct. A large entrance gateway is flanked on either side by waiting-rooms, into one of which we had walked before we noticed that a corpse, dressed in clothing and boots as usual, was lying on the table. As there was not a living soul to be seen, we never dreamed that a dead body would be lying there unattended. It was uncovered, too, so if death resulted from an infectious disease, it was scarcely a safe way in which to leave it. Private chapels and tombstones are round part of the wall of the cemetery, while the other half is on the mausoleum system.

Round this is a gallery by which the upper mausoleums are reached. As we walked along the mausoleums we encountered the most awful odours, and noticed innumerable cracks from which they no doubt issued. We fled to the centre, where were four bare plots of ground, which, we learned later, are reserved for the poor. They are entirely destitute of monuments of any kind, save a few trees and wild geraniums. Everywhere the ground is giving way and sinking, and the cemetery appears much too small for the requirements of the population. Reaching the further side we heard hammering going on, and looking round, perceived a man chiselling at a stone on the mausoleum gallery. Thither we wended our way. Perceiving that he was opening a grave, we asked why. The man was taciturn, not like the loquacious gravedigger in *Hamlet*, and simply lifted his hand and twitched the two first fingers and thumb together. This, we knew, signified money, but what money had to do with opening the mausoleum we could not tell. At last, after further questioning, we elicited the same movement and the words " No page " (" Do not pay "). Consulting together, a horrible idea struck us, and we questioned further to ascertain the truth. " How long has the person in that tomb been buried ? " " Two years," was the answer. " And what are you going to do with the body ? " To this we only received for reply from Old Mortality an indication of the thumb over his shoulder towards one end of the cemetery. So we concluded, erroneously however, that the bodies when turned out were buried in one common grave. It seems that these square holes, just large enough to contain a coffin, are rented by the year, not purchased. Therefore when the relations of the deceased, either through poverty or neglect, fail in their payments, the corpse is evicted for non-payment of rent. This is a horrible custom, and revolting to the feelings. Even the Guanches were more civilised, giving not only decent, but permanent, burial to their dead. Close by, where the man continued his excavations, was another recess already opened, and looking in, we could see the corpse of a child half decayed, in a blue dress. No doubt this was about to be removed too. Odours, awful odours, were around, and we fled horror-struck from the mausoleums.

The tombstones, covered by wreaths and immortelles, were less trying to contemplate, and walking round the pathway by the further side till we reached that by which we had entered, we proceeded to leave the place. John was a little in advance of me, and finding a path leading behind the tombs which lined the walls, he walked along it. I followed at a distance, and saw him standing half-way up some steps, looking over a wall. He beckoned to me to come, but instinctively I hesitated. " If it be anything horrible," I said, " I really won't go, for I have had enough horrors to-day to do me for a lifetime." He urged my coming, but wisely never told me what was to be seen. So I went. Ascending a few steps, I looked over the wall upon a scene I shall never forget. Between four walls were heaped all sorts and conditions of men in all stages of decay. Here lay bones, there broken pieces of coffin, here skulls with the teeth grinning in ghastly rows, pieces of dress, boots encasing shrivelled and worm-eaten legs, a hand with the skin still clinging to it, locks of hair intermixed with earth and rubbish, while lying on the top was a child in a broken coffin, one side of the face gone, and a little further a woman, perfect though shrivelled, disinterred before her clothing had lost its colour. Fascinated and spell-bound, we stood looking at the horrid scene. Here then was the spot where the evicted were put, not into a decent, if common, grave. The charnel-house was nearly full. What would happen then ? Would these poor remains be cast into the sea, or what would be done with them ? Thanks to the magnificent climate, but little effluvium arose here, such as we encountered at the mausoleums. The sun was drying the bones and withering the flesh without harm to the living. It is only in such a dry climate that pestilences can be thus defied. Horror-struck at this last and worst sight, we hurried from the cemetery, and drew a breath of relief as we reached the sea-shore and its

fresh breezes, after the above abominable sights. Our attention
was distracted by a man walking along the beach dragging on
his back a huge turtle, which he had just captured, large enough
to make turtlesoup for the town, a dainty, by the way, we are
not given at the fonda, and which must be easily got if turtles
are so readily procured.   It was with some difficulty we found
the carretera by which we walked back.   Several days elapsed
after this before we felt certain that we had escaped typhoid
fever.   The remembrance of that awful burial-ground did not
disappear quickly.   Dinner was unpalatable that evening, and
nightmares haunted the hours of darkness.   Time has scarcely
effaced its horrors, but I am glad nevertheless, as John knew I

CABLE HUT, SANTA CATALINA, LAS PALMAS.

should be, to have seen in order to write of the sight.   It is no
wonder indeed that the isleños put their burial-places far from
the haunts of men, that they desert their corpses on its threshold,
and that, never entering them, they care not what becomes of
the once-loved clay.   How vastly better would be cremation than
such disgusting and dangerous places of interment.   It is a
disgrace to a town of the size and importance of Las Palmas
that such doings should not only be allowed, but be looked upon
as unavoidable.   It drives one to think favourably of cremation
when one sees such sights and is assailed by such dangerous
odours.   It is no wonder that, when pestilences did reach their
shores, the islands were half depopulated.

January 3rd, Thursday.—The thermometer is still steady at 66° F. (19° C.) at nine in the mornings. We drove out to-day to the wooden hut which the cable company have erected on the east side of the isthmus preparatory to landing the cable from Lanzarote. Knowing as we do all the gentlemen connected with the laying and starting of the cable here, it makes a pleasant little community, and gives life and society to us during our prolonged stay.* The acquaintances one makes in a foreign land partake more of the character of friendships. People are thrown together, and being isolated by nationality and customs among the nations with whom they are sojourning, a community of feeling is engendered frequently productive of warm and lasting friendships. The icy reserve in which Englishmen encase themselves being forced by circumstances, they find that, the national coldness once removed, they are like others, and consequently become natural. A travelled Englishman is a very different being from the narrow-minded stay-at-home.

> " How much the boy who has been sent to roam
> Excels the boy who has been kept at home,"

is an old adage, but a true one of any individual as well as nation. Living as we do on an island, our insulated position renders us more impervious to outside influences and still more unable to see the good in all from want of contact with other nationalities.

The lad who drove us in his van to the isthmus we presented with an orange, whereupon, not to be under a compliment or from native politeness, he presented John with a cigarette. He looked as if he thought of offering me one, but finally decided not to do so.

Some of our fellow-countrymen generally drop in during the evening for a cup of tea and a chat, which we enjoy.

---

* One gentleman, the engineer, has since succumbed to typhoid fever in Santa Cruz. He had travelled much, and had had typhoid fever several times, and always said he should die if he ever had it again. So when he caught it he gave in at once, and consequently, poor fellow, is gone.

Afternoon tea is not an institution here, so the far pleasanter after-dinner dropping in takes its place.

January 4th, Friday.—It was warmer to-day, being 68° F. (20° C.) at 9 a.m., notwithstanding which it rained the greater part of the day.

I was much troubled by being told by residents here that after my illness it would be suicidal to return to England before May. We have been longer here than we originally intended, and the prospect of such a prolonged stay, much as we like the islands, does not suit our plans. An appeal on the subject to our home doctor as well as to Don Gregorio has decided the matter in favour of our return. So we are only now waiting for a steamer to take us to Lanzarote. Many people, everyone in fact, said I was exceedingly foolish to go through the remaining two islands yet unvisited. I appealed again to Don Gregorio, who, in his deliberate and dignified way, said, " No, Señora. The air of Lanzarote is the most bracing in the whole archipelago, and will completely restore you to health." So, backed by my doctor, we made preparations for our departure. We think it foolish, however, to tempt the hardships of a correo schooner, so intend going by the French steamer which touches at Lanzarote on its way back to the African coast and Marseilles.

January 5th, Saturday.—64·4° F. (18° C.) at 9 a.m. We made inquiries as to when the arrival of the French steamer might be expected, got some money, and did some shopping. We have ordered a large box of Canary pinewood to be made to carry our extra possessions to England. This wood is so resinous, that no insects will touch it, nor will damp affect it. It is therefore invaluable, and was the wood used by the Guanches on which to lay their mummies.

When paying Ramon upon one occasion his hotel bill, we gave him a Bank of England note. He had never seen one before, and doubted if it meant money ; so we told him on our return—we were going into the interior—if he could not change it we would pay him in coin. When we came back, we found, however, that he had discovered it was a marketable commodity. There are not many civilised places in which a Bank of England note is refused.

The cable was opened to-day to the public, so messages can now be sent by anyone for payment.*

January 6th, Sunday.—63° F. (17·5° C.). Don Gregorio called this morning, a sort of farewell visit, as he considers me quite out of his hands. I have received much kindness and consideration from the medical profession, but Don Gregorio's in positively forbidding any mention of remuneration for his prolonged attendance upon me has created a debt of gratitude I shall never be able to pay. "No, Señora, no. You write, and so do I. We have a common bond of union which unites all nationalities and should make us help each other in every and any way." And, with all the courtesy and dignity of a gentleman, the subject was tabooed.

. During the day we were requested by Mrs. Quiney to accompany her to the new house she and her husband are about to take and convert into a hotel. The house is light and airy, and situated in the business quarter of the town, not far from the mole, so will no doubt be convenient for those who prefer to be in an English hotel.

Gunfire this afternoon announced the arrival of the Cadiz mail. Not many letters come that way, but it is the most certain and direct route by which to post to England.

The cockfighting most unhappily always takes place on Sunday, so, as the first tournament of the season was to be to-day, John went to see how this barbarous amusement was conducted, of which he has given me the following account:—

"Cockfighting as a legitimate pastime is unknown in England, but in the Canaries it is almost the only amusement which

* The rates at first were almost prohibitive—they are settled by the Spanish Government—but have since been reduced.

arouses the enthusiasm and kindles the fire of the mixed Spanish and Guanche blood of the natives. The regular season for the sport commences on Carnival Sunday, and continues on successive Sundays. The training and preparations for the many tournaments involve the expenditure of much money, and give occupation to many people. The town of Las Palmas, has two cock-training establishments, for the development of the warlike instincts and powers of the cock is a most elaborate and carefully thought-out art. Turning down the Calle Puertas I rapped at the door of an ordinary dwelling-house, and readily obtained admittance. Before my eyes could become accustomed to the comparative coolness and darkness of the interior after the heat and glare of the street, my ears were assailed with the unmistakable sound of spasmodic cock-crowings. The rooms of the house had been converted into dwellings for innumerable cocks. The walls were lined with boxes about the size of tea-chests, placed one above another, for some four or five tiers. Each box had wooden bars in front, and nearly all contained cocks. Perches, I found, are only put in at night for roosting upon. On the day of my visit one hundred and sixteen birds were undergoing the course of training, though the manager informed me that before Easter he would have to provide one hundred and fifty in order to match a similar number now being trained at the rival establishment. Fifty prime cocks were to be selected from this house to meet in mortal combat fifty from the other house in the town, to fight in matched pairs. The fighting weight is from three pounds twelve ounces to four pounds two ounces, and the object of the training is to bring each bird within those limits, and at the same time to keep their health and physique good and robust. Feeding-time is two in the afternoon, when each bird is served with a carefully weighed-out quantity of grain, water, etc., in accordance with the desire of the trainer to increase or reduce a particular bird's weight. Our English expression of 'living like a fighting-cock' would seem to be inapplicable here, for, so far as I observed, no bird was allowed to gorge to his heart's content. The system of feeding the fighting-cocks in England would appear to have been different, or the proverbial saying could scarcely have arisen. Once a day the birds are taken singly from their cages and sunned for a short time on the azotea, or flat roof, this exposure to sunlight being essential to the maintenance of a healthy condition. From the azotea the bird is taken downstairs to a yard at the back, where he is allowed to scratch and pick about in a cinder-heap provided for the purpose.

The main consideration in the breeding of gamecocks in the Canaries is good game parentage, colour being of no account. I saw cocks black, brown, speckled, white, and others of almost every variety of mixed hue and shade.

The training bin was in the centre of an upper room, solely devoted to its use. This is a round railed enclosure on the floor, eight feet in diameter, surrounded by tightly stretched canvas eighteen inches high. This miniature circus is where the cocks are made to exercise for the reduction of weight, and where sham fights occur in the course of training. The bird whose weight has to be reduced is placed on the sanded floor of the enclosure. The trainer, taking another cock under his arms, which he first allows the cock on the ground to see and become excited over, walks round and round the circle, where he is followed closely by his adipose *confrère*. This wholesome discipline soon reduces weight, and also improves the stamina of the leg muscles. Sham fights, to teach the birds the use of their spurs, take place in the same bin, each spur being encased in a little padded bag, the *botona*, a device exactly corresponding in use to boxing-gloves. When a specially game bird's education is desired to be pushed forward and perfected, it is considered worth while to let him taste blood, for which purpose he is matched in the bin on several occasions with inferior cocks. The weaker birds of the establishment are thus one by one sacrificed for the benefit of the most promising.

When a good gamecock loses a spur by accident or in a

fight, a not unfrequent occurrence, it is replaced before a tournament by a spur taken from the leg of a dead cock. The new spur is tightly strapped on. I saw a table-drawer full of fine spurs preserved for this purpose, for in the Canaries the keen steel spurs so common in Mexico and Peru are never used. There can be no question that the use of artificial spurs is a more merciful method of cockfighting, for when the birds use their natural weapons, the combats are much more protracted, and therefore more cruel.

The crests and comb are cut off in the Canaries at the age of one year, for a gamecock must have nothing which his adversary may lay hold of. In order that the birds may be cool during the combat, all the fluff around the thick ends of the quick feathers is cut off. A curious semi-naked appearance is the result of this treatment.

The fighting age begins at two years. The ordinary value of a bird of known parentage is two or three dollars. If the parentage be not known, the bird is practically valueless. Recently a remarkably game cock sold for ten pounds, but that was quite an exceptional price.

The cock-pit, adjoining the training establishment, is a circular building, with tier upon tier of benches, capable of accommodating about four hundred persons. The actual pit is a circular enclosed space, eighteen feet in diameter, elevated two feet above the floor, in the centre of the building. It is surrounded by wooden railings, with two doors opposite to each other for the introduction of the rival birds. Suspended by a string from the lofty ceiling above this circular pit is a pair of scales, ready for weighing the cocks at the last moment before the combat, for the birds pitted against one another must be of equal weight.

Seven duels take place at a tournament, and the two establishments in turn inform one another of the respective weights of the seven birds which will be produced. Three onzas (ten pounds) is staked on each duel by either establishment, so that the stakes for a tournament amount to one hundred and forty pounds. The gate-money, one peseta a person (about ten-pence), is divided into three parts, one part going to the owner of the cock-pit, the other two parts between the two cock-training establishments of the town. Betting goes on freely during the fights, but there is very little shouting or uproar. The Spaniards are too dignified and sedate to allow free vent to their feelings. Sometimes several men combine to bet together ; they form a *vaca* (cow), and, placing their money together in equal quantities, permit one of their number to do all the betting for the lot. The origin of this curious name for co-operative betting at cock-fights is uncertain.

As with most other sports where betting contributes to the excitement and popularity of the amusement, cheating is not unknown in cockfighting. There are two modes of obtaining unfair advantage in the sport, which are especially odious in the eyes of the spectators ; one consists in putting grease upon the feathers, the slightest amount preventing the opposing bird getting a good grip with his beak. The other and even more heinous crime is putting poison on the spurs. For instance, if the spurs be run into a garlic bulb before the fight, they will instantly cause swellings on the antagonist's body from a mere scratch.

The tournaments take place at noon on Sundays, and I never saw women present. A bird is brought down into the arena by the representative of each of the training establishments. A piece of string is passed under the body and tied over the back ; the scales are lowered and the birds weighed in the presence of the spectators. Both sides being satisfied that the weights of the two combatants are the same, a man advances into the pit and carefully wipes each bird's spurs with a sponge dipped in vinegar, or runs them into a lemon. Then the strings are untied, and the birds, still grasped firmly, are held near to each other. They at once become excited, when, the cock-pit being cleared and the doors shut, they are placed on the ground opposite one another, in the centre of the enclosure.

One can never be 'cock-sure' as to what the birds will do,

or which will be the winner. Sometimes directly they touch
the ground they rush together with a mad impetus, meet,
cannon, rise in the air with wings partly extended, and rebound
to the ground on their feet. Sometimes when liberated they
at first stretch out their necks to the fullest extent, and for a
second or two remain thus motionless, as if in a mesmeric
trance. Then commences a stern fight, generally to the death.
The policy of each bird is to get above the other in order to
get a downward thrust with his spurs into the antagonist's
head. To do this, they try their utmost to seize one another
by the nape of the neck, and in their furious peckings drive
their bills deep down into the flesh, which soon becomes swollen
and bloody.

Now and then a well-trained cock kills his enemy at the
very first onslaught by a well-directed spur-thrust in a vital
part. I timed some of the combats, and found that they lasted
for some ten, fifteen, or even twenty minutes, the birds, as a
rule, fighting till one or other fell down dead, the conqueror
in some instances only surviving a few seconds. In some
of the well-sustained fights the birds, apparently by mutual
consent, retire from one another for an interval to enable their
panting sides to become tranquillised before recommencing.
Now and then in a tournament a cock will suddenly turn tail
and run as fast as his two legs can carry him round and round
the enclosure, closely followed by the other. This sudden
resolve, perhaps after a most plucky stand-up fight, was sometimes a most comic spectacle. The retreating bird seemed to
say, 'I see you are stronger than I; I haven't a chance; I
must go; good-bye: I'm off.' I realised fully the force of our
expression 'turning tail.'

The most sickening sight I saw was when a cock, tired
even unto death, was holding its head low down on the
ground, its bill buried in the sand, and its body quivering in
the death agonies, while the other was piercing and piercing
its neck until the sudden roll over announced that its fighting
days were over. I never visited the cages above the pit

after the tournaments without finding several cocks which had been removed as conquerors lying dead in their places, such birds having, in sporting parlance, evidently died game. I need not say that the combats, even the best fought out, are brutal and unpleasant, and that we lose nothing by forbidding them in England.

The sport, however, is one peculiarly adapted to the Spanish temperament and character, requiring no physical exertion. The menial part of the business can be performed by hirelings, and the spectacle is compatible with a cool, gentlemanly, unruffled demeanour."

CHAPTER XII.

CAVE DWELLINGS—WALKS ABOUT LAS PALMAS— TELDE.

Dry blows serve in lieu of provender in Spain for all beasts of burthen.— WASHINGTON IRVING.

The sea-shore always presents a great attraction for naturalists. The sea is a wonderful nursery of nature. The creatures that live in and upon it are so utterly different from those which we meet with by land. Then everything connected with the ocean is full of wonder.—SMILES.

January 7th, Monday.—Last night there was a fearful storm, accompanied by rain. The wind was from the south-east, so blew direct into the Puerto de la Luz. It is not often that storms blow from this quarter, but when they do, there is no shelter for vessels. The greater number run round the Isleta, and anchor in Confital Bay, but some are unable to weather the point, so have to ride it out, and are occasionally driven ashore.

When buying some stamps to-day, we wanted one for England. The shopman had not a twenty-five centimo, but gave us a twenty and a five, carefully and elaborately explaining that it would be the same thing if we put both on the letter! It showed that such explanations were evidently necessary for the natives, or was it he thought Ingleses obtuse?

The French boat is not in yet, for which I am thankful, as it is exceedingly rough. Every morning we go upon the azotea as soon as we rise, to see what vessels have arrived. By looking at the flags flying from the consulates one can see the nationality, and if upon the azotea when the gun is fired and the flag hoisted on the Atalaya or signal-station, one can tell exactly, if one have a key to the signals, what vessel has come.

January 8th, Tuesday.—No mail has arrived from England this week. The mail-boat is supposed to have passed owing to the gale, though frequently the vessels are said to pass in winter without thinking it worth while to drop anchor.

The English population in Las Palmas all told amounts to forty souls. Of these of course many are children. Still we were able to muster a fair congregation on Sunday at the consulate for the clergyman, who read the morning service. The congregation, owing, however, most unhappily to events during the week in which the clergyman—we will hope, for his own sake as well as for ours, that he was not really in orders—was concerned, dwindled to a very small number the following Sunday, and the services were subsequently entirely abandoned.

We went to the Puerto de la Luz this afternoon. It was still blowing hard, which made the sand exceedingly disagreeable. Most of the ships and steamers are in Confital Bay; two schooners are ashore, and a lighter, filled with coals, sunk. No lives have been lost, fortunately. The sand lay in drifts, like snow, and the entire contour of the ground was altered almost beyond recognition. The wind is still from the south-east, but steadily lessening in force.

I had an amusing conversation with Maria this evening, during which she asked me " if English children spoke English " ! The language seemed so difficult to her, no doubt she marvelled that children should master it. She also informed me that it was thought when we came that "the English merchants had paid us to come"! When in the interior, we heard that we were supposed to have been sent by the Government. That anyone should come and travel through the islands, going to the most out-of-the-way places and procuring information, for the pure love of seeing beautiful scenery and new customs and transmitting the same to paper, was to her and the peasants generally quite impossible to be understood.

The past two days the thermometer has registered 64·4° F. (18° C.) regularly at 9 a.m., but on the 9th it fell to 62·6° F. (17° C.), rising again on the 10th to 64° F. (17·8° C.), where it remained steadily until the 16th.

January 9th, Wednesday.—When driving to Arucas, we had noticed upon leaving the city some cave dwellings, burrowed in a cliff beneath the fortress, which we determined to visit on foot upon the first opportunity. To-day, having a desire for a walk, thither we bent our steps. We cross the barranco by the stone bridge, and looking over, see that it is nearly full of reddish, muddy water, rushing down to the sea, which it discolours for a considerable distance. When the water is this terra-cotta colour, it comes from the cumbres. When the rain has only been lower down, the water is the colour of dirty soapsuds. We are now in the Calle de San Francisco, a long, straight street, beginning here in an open square, bounded on one side by the barranco, on the opposite by the façade of the casino, and on the other two sides by shops, chiefly chemists'. When we reach the other end of this street, we turn and look back, for the view is picturesque. A variety of balconies break the monotony of the straightness, and being painted in various colours and made of different materials—light iron tracery of delicate patterns, plain wood in thin laths crossed, and so on—the sides of the street are not wanting in light and shade effects. The vista ends charmingly in the Plaza de Cairasco, to which I have already alluded, with its wealth of foliage, backed by the towers of the cathedral, rising above the leafy surroundings. The water-spouts from the roof-tops, some quaintly made of wood and roughly carved, some of stone, and some of a mixture of these two materials, project over the pavements on either side all the way up, and impart a peculiar feature to the thoroughfare, but which is more or less common to all the

streets here. The more remarkable point about these gargoyles is that they always project sufficiently to exactly play
upon the heads of those walking in the middle of the pavement.
When therefore it rains, one has either to walk close up to
the wall, or take to the road. We notice several boys flying
kites from the house-tops, a favourite amusement here with
the juvenile population, especially on Sunday, on which day also
the bakers' shops do an active business.

The end of the Calle de San Francisco we find unfinished,
so, in order to gain the carretera which goes to Arucas, we
have to clamber over loose heaps of stone and rubbish.
Turning then to the left, we pass beneath the fortress into the
district of the town called Matas, and turning again after a
few yards sharply to the left, past the obnoxious, sentry-like
box of the *fielato*, the man of which was just then rummaging
the contents of a peasant woman's donkey saddle-bags,
strike a path leading upwards towards the fortress. This soon
brings us to the object of our walk, the colony of cave
dwellings rejoicing, why we have been unable to ascertain,
in the name of "Caves of the Prophet" (Cuevas del Provecho).

The mountain side is mainly composed of a loose kind of conglomerate, in which large boulders are here and there embedded.
In this dangerous stratum many caves have been hollowed out,
and here live a number of men, women, and children. The
caves are of a much lower order than those of Artenara, and
are even more squalid than those of Atalaya. They are not so
square, neat, clean, or so well-to-do-looking. The people are
of the poorest, though poverty in this climate never takes the
distressingly piteous form to which we are accustomed at home.
The Spaniards tell us that the worst people of the island live
here, those who have been turned out of more respectable
dwellings. There is no rent to be paid for the caves. When
one tenant leaves, another simply takes possession. Upon the
lintel of each entrance there is painted a large Government
number, and in the upper tier of caves we noticed that the
last was 32. There are also a few even more squalid dens,

burrowed out below the caves proper, and some are actually
beneath the carriage road. The roof of one of these dens
fell in a few months ago, and some of the troglodytes were
killed. The whole place is a dangerous rookery, which should
be cleared out and closed. Though chiefly in the conglomerate,
some of the caves are made in a reddish sandstone, of which
some parts of the mountain side are composed. The people
were very brown, even African-looking, and the women were
engaged at domestic employments, fanning up their braziers,
sorting maize, etc. The doors of those caves which had such
a luxury were open, so that we could see into the interiors.
The furniture in the best caves consisted of a table, bed, large
wooden chest, and a chair or two. Many of the caves seemed
to be destitute of anything to which the name furniture could
be applied. There were odours about the place not at all
savoury, and, as far as we could judge, there were more than
the usual five children to a family.

Leaving the Cuevas del Provecho, we cross the carretera and
ascend by a new road, which goes round the brow of one of
the cliffs behind the town. Las Palmas is not a pretty town
from any point of view, and certainly not to look down upon;
the houses all look as if waiting for the next story to be built.
The Isleta to-day is completely hidden by a haze, or rather low-
lying sea-fog. Immediately beneath the road are fields of
cochineal, for we are on the outskirts of the town. If this
carretera were only finished, it would prove one of the prettiest
drives or walks in the neighbourhood, for from it one gets an
uninterrupted sea-view, which with the Isleta forms a pretty
scene. We encountered two young Spanish ladies during our
walk, and, marvel of marvels, they were alone. Even this
slight attempt at breaking through the restrictions of absurd
customs was gratifying to see. We pursued the carretera
until it stopped unfinished, and we then went down to the
plains below by a path past some houses. Encountering a
peasant, we asked the way to the town, whereupon he giggled,
said "he did not know the road," and walked away. Meeting

another more respectable-looking individual, we accosted him, and he showed us our way, for we found we had got among private paths leading to houses.

Maria came into my room this evening talking volubly to somebody or thing, but she is so big herself, that one can never see anything else when she is present. Hearing a pattering, however, I discovered a tiny white dog, a sort of half Maltese terrier, pure white and spotlessly clean. It seems Maria adds to her other duties the washing of this animal, which is devoted to its black mistress. I regaled him with biscuit; consequently he could not be induced to leave the room, and hid beneath the beds and tables, until at last Maria caught him, and tucking him under her arm, departed smiling. The white dog, surrounded by a black arm and fat, good-humoured black face above it, with a row of shining ivories, formed quite a picture.

January 10*th*, *Thursday.*—A certain amount of sugar is no doubt necessary to the system. Deprived as we are here of the sweets to which we are accustomed, we crave in a perfectly childish fashion for something sweet. The Spaniards supply it by half filling their coffee cups with sugar and by occasionally eating luscious conserves. Marmalade is an item difficult to procure, and can, in fact, only be bought at the English shops, where one pays a peseta (tenpence) for a small tin. It seems like bringing coals to Newcastle, the importing of marmalade to the Canary Islands, where both the oranges and the sugar are grown, and that duty-free.

January 11*th*, *Friday.*—This season proved unusually good for walnuts, which were to be seen lying on every house-top. Perhaps it was the abnormal amount of wet and cold weather that produced this result. Though I have had occasion to mention the wet weather frequently, in reality there was but little of it compared with what we consider wet in England. Its effects also were unobtrusive. As a rule, the rain came during the night, so that one was enabled to enjoy the day, and if it did rain during part of the day, the moment it cleared the streets were available for walking. The necessary rainfall thus produced the minimum of inconvenience.

January 12th, Saturday.—The sky is cloudy, and the wind blowing from the south-east. We went out to the Isleta, and found the water on the east side very rough, while that on the west was quite smooth. We have been employing our time these past few days in packing for England, for upon our return from the Purpurariæ—as King Juba II. called Fuerteventura and Lanzarote, owing to the orchilla from which a purple dye is extracted being found there —we intend to start immediately for home, by way of Madeira.

January 13th, Sunday.—There is a small plaza in front of the mole called the Plaza de los Ingleses, in which are some seats and a few trees and shrubs. The opposite side of the street is occupied by an immense house, intended for the occupation of the Governor of the archipelago. This official, however, resides at Santa Cruz, and there is apparently no reason why he should not continue to reside there, except that the Canarios make unceasing efforts to have the seat of government removed to Las Palmas. The Governor's house being built before the arrival of the Governor is rather suggestive of preparing a wedding breakfast on the chance of there being a bridegroom! Las Palmas in being the head ecclesiastically of the islands might be content. Since the first see established in Rubicon, Lanzarote, was removed here, this town has always been the residence of the bishop. It was here, too, that the Inquisition held its sway. In Church matters Las Palmas was and is supreme. Let Santa Cruz remain the civil head, a very fair arrangement and division between the two most important islands.

The worst of sitting in the Plaza de los Ingleses is that, numbers of the inhabitants doing likewise, one is nearly sure to arrive home *plus* a few pulgas. We did to-day.

Don Alejandro Rodriguez y Silva, kindly called, and gave us a sketch map of Lanzarote. He generally lives at the fonda in Arrecife, and has promised to write and order his rooms to be placed at our disposal, as he says they are the only good ones in the place. We have endeavoured to obtain information about the Purpurariæ without much success, although we have come across a few who know the islands, but we have been given letters innumerable to the residents there, who, though poor, are said to be most hospitable. Don Felipe Massieu owns Fuerteventura almost entirely, and from him we have most kindly received recommendations. So now we only await the steamer, which, out of pure contrariness, has elected to let a week pass without calling. As we shall ride camels entirely in those islands, we do not take our saddles with us.

It is surprising the llama has not been introduced here. It is used extensively in Peru and Bolivia, where it costs about eight or ten shillings, and carries fifty pounds weight. It would be very suitable for all these islands, as it can go without water for a lengthened time and is accustomed to heat.

It is curious to see carpenters sawing with the teeth turned away from them. They do not look as if they could get pressure upon the wood. Everything is used in a different way from what we are accustomed to see. The road-men use hoes instead of spades, and hammers for cutting the stones, or rather the cobbles, square.

January 14th, Monday.—We drove out to the Puerto this morning, and on the way saw potatoes being dug. New potatoes are easily procured in January. What a treat! Soldiers were being drilled on a large piece of ground. They looked as if raw recruits. The sand hills are perceptibly lower, owing to the wind. As we returned at sunset we noticed an extraordinary, transparent-looking blue light, inclining to purple, in the sky to the eastward, which continued until a little after sunset.

January 15*th, Tuesday.*—Last night before going to sleep I heard the sereno calling, " Cloudy!" There has been a little more variety lately. It has not been always serene. The night before we had *viento* (wind). Clouds here mean rain. It is not like England, where although unable to see the sun for days, we yet have no wet weather. So this morning, on going out at 8 a.m. to the market, we found the streets a little damp, but the sun shining and the air deliciously fresh and clear.

The markets here are fine buildings. That for vegetables is a stone structure, which, though substantial and solid, does not compare favourably with the lighter and really elegant fish-market. The walls of the latter are formed almost entirely of Venetian shutters, painted yellow, capped by a light dome, also of wood. Slight iron pillars support the dome in the interior. Passing through an ordinary-looking doorway, we enter the vegetable-market. Round the walls and in the middle of the building are counters, where much the same produce is presented for sale by all. This is considered the least productive month of the year, so we walked round to see how we could supply a house—if we had one here. Young potatoes, cabbages, French beans, peas, cauliflowers, lettuces, pumpkins large and small, tomatos, sweet capsicums, and various herbs for seasoning comprise the fresh vegetables. Oranges, bananas, and apples are the fruits. Guavas and mandarin oranges ought to be for sale, but they are chiefly in private gardens, and seldom appear in the market.

One side of the building is devoted to bread, brought in by the country people. There are, however, regular bakers in the town. Three kinds of bread are made. One is white and close, of foreign flour, another open, and made from home wheat. The third is also home wheat, but darker, and considered common. Many, however, prefer it, as it has more flavour. With some difficulty we succeeded in introducing the last-mentioned variety at this hotel, and now very many others use it too. The bread is generally baked in half-pounds or pounds, and is sold for seven, eight, and nine quartos the pound. Eight quartos make twopence-halfpenny. A disadvantage to some of this form of baking is that there is a crust entirely round the bread, and as it is generally overbaked, one gets a great deal of hard crust, more even than that of the "yard" bread of France.

Another side of the market contained the butchers' stalls. Here one can buy beef, mutton, veal, pork, and lamb, and every thing and part that appertains to fresh meat. Cow's milk may also be bought, the price varying with the season from twopence to threepence the quart. A new product now offered for sale in the streets as well as the market is sugarcane. It is cut in small lengths, and is much eaten, or rather sucked, by children.

Passing out of this building, we cross over to the fish-market, before reaching which we notice many stores of salt fish piled in the basements of houses. Entering, we find a fair quantity of fresh fish, although it is now comparatively late in the day. All are different from those caught in northern seas, and none are as good to eat. There are red fish like mullet in appearance, but not in taste, others like haddock and cod, piles also of pilchards. Names, however, convey nothing, for the flavour is totally distinct. In fact, there is but little variety to the palate, and if one's eyes were shut, it would be impossible to tell which was which. This may however be due to the manner of cooking. The floor and counters of the market are made entirely of marble, while in the centre there is a fountain of running water. We passed out behind the building, and found ourselves on a flat, walled-in yard close above the sea, part of the fish-market premises. The view from here of the ships in the offing, the calm sea, and Isleta beyond was beautiful this fresh morning.

What a lasting shame it is that the best views in the town are completely hidden from sight! Can anyone imagine a town council so utterly idiotic as to allow the backs of the streets to be built close to the sea? There still remain places where, by building a sea-wall, a road might be constructed. It is short-sighted policy to make a town ugly when it might so readily be made attractive.

Between the vegetable market and the barranco is a wide space. This is also taken up with the business of a market, and here in the mornings may be found men and women sitting and standing selling their wares, intermixed with donkeys, mules, and horses interminable. The poorest men here, except the actual beggars, have donkeys. Very pretty animals they are, too, and of every shade from white to dark brown. Some, like those of the Peninsula, are very large. They are very seldom shod, yet retain good sound hoofs.

The most distressing sight in these islands is the great cruelty shown to the animals. To-day, returning from a walk on the mole, the only place in the town where one can get near the sea, I saw a shockingly wanton and premeditated instance. Near the pier the hack waggonettes were drawn up at one side of the road. At the other, across a good width of street, the drivers were sitting and standing, waiting for "fares." Foot-passengers are thus obliged to pass along the centre of the road. As I approached I noticed one of the drivers, a tall, powerfully built man, with a long, heavy whip in his hand, stepping out cautiously into the road. Opposite were a horse and mule, both small, cowed-looking animals, in a waggonette, standing motionlessly, rather drowsily perhaps. I was struck by the man's manner of walking, so watched him. He crossed the road slowly and softly, on tiptoe, and when half-way over, he equally quietly, slowly, and cautiously raised the long, thickly knotted whip in his right hand, and brought it down with all the force of his powerful frame across the nose of the near horse. The poor brute staggered awake, and he then stood and lashed its hind-legs in the tenderest parts and in the most approved fashion of brutality. The whole action was uncalled for and wantonly brutal, and could only be the outcome of a brutal, vicious mind. It was sickening. Words I could and did use, much to his astonishment, but a horsewhip would have enforced my meaning better. The man and his whip were so large, and the animal so small, thin, and cowed-looking, that none but a coward could have acted so. Bullies are invariably cowards. Ineffectual in a great measure as societies for cruelty to animals are, surely one here would do some good. It would be almost useless, however, to expect the natives to start such a thing, for even the best of them are more or less blunt in their feelings with regard to animals. Cock-fighting, which here flourishes, shows that, and it is want of power, not of will, which prevents bull-fighting. What can be expected of a people whose national pastimes are these ? Not, at any rate, societies for the prevention of cruelty to animals. Surely, surely, English residents and strangers might do much.

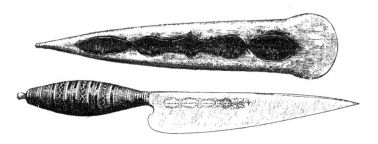

DAGGER AND SHEATH OF NATIVE MANUFACTURE.

Example is better than precept any day, and a consistent discarding of exceptionally brutal men and boys—for, alas ! they are all more or less so—would go some way towards lessening cruelty. Brutes can only be appealed to through their pockets. If therefore the most cruel men were not employed by the English, as, I am glad to say, they are not now by many in this hotel, some beneficial effect must accrue in the end. No action, whether for good or evil, ever dies fruitless. There is one good point at any rate about the isleños. Nearly all the men and boys carry daggers, which, when a quarrel is about to begin, are invariably flung away. If this custom were not well recognised, the hot Spanish blood might cause many fearful tragedies.

January 16th, Wednesday.—It does not do to come to the Canary Islands with the fixed purpose of returning home or moving from one island to another at certain dates. The steamers which touch here are supposed to do so at regular intervals. They seem, however, to have caught the always-behind-time infection from the Spaniards, and are not to be depended upon. Before Christmas we had our letters ready, as usual, for the English mail-boat, but it passed us by one week, and our letters had to wait. A French steamer comes here once a fortnight, and as it takes Lanzarote on its homeward voyage, we purposed going in it to that island. The vessel was due the beginning of this month, and we have been waiting patiently day after day for its coming, never knowing when we wake each morning but that it may be lying in the offing, and we shall be obliged to start that night. To-day a telegram came from Santa Cruz to say it was in there, and we commenced preparations forthwith, when another telegram arrived to say it was an extra vessel put in for coal, so we had to unpack again.

A poor child in a house opposite has just died of what is called diphtheric croup. There is a good deal of it, I believe, in the islands. I am only surprised they don't have every disease possible, in consequence of the bad sanitary arrangements. The drainage is *nil*. The natives never seem to know when there is a smell. Their noses, being always accustomed to ill odours, are not able to discover it. Seriously, however, if it were not for the dryness of the climate, typhoid and diphtheria would rage unchecked.

Perfectly pure, however, is the air on the isthmus and Isleta, and thither we wended our way to be refreshed and braced. We stopped this time at a new hut of wood for the Lanzarote cable, which has been erected near the road on the Las Palmas side of the bridge. The hut is built upon a high bank of sand, and below this we found a bed of broken-up seaweed, which at places was quite six feet deep. The storms of the past ten days and the south and south-east winds had driven a heap of sea-weed and drift against the east shore of the Isleta and isthmus. Here, if one had been a marine zoologist or an algæ-fancier, were rich fields. We came upon a stranded dead specimen of the Portuguese man-of-war, looking just like a bladder, but with the most vivid pink and blue colourings. It was six inches in length, and was very noticeable and beautiful as it lay on its sea-weed bed. Besides this we found the storm had landed high and dry a vast quantity of small rounded pieces of pumice stone, both white and dark brown. There were also millions of a delicate white spiral shell scattered all over the sandy shore. Bits of sea-worn wood, bleached white, formed quite small heaps, and in those we found, besides many seeds which we had not before seen, a large dead chrysalis of the Eyed Hawk moth and small bits of charcoal. The unfortunate Hawk moth must have been unearthed and washed out to sea by the rains to find its death in the ocean. We also found an extremely delicate bivalved pink three-cornered shell, with recurved hooks upon the surface, which, owing to not having any boxes with us, we could not bring home intact. These jetsams had perhaps come from many, many thousands of miles, driven by the steady, furious blasts of a southerly gale.

It was a pleasant day, the thermometer having registered a maximum of 67° F. (19·5° C.) and a minimum of 66·5° F. (19·2° C.), whilst the difference between the wet and dry bulbs was 5° F.

Getting tired of wandering along the shore, I left John to explore alone, whilst I sat on the sand and revelled in the pure air, the sunshine, and the ripple of the waves on the beach at my feet. Think of it, ye who shiver in our northern clime, cowering over fires or buttoning your coats closer to your chins as you turn the corner of the street and encounter a blast that would pierce twenty coats like a knife. This is the 16th of January. January—the bitterest month of all the twelve! January—that makes even the miser bestow some goods to feed the poor! January—when infants shiver at some crossing whilst we hurry homewards to our comfortable fires and slippers! Ah, there is no poverty like the poverty of northern climes. The happy children of sunny skies know not the meaning of long, cold nights, of wet, wet days, when the scanty rags that hide the limbs, but keep out none of the biting, bitter cold, are soaked with rain or snow, when the little blue feet trudge wearily homewards, and the scanty garment is strained tighter and closer across the little breast. Poverty is ugly in adults; in children it is piteous. Here are we happy English people revelling in warmth and beauty, our hearts unharassed by scenes of harrowing sorrow, enjoying the glorious blue of sea and sky, sitting in the pure air of heaven, as if it were July instead of January, and still—well, we sigh for home, yearn for the English mail, which cometh not, and feel that after all, be it January or July, there is no place like England, " where English minds and manners may be found."

We wandered on amid the rocks to the old castle of Santa Catalina, one of those built when the island was conquered. It stands on a rocky point of land, which is an island at high water, but to which one can cross at low tide. The rocks and pools, although by no means destitute of life, do not teem with interesting objects, as do, for instance, the Channel Islands, where more than anywhere else marine beauties are to be found. Could anything be more exquisite than the colours in the Gouliot cave in Serk ?

Santa Catalina is a small castle, each wall built in a wedge shape. A flight of steps leads upwards to a door, but some distance from it,—the drawbridge which connected them being gone,—and the steps, a solid bit of masonry, stand alone.

January 17*th, Thursday.*—As we were sitting at early break-fast this morning, being bound for Telde, we heard the gun fired, and found that the steamer from England had come in at 7.15 a.m. That homeward bound also arrived early, but there is no sign of our French vessel. We had promised, if we possibly could, to return to Telde, so this morning we left by the eight o'clock coach for that town. It was a lovely day, and as we drove along the carretera, we could see the vessels lying on the blue sea, looking at this distance perfectly placid. As we walked through Las Palmas to the coach office on the outskirts of the town on its southern side, goats were being led round to the various houses and milked at the doors. It certainly simplifies the office of milk-vendor, and also ensures no adulteration, a thing much to be desired. Numbers of people, comparatively speaking, were going to and from market. A parcel of some sort was entrusted to our driver, together with money for the *fielato*, which, however, was not given when we stopped at the *transitu de consumos*. As we sat outside we were thankful we were not harassed by the awful scenes we had witnessed in our coach drive between Orotava and Laguna. These horses were fairly good, better than many in the island. The road is much cut up by the late rain, which has in many instances forced its way across the road, regardless of the drains made for its passage.

Don José Padron met us at the coach at Telde and escorted us to his house, in the lower part of which he keeps a school. His three daughters waited upon us while we had breakfast, or what it really was to us—luncheon—and were much distressed at what they were pleased to consider our indifferent appetites. Don José took us to see many fincas and some good houses and gardens. This is considered the worst time of the year to see the gardens, but even now there are quantities of roses and other flowers. We also went to the house of the Conde de la Vega Grande or Don Fernando del Castillo, brother of Don Leon, the representative in the Cortes. Don Fernando is the engineer of the roads in the islands, and must be congratulated in many instances on the skill he has shown in laying them out. He had given us letters to his agents in the south of this island, which we were unfortunately unable to use, owing in the first place to lack of time and subsequently to my illness, by which I fear we much, though unintentionally, offended him. In the garden is a pond full

of fish and a big dragon tree, while the borders to the beds
are of myrtle.

> " And what a wilderness of flowers !
> It seemed as though from all the bowers
> And fairest fields of all the year
> The mingled spoil were scattered here."

Outside the gate crowded a number of beggars waiting for
alms.   The barranco on which Telde is situated is a small
gorge, and romantically wild.   It is in Telde that the best
oranges in the archipelago are said to grow.   I have had many
sent to me in England from thence, and they certainly are most
delicious.   Don José urged our remaining for dinner, but,
thanking him for his kind hospitality, we returned to Las
Palmas by the afternoon coach, arriving at 5.15 p.m. to find
English letters awaiting us.

January 18*th, Friday.*—We took a walk up the road to Tafira
and San Mateo to-day, and found everything looking fresh and
green after the past rains.   The walls are much broken by the
water.   They are formed of large stones and usually built without mortar, even when attaining a great height.   The present
race of Canarios seem to have inherited the art of building these
walls from their predecessors and to succeed marvellously well.

When returning from tea at the vice-consul's to-night, we
encountered the sereno in the street just as he was about to
call the hour.   Putting his lantern on the ground, he stood in
the middle of the road, and raising both hands to his mouth,
bawled at the top of his voice, " It has gone eleven, and fine."
It was really deafening to be so near him.   His occupation and
accoutrements are an anachronism, the modern bull's-eye
lantern being quite out of keeping with the hooded coat, long
staff, and the calling of the hours.

January 19*th, Saturday.*—We are yet another day without
the arrival of that steamer, and begin to think she is not coming
at all.   When buying some stamps to-day, we found the little
shop full of masks of all sorts.   It is getting towards Lent, and

the Carnival will be taking place, besides which masked balls are occasionally given.

I saw some delicious pineapples being sold in the streets to-day. It is a never-failing source of momentary astonishment to come across what are rare fruits at home being thus a common and cheap commodity elsewhere. It is true that pine-apples are sold in the streets of London, but they are so poor as not to be worthy of the name of the King of Fruits.

Driving out to Confital to-day, we met a woman carrying half a hundredweight of flour on her head! As we surmount the sandy hill which we cross to reach the strand, a splendid view of the Peak of Teide, entirely snow-covered, bursts upon us. How unapproachable it now appears.

January 20th, Sunday.—There was service at the consulate, twenty-two being present, after which we went once more to Confital Bay, to say farewell to it. We have a positive affection for the place, it is so quiet and soothing, and totally destitute of one's fellow-creatures. Solitude, especially that of the sea, is very soothing occasionally. To-day the solitude, though not the silence, was broken by a few men, who stood barelegged upon the rocks in the sea, fishing. The only regular haunter of the isthmus is a goatherd, a tall, lean individual, who wanders silently among the sand hillocks, like the spirit of a departed Guanche. His usual, and indeed constant, dress is a pair of white trousers and a blanket cloak. Mr. Béchervaise tells us that he continually hovers within a little distance of the hut, but never approaches. Perhaps, as a spirit, he resents the desecration of his happy hunting-grounds by the hand of man, and is not the electric wire an extreme result of civilisation? Or, as a mortal, does he fear to come too near to the enchanted hut, where are forces to him unknown and not understood, and which to his simple island mind consequently partake of the marvellous?

January 21st, Monday.—We ascended to the top of one of the square towers of the cathedral to-day, from which there is a fine view of Las Palmas and its surroundings. The view, however, though from a higher point, is one already well known to us, one which we have frequently seen from the summit of the Museum and from the azotea of the hotel. The steps are two hundred and eighteen in number, broad, and of good stone. At their foot sits " blind Juan," a poor sightless youth, who is employed to pull the bells which ring so unceasingly. His knowledge of the voices and even footsteps of those who enter the church is said to be wonderful.

The correo left to-day for Lanzarote, but as the steamer is really expected soon, we did not venture in it. The schooners leave this upon the 6th, 13th, 21st, and 28th of each month, and remain some twenty-four hours at Arrecife before coasting southwards to Fuerteventura.

The gathering in our room to-night will be a farewell one, for at last we hear the French steamer is in Santa Cruz, and will be here to-morrow. We have laid out our plans to return to Las Palmas just in time to catch the homeward mail to England, a fortnight hence, but whether we shall do so or not remains to be seen.

January 22nd, Tuesday.—Vainly this morning we searched for biscuits throughout the town, as we wished to take a few with us. Sweet ones we can obtain, but none of English make. Some are kept at the English shops occasionally, but there are none just now. We had to ask Mr. Miller to change money for us. It is remarkable that there is not a bank of any sort in the islands, so one has to make bankers of one's consuls. The simplest way is to take Bank of England notes, which are always negotiable, and which the English firms are glad to have for remitting money to England. We left the hotel at 4 p.m., hearing we were to sail at five o'clock. We had to stand about the mole, however, until 7 p.m., when the boat at last started for the *Vérité*. It was 8 p.m. when we weighed anchor, the captain promising that at 8 a.m. we should be in Arrecife.

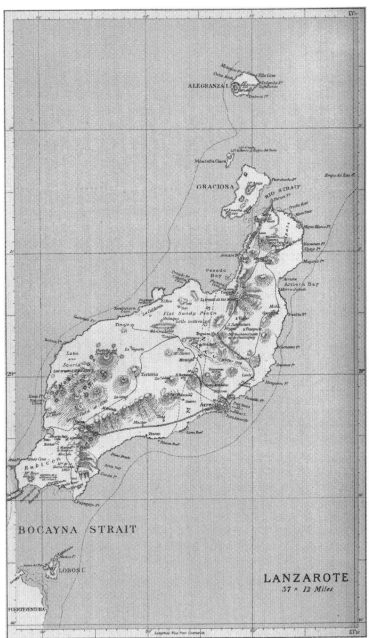

CHAPTER XIII.

> Oh fair to be, oh sweet to be,
> In fancy's shallop faring free,
> With silken sail and fairy mast
> To float till all the world be past !
>
> Oh, happy fortune on and on
> To wander far till care be gone,
> Round beetling capes, to unknown seas
> Seeking the fair Hesperides !
>
> Lewis Morris.
>
> Now dawns the rising of a brighter age.
> Rivers of gladness water all the earth,
> And clothe all climes with beauty ; the reproach
> Of barrenness is past.   The fruitful field
> Laughs with abundance ; and the land, once lean
> Or fertile only in its own disgrace,
> Exults to see its thistly curse repealed.
>
> W. Cowper.

January 23rd, Wednesday.—As the captain predicted last night, we made the voyage to Lanzarote in exactly twelve hours. We weighed anchor last night at eight o'clock off Las Palmas, and it was on the stroke of eight this morning when we dropped it again in the harbour of Arrecife.   This is the longest voyage between the islands, unless indeed that from Gomera to Hierro be longer.   Of that, however, we can scarcely judge, as we went thither in a sailing vessel, at the mercy of wind and tide.

   As soon as daylight appeared we found we were leaving Fuerteventura behind and running up along the east of

Lanzarote, having passed through the Strait of Bocayna in the early morning. Both islands appeared as a series of dwarf volcanic peaks, the valleys green with young corn. From our deck cabin, as we lay in our berths, we could see the sun rise like a globe of fire out of the sea, a sight always beautiful. Leaving Fuerteventura and the high rock of Lobos Island behind us, we came in sight of Arrecife, its little castle, on a rocky islet, standing prominently in front. The capital of Lanzarote is built close to the sea, in the middle of a plain completely surrounded in the background by a semicircle of low volcanoes. Owing to the recent beneficial rain, this plain is green, but the mountains in the distance are bare and rugged, and not a tree is visible as far as the eye can reach.

The harbour of Arrecife is the only natural one in the islands. Although the outlying rocks are low, bare, and rugged, yet, both from the sea and land, they have a certain picturesqueness, just now enhanced by a scanty clothing of herbage.

As we entered the boat for the shore, a sharp shower of rain fell, a curious and unusual welcome to Lanzarote. There has been more rain here this year, we found afterwards, than for the past century. We had no trouble in landing, and two men civilly offered to carry our baggage to the fonda, where, after securing rooms, they further showed us the way to the house of Mr. Topham, the English vice-consul. Whilst enjoying some details of much interest upon the island from Mr. Topham, the rain came down in torrents, as though a huge jug were being emptied in the heavens above. That shower was the heaviest rain there had been here this season. Mr. Topham tells us that all the cisterns are full of water already, and if they should get no more, there is enough to last for three years. Every house of any size has a large tank beneath the patio, into which the water off the house-tops runs. The year 1877-8 was a very disastrous one from lack of water. Ships came laden entirely with the precious fluid, and 8,000 people emigrated from sheer hunger and thirst.

When there is a good year, which means when enough rain has fallen, there is so much grain, that it is exported to Tenerife and Palma.

Leaving Mr. Topham as soon as the rain moderated, we returned to the fonda for breakfast. This is the only fonda in the island, and although a small, one-storied building, is clean, fairly comfortable, and the food good. Our rooms, each containing a single bed, open out of each other. The front room has a window, but the back only borrowed light.

A Syrian prince, in flowing, bright-coloured Oriental robes and turban, was on board the *Vérité*, and landed here, but did not take up his quarters at the fonda. He engaged an empty house, where he was waited upon by his servants, of whom he had several. What his object in settling down for some days in such an out-of-the-way place could be was a matter of astonishment, for he did not travel through the island, and indeed spent most of his time sitting at the window smoking. Though apparently a devout follower of Mahommed, he was a singularly well-educated man, knowing French thoroughly, and liberal in his views and ideas.

The rain ceasing as suddenly as it began, and the sun shining, we went out to see the town. Turning naturally to the landing-place, we found what must have been an unusual amount of animation prevailing. Several camels were being laden with barrels just unshipped, one on either side. But the most unusual sight—one, in fact, not seen for at least thirty years—was immense pools of water lying in the depressions of the road. The wharf is broad and roomy, so the few camels and men, with the equally few imports lying around, only increased the generally deserted appearance, instead of rendering it one of bustle and business. Very few visitors come to Lanzarote, it and Fuerteventura being considered quite beyond the pale of civilisation, especially the latter island. Owing to the fortnightly call of the French and the monthly touching of Forwood's boats from London, a few people have seen Arrecife, and thinking that they have therefore seen the whole island, have included it in meagre and uniformly incorrect descriptions. When one knows and remembers that it was this island that was first conquered in 1402 and that it was here Bethencourt first settled, that earlier still, probably in the thirteenth century, one Lancelot Maloisel, a Genoese, discovered and built a castle, giving to it and the island his name, and that later, owing to pirates and invaders from Barbary, this island has been one continual battle-ground, it will not be wondered at that we refused to leave the archipelago without judging for ourselves if it were worth while to visit a place full of so much

WHARF ARRECIFE AFTER RAIN.

historic interest.   Yet again it contains one more point that should render it of intense interest to English people.   It was perhaps the island best known and most often visited by that accurate observer and unfortunate mariner Captain George Glas. His descriptions of this island and its inhabitants, although published in 1764, are the best yet written, and apply, almost without correction, to the Lanzarote of to-day.   One change, however, there is in the rising of the port of Arrecife from consisting only of "some magazines where corn is deposited in order to be ready for exportation" into the first town in the island in size and population. Like the rest of the islands, Lanzarote increased in importance and wealth during the reign of cochineal, and, like the others, it now shows signs of past prosperity in empty houses and desolate wharves.

Miss Topham most kindly escorted us in the afternoon to the various spots in and around the town. It is not only possible to get one walk, but many, here, and owing to the rocky islets, the placid lagoon in which pleasure-boats can sail, and the bridge causeway dividing the harbours into two, the scenery is novel and totally different from that of any of the other islands. The place where we landed is the Puerto de Arrecife. It is not so deep as the Puerto de Naos, to the north of the town, but was sufficiently so to allow of the entrance of the French steamer, which, however, had to await high water for its exit.

Walking along the wharf, we turn off to the right upon a causeway road, which conducts to the island of Los Franceses. High walls are on both sides, and about the middle we reach a drawbridge. Two tall grey stone pillars mark the place where the portcullis ought to be, but is not. There is sufficient room beneath the bridge for small boats to pass, and by raising the planks a schooner could get through. The further and island end of the causeway is, or rather was, guarded by a castle, that of San Gabriel, now fallen into disuse. It has seen service, however, during the Moorish invasions, and two English privateers, the *Hawke* and *Anson*, in 1762 silenced it with their guns, but were unable to find the entrance to the harbour, so had to land elsewhere. There are three other castles in the island: another guarding the town, and that of Santa Barbara, overlooking Teguise, and of Aquila, in the south of the island, built by Bethencourt. The castle walls of San Gabriel are now chiefly useful in forming a point from which one can obtain a good view of Arrecife. The town stretches along the shore, and runs a little inland. It is small, compact, and low. The land on which it is built being level, one cannot see the back of the town, which thus appears even smaller than it is really. A road runs close to the sea along the front of the houses, a vast improvement on Las Palmas, where one is never aware of the proximity of the ocean. It seemed really like going to the seaside from town coming to Arrecife after Las Palmas, and we enjoyed the change as much as if we had really been inland. Behind and to the right and left of the town the ground rises gently towards the chain of volcanic cones which bisects the island lengthways. The little town of San Bartolomé glints white in the sunlight at the foot of one of these hills. Montaña Blanca is on our extreme left. To the right of it is the Caldera, between which and the Montaña de San Bartolomé is the town of the same name. As nearly every mountain one sees is a caldera, it is a rather puzzling, but unfortunately very usual name for the nearest crater in each district. Tahiche, a rounded cone on the right, of reddish soil, reminds one both in colour and form of the Peak of Galdar, but has by no means the bold lines of that noble mountain. Immediately at our feet to right and left lie the ports of which Lanzarote is so justly proud. That on the north of the town, Puerto de Naos, has two entrances, and is guarded by the island of Los Cruces, which acts as an effective breakwater, inside which ships anchor peacefully and can be beached if necessary. A short time ago during a gale Her Majesty's gunboat *Ceres* ran for the harbour, and entered safely. The other entrance to this port has a guide in two lights on the mainland, by getting which in a line a ship can run in safely. Not a house in Arrecife has more than two stories, most have only one, and all are flat-roofed. A feature of the landscape is the innumerable windmills rising from the plain behind the town.

Leaving the little islet of Los Franceses, we returned to the mainland, and walked along towards the Puerto de Naos, crossing on the way a couple of small bridges over inlets of the sea, which laps half round the town on its northern side. Here there were a few ships, but desolation reigned supreme, the port, like the town, being asleep, waiting for the magic touch which should awaken it.

We were much astonished to get not only a fairly good dinner, but to have a pudding served, and a very good one, too.

Mr. Topham kindly invited us to go to his house in the evening, which we did, and received much valuable information. Later, on our return to the fonda, Don Antonio Maria Manrique, a *notario publico* and amateur geographer, who knows the island well, kindly indicated for us our best route, and marked on the Admiralty chart the principal places.

We noticed in passing through the town to-night that in the main street, called Principal Calle, there were only three lamps. There used to be ten, we are told, but as they were all private illuminations, their dwindling to three may be taken as yet another instance of the faded prosperity of Arrecife.

The great drawback to the advancement of Lanzarote is of course the lack of water. A company was a short time ago formed for the purpose of digging for water. Hoping to make an artesian well, they of course failed utterly, and sank their money in volcanic soil. An extensive system of cisterns is the only plan available, but the poverty and paucity of the inhabitants prevent much being done. That they might easily be wealthy if they only had water may be imagined when two bushels of wheat planted in virgin soil yielded 240 per cent. ! This is truly more than " a hundredfold."

January 24th, Thursday.—We had ordered a camel for our projected journey to the north of the island, to Haria, which, with its owner, arrived at 7 a.m. at the fonda door. We told the man we should not leave until 9 a.m., whereupon, instead of taking the camel away for the two hours, he simply made the beast kneel, and tied the halter round its bent knees to prevent its moving, and went away himself until we were ready. We had some difficulty in procuring a little food to take with us, but at last started at 9 a.m. I shall never forget my first experience of camel-riding. We did not have proper chairs to sit upon, but only the ordinary pack-seats, on which barrels, or packages, or stones are carried. They are simply frames made all in one piece, and are placed over the hump in the shape of two V's turned upside down, the lower legs being continued nearly horizontally, and joined by bars top and bottom. The seats are some eighteen or twenty inches square, but hollow in the centre, save for a bar of wood; that is, they are simply frames, so that if sitting upon them one is merely resting on the bars of wood of which they are composed. Looking at these seats, we thought they seemed very hard and uncomfortable for a long ride, so proceeded to remedy the defect. Our portmanteaus fitted very compactly under the frames, where they were secured by ropes. We then placed our rugs upon the bars, and so had rather comfortable seats. Sitting upon a shawl, I wrapped it round my knees, and was very snug. It was quite cool enough to wear a jacket and cover one's knees with a rug. The next performance was to get upon the seats, which when the camel was lying down were about the height off the ground of an uncomfortably high chair. We had both to sit down together, a sort of " One, two, three, and away!" arrangement, or the frame would have slipped to one side, if not off the camel, as no undergirth fastens it. All this, however, is child's play to the sensation of a camel rising. The landlord of the fonda, usually a phlegmatic individual, and the arriero, or camel-driver, both urged with much vehemence that we should hold on tightly, and it was not until the camel was on its feet that their faces were freed from anxiety. I sat on the right side and John on the left on this occasion, the heaviest portmanteau being placed beneath my seat. It is very necessary to be properly balanced, and if one side have a heavier load than the other, the lighter one has stones added. Holding by the bar at the top of the reversed V with one hand and by the bars on which we were sitting with the other, we told the man we were ready, and the camel was ordered to rise. This was accomplished by three distinct jerks, each one of them sufficient to send us flying into the road if we had not been holding on. Grumbling and grunting, the camel rose on his fore-knees, a position that nearly doubled us in two, then, with a great jerk, he raised his hind-legs until he stood upon his hind-feet, which made our seats incline forward at an angle of forty-five degrees. A final plunge brought the creature from his fore-knees on to his feet. The whole was done in as short a time as it takes to read of it, and we found ourselves safely swinging in the air some five feet from the ground and thoroughly shaken by the process.

It was blowing strongly, and the temperature 60·8° F. (16° C.), at 9 a.m., when we set out. We were told by many that the motion of riding on a camel would produce a kind of sea-sickness, by others that we should get so tired, we should get off and walk, so I rather dreaded the journey, not knowing what I might have to endure. The camel-driver asked three pesos (nine shillings) a day and his food. As the usual charge for a camel is two shillings and no food, we treated this mild request as no doubt the man expected, and gave him a dollar (four shillings), to include everything, just double his proper fare. Mr. Topham sent his nephew, a lad of about fifteen, with us, to help us to procure information and to make the youth practise English in speaking to us, as he had very little opportunity of doing so. He rode a horse, so did not start until some time after we did, for a camel's pace is slow. It appears very much slower than it really is, being about two and a half to three miles an hour. One could ride through these islands much faster on horses, but they are not procurable. Of course camel-riding is much less expensive, for when we had horses, three were necessary, whereas one camel easily carried both ourselves and our luggage.

Owing to the rainwater lying about in pools in many of the streets, we had to go round the byeways in order to reach the carretera, the camel refusing to pass the water. Just where the carretera to Teguise joins the town is a deep ditch, now full of water, the final juncture not having been completed, thus rendering the road useless. The carretera is a fine broad road, the land on either side being flat and stony. The view of most interest and novelty at present to me is that immediately in front and at my feet. A huge shoulder of thick hair moves to and fro, and swinging out from it like a pendulum in a socket is the long, narrow, deep neck, first sinking and then rising till it ends in the head. The nose and forehead are on a level with the hump. The thick, bushy hair on the forehead and short ears look as if they might belong to a Newfoundland dog. The horizontal position of the nose, elevated as it is on a line with the forehead, causes the eyes to look down on one obliquely, and, with the overhanging eyelids, gives that cynical look so frequently attributed to the camel. It is a subject of much discussion as to what is a camel and what a dromedary. Some say a dromedary is only a camel trained to go fast, thus naming both the single and double-humped animals camels, others that the two-humped is a camel, the one-humped a dromedary. Sir Samuel Baker, in his "Nile Tributaries of Abyssinia," comes to this former conclusion, but the one held in these islands among the better classes and educated is that, though the animal here is commonly called a *camello* (camel), it is really a dromedary. A riding dromedary, which Sir Samuel Baker measured, was seven feet three and a half inches to the top of the hump, but he states that it was above the ordinary height. Its pace was greater than that usual here, being five and a half miles an hour, and of the riding he says, "Of all species of fatigue, the back-breaking, monotonous swing of a heavy camel is the worst." Here they are trained for sure-footedness and to climb hills in zigzag fashion more than for speed, but we rode one animal in the neighbouring island that trotted. They were imported originally from the coast, and are still occasionally, but they breed freely in these two eastern islands, so that it is not necessary to bring them from Africa. In character and temper they are much superior to the continental camel, and are more domesticated. If Mr. Ensor had seen the dromedary of these islands, he would not have been so severe in his remarks as he is upon those of Nubia and Darfoor. He is in the main correct, however, especially in saying of a camel that "his virtues are exhibited on his journey, his vices directly he comes into camp. He is essentially a traveller. Rest for him is an abnormal condition. . . . Directly the day's journey is over, and he has to stop, he begins to growl, to snarl, and sometimes to bite; it is the kneeling down, the sudden fall on the front knees, that he objects to. The climax of his ill-nature is reached in the morning, when he is again brought into camp to receive his load; the noise he makes is like that of many angry lions. Once on his legs again and started on his journey, he is quiet and happy." *

We met a camel with a load of Palma Christi piled on his back, so that he looked like a walking haystack. Three other camels and their drivers joined us, and we all proceeded in single file along the wide and desolate carretera. One of the men wears sandals of leather, the hair still upon the hide, and thongs that cross the foot. All have the same type of face, round, and covered with short hair, and on the whole plain, the nose of the kind that is generally designated as shapeless, not even a respectable turn-up, and the eyebrows heavy. Their figures are rather small, but sturdy and compact.

The carretera passes through a lava stream which has been a subject of interest to us for some time in the distance. It is as black as ink, quite infernal in appearance. Coming from a westerly direction, it crosses the road—or rather the road crosses it—and it flows into the sea on the east coast, a few miles north of Arrecife. It was one of the numerous streams of lava that devastated the country during the frequent eruptions of 1730 to 1736. They all took place, however, on the western side of the island, where there are innumerable craters, called collectively the Montañas del Fuego, and this is the only stream which flowed easterly. One that nearly destroyed Tiagua in July, 1824, was said to have been stopped miraculously by the procession of Nuestra Señora de los Dolores which met it. Unfortunately the sceptical say it was the hill in front of Tiagua that effected this desirable result. The eruption of the previous century, however, flowed from the same crater, near Tiagua, in this easterly direction. It is said that for five years it never ceased moving slowly onwards to the sea, a black, burning

* "Journey through Nubia to Darfoor." By F. S. Ensor.

mass. It is in Lanzarote that the latest eruptions have taken place, that of 1824 being the last in the archipelago.

We met a few peasants carrying earthen jars containing fish, one surmounted by a pair of boots. Our elevated position enabled us to look down upon their heads and see the contents of the jars.

Gradually we are rising, and at 10.20 a.m., as we leave the carretera, turning off upon the right, we find ourselves 300 feet above the sea. We are close to Tahiche. Juan Topham overtook us here, having left some time after we did.

We have not taken to our feet yet, though just in the middle of our backs, beneath the shoulders, is a spot that aches from the unusual swaying motion. A camel's walking pace causes a double motion of the body. Neither motions, however, suit the angles of the human frame, but move one, as it were, diagonally. A little studying of the best mode of sitting convinced us that camel-riding must be treated as one treats an Irish car. The body must move and give way to the motions of the camel, and sway with it. An endeavour to remain still is not only fatiguing on a camel, but is apt to render one's seat dangerous. A couple of days made us *au fait* with camel-riding, and it proved not only comfortable, but less fatiguing than riding on a horse. We had ample leisure to look around ; writing notes was easy ; we could converse, being only a foot or two apart ; and, with a little basket placed on the hump between the bars, we could partake of luncheon when we wished. I know that many people would scarcely credit that we wrote, much less ate, suspended from a camel, it being thought too difficult and uncomfortable to do so. We, however, really enjoyed our camel-riding, and look back to it with pleasure. A rope halter thrown over the neck of the camel is its only means of guidance, and a rope crupper to keep the saddle from getting forward is the entire harness, unless a small bell hanging from its neck, and giving a gentle tinkle, be included.

The land around Tahiche is more or less cultivated. Some is

in a kind of common. White and purple flowers deck our path, and abound everywhere.

Tahiche is a small village of ruins. We passed through it, and on the further side came to better houses and slopes covered with growing grain. The general appearance of the country is as of vast plains and rolling slopes, rising here and there to bare peaks and cones. Flat-roofed white houses in groups dot it at intervals, also brown huts, both of plastered and loose stones. The dividing walls of fields are built entirely of loose stones.

There is a good deal of costume left still in Lanzarote. The montero, or cap, such as we saw in Palma, of blue, bound and turned up with yellow and red, is common. We met a goatherd wearing one. He was dressed in a white linen smock, woollen garters, sandals of hairy hide, and carried a lance and bag on his back. There are a great number of goats everywhere.

We passed along, over, around, and among the undulations of the ground, sometimes 300 feet and sometimes 200 feet above the sea, towards which the land sloped gently. Feeling hungry, we stopped at 12.30 p.m., and dismounted, eating our luncheon under the shelter of a wall, sheltering from the wind which blows, not from the sun. The man gave a twist to the rope round the dromedary's knee, which then lay perfectly still. He objected to our remounting him, grumbling and growling, but of course was powerless to move.

This method of, as it were, tethering a camel to itself is, according to travellers' accounts, prevalent in the deserts of Africa. There, as here, the animals when on a journey are fed in this posture.

The undulating nature of the ground ceased, and on surmounting the highest and last elevation, we saw Guatiza lying beneath us, which we soon reached. The village is situated on a flat plain between hills, those on the left being bare and of a slatey grey colour. The ground, which had been yellow scoriæ, is now covered by a coating of grey mould. It was here we saw for the first time extraordinary cone-shaped stacks, twelve to twenty feet in height, in the hollow centre of which grain was stored. The top, which is removed each year to admit the grain, was here of red clay, which dries to a lighter colour, and looks like a monk's shaven head. We reached the church at 1.15 p.m. (350 feet). The road is a wide path between broad, low walls of grey pumice stones, and winds in and out and round the farms and farmhouses like a maze, for one frequently turns to the left in order to reach one's destination on the right. Cochineal is the chief product, and everywhere the ugly cactus rises from amid the dry, bare lava. The fields are simply composed of black cinders. What a burning, smothering furnace this place must be in summer, when even to-day the winter sun feels strong! The people wear immense broad-brimmed straw hats, and we met a man dressed completely in white clothes, and carrying a white umbrella. Beneath the village is a windmill of the regular Don Quixote type, and so low down, that we can readily understand that individual charging it! Near the windmill is an earth quarry, for in this plain of lava, once no doubt a fruitful valley, mould has to be dug from beneath the slag. The quarrying has gone down some twenty feet, leaving here and there monoliths of lava, pillars standing upright, originally on a level with the ground. As we pass the scattered houses of Mala we see the dromedary put to the oddest use. He is ploughing. Two pieces of wood crossed over his neck form a yoke, and attached to them are on the left side a shaft and on the right a trace. A gap in the hills on our left shows us a few fig trees, the first trees of any sort we have seen. We get near the sea now, after having taken a short cut across the country, with hills between us and the sea. There is earth banked up on the sides of these hills, which is, I think, to keep the water from flowing off them, but our arriero seemed to think we were foolish to ask such a silly question as to the uses of these banks, and would not deign to answer. Piles of stones are laid at intervals down the fields as boundaries, and we are immediately reminded of the old Jewish command, " Remove not thy neighbour's landmark." There is a curious sugar-loaf mountain, with the top cut off, as it were, on the left of which we turned up a gully and made for two windmills on a hill, behind which lies Haria.*

Our path now led upwards by what would be a gentle incline to a horse, but is steep to a camel. A dromedary was kneeling to be laden half-way up, so we had to wait until the man finished before we could pass. The top reached, we found ourselves 900 feet above the sea, and in the vicinity of the usual cemetery. Haria is a prettily situated town, surrounded by hills which are cultivated. Numbers of palm and fig trees rise from amid well-to-do houses. Our letter of introduction was to Don Salvador de la Fone, whose residence being unknown to our arriero, we made inquiries at a shop; there were only two or three in the place. As we entered the town we were greeted by the inevitable tin-rattle business in the church.

Don Salvador's wife received us kindly, and made a great fuss over us, immediately preparing some dinner, consisting of black sausages and eggs, which we ate in a little doorless room opening off the courtyard at 4 p.m. We then went for a walk round the town, at the further side of which is a fine and extensive view. A broad and undulating valley, an oblong basin, dotted with a few houses and well cultivated, lies beneath and sweeps onward to a mountain, the Corona, which verily crowns it on the farther side. The grand roll of the ground and its general contour, with the noble lines of the mountain beyond, render this scene deserving the name of splendid, tame though it may seem in detail.

Haria has always been a noted spot. It was in the old days of its ancient inhabitants the residence of one of their kings or chiefs, the neighbouring cave, now called Cueva de los Verdes, having been the royal residence, it is said. Later days have seen the sacking of the wealthy Haria by pirates from the coast of Barbary. Glas's first visit to Lanzarote was to this town, and he gives an amusing account of how he could not

* The *h* at the beginning of a Spanish word is always dropped. It is as incorrect to pronounce it in Spanish as it is to omit it in English. *Haria* is therefore pronounced '*Aria*.

get anything to eat, there being no shops, and the people, as he thought, being inhospitable. In reality, however, he arrived past their morning meal, so had to wait until their dinner and his supper-hour. A curious story in connection also with Haria is that the people objected to taking the life of anyone who deserved capital punishment, so in order to kill the offender they had to invent another method. They had therefore a square place, the walls being very high, in which the prisoner was put. He was given his choice of either food or drink, and then left to perish from starvation or hunger. The unfortunate man usually chose water. One, however, who was conducted to this place of death, was told by his godmother to ask for milk. He followed her advice, and of course did not die. So this manner of disposing of criminals failed. There is something peculiar about the story. For instance, whoever the woman might be, it is not possible she was his *god*mother, for the old inhabitants were not Christians. However, it is a pity to spoil a good story, so I leave it as it is.

Considering this was my first journey since my illness, I felt tired, though only healthily so, therefore went to bed at 7 p.m. ! Before doing so I asked for a basin and water, and the good people wanted to know if I would have it in the comedor ! I succeeded in getting it in my bedroom on a chair, though with some difficulty. Our room was on the ground floor, a large one, and, I fancy, vacated for us by our hosts.

January 25th, Friday.—It is tolerably chilly up here among the hills, and at 8 a.m. we found it was 57° F. (14° C.). We rose at 7.30, and were conducted to another house for breakfast, the owner of which was a poor man, with but one leg. He was the greatest character we met with almost in our wanderings. His wife did the cooking, and he did the laying of and waiting at the table. As, however, he used no crutch, he was obliged to hop everywhere ! With shirt-sleeves turned up and a beaming, fat face, this individual as he hopped through the room, carrying now a plate or knife and then a cup, steadying himself with a finger upon the table or leaning against the wall, formed the most pitiable yet laughable of spectacles. His own bright face banished somehow the idea of commiserating him upon his misfortune, and only brought up the ridiculous side of the picture, while his being a man of about fifty or more added to the ludicrousness. The room contained a bed. The floor was cemented, and the walls whitewashed. One door led into the kitchen, and the other into a little shop which he kept. Painted deal chairs were placed round a table in the middle of the floor. The roof was of bare rafters and laths. The breakfast was long in coming, but very good. We had one of those substantial and not to be despised omelets of chopped ham and potatoes, besides other things. Our forks, of steel, were, alas! very dirty, and we surreptitiously wiped them between the appearances of our hopping waiter. We produced a little tea of our own, and requested we might have boiling water, laying great emphasis on the *boiling*. It was boiled in a saucepan, and the tea made in the bottom of a coffee-pot!

It was our wish and intention to go to the Cueva de los Verdes to-day, and to El Risco, sleeping in Haria again to-night, and going back to Arrecife by another route to-morrow. We started therefore for the cave at 10.10 a.m. When our hostess where we slept saw that we had only rugs upon the camel frame, she was horrified, and running into the house, produced two pillows, that made very comfortable seats.

We left Haria by another and different gap in the surrounding hills from that by which we had entered, and proceeded towards the sea. Quite a little cavalcade started, for Don Salvador, riding a donkey, kindly accompanied us, as well as a guide to the Cueva, the entrance to which is difficult to find. Then there was Juan Topham, on his horse, our camel and selves, and the arriero. Don Salvador carried a long barrelled gun slung across his shoulder, wore a belt containing powder and shot round his waist, and was accompanied by a dog. Sylvestre, our guide, a tall man, was a striking figure, with a lantern in one hand, his lancia in the other, a rope twisted round his shoulders, and shod in sandals. The donkey insisted on braying, and the horse was lively. The camel being the slow goer, made the running, leading the way in stately, swinging fashion. As we leave Haria it becomes much warmer, and the thermometer in the shade marks 68° F. (20° C.). We are descending, and also are passing through volcanic ground, and the lava walls reflect the heat. The land is stony, and nothing grows upon it but the cochineal cactus, divided by the low walls of lava and occasional heaps of lava piled here and there as they have been gathered off the land. The dog, which roams far and near, gives an occasional yelp as he treads upon a " Christ's thorn." Our camel insists upon stopping to eat the cactus, the only animal I ever saw eating those thick, hard leaves. Presently we walk over a vast surface of smooth rocks, lying in broken pieces, among which the euphorbia chiefly grows, but every niche and cranny where there is a trace of soil is covered by small flowers and weeds. Even on this bare, rocky surface we move noiselessly. The camel is always noiseless, as he treads with thickly padded feet, but the horse and donkey are shoeless, and the men, wearing simple pieces of leather turned up over their insteps, and fastened by thin strips of leather, sandal fashion, the whole guiltless of heels or nails, are also perfectly noiseless in their tread. We pass now along a cinder path through a vast extent of broken masses of lava, interspersed by nothing but quantities of euphorbia and grey lichen to relieve its monotony. This is a malpais, and very bad walking it is. Not a square inch of the surface is even ; all are jagged, ragged lumps of thoroughly smelted and fired stones. Below on our right lies the sea, and on our left the Corona, the outline of which from here is much serrated and broken. It is the end of the chain in the north of the island, and is a fine and singular object in the landscape. It was 11.45 a.m. when we arrived at a hole in the ground, which, after some searching, our guide, Sylvestre, had found. Holding the halter, the camel-driver stood in front, and uttering "Tutchi! Tutchi!" many times, induced the camel to lie down on a small surface of level ground that he had found, when we dismounted. The hole was not the best entrance to the cave, so we walked a little distance until we came upon a large, round opening, into which we descended. Out of this central hole, somewhat like a disused quarry, two caves open, and into one of these we entered. The ground descended rapidly, and we walked on until we came to a precipitous descent, needing a rope. Ascertaining that there was nothing to be seen beyond the cave itself, though that is of the greatest interest, and that it would take the entire day to penetrate its recesses, we did not venture farther. This was the main entrance, but there is another near the sea, the one doubtless by which individuals entered secretly with provisions. The story goes that on the 1st of May in the year 1618 a fleet of Algerine corsairs, consisting of sixty vessels, commanded by Taban and Soliman, disembarked five hundred men in Lanzarote. The Conejeros (people of Lanzarote), thinking only of saving their lives, fled, some to Fuerteventura and some to the caves. The greater part, nine hundred persons, hid in this cave of Los Verdes. The corsairs, believing that in guarding this entrance they had them secured, and that they must succumb to hunger, were all unconscious that by another outlet the people were going and coming freely with provisions. One man, however, on one of these errands was taken prisoner, and, under threat of immediate death, showed the private entrance of the cave, which the Moors then closed, forcing the unfortunate people to surrender. They carried them away captive, and it is almost a satisfaction to know that the traitor and his family were likewise carried into captivity. As the Spaniards broke faith with the Guanches time after time, so the Moors now broke faith with the descendants of those first invaders. Who can say it was not deserved? The prisoners and booty were safely conveyed to Algiers, notwithstanding that a Spanish fleet was sent to intercept them in the Straits of Gibraltar. The King of Spain, however, ransomed the people later, and sent them back to Lanzarote. Another attempt was made by the Moors to land in 1748, when the Spaniards showed more pluck. They allowed the corsairs to land and get well into the country, when they intercepted their retreat to their boats and killed them all, save those upon the vessels. These went home to tell the tale of their disasters, and ever since the island has been left in peace by the Moors. What with several English attacks, the first in 1596, and the numerous landings of the Moors, this unfortunate island has

ENTRANCE TO CUEVA DE LOS VERDES, LANZAROTE.

suffered severely, and without respite since the conquest until the end of the eighteenth century. Even before that date its shores, so easy of access, and its proximity to the continent seem to have induced invasions of all sorts of people. Little as Lanzarote and Fuerteventura are valued by Spain, she would find them a sore in her side were they taken by any other nation, for from them invasions of the richer and more valuable islands could readily be made, as the Spaniards did formerly, and thus a second conquest be accomplished, were the nations of Europe at war.

Herr von Fritsch, who entered and examined the Cueva de los Verdes, gives an exact description of the interior. "Cavities lead into the high, vaulted subterranean galleries of the great Cueva de los Verdes. These galleries are here piled one above another like stories. Where even the roofs of these natural tunnels (they are masses of lava, usually as much as a metre in thickness) are broken it is possible to climb up from one gallery to another or else to descend from one to another by means of a rope. In most places the height of the galleries exceeds ten metres (about thirty-two feet), and their breadth in the middle may be reckoned at eight metres (about twenty-six feet). In some places the roof comes nearer the ground, or the side walls approach each other more closely, so that, especially in the lowest story, it is hard and then difficult, if not impossible, to go farther. The side walls either rise straight up to the vaulted roof, or else resemble a staircase turned upside down. From the roof, as from the overhanging ledges of the side walls, hang small pointed lava stalactites, and in many cases the side walls and roof have an encrustation of gypsum, sometimes in a firm, but at other times in a more pulverised-looking, state; at the lower part of the side walls, plates of lava run, of irregular length, now like a piece of wainscotting and now like veneer; and in many places regular tables of lava may be seen on the floor of the cave, at a little distance from the wall. These are from one to two decimetres (about 3 to 7 inches) in height, and are from three to four decimetres away from the wall. They lie in rows. Elsewhere the floor is formed of slabs or covered by pieces of slag, or with great lumps that have fallen from the roof. The natural tunnels are formed with a marvellous regularity for long distances. In one place we walked along almost straight galleries for six hundred and eight hundred paces, fourteen hundred in all, or rather more than a kilometre. This cave is incontestably the largest lava grotto that is known. It is formed by the inner mass of a lava stream (which remains liquid longer than the outer), continuing its course under the hardened upper crust, when, no new lava flowing after it, empty spaces, or caves, are left behind.   A cave formation such as this would be very well formed in a lava stream that filled a glen, but the existence of a tunnel like those I have just described would necessitate the presence of a barranco."

The second cave opening out of the quarry-like hole was said to be tenanted by pigeons, so Sylvestre entered, Don Salvador waiting gun in hand. Numbers of rock pigeons flew out, but none were killed. John took a photograph of the mouth of the cave as we rested after our scramble in the interior. It was 12.45 when we left the Cueva de los Verdes and rode back towards Haria.

Our arriero's sandals are the worse for wear, and at the toes and heels he is really walking on his bare feet. The camel had been supplied with fresh food this morning before starting, with which it must have swallowed some caterpillars, for while walking along chewing the cud, it made a gurgling and grunting and blowing noise, closed its nostrils, and then with a puff ejected the caterpillars which had been in its stomach. It was curious to observe how neatly it did this, not sending any particle of food out, but only the caterpillars.

It was but 2 p.m. when we reached the road near the spot where the ascent to Haria begins. We suggested to Don Salvador that we should now go to the Risco. He was much surprised at our proposing to do any more to-day. However, on inquiry we found, as we thought, that we could get back before dark, an hour and a half at camel's pace taking us there. We begged Don Salvador not to accompany us if it inconvenienced him or if he were tired, but he indignantly denied all fatigue, and kindly went with us. Turning off by the village or hamlet of Magnes, upon which we had looked down the previous evening from Haria, we ascended by the foot of the western side of the Corona. Two hills, with large craters, lie on our left, their edges broken and beneath them is a perfectly flat plain, entirely cultivated. Numbers of holes in the land have green vegetation inside. How it gets there is difficult to say, but the effect is curious from a distance, the bright green spots against the brown land. We picked many flowers on the way : *Silybum Marianum, Salvia Bronsonetti, Aizoon Canariense, Aizoon Hispanicum, Helianthemum pulchellum, Erucastrum Canariense,* and *Spergularia media.* Ascending, we reach a ridge 1,400 feet in height, from the top of which we gain a fine view of two perpendicular rocks, upon which the sun shines, and at whose feet the sea breaks. We think they are Santa (or Montaña) Clara and Alegranza, but as we immediately commence descending, lose sight of them. The Corona is now near us on our right, gaining, and not losing, by a closer inspection. Its steep, sloping sides are perfectly bare, but at its foot are a couple of stone huts. Our attention is fully occupied, at present, with the endeavour to hold on, for, owing to the steep descent, our seats are sloping most uncomfortably forward, and a fall from this height would not be pleasant. These dromedaries seem much larger than those common in Egypt and elsewhere, and our seats are generally some six feet from the ground.

Glas tells of an amusing adventure which occurred to his carpenter and boatswain, who, like their captain, visited Haria and were unable to get any food. Being tired and faint therefore on their way back to El Rio, where the ship lay, they asked a man who was riding a camel to allow them to mount and ride to the brow of the cliff. The camel when half-way there shook himself, and the tars, proverbially bad riders, were tumbled off, as much to the surprise of the arriero as of the sailors, who preferred to walk the remainder of the way.

Very slowly did our camel descend, and rather unwillingly, his short body and long legs not being adapted for hills. Fields of peas and beans, the former in flower, reminded us of England several months hence. Some volcanic rocks of octagon formation, and hollow, attracted our attention. Next we reached a sloping limestone rock, nothing growing on its white surface but "Christ's thorn." The rocks sloped very abruptly upwards upon our left hand, so that, although but a few yards from their summits, we were totally unconscious of the surprise in store.

Reaching now basaltic rock, we dismounted, and walking up to the top, only half a dozen yards distant, we were struck dumb by finding ourselves on the brink of a precipice, with one of the most magnificent seascapes spread below. The two cliffs we had caught a glimpse of previously, we found were Alegranza and Montaña Clara; but between them and the mainland lies Graciosa, with its three humps, the northern one, or rather two, being named Montaña Aguja, and the southern Amarilla. Around the hills, appearing only hillocks as we look down upon them—for we are just double their height—is ground usually nothing but sand, but now partially covered by verdure, giving it a grey appearance, which presents a beautiful contrast to the blue sea. From this height we can see each grey island standing out clearly, edged with a narrow ribbon of white surf, and encircled by a band of blue sea. Even these three islets Nature disdained to fashion after the same pattern. Alegranza, the farthest from here, has a perpendicular buttress, with crater summit, dropping into the sea at its south-western side. One end of this crater is deeply serrated down its face, which from here appears lined. The eastern side falls rather abruptly landwards to a low level, until it ends in three small peaks, on the outermost of which is a lighthouse. The whole island is rather like a tadpole in shape from this point. Montaña Clara is composed almost entirely of one rock. There is, however, a little low-lying land on its southern side. North of it is the rock called Roque del Oeste, some twenty feet high, and scarcely worthy of mention but that it forms the thirteenth island of the archipelago. Graciosa, with its three hills, lies at our feet.

Seldom have I seen anything more beautiful than these rugged grey, red, and brown rocks, dressed in blue. Taken separately, there is nothing in each island, bare and treeless, to extort admiration, but what constitutes the beauty must be seen to be admired. It is the marvellous colouring, blue sky and fleecy clouds, and these rough, strongly coloured, barren islets, set as if precious gems in a turquoise sea.

A few white houses on the strand on Graciosa, just opposite us, mark the late fish-salting depôt, and on a sandy point at our feet lie the Salt Works. El Risco, on which we stand, has most unworthily fallen into the background of our thoughts, owing to the beauty of the islands. A precipitous cliff is at our feet, sufficiently sloping at the spot where we stand to admit of a descent by a path which leads to the narrow, flat strip of land lying close along the sea-shore. The path zigzags downwards, and we can scarcely follow its wanderings, for it is a mere goat-track. It was up and down this path Captain Glas climbed, and it was in the blue, still waters of El Rio—so called from its narrow, winding nature between the islands—that his good ship lay at anchor. "This is a convenient place," he says, "in the summer season for careening large ships, for a man-of-war of any nation that may happen to be at war with Spain may come in here and unload all her stores, etc., on the island of Graciosa, and heel and scrub. Or if two chance to come in together, the one may heave down by the other, in doing which they need not fear any opposition from the inhabitants, for there is neither castle or habitation near this port. But the water here is not so smooth as in Porto de Naos, especially if the trade-wind happens to blow hard from the east, which sends in a swell that makes it very troublesome, if not impossible, to careen a ship properly. But the wind does not often blow from that quarter in this part of the world. That which prevails most is the north or north-north-east trade-wind. In mooring here great care must be taken to have a good anchor and large scope of cable towards Lanzarota, for in east or south-east winds heavy gusts or squalls come from the high land of that island. In the winter the wind here sometimes shifts to the south-west, when it is necessary to weigh and run back to the eastward round the aforesaid shallow point, until the ship be land-locked from that wind, and there anchor." I give these practical directions

at length because his book is difficult to procure—and who
knows but that they may be useful some day to our countrymen?—and because Glas in such matters is implicitly to be
relied upon.   Then, as now, the salt works on the littoral
existed.   "Here is a salina, or salt-work, being a square
piece of land, levelled and divided by shallow trenches about
two inches deep.   Into these they let the sea-water, which,
by the heat of the sun and the nature of the soil, soon turns
to salt."   Of the path Glas also says that it is "narrow,
steep, and intricate, . . . scarce possible for a stranger to
ascend it without a guide, for if he should chance to wander
from the path, he could not easily find it again, and would
be in imminent danger of breaking his neck."   The spring
of water to the north of the salt works appears from Glas's
description to be a chalybeate spring, for his crew suffered
from it on first using it.   He says, however, that it is good
to use for drinking and keeps sweet at sea, and that "it is
easy of access, lying close to the waterside," and "yields
enough to fill two hogsheads in twenty-four hours."

There is yet another islet, a rock lying to the east of all these
others and to the north-east of Lanzarote, called the Roque
del Este.   Numberless have been the wrecks, known and
unknown doubtless, upon the inhospitable shores of these
lesser islets.   They are all destitute of fresh water, so that
shipwrecked mariners only escape a watery grave to perish
by thirst.

About the middle of the eighteenth century an English
ship ran on Alegranza during the night, and was soon
beaten to pieces.   The crew, however, got ashore safely.
There was not a lighthouse then upon the island, and the
unfortunate sailors strove in vain to draw the attention of
the inhabitants of Lanzarote.   This, we can readily understand, failed, for El Risco completely hides the main island
from view, and no one lives on the strip of littoral below.
After subsisting for some days on rainwater they found in
holes in the rocks, and provisions saved from the vessel, the

captain made his escape in a curious way. The sailors had noticed that the wind blew steadily from Alegranza towards Graciosa, so, making a raft, on which they erected a mast and sail, with an oar for a rudder, the skipper sailed away and landed safely at Graciosa. Here, as it was winter, there were a few shepherds and fishermen, and the latter "immediately went off in a boat to their relief, and brought them all safe to Lancerota."

The Risco reminds one a little of Las Playas in Hierro, but is not so precipitous, and, unlike it, is crowned with limestone. Two sheltered and pretty little bays are near Amarilla, on Graciosa ; at least, they look charming at this distance. After looking for some time with close attention at the littoral and less precipitous parts of the Risco beneath, we discover moving objects that might be toy animals out of a Noah's ark, but prove ultimately to be dromedaries, horses, cows, and donkeys grazing.

Reluctantly, with more reluctance than we ever experienced before, we felt compelled to leave this scene, as time was passing, and nightfall might overtake us unawares. Perhaps it was the novelty of the view that was so enticing, for it is difficult to imagine a treeless landscape being beautiful ; or more likely it was the sea, which lends a charm to the most arid and uninteresting scenery, and gives that ever-changing and restless yet soothing idea of motion, the knowledge of a great force kept in restraint.

> " Watching at eve upon the giant height,
> Which looks o'er waves so blue, skies so serene,
> That he who there at such an hour hath been
> Will wistful linger on that hallowed spot,
> Then slowly tear him from the 'witching scene,
> Sigh forth one wish that such had been his lot,
> Then turn to hate a world he had almost forgot."

Three paces downwards, and the scene is lost, gone for ever, and we sigh as one sighs after anything beautiful, as the last chord of the moonlight sonata dies away under a master hand, or the notes of a perfectly trained and melodious voice cease to hold us enthralled, or the glorious hues of a sunset fade and disappear as the night draws on. After each and all we waken mentally, as a dog sleeping and dreaming of canine delights wakens, and shakes himself, and is ready for the present life, either kicks or cakes.

We were glad to walk part of the way back to Haria, having been riding all day. We saw an unusual number of birds, and many of them strangers, visitors from the adjacent coast of Africa, only sixty-six miles distant. A tabobo alighted on a neighbouring wall but a short distance away, and Don Salvador, anxious to show he could kill something, shot the poor little wanderer. They are pretty birds, these tabobos, dun-coloured, with black-and-white bars on the wings and fan tail. The feather tufts on their heads are also black-and-white, and the beaks are long and narrow. They are about the size of a small pigeon.

Innumerable legends and tales are connected with the bird, arising from its crown or tuft of feathers. The original crown, says tradition, was of gold, granted by King Solomon, though against his advice, for services rendered by the birds to that monarch. Its value, however, caused the unlucky tabobos to be ceaselessly pursued and ensnared, so that they besought Solomon to remove his too costly gift, which he did, substituting feathers.

Most of the day had been cloudy, a grey day in fact, which made travelling pleasanter. We left El Risco at 4.10 p.m., and reached Haria at 5.45 p.m., where we got dinner at the venta. The schoolmaster came to see us during the evening. The pedagogue in each village generally paid us a visit, urged thereto perhaps by the villagers, as the one man amongst them who was able to cope with such learned people as we were—we could read and write, and so could he! The priest of course took precedence of all, but that dignitary could not be expected to call upon strangers without a letter of introduction, so his curiosity had to remain unsatisfied, and news of us could only be obtained second-hand. As we were frequently the only visitors within the memory of man to many of the hamlets and villages, this dignified reticence must have been difficult to maintain, and was quite worthy of a Spaniard.

Having been treated as an invalid until within the last day or two, and having eaten meals frequently—and how rapaciously only those who have ever had a fever can tell—I find it rather trying to be suddenly reduced to two meals a day, and to-night screwed up my courage to ask our hosts if I might have some *leche sopa* (milk soup), as boiled bread and milk is called. They fortunately had some milk, and were only too happy to give us anything they could.

CHAPTER XIV.

TEGUISE—THE MURDER OF GLAS—MEDAÑOS—YAIZA.

> By my life,
> These birds have joyful thoughts! Think you they sing
> Like poets, from the vanity of song?
> Or have they any sense of why they sing?
> And would they praise the heavens for what they have?
> And I made answer, "Were there nothing else
> For which to praise the heavens but only love,
> That only love were cause enough for praise."
>
> TENNYSON.

> Foul deeds will rise,
> Though all the earth o'erwhelm them, to men's eyes.
>
> SHAKSPERE.

> Pleasant my days pass, filled with household cares.
>
> EDWIN ARNOLD.

January 26th, Saturday.—A glorious morning, with the thermometer at 59° F. (15° C.) at 8 a.m. John went to see a photographer, for there is actually one here, though his apparatus of course is very primitive. He has never heard of dry plates, and, in fact, chiefly uses tin types.

The room that we have had here contains a large fourpost and a small iron bed, a wardrobe, and two small tables, and is divided by a glass door from the next bedroom. The windows are glazed in the upper part, but there are no sashes in the lower, only fixed venetian shutters. The door opens into the yard, where there is the usual cistern, paved over, and a few old soap cases, now containing plants, of which the good woman is very proud, and justly so in a land where water is scarce. Our aneroid had been left out this morning for a little. We generally carry it with us or lock it up, and on our return found it indexing 7,000 feet, an altitude probably attributable to the exhilaration of childhood. The rapid change of the index was unfortunate, as we could not set the instrument again correctly until we reached the sea-level at Arrecife, though we could make a guess at what the altitude had been. By an unfortuitous circumstance we had omitted to take the altitude of Haria upon our arrival, and now we could not, but it must be about 700 or 800 feet.

We left at 9.40 a.m., our friends very anxious we should take pillows to sit upon, but the difficulty of returning them was insurmountable. We intend riding along the ridge of which El Risco is the northern end, until we reach the plain in mid-island, to which we shall descend upon Teguise, the ancient capital, and thence to Arrecife. Passing out of the town, whose most noticeable features are palm trees and the curious conical grain-stacks, or *pajeras*, we ascend a steep and stony road on one side of the valley which extends southwards from Haria. Our camello is again getting rid of caterpillars this morning. The almond trees are covered with beautiful white blossoms, but destitute of a leaf. The valley is terraced as high as possible, above which all is bare and rugged—nothing but stones and lichen-covered rocks. We met a respectable old man in a black coat and white shirt, leading a grey donkey, on which was laid a very gay saddle-bag. Presently we met another individual in a bright red plaid, seated on a saddle-bag of all colours of the rainbow. There has been a heavy dew or a mist during the early morning—more likely the latter, as dew falls rarely and then only lightly in these islands—which still clings to and refreshes everything. Whether the dromedary objects to the moisture or is lazy with his recent supplies of green food I know not, but he is going so very slowly, that his owner apostrophises him and suggests, "If you step like

this, we shall be three days going to La Ciudad" (the town).
Further up the road winds sharply backwards and forwards,
and from this vuelta we gain a fine view of the valley and
Haria beneath, the Corona, of curious shape, and beyond,
in the sea, the Roque del Este, the only one of the islets
visible. It is a grand view, the sweep of country covered being
extensive, while Haria lies embosomed in the hills, various
valleys leading out from it to the adjacent country. As we still
ascend higher the path becomes of the stone wall species—that
is, paved with cobbles—and on either side of it is steep, rocky
ground, verdant now with short, sweet grass and beautiful
flowers. One lovely purple flower of the iris order, with delicate
sword-shaped leaves—*Romulex bulbocodium*—grows luxuriantly,
while another white one crops up from amid the stones upon
which we tread. A cross erected at some 1,750 feet up, where
a woman fell over the cliff and was killed, has more reason for
its erection than is often displayed. We have now reached
the highest ridge in the island, the height of which Fritsch
gives as 684 metres (about 2,223 feet), and look over into
another valley, terraced on each side to the summit. The wind
is strong here, as it is almost everywhere in Lanzarote, except
of course where sheltered by mountains. Many attribute
the healthy condition of the island and its exhilarating climate
to this cause. Glas remarks that " the climate of those islands "
(Lanzarote and Fuerteventura) " is exceeding wholesome,
which may be owing to the driness of the soil and the strong
northerly winds that almost continually blow upon them, so that
the inhabitants in general live to a great age." The wind,
though so beneficial in many respects, is charged with preventing the growth of trees. There be many other causes
which produce this result, such as the droughts which are so
frequent, and the quantities of rabbits, which some say have
caused the Spaniards to christen the people of Lanzarote
conejeros.

The orchilla-weed, before mentioned, although it grows
in all the islands and is of an inferior quality in the two

eastern, has yet been more connected with these islands, owing no doubt to its being the chief support of many of the people. It was a royal monopoly until the year 1814, since which date it has been free. It used to be sold for about eight or nine pounds the quintal (one hundred and four pounds) and exported to Europe. About thirty or forty years ago it was ten pounds a ton; now that quantity is worth only two pounds. It is said that, being found in great abundance in Africa, the price went down here. The orchilla of Gomera and Hierro is the best. It grows principally on the faces of the steepest rocks, and men went, and still go, over the cliffs, to gather it, putting the little plant, of some three or four inches in length, into bags round their necks. The origin of the generic name of these lichens is supposed to be from the noble Florentine family of the Rucellai. This name by corruption became Rucellari, and so passed into Rocella. The family, it is said, possessed the secret of dyeing with *orciglia*, which was introduced for the first time into Italy from the Levant by one of their ancestors, about the year 1300. The dye was used in dyeing English blue broadcloths, which showed a purple hue when viewed against the light. Glas says, "Upon the rocks on the sea-coast grows a great quantity of orchilla-weed, an ingredient used in dying, well known to our dyers in London."

A little yellowy-red flower—*Adonis Pyrenaica*, a native of the Pyrenees—like a ranunculus, we found at 1,900 feet, also a fine yellow ranunculus (*spicatus*), a native of Algiers, and a cluster of whitey-pink flowers at the top of a long stem, at whose base was a bulb (*Allium roseum*); the colour varies from white to dark pink, and the leaf is variegated like holly. A blue labiate and thyme were also plentiful. The dark mauve iris grows but a few inches above the ground. Owing to the recent rains, the seeds, which may have been sleeping for years, all seem to have burst forth and carpeted the ground with a beautiful and varied colouring. We had hoped that upon reaching the summit of the ridge we should once more see our lovely islets, but were disappointed. El Risco was too high

for us to see over it, notwithstanding our own elevation, and
the islands lying too closely beneath its shelter. The road is
tolerably level and very broad; in fact, I think it is as nature
made it, the centre, a path about five or six feet wide, of
large, uneven stones, alone being man's handiwork. The stones
are carefully avoided, however, and on either side of them is
a beaten path, along which our dromedary swings. We
descend a little, and an extensive view opens out of masses
of peaked cones and a vast plain of whitey-pink sand. A flat
promontory or islet lies on our right, as it is marked on the
chart, a square, jutting-out piece of land, almost an island, a
passage for boats lying between it and the mainland. Our
road lies on a high isthmus, as it were, the cliffs upon the
right and left dropping over a thousand feet into the sandy
plain beneath. Originally perhaps the sea washed below, but
has now retreated, leaving a vast plain of sand. Many of the
hills beneath are so low, that we can look into their craters.
We reach, at about 1,950 feet, a little church, and, as is usual
with a chapel on a mountain, it is named La Ermita de las
Nieves—the Snow Hermitage.

Our path is literally strewn with flowers, an expression
generally employed metaphorically, but which here is prosaically
correct, every footstep of our dromedary crushing numbers of
delicate petals. The plants do not, however, dazzle one by
their colours, for the background on which they rest is not
green grass, which would throw up pink, mauve, and white
to perfection, but yellowy-pink or whitey yellow-ochre scoriæ
and sand. Presently, however, we cross a sort of common,
partially green, where stones are plentiful, and fired rocks crop
up in abundance. Here are bright orange dandelions, with
claret-coloured eyes, growing abundantly, and looking rich and
beautiful.

As we descend and are sheltered from the wind, we are
suddenly greeted by sweet, low, melodious singing, and for
some seconds look in vain for the songsters. At last, close
to the stones, and partaking of their colour, at a little distance

we distinguish a flock of canary birds. Their song carries us homewards, but the familiar little yellow captive can never again occupy its place in our minds as being the true canary, although its song is the same, though not so sweet, as that of its wild progenitor. As if on enchanted ground, the sweet, wild song accompanies us onwards, though the singers are seldom seen. The yellow roads of scoriæ and rock emit a great glare.

We descend by a rough path into a well-cultivated plain of rich red soil. I can tell how rough the path was by the hieroglyphics in my note-book! A hill on the further side is surmounted by a castle, that of Santa Barbara or De Guanapay, of historic fame. Three yoke of oxen and a camel are plough-ing near us, and there are others further off. There is only one house, which is, we suppose, Valler. Part of the valley is in wheat, which gives a rich green colour to the landscape. A slight ascent faces us, on whose summit is a windmill, betokening the presence of a town; two more come in sight as we rise higher, then a couple of yellow pumice hills, hiding Teguise. Between the hills is a large cistern, now over-flowing and filling the little valleys with the welcome fluid. During the great droughts people came from far and near to this cistern for water, and were relieved, except the inhabitants of Arrecife, to whom all aid was refused. It did not cost much to construct, for the contour of the hills lent itself to the project. Round another pumice-heap the town came in view. We dismounted at 12.45 p.m., and sat down to eat some luncheon under the shelter of the hill behind the cistern.

Teguise is decidedly disappointing. It is a small and in-significant village. The prevailing colour is dull terra-cotta, the same as the surrounding earth, which is suggestive of mud walls. There is a background of hills on the south side, while beneath the town to eastward is a plain of sand. The crowning position and interest, however, is the castle of Santa Barbara, which guards and overlooks the town on its north-eastern side on the summit of a low crater. The roofs of the houses, tiled or of clay, impart a quaint and pretty, if poverty-stricken, aspect to Teguise, and are far preferable from an artistic point of view to the flat roofs of Arrecife. There are three churches, which alone remain to tell of the past glories of the place, now wrested from it by the newer and more prosperous port.

Teguise has, however, a history of which to boast. Was it

TEGUISE, LANZAROTE.

not sacked by the English in 1596, when a small squadron, commanded by the Earl of Cumberland, landed five hundred or six hundred men, under Sir John Berkley, in search of a rich marquis and his property ? They found neither the nobleman nor his reputed wealth, but they reached Teguise while pursuing the flying Spaniards, who even abandoned Santa Barbara, which, it is said, "was so strong, that twenty men could have defended it against five hundred," and made themselves ill partaking of the wine they found in the village.

The early history of the island, when Bethencourt landed, is connected almost entirely with the south of Lanzarote. The island, it is said, was then called Tite-roy-gatra, and owing to the raids of pirates, although formerly well peopled, was reduced at the conquest to but three hundred people. To give the entire and interesting history as related in the quaint language of the two priests who accompanied the expedition would take too much space. It is better to read the chronicle as translated and annotated by Mr. Major in his valuable work for the Hakluyt Society, than which a more interesting and instructive relation of middle-ages conquest cannot be found.

Now that we had reached the carretera, our young friend rode home to Arrecife, while we came after in stately fashion, our dromedary not being a trotting individual. Passing behind the sleepy little town, with its Guanche-like roofs, we come on the new high-road, a remarkably good level and broad highway. The surface is covered with cinders, and two rows of stones, about the size of a man's head, placed alternately at the sides form the only obstacle to prevent one's carriage going over into the lower levels of the plains on either side. As, however, no carriages traverse this mighty solitude, it does not matter at present. It is like a house swept and garnished, and with no one to enter in and take possession. At one place the recent rains have broken the road away. The bottom of the valley or plain into which we look down from Teguise is sandy, but on either side the land is cultivated. This plain stretches in a slight curve from one side of the island to the other, interrupted only by a few low cones.

Certainly the most noticeable feature is the absence of inhabitants. The country seems deserted, so thinly is it populated. Even the villages appear half depopulated. The area is large, and the island, thirty-seven miles by twelve, contains only some fourteen thousand souls. Yet there is much cultivation. We passed through miles of corn to-day. In a rainy year like the present there are not sufficient people to cultivate the land, but in a year of drought there are too many to live upon the scarcity.   One understands, when passing through a country such as this, how there could be seven years of plenty and seven of famine without the least contravention of natural laws.

The road, as painfully straight as one of the Roman species, is grass-grown, and guiltless of wheel-tracks.   As we were likely to meet other camels, our driver, with much expostulation on the part of the camello, put a nose-cage or sort of muzzle on him.   It seems that in the spring, when grass-fed, the camellos become occasionally troublesome and cross with each other.   More birds in flocks beguiled our way with their music, and one little fellow, sitting on a stone by the roadside, watching us with his bright eyes, sang until we thought he would burst, ruffling his breast and raising his crest as he poured forth his sweet and jubilant notes.   Between Teguise and Arrecife we met one man on horseback, two women walking, and a flock of sheep and kids—no lambs—herded by a very small boy in a very big hat.

It is just six feet across the camel from edge to edge of the saddle, so a good deal of room is required for a couple of laden animals to pass each other.   Our man says this dromedary cost him seventy pesos (ten pounds ten shillings), a little more than the usual price.

We passed a carefully made stone pit, long and narrow in shape, on the right of the road, but could not get our camellero to say for what purpose it was made.   Describing it later to friends in Arrecife, they were unable also to suggest its use.   We soon after passed on our left the brown stone and mud huts of Tahiche, with its one good, whitewashed dwelling, and turning an angle, reached the same part of the carretera along which we had ridden when going to Haria.   A few eucalypti are planted, an endeavour being at last made to get something to grow.   Early to-day the sky was cloudy, but it is blue now.   We pass once more the lava stream and ride into the town, where we arrive at the fonda just in time for dinner.

We find here several Spaniards, also an American, Mr. B——, who is endeavouring to establish a tunny fishery in the south of the island. The difficulties thrown in the way of strangers getting any concessions are immense. For years Mr. B—— has been endeavouring to obtain a strip of sea-shore on which to build a shed. He went to Madrid and hung about there for months, hoping to hasten matters by his personal presence, but official one sent him to official two, and official two to official three, and then the process was reversed, and the little game played backwards until he reached official one again. He has not yet got permission to establish his fishery, which would be so beneficial to the inhabitants by giving employment whether it rained or not.

The adjacent sea between these islands and Africa near the coast of Barbary is a good and plentiful fishing ground, especially for bream and cod. Some say it is the best in the world, better even than Newfoundland. Glas thought so, and it was his knowledge of this fishing ground in his journeyings to and fro that first made him think of settling on the adjoining coast. He chose the bay and castle of Mar-pequeña, originally established by the Spaniards—a fact unknown to him until he discovered some coins and ancient foundations—and sailed thither from England in 1764, just after publishing his book, intending to establish a port there for the barter of goods with the natives. He renamed the spot Port Hillsborough, after the earl of that name, who was then a member of the Government, and who had approved of Glas's project. Unfortunately he found that the wind during the greater part of the year did not serve to carry large vessels out of the port. He therefore in his long-boat, with only a few sailors, set sail for Lanzarote, where he purposed purchasing a small schooner or brigantine, such as ply among the islands. Being unable to procure a suitable vessel in this island, he sailed on to Canaria, sending his boat back to Port Hillsborough. Meanwhile the Spaniards had become alarmed through their ambassador in London, who had heard of the projected settlement on a spot they still considered theirs, though abandoned by them for two hundred and fifty years, and orders had been given to thwart Glas in all his plans. When therefore Glas, all unconscious of their hostility, landed at Las Palmas, he was taken prisoner and sent to Santa Cruz, where he was secretly confined for a year. Meanwhile his settlement was sacked and pillaged by the Moors, and his wife and daughter, a beautiful child of eleven, and a few other survivors succeeded, after many privations, in reaching England. Glas tried to make some knowledge of his imprisonment public, and at last succeeded by throwing a biscuit, on which he had written in charcoal, out of his window. This was carried to the captain of an English man-of-war lying in the harbour, who reported the occurrence in England, and after much difficulty and many negotiations, the Spaniards, expressing great surprise that so much trouble should be taken over an ordinary sailor, at last liberated Glas. He continued in Santa Cruz until his wife and daughter, for whom he had sent, arrived from home, when, in November, 1765, they sailed in the *Sandwich* from Orotava, the commander of which was Captain Cockeran.

Glas was a native of Scotland, and had been originally intended for a surgeon. He was evidently a powerful man, for during a former voyage he is said to have been "greatly superior in strength to any in the ship." His strength, however, did not now preserve him from an awful fate. The *Sandwich* had treasure on board to the amount of about £100,000, and Glas, as subsequently appears, must have also had with him a considerable amount of money and valuables. The treasure attracted the cupidity of the crew, and George Gidley, cook, Peter Mackinley, boatswain, Andrew Zekerman, and Richard St. Quintin conspired together to obtain it. Captain Cockeran and Glas seem to have had some suspicion of their intentions, and thwarted their designs for three successive nights. At last on Saturday, November 30th, 1765, at 11 p.m., the four assassins killed Cockeran and then the two other sailors who were not in the conspiracy. Glas, awakened by the noise, got out of his bunk, and seeing what was the matter, rushed back to the cabin for his sword. When again leaving it, Mackinley, who had concealed himself behind the door, sprang on him from behind and pinioned his arms, at the same time shouting to his companions for assistance in his murderous design. Glas was overpowered, chiefly because he had thrust his sword through the flesh of Zekerman's arm, whence he could not withdraw it. The plucky Scotchman fought furiously, but the four scoundrels were eventually too much for him. The sword was wrested from his hands, and with it he was repeatedly stabbed, till he died. His dying groans brought his wife and daughter upon deck, who, seeing what had happened, vainly implored on their knees with clasped hands mercy from the murderers. Telling them they must die, the unfortunate mother and daughter clung to each other in a last embrace, when Mackinley and Zekerman caught them both together and flung them overboard. There now only remained two boys besides the four murderers. The murders took place in the British Channel, as the ship sailed to London. The miscreants changed the vessel's course, and steered for Ireland, where on Tuesday, December 3rd, 1765, at 2 p.m., they arrived, within ten leagues of the harbour of Waterford and Ross. Here they determined to scuttle the ship, but first loaded the "cork" boat with dollars "to the quantity of about two tons," and then, knocking out the ballast port, quitted the ship, with fiend-like nonchalance leaving the two boys to perish in the doomed vessel. One lad jumped overboard, and laid hold of the gunwale of the boat, but one of the ruffians gave him a blow on the chest, so that he loosened his hold and was drowned. Before they left they saw the vessel heel over and the other boy washed out and drowned. All witnesses of their atrocious deeds thus destroyed, they rowed up the river or estuary and landed two miles from the fort of Duncannon, in the county of Wexford, where they buried most of their treasure between high and low-water mark. Next day (December 4th) they proceeded to Ross, where at a public-house they exchanged twelve hundred dollars for current gold, purchased pistols, and hired six horses and two guides to take them to Dublin. What a touch of the times we here get! No roads, only paths, and these no doubt in places not safe against highwaymen. Arriving in Dublin on the 6th, they put up at the Black Bull Inn, in Thomas Street. Meanwhile a totally uncalculated-for event took place. The good ship *Sandwich* after all did not sink, but was driven ashore in the county of Waterford, and having no one on board, and doubtless still bearing witness to signs of violence having been committed, was connected with the strange travellers who had been so reckless and extravagant with their money in Ross. An express—which meant then a messenger mounted on a fleet horse—was at once sent off to Dublin, arriving on Sunday, the 8th, at 3 p.m., with the result that St. Quintin and Zekerman were apprehended the same day at 8 p.m., and being examined separately, as was then the custom, confessed the murders, and gave full particulars of the awful occurrences. Mackinley was seized in Dublin on Monday as he was receiving payment from a goldsmith for three hundred pounds worth of dollars. Gidley, who had set out in a post chaise for Cork in order to take ship for England, was captured at Castledermot, County Kildare, on the 10th. Thus in ten days from the annihilation of the Glas family the murderers were caught. The treasure was subsequently found, and the murderers met their deserts.

> "Blood, though it sleeps a time, yet never dies;
> The gods on murderers fix revengeful eyes."

A more pathetic and frightful tale could scarcely be conceived by the most inventive writer of nautical fiction. One point is noticeable, and requires explanation. The murderers spent more than the money alleged to be missing from the treasure; therefore a quantity of Glas's private means must have been

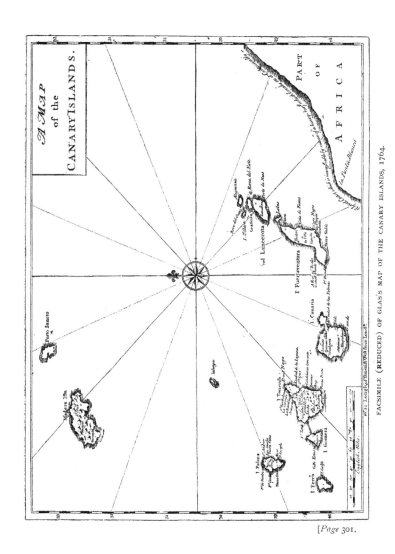

A MAP of the CANARY ISLANDS.

PART OF AFRICA

FACSIMILE (REDUCED) OF GLAS'S MAP OF THE CANARY ISLANDS, 1764.

spent. What has become of the remainder? There is also apparently lost to posterity a MS which Glas was about to publish upon the West Coast of Africa, and which he mentions in his work on the Canary Islands. If he carried it with him, was it taken out of the ship when it came ashore? If he left it in England, where is it? Glas's map of the islands must have been invaluable in his day, and, still being of great interest, it is reproduced here in facsimile.

Though I have prosecuted every inquiry in both County Wexford and County Waterford for relics and traditions of the unfortunate captain and the ill-fated *Sandwich*, I have met with little success. A small, low, sandy bay between Duncannon Fort and Hook Tower has been called Dollar Bay since 1765. The people in the neighbourhood have heard their fathers and other old men tell of many persons who searched for and found a few dollars at this spot. Tradition—and there is every probability of it being correct—says that as the murderers approached the shore they threw out a chest to lighten the boat at Barrow, up the Ross river. This chest was for many years an object of search, but whether it has ever been found tradition sayeth not. A sea-captain told one of my informants that he had once touched the lid of an iron chest in the place indicated, and would have tried to raise it had he not been driven away by others who were watching and searching for it too. The story of the murders and wreck is still related at the little village of Felthard, three or four miles from Dollar Bay.

But though so completely wiped out of men's memories, that at the place where his murderers landed his name is unknown, Captain George Glas will ever live in the minds of all interested in these islands. His careful scientific powers of observation were far in advance of his time. His recorded observations of habits and customs are fresh and real. His sailing directions, exact and practical, are valuable at the present day. His plain, even if blunt, way of dealing with and exposing imposture, arrogance, and bigotry, shows him to have been a man of a well-balanced and liberal mind. Physically strong and mentally healthy and vigorous, Glas was a typical specimen of those old sea-captains who made the name of our native country known and revered in foreign lands.

There is another gentleman here whose father is about to establish a salt-fishery once more at Graciosa.*

We walked along the beach in the evening after dinner. There was a lovely sunset, and peace and calm brooded over land and sea. Somewhere, perhaps upon the spot where we now stand, a Protestant Englishwoman was buried in the sand by the sad sea waves not so very many years ago, Christian burial being quite forbidden for foreigners and heretics on sacred soil belonging to Rome and Spain. Now, however, things are changed for the better, and if other places of worship are not tolerated, at least foreigners are not interfered with as to their consciences, and cemeteries in each island for the burial of their dead are permitted.

January 27th, Sunday.—We turned in to the church this morning, which is a plain edifice, with pillars and arches painted to imitate marble. There are two aisles, the rafters are whitewashed, and the floor is of stone. The choir as well as the altar and reredos are of carved wood, painted white. There is a little organ in the loft. The windows are of square pieces of glass, coloured red, green, yellow, and blue. Seventy chairs, with the names of their owners painted on the back, were all the seats the place contained.

Don Ruperto Vieyra, to whom we have a letter of introduction, called. He has a house at Yaiza, where he has kindly invited us to stay while visiting the southern part of the island. As there is a carretera to Yaiza, and as he possesses one of the only two vehicles in the island, he proposes driving us there

---

* These fisheries seem as yet ill-fated in one way or another, for some time after we left the islands we heard of the sad death by drowning, in one of his own vessels, in which he was returning to England, of the elder gentleman, once more causing the Graciosa establishment to be in the market.

to-morrow if he can find a horse to pair with his, his second animal being ill.

Barilla was at one time a source of much profit to these eastern islands, where it was carefully cultivated. It was used chiefly as a source of carbonate of soda. Previous to the year 1793 the whole of the carbonate of soda of commerce was obtained from the ashes of sea-plants, the chief source being barilla. But the ash of this plant contained only about one-fourth of its weight of carbonate of soda, so the required salt was thus imported from Spain, at a great expense, and consequently the manufactures of glass and soap, in which it is indispensable, were much hampered, and those commodities rendered proportionately dear. During the wars of the French Revolution the price of barilla had risen so much, that Napoleon thought it advisable to offer a reward to the French chemists for the obtaining of all the materials necessary to the making of the carbonate in their own country, "so as to render vain the efforts and hatred of despots." A commission being appointed to investigate the subject in 1794, it reported upon no less than thirteen different processes for the manufacture of soda-ash from common salt. From that day barilla as a source of carbonate of soda ceased to be of importance in the commercial world. Now this important salt is made on a large scale by what is termed the "salt cake process," in which sulphuric acid and common salt are the chief actors in the chemical reactions. Thus, as in the case of cochineal, chemistry has been the innocent means of taking a source of wealth away from these islands. So, instead of, as in 1818, during the Peninsular war, a ton of barilla costing one hundred and sixty-five dollars (thirty-three pounds), it has fallen as low now as nine or ten dollars (thirty-six and forty shillings) a ton. A quintal (one hundred and four pounds) can now be bought for a peseta (ten-pence). The plant is no longer cultivated, but picked up on the mountains, and what small export trade there is in it is with Barcelona.

There are very few birds in cages here. We saw one, a

capirote, in a shop. The little Canarian nightingale is not
found in this island, this one being imported from Canaria.

We took a walk to Los Cruces island. The islet is entirely
cultivated, and there is not a cross to be seen, so wherefore its
name ? It is circular in form and rather low. Round the edge
the rocks are of black lava, of octagon formation, like the
columnar basalt of the Giant's Causeway. We saw cuttle-fish
and innumerable pools, containing prawns and other living
things—

> " Fish, that, with their fins and shining scales,
> Glide under the green wave."

It was quite enjoyable dabbling among the rocks and sitting on
the southern side to leeward. Here, as we sat motionless,
basking in the sunshine, enjoying the quiet, with the ripple of the
waves at our feet, we saw lizards, large and small, that watched
us with their bright eyes, and finding us harmless, came out
also to bask on the warm sea-shore. We returned by a windmill, which was grinding away as if it were not Sunday. Seeing
a woman and some children seated at the open door of the
lower room, some six or eight feet from the ground, we asked if
we might come up, and on receiving a hearty invitation climbed
the ladder. The mill was similar to those we had already seen,
so we soon took our departure, after chatting with the smiling
mother, who seemed quite happy with her children, notwithstanding their close proximity to the unguarded door, a fall from
which seemed imminent to me.

The women here are not good-looking. There is not nearly
so much smoking among the men, but it may be their poverty,
and not their will, that prevents the use of tobacco. Serenos
break the stillness of night, as in the other islands. We
returned by the old part of the town, chiefly a fishing village.
The streets are of rock, upon which the houses are built,
and the sea laps them a few yards from the cottages. A
block of good Carrara marble lies near one of the bridges,
which has lain there a hundred years. A ship laden with the
marble sank in the harbour, and this piece alone was brought

ashore. As we walk up the Calle Principal we see a sun-
dial on one of the houses. Altogether Arrecife is a study.
A mixture of the new and clean, the old and quaint, situated
close to land-locked bays, islets sheltering it from the sea,
strong breezes blowing all that is disagreeable across the
Atlantic, so that even the fishing quarter smells sweet, Arrecife, with curiously coloured hills in the background, forms a
pleasant picture, and is a place where one could linger and
dream away the days, let the time slip past and the years
follow each other in peaceful succession, until aroused at last

CALLE PRINCIPAL, ARRECIFE, LANZAROTE.

too late to find youth gone, grey hairs come, life past, and
nought accomplished.

They marry and are given in marriage here, however—there
seems enough energy for that—and on the days when a girl is
called in church, it is the custom for her friends to go and see
her.

January 28th, Monday.—This morning we visited the fish-
market at the end of the Marina, but fish was conspicuous by its
absence. We then went along the Marina past the casino and
barracks, in which there are six soldiers to defend the port, to

the market. One animal killed each day suffices to supply with meat those who can afford the luxury. Three women were selling radishes and young onions, the sole native vegetables procurable at present. We next visited a shop, where we bought a basket to put on the camel in Fuerteventura with eatables, and saying good-bye to our kind friends, walked to the carretera, where we found Don Ruperto and his nephew awaiting us with a four-wheeled trap.

It was 10.55 a.m. when we started for Yaiza. The modern cemetery, twelve or thirteen years old, we passed a long way outside of the town, at the end of the sandy beach, the older cemetery, nearer the town, being now disused. There are twenty-two kilometres of completed road to Yaiza, made in 1862, and eleven kilometres northward to Teguise.

Lanzarote is an island of curiosities, and we were now to encounter a peculiarity. About the fourth kilometre we were brought up by a sand-hill in the middle of the road. These sand-hills are caused by the wind blowing steadily in one direction. They are called *medaños*, and in this island they cross from Penedo Bay in the north to the spot we are now traversing in the south. There are numbers of them, and they move slowly forward year after year, like living creatures, until they are finally blown into the sea on the south-eastern shore. They always take the same course, a broad, direct road in a straight line from one side to the other. This one on the carretera will take three or four years to get over, and meanwhile the traffic has to go round it to windward. We suggested that the obvious course would be to hasten its movements by human labour, but Don Ruperto laughed, and said, " There are only six or eight carriages in the island, of these but two are capable of being used, so it is not worth the trouble and expense, for camels and horses can walk round it." So we got out of the carriage, and the horses were led round the medaño. It was about twelve to fifteen feet high, and circular in form. It is only in this one place that the medaños cross the road.

A few trees of the tobacco family strive to grow, protected by banks of stones, along this bare tract of country. Single trees are always difficult to cultivate in windy positions; they require to be planted thickly to protect each other, and then the plantation thrives. Sometimes the banks were covered by a pretty mauve flower. We also found on this road the *Rhytispernum arvense* and the *Malcomia litorea* and *Calendula arvensis*. We were surprised to see black sand constantly spread over the land. It seems, however, that this volcanic sand retains the moisture better. The country is more or less green if there be rain from November until May, but there is only a little rain in February, March, and April. January though it was, we were glad to put up our white umbrellas, the sun shone down so powerfully.

The horses did not go well. Don Ruperto's own animal was a fine, plucky little horse, but the other had never been in a vehicle before, and pulled backwards instead of forwards, and was frightened at the pace at which his companion obliged him to go, and at the continual rumbling behind him. It was in vain for Don Ruperto to urge him with voice and stick, for he did not understand pulling, so the other poor horse did all the work, and this one had all the blows. The owner of the strange horse said that the animal had pulled a well-wheel, so it was thought he would understand pulling on the collar! We stopped to rest the horses, the one from its double work and the other from fright, at a ruined house eight kilometres from Arrecife. Flocks of small brown birds, with red beaks, frequent this district. There are a few huts of dusty-looking grey and brown stones, with mud roofs, struggling up the hillside on our right to a church which crowns the summit, the whole designated by the name of Tias. We notice that spades are used here, not the hoe, so the Conejeros are actually more civilised than the Canarios. What would the latter think if they were told this? for they have a supreme contempt for everything connected with these eastern islands, looking upon them as hopelessly poverty-stricken and almost beyond the pale of civilisation. Can any good thing come out of Lanzarote? Nevertheless I venture to say that the Purpurariæ are a very integral part of the Province.

Our strange horse at last succeeded in kicking over the traces and getting astride the pole. We were forced to stop and take him out. I thought of course that we should put the animal in again and drive on, but our friends were afraid of him, and handled him delicately, as if he were combustible, and finally led him to Macher, the other horse drawing the vehicle while we walked alongside. Here we found another horse, which, it was hoped, would work better in harness, and the strange horse was unharnessed, discarded, and left to manage himself or return ignominiously to his former position.

We are driving along a straight road constructed on the littoral, a chain of craters on our right-hand side. It is a vast extent of black country, the volcanic soil of which is most productive. There are some fig trees in pits, with walls raised round them to shield them from the wind. Near the few houses we pass are immense yards, like tennis-courts, of cement, to catch the rain-water and run it off into cemented cisterns. A long scoop of cement on the side of the road, and running quite two or three hundred yards down a gentle elevation, conducts the rainfall on the road to the cistern of a house. Every drop of water is precious. The road is a cinder avenue, straight, level, black. It is 1.35 p.m. as we reach the fourteen-kilometre stone. We met a dromedary and its young one, a pretty little thing, a flock of goats and kids, and a few sheep, white and woolly, like the newly bought " baa-lamb " of a baby.

Large tracts of flat or undulating land are now green with the coming grain. This island is one bed of grain, the level surface being suitable for its production. Having heard that in a good year grain can be exported to Spain, I asked Don Ruperto if he thought this would prove such a productive season. He says, however, that never during his lifetime, fifty years perhaps, has he ever seen a year in which grain could be sent away. We turned off to the right at the twentieth

kilometre by Uga, which lies at the foot of the Montaña del
Fuego, a hill with a red, a fiery red, top, a black base, and
surrounded by black lava. Some of the houses even are black,
built of the lava stones. The road here passes through the
line of craters that we have had on our right. The name
Moñtana del Fuego, marked on the Admiralty chart as much
further north, is very misleading. It is in reality a name
applied in the southern part of the island collectively to all the
craters, which congregate here by the dozen, I had almost said
hundred. My friends named the crater on our right thus, but
the numberless craters which lie in front of us are likewise
called Montañas del Fuego. As we drive through the pass, we
see beside the first crater another, wide and open-mouthed ; in
front is lava, piled in broken masses as far as the eye can reach
to north and south, like a black glacier. Beyond its blackness
to westward rise the craters, red as if sunset hues were athwart
them, or as if the glow of the subterranean fires there were
still uncooled. A few black or dark places appear, as if clouds
were flitting across the red hills.

We are scarcely out of Uga when we reach Yaiza, consisting of straggling huts placed here and there on the edge
of the lava glacier. A few whitewashed houses relieve the
brownness, and above and beyond the village rises the fine,
spacious, and picturesque dwelling of our host, Don Ruperto
Vieyra. It is 2.30 p.m. as we enter through gates into a
courtyard or garden, for the house has wisely been built with
only three sides, allowing of views from all the windows. A
fountain and flowers and plants adorn the patio through which
we are led into the house. Here we are cordially welcomed
by Don Ruperto's sister, Doña Clodosinda Vieyra, and, after
resting for a few minutes and recounting the experiences of
our drive, we go out. First, however, we are taken to our
rooms to see the view, which is magnificent, different from any
I have ever seen. Don Ruperto's house and grounds stand on
sloping ground 650 feet above the sea, a hill rising behind.
This slight elevation above the plain gives a commanding and

extensive view. Mountains are all around, those lying in front being *par excellence* the fire-mountains both in their nature and colour. To the left, at the foot of one fiery crater, was a village, but the lava came, and now only a black sea is left. At our feet lies the lava, which stretches to the base of yonder red mountains. It is an awful as well as a magnificent sight—

YAIZA, LANZAROTE.

infernally suggestive. Yaiza is a curious village, scattered, as are most. Here, however, the houses are actually built in and about the lava, and being constructed of dark stones, the appearance of the place is totally different from that of any other. A few of the larger dwellings are whitewashed, so stand out vividly from amid their dark surroundings.

The priest kindly showed us over the church, which has a stone floor and dark wooden roof, and is poor.

Don Ruperto has a garden and several cisterns, the roofs of which are cemented, to allow of the water draining into them. There are also cemented paths leading from the hills behind, and from every available spot where there is sufficient fall. The fields are square and sunken. They are surrounded by broad walls, along the top of which we walk, the fields lying from six to twenty feet beneath. Doña Clodosinda accompanied us on our walks. She tells me she likes being here much better than in Arrecife, that she is much out, all day nearly, wandering in and out, looking after her garden and animals, and superintending generally. Her life reminds me more of English country life than that of anyone I have yet encountered. The result in happiness to herself is apparent in her bright, contented countenance and active movements.

After dinner and tea, served as in any other gentleman's house in the archipelago—for be it remembered that the Vieyras date from the conquest and were previously "blue blood" in Spain—we ascend to the azotea to catch the sunset. We have of course in travelling partaken of the hospitality of all classes, given kindly and ungrudgingly, but intercourse with the aristocracy of these islands has not proved the least pleasant part of our journey. The gentlefolk of the archipelago are proud of their lineage, and justly so, for the blood that runs in their veins is very "blue." Shut out as many of them are from much, if any, intercourse with the outer world, the natural polish and delicacy of feeling inherited from generations of aristocratic ancestors is still forthcoming in mountain solitudes or amid lava-strewn plains.

We had a suite of rooms in a wing of the house, which, after the way we have to rough it so frequently, was quite luxurious. Every article necessary, or likely to be, for the toilet was, as is customary, provided.

CHAPTER XV.

*THE BURNING MOUNTAINS—THE SALT LAKE—
BETHENCOURT—PAPAGAYO—BOCAYNA STRAIT.*

> No thunders shook with deep, intestine sound
> The blooming groves that girdled her around,
> Her unctuous olives, and her purple vines
> (Unfelt the fury of those bursting mines),
> The peasant's hopes, and not in vain, assured
> In peace upon her sloping sides matured.
> When on a day like that of the last doom,
> A conflagration labouring in her womb,
> She turned and heaved with an infernal birth,
> That shook the circling seas and solid earth ;
> Dark and voluminous the vapours rise,
> And hang their horrors in the neighbouring skies ;
> While through the Stygian veil that blots the day
> In dazzling streaks the vivid lightnings play.
>
> W. COWPER.

January 29th, Tuesday.—The deliciously comfortable beds must be answerable for our oversleeping ourselves this morning and only rising a little before seven o'clock, so it was 7.40 before we left for the Montañas del Fuego, on the opposite side of the lava glacier. Donkeys are the only animals that can scramble over this dreadfully rough ground, a veritable malpais, so two had been procured. A lady's saddle was not to be got, however, for love or money, though there was a gentleman's. Doña Clodosinda looked in despair. What was to be done? "Oh, I can ride bare-backed," I said. "It is not the first time." An albarda was, however, put on the donkey. This is a straw pad with a rope crupper, and with a piece of string for girth, on which everything a donkey carries is usually packed. The donkeys were very small, therefore easily mounted, and, much to the amusement, as well as a little to the anxiety, of our friends, we started, accompanied by a guide.

Turning to the left out of the village, we soon reached the last hut and decent path, and prepared to cross the black desert, " the colossal black lava field of last century." There is a kind of path which winds in and out of the larger lumps of cinders, just broad enough for one person or one animal. It is only made by removing some of the larger pieces of lava and filling in the holes. The lava, from being trodden upon, has been more or less broken. Even, it is not, and frequently our poor little donkeys stumbled or put their feet in holes. Mine was the stronger animal, so John was the first to rest on mother-earth, or rather subterranean lava. His donkey's hind-feet stumbled, and he dropped on his hind-knees, where-upon his rider quietly slipped over his tail and sat on the ground behind him! A little further, and the same donkey put a fore-foot into a hole, and went down on his knees, whereupon John slid off right over his head! That donkey's thoughts must have been worth something, as first its tail and then its ears were thus crushed earthwards. Frequently it fell without these rocking-horse movements, when John would simply stand and pull the animal up under him again! Though I could afford to laugh now, I came to grief later on. At any rate, it proved a merry ride to us, but not to the donkeys. The young one was really too young for the work, and it was pitiable to see its poor little legs all cut and bleeding from the jagged edges of the lava. The reins were halters simply noosed round the animals' noses, so that, if not held tightly, they would slip off. The road was so very rough, and my seat so insecure, that, for the first time since we came to the islands, I was unable to write as I rode. I have five lines in my note-book where I made the attempt ; certainly I can read them, but with difficulty.

The large masses of rock took curious shapes and forms ;

here was a rhinoceros, and there an elephant; there were also several flat places, as if of frozen treacle. Fifty minutes after starting we came to the end of the malpais, and passed on to a smooth plain or lake of black lava, as fine as sand, and as smooth, and absolutely devoid of vegetation. The poor little donkeys' feet sink over the fetlocks in this loose soil. One solitary plant which was in flower we appropriated; its root came up readily, as it had no hold in the soil, a miserably stunted species of *senecio*, four inches in height. Odd pieces of lava and an occasional hillock of it rise from the black plain like rocky islets.

We reach the foot of the first crater at 9 a.m., where, dismounting, our animals are tied to some lava, and we commence the ascent. It is tolerably steep, but fatiguing, owing to the loose, cindery nature of the soil, in which one's feet sink as they did on the Peak of Teide. This ascent was short, and we gained the summit in fifteen minutes, 1,350 feet above the sea. We are standing on a ridge from which we can look over into the crater beneath. The blackness, but not the depth, is very great. From this point we can see innumerable craters all around, with wide, gaping mouths; in front lie five tolerably perfect, on the left three running into the sea, and to the right two. Those to westward on our left are the craters of 1824, where the latest eruptions took place, the furthest cone near the sea being El Cochino, the third which then burst forth. A high hill intervenes to the north-west, the Montaña del Fuego of 1736, or one could doubtless see many more craters on the ridge to northward. The sides of the craters are mostly composed of black cinders, the topmost edges being red, while from their bases to the sea is one mass of lava, except to the east and south, where it has rolled along partly to the sea and partly stopped near Yaiza. The bright, vivid red patches of ground against the black fluid from the bowels of the earth are suggestive. The stillness is oppressive and awful. Nothing moves; there is not a twig to denote which way the wind blows; all is the barrenness of desolation. Two black crows suddenly appear, and as they soar above us we can hear the swish of their wings. They seem like birds of prey waiting until death should overtake the rash intruders into this awful wilderness.

Where we sit the small stones forming the scoriæ are red, yellow, blue-grey, and brown in colour, and there are large surfaces of flat yellow-red stone, red underneath, and some few inches in thickness, that when stood upon crack and give way as caked clay would.

We found precipitated salt lying in many places on the ground. It was near here that the last eruption in the archipelago occurred, that of 1824. But it was the earlier eruptions of 1730-36 that caused the greatest devastation, ruining fruitful valleys and destroying houses. The lava streams of 1824 have in many places surrounded the older craters, which rise like islands, and are green with euphorbia bushes. Near Yaiza " Pele's hair " is found, a sort of thread-shaped lava. The northern and weather side of the immense lava field at our feet is slightly sprinkled with lichen, but devoid of any other sign of vegetation. Our guide wears blue linen trousers, patched with brown, and a white smock. Any colour that differs from the black, yellow, and red around stands out in remarkable relief. Descending into a hollow between the craters, we dug out holes with our hands, and buried some potatoes and eggs a few inches beneath the surface. Our guide, however, was not aware of the hottest part, so, although half cooked at the end of twenty minutes, they were not so thoroughly done as they would have been had we hit upon the right spot. The cinders under the surface were white with heat, and on lifting one out I had to toss it backwards and forwards in my hand like a hot potato, unable to bear the heat. Some rocky lumps afforded us seats, where we could lift our feet for a few minutes off the burning surface which scorched them. The entire surface of the ground in this region of craters is hot, in some spots very hot. The subterranean fires must be near the surface in order to keep up this heat.

Walking was heavy and fatiguing, so we did not wander further amid the craters, but returned to our donkeys, and remounting, set off homewards.   Donkeys are proverbially willing to go home, and mine was no exception, for on going down a sloping place on the black sand it set off at a gallop. I sat on for some time, but was at last obliged to half jump, half tumble off, and run alongside, holding on to the halter until the little animal thought fit to stop.   It was John's turn to laugh now, but the arriero looked scared, why I don't know, for even a fall on that yielding, cindery sand could not have hurt.

We returned by the same tortuous path, the entrance to which would be difficult, if not impossible, for a stranger to find, and which when once found must be strictly followed, as one would keep to the path across a morass.   The colt was so frequently on her knees, that she was abandoned and allowed to walk home riderless, and I walked most of the way, as we could then keep up a faster pace.   We reached Yaiza at noon, where we found almuerzo awaiting us, and serving us as luncheon, after which we set out on another expedition to Januvio.   We should like to see the lava grotto, the Cueva del Mojon, which is worth a visit, but find our time too limited, a day being necessary for the expedition, and as we have written to a gentleman in Fuerteventura that we are coming to-morrow, we must not remain.

Fritsch, who visited the grotto, states that there are gypsum stalactites in it, and its two entrances " open at a sea cliff that must once have been twenty metres high, and from the foot of which the sea has been forced back by the lava of last century. This foreland resembles a mass of water that has been petrified when its angry billows were at their full height.   The grotto forms a high dome, whose roof is somewhat broken, so that the light penetrates from above through an almost circular opening. The passage from this vaulted beginning commences high and broad, and shaped like an elbow sharply bent.   Thus it advances for some distance into the mountain, then it narrows to a sort of split, and after that it is said to grow wide again and proceed in an upward direction."

Places of interest, not of the stereotyped sort, are numerous in Lanzarote. The salt lake of Januvio is one of these. A horse and the two donkeys being procured for the expedition—for Juan Topham accompanied us—we started at 1.20 p.m. The first performance of my donkey on leaving the gates was to cut sharply round the wrong corner towards its home, an action which sent me flying on my feet in a more forcible manner than is usual. Don Ruperto and Doña Clodosinda, who were watching our departure, rushed towards me to see if I were damaged. They were not accustomed to the freaks of the donkey, but I was, and soon jumped on again, and got round the left corner, which was the right one, this time in safety. Following a broad path like a lane, we turn off presently across the open, and descending a low cliff, get into a wide, flat bay, like a Jersey bay. The salt water, however, is enclosed on the further side by lava. In the centre of this lake are several hundred wild ducks. The left side is bounded by low cliffs, the right by the lava-flow of last century, which found its exit to the sea here, and nearly enclosed the bay. We dismounted and walked along the sand to the right to reach its further side. *Patos* (large water-birds) patronise the place, and a huge sea-gull, perched on a tiny rock in the lake, eyes us without moving. Very handsome he looks in his white plumage, with a background of blue lake and mountains. At the side next the sea a little water trickles into the lake, like a streamlet, which I tasted to make sure it was salt, it looked so like fresh water. Walking on, we cross a high bank of large black stones, till we reach the sea. The surf here roars in a totally unnecessary manner, as if much disturbed at the limits of its kingdom being curtailed. Very mysterious appears this lake as seen in the chart, but the mystery is easier to solve when upon the spot. The lava which destroyed the valley at Yaiza entered the sea at one side of this bay, and flowing round, choked the entrance, across which stones have later been thrown by the surf. The water of it still ebbs and flows a little with the rise and fall of the tide, but the lava is an impenetrable barrier to its being ever either emptied or further filled. When the sea is very rough, we are told that more water goes in by the underground entrance.

The view as I sit on the top of the stony bank, with my back to the sea, is very fine. The black mass of stones extends from my feet to the calm blue lagoon, dotted with birds. A high bank bounds the further side of the lake, beyond which a chain of volcanic peaks is clearly cut against the blue sky. In contrast with this peaceful scene, to which the blue lagoon and birds mainly contribute, is the roar and thunder of the white surf on the black beach behind and to right and left. The huge mass of black lava to the immediate north is a silent, though to the senses a powerful, contributor to the stormy side of the picture, for it looks as if endowed with latent force which might become active at any moment. The lava stones on which we sit, rounded by the action of the sea, contain a quantity of green, sparkling pieces, which contrast with their black setting.

Leaving the inky barrier and roaring surf, we walk back over the rough stones to the sand, the original bay, and the foundation on which the stones now rest. It is scattered over with a few rounded lava stones, a quantity of shells, whole and broken, and castings of worms.

When riding to Januvio, we noticed a great number of crosses on the way, placed there by the inhabitants of a village whose burial-ground being at Yaiza pass thither with their dead, and where the coffins rest, erect a cross. Returning, we saw two young dromedaries. They looked pretty creatures, with their fawn-coloured coats. Cisterns abound here, even the smallest house having one. It was with interest we saw barilla growing wild by the wayside, for it is not now cultivated.

I have seldom seen a more wonderful instance of the power of man over drought, that enemy to all vegetation, than is shown by this country seat of our host. It is a perfect oasis in the desert. Rising in front of the house are palms, one in particular a fine and stately tree, which must have waved its leaves over many changes in the valley below, scenes of beauty, a valley well cultivated and rich in agricultural wealth, houses well built and numerous, all overwhelmed by the approach of a thick, dull, slowly moving, but irresistible mass of molten mud. Now only the edges of the valley remain where the mass could not flow upwards, so the stately palm waved untouched while destruction flowed onwards a dozen yards below its feet. When, in the course of years, the lava field cooled, the very poorest of the islanders built themselves huts on the edges of the lava itself, for it was "no man's land" now, and gradually Yaiza became populated, it and its district numbering some fifteen hundred souls. The neighbouring village of Uga, which is included in these numbers, has more country houses of the better classes, and lying further back from the valley of desolation, contains more gardens. But it is in Yaiza that one gets such a wonderful combination of the sublime and beautiful, the fire-mountains and the placid lake, and in proximity to these wonders of nature, the hand of man has wrought a garden in the desert, where good Samaritans take pity on the passing strangers wafted to their shores, bid them welcome, entertain them royally, and send them on their way rejoicing.

If Nature be inhospitable to look at, her sons make up for her lack of kindness. The men of Lanzarote are very civil and polite, and rich and poor are on hospitable thoughts intent.

January 30th, Wednesday.—It was with real reluctance we left our kind friends and prepared to start for Fuerteventura. A *silla Inglesa* had been provided for the dromedary we rode, for there was a second for the luggage, so we were in luxury to-day. This consists of two legless arm-chairs * with low backs and swinging boards, attached by ropes to the chairs, on which to place the feet. Beneath the seats are drawers, and as I was the lighter weight, a few stones were placed in mine to make the balance even. So at 8.5 a.m. we said

* See Title-page.

good-bye to Yaiza, and turned round by the back of the
house up a cultivated valley between low hills, in which there
was a small crater, open, as usual, to the north.

I notice that the men have short necks in this island.   The
camellero to-day is called Matias.   Our dromedary's mouth is
covered with froth, the result of green food, we are told.   We
ascend the valley, and cross over a dip in the hills at its
upper end, and passing round the outer and western edge, gain
a good view of Januvio, the surf breaking on its lava-bound
shore standing out clearly in the sunshine.   Beneath and in
front of us lies a flat plain, the upper part of which is
cultivated, and over which the yellow-brown houses of Breñas
are dotted.   Nothing further breaks the level monotony as the
eye travels southwards, until it is stopped by Montaña Roja,
rising at the extreme end near the southern shore.   Beyond
this is the Bocayna strait, looking from here but a narrow
strip, in which Lobos, like a tadpole, floats, and rises black
against the lines of hills in Fuerteventura.   A long stretch of
white strand bounds the northern shore of the longest island in
the archipelago.

Here we look down upon historic ground, for the district
below is Rubicon.

> " The mountains look on *Rubicon*,
> And *Rubicon* looks on the sea,"

if one may be permitted to substitute one name for another.
San Marcial lies amid the hills on our left, and we pass the
outskirts of its few houses.   Once it was the headquarters of
the Church, and it was here the first church in the archipelago
was built, and where Guardafia, the King of Lanzarote, was
baptised.   The bishopric of Rubicon was established in
1408, and the first bishop who resided there was a Franciscan,
Alberto de las Casas.   This settlement and the castle of
Aquila, near to which we shall embark to-day, were the headquarters of the Spaniards until Gran Canaria was finally
subjugated, three-quarters of a century later, when the see

was removed to Las Palmas, and the wars and intrigues moving further westward, Lanzarote sank once more into comparative obscurity. Raids of pirates and attacks by English ships, which, to all intents and purposes, were equally piratical, brought occasional and unenviable notoriety upon the island, but since the eruptions of its volcanoes little has been heard or thought of Lanzarote, whose existence, much less its name, is scarcely known to the nations of the world.

It was with only fifty-three followers that Bethencourt reached the island of Graciosa after leaving Cadiz. They apparently sailed on to the south of Lanzarote, where they landed, and finding no inhabitants, encamped. However, the Conejos seeing that the French—for Bethencourt * and most of his followers belonged to that nation—were quietly encamped, some of them ventured to go to the strangers and actually assisted them to build a fort, that of Rubicon, or Aquila Tower, the one we see lying beneath, and near to which, where the invaders landed, we shall presently embark. As the explorers were so few in number, Bethencourt himself was obliged to return to Spain for supplies. Failing to obtain aid from France, he applied to relations whom he had in Spain, but was assisted chiefly by Henry III. of Castile, who also granted him the title of King of the Fortunate Islands.

There is a significant and curious story about Guardafia, the King of Lanzarote. There being war between Spain on the one hand and Portugal and England on the other, a fleet was fitted out by the former in 1377. These vessels encountered a storm, in which the admiral's ship ran before the wind until she anchored at Lanzarote. "Here the Spaniards landed, and were kindly received by the natives, who treated them with the

---

* "Messire Jean de Bethencourt, Knight, was of noble birth, and held the title of Baron in right of the Barony of St. Martin le Gaillard, in the Comté d'Eu, where he had a strong castle, which was taken and retaken several times in the wars with England. Monstrelet speaks of its final siege and ruin in 1419. It came by inheritance to Messire de Bethencourt from his grandmother, Dame Isabeau de St. Martin" ("The Canarian," page xlii., Hakluyt Society).

best that the island afforded." The King then was one Qonzamas, with whom the admiral, Don Martin Ruiz de Avendano, lived, in return for which hospitality he had a daughter by the King's wife, Fayna. This girl, Yco, who was very fair, married one of the royal family of Lanzarote, who ultimately became king, and her son was Guardafia, who was king when Bethencourt landed. He had not obtained regal power without dispute. For the natives insisted that Yco was not noble, being the daughter of a stranger, and not of Qonzamas. Her complexion seems, however, to have led to this conclusion, so it was decided to put the matter to a test, and Yco and three female servants were shut up in Qonzamas's house and there smoked. Yco stood the test of nobility from having secretly conveyed a wet sponge into the house, which she held to her mouth, and thus lived while the servants were suffocated. Guardafia was therefore pronounced noble and allowed to reign.

But to return to sub-conquest history. Gadifer seems to have considered that one of the ships of the expedition belonged to him, and upon one occasion the sailors mutinied and refused to take him or Bethencourt on board his own vessel. There is a curious drawing from the original work in the possession of Madame de Mont Ruffet of this event, which was photographed by the Hakluyt Society, and which they have courteously given me permission to use. Its chief value lies in the fact that the arms of Bethencourt and the Chevalier Gadifer de la Salle, the latter having a cross, are depicted in the engraving.

When Bethencourt started for Spain, owing to the above mutiny, he left in charge of the garrison one Berthin de Berneval, who appears to have been under the civil jurisdiction of Gadifer de la Salle. Berthin, however, seems from the beginning to have entertained ideas of his own about the conquest, and made a party among the men of the expedition. After Bethencourt had left, a ship arrived at Lobos, to which Gadifer sent Berthin, thinking it was the *Tajamar*, with whose captain he was intimate. It proved to be another, the *Morella*, and Berthin tried to persuade the captain and crew to help him against the Conejos, a piece of treachery against Bethencourt in which they indignantly refused to assist. Meanwhile Gadifer, unsuspicious of treachery, set sail, with one Remonnet de Leneden, from Rubicon to Lobos, to procure seals to make shoes for the crew. They remained in Lobos several days, until, provisions failing, Gadifer sent Leneden to Rubicon for food. Meantime Berthin on Lanzarote had behaved very treacherously

HOW THE MARINERS' REFUSED GADIFER ADMISSION ON BOARD OF HIS OWN SHIP.

to the inhabitants, and had entrapped a number of them and, with various excuses, put them on board the *Tajamar*, now lying at Graciosa. The King was among the prisoners, but by his prowess escaped. Berthin stayed on the *Tajamar*, but sent some allies to Rubicon for provisions. These, finding the boat had returned from Lobos, took possession of it, and, with more of Berthin's confederates, sailed to Graciosa, notwithstanding the prayers of Gadifer's friends on his behalf. The *Tajamar's* boat, with Berthin's men on board, came the next day to Rubicon, and was soon followed by Berthin in the other boat, when a scene of pillage of stores and frightful treatment of some French women occurred at the castle. The two boats laden with provisions, arms, and various private goods belonging to Gadifer, set sail to the *Tajamar*. Gadifer's friends were in despair about him, and sent the two chaplains and two other gentlemen to beg assistance from the *Morella*, which was now also lying at Graciosa, praying the captain to relieve Gadifer and his eleven companions, who must be at the point of death, "having been eight days without provisions." The captain of the *Morella* accordingly sent Ximenes to Rubicon, where, accompanied by four friends of Gadifer's and provisions, they crossed in a little cockboat, which had been left without oars at Rubicon, to Lobos. The two chaplains, seeing from the deck of the *Morella* the two boats full of provisions approaching the *Tajamar*, begged the captain to go with them to that vessel, where they confronted Berthin, who, however, maintained that all he had was his own. In the end Berthin set sail, first, however, wisely putting his accomplices ashore, in case they should tell tales to Bethencourt. These traitors, afraid to brave Gadifer's wrath, sailed to Barbary, where their boat was upset, and ten out of the twelve drowned. Berthin arrived at Cadiz safely, but on board was a friend of Gadifer's, who cast Berthin and his friends into prison, and told Bethencourt, to his astonishment, of all the doings at Lanzarote. He then sent a vessel with provisions to Gadifer's relief, at the same time telling him that he had done homage to the King of Spain for the islands. This communication was not welcome to Gadifer, who hoped to have shared in the possession of the islands.

The bad faith of Berthin in stealing the natives made them look with suspicion on all their new friends, against whom they turned. There was, however, a traitor among the Conejos, one Asche, who, aspiring to be king of Lanzarote, came and spoke to Gadifer, telling him that as long as Guardafia lived there would be no peace, and that he would help to give him into their hands. Asche meant not only to betray his king, but also to take Gadifer and his people prisoners. The plans miscarried, and although for a short time Guardafia was made prisoner and Asche reigned, the latter was killed in the end. European blood had been shed—that of one man—for which reason the invaders thought themselves justified in waging a relentless war against the natives, nominally to punish them, but their real purpose is quaintly indicated by the dual chroniclers, who state that "they used all their efforts to make captives, for it was their only solace till the arrival of M. de Bethencourt"!

When the relief ship arrived from Spain, Gadifer sailed in her to Erbanie (Fuerteventura), where he landed and met with some adventures. He then sailed round the other islands without landing, and returned to Lanzarote, anchoring this time at Aratif or Alcatif (? Arrecife), when the vessel returned to Spain. Bethencourt now arrived at his kingdom, where he was welcomed in a truly loyal manner by both Christian natives and Europeans. The Majo king, finding he could not contend against the superior forces of the invaders, also became submissive once more, and the remainder of his people following his example, Lanzarote was finally conquered, or, as the pious priests write, "M. de Bethencourt and Messire Gadifer then went and spoke together apart, and embraced each other, weeping for joy at having been the means of bringing so many souls into the way of salvation, and then arranged how and when they should be baptised."

After this Fuerteventura was visited and conquered, and the fort of Richerocque built. Then Gadifer and Bethencourt fell out, because the former thought his services deserved more substantial remuneration. Both went to Spain, and the matter ended in Gadifer retiring to France and being heard of no more, while Bethencourt returned to his kingdom. Here he settled many affairs, especially in Fuerteventura, which he completely conquered. He then revisited France, where he persuaded a number of people, including nobles and their wives, mechanics, and musicians, to join him and return with him to Lanzarote.

His retinue was now so magnificent in the eyes of the simple inhabitants, that they thought still more of their new king ; and the settlers he had brought with him were well pleased with the country, which at that time seems to have been wooded and watered, several springs being mentioned by the historians. Crossing to Fuerteventura, Bethencourt went to his other fort of Baltarhayz (Val Tarajal). Here, a child being baptised in honour of his return, "some vestments, an image of Our Lady, and other church furniture, as well as a very beautiful missal and two little bells, each weighing a cent," were presented to the chapel, which Bethencourt ordered to be called "The Chapel of Our Lady of Bethencourt," and Le Verrier, one of the chroniclers, was established there as cura. This is probably near the present town of Betancuria.

It was after these events that Bethencourt visited Gran Canaria and Palma, Hierro and Gomera, establishing colonies in the two last. He found houses for the settlers by the simple but doubtful means of taking the natives prisoners and giving the colonists their habitations ! Bethencourt then returned to Baltarhayz, where he arranged the civil and military affairs of the newly conquered countries. His nephew, Maciot de Bethencourt, he made governor of all the islands in his absence, for he intended returning to France for a time. Before going he allotted land to the late kings of Lanzarote and Fuerteventura and to all his followers, and, it is said, succeeded in pleasing everybody. Lastly, he gave a great feast in his castle at Rubicon, to which all the gentlemen and the three kings were invited, when he made a speech and presented Maciot as his representative, whom they were to obey.

When Bethencourt arrived in Spain, he went to the court, where he was well received and sent on to Rome to procure a bishop for the islands. He then retired to his estates in Normandy, where he was enthusiastically welcomed, and where he remained until his death, in 1422, without revisiting his Canary kingdom.

Thus ends the history of a most remarkable man, and one

who seems to have been as much loved as feared. The dual chronicle of the brother-priests ends also here, and it is to the MS translated by Glas that we must look for any further accurate information. There have been MSS found from time to time, especially in the Purpurariæ, but they have all been lost or destroyed during the invasions from the coast of Barbary.

I am indebted to the Hakluyt Society for permission to reproduce their portrait of Bethencourt. Concerning this like-ness of the conqueror of the Canaries, the Society says, "There is no warranty for the authenticity of the portrait. The best arguments in favour of the supposition that it may have been derived from a genuine original are the following. 1. The conqueror survived his return from the Canaries to Normandy nineteen years. 2. The distinction which he had earned for himself, as one who was to live in the minds of men, would suggest the desirableness of a portrait of some kind. 3. The engraved portrait was issued with the sanction of Galien de Bethencourt, the hereditary possessor of the family documents. 4. It exhibits a remarkable distortion in the left eye, which, if unwarranted by a prototype, would be a needless defect, very unlikely to be fancifully inserted in the portrait of an otherwise handsome man."

It is upon the ground of these adventures that we now tread, and look upon the scene that Bethencourt knew so well. We passed numbers of flocks feeding on the vegetation which has sprung up with the winter's rain. As we neared Papagayo we rode in and out of sand hills, and at the bottom of one of these came to a well. A herd, long, lean, and scantily clothed, looked like an ancient inhabitant as he tended his goats. He drew water from the well, and filled two stone troughs, at which the goats eagerly drank. The scene was very Eastern, the drawing of water for the animals, of which one often reads, and scarcely understands the allusion. The two troughs had also a meaning, for one was for goats, the other for sheep, the shepherd carefully dividing them from each other.

Boccaccio in his narrative already quoted, though he must

have seen Lanzarote—for he landed on Fuerteventura—
gives no account of the inhabitants of the former island. But
of the Majos he says that they were naked, and like savages
in their manner and appearance. Azurara's account of the
people in these two, being subsequent to the conquest, is of
little use, for we have the earlier account of Bethencourt's
chroniclers. Indeed, Azurara scarcely mentions the customs or
habits of the already-conquered islands. Bontier and Le Verrier
state that the people of Lanzarote were tall and brown, " a fine
race. The men go quite naked. Excepting for a cloak over
their shoulders, which reaches to their thighs, they are indifferent
to other covering. The women are beautiful and modest.
They wear long leather robes, which reach down to the ground.
Most of them have three husbands, who wait upon them
alternately by months. The husband that is to live with the wife
the following month waits upon her and her other husband the
whole of the month that the latter has her, and so each takes
his turn. The women have a great many children, but have
no milk in their breasts. They therefore feed them with their
mouths, and thus their under-lips are longer than their upper
ones, which is an ugly thing to see." Polyandry seems to have
been practised only in this island, though it may have been
also in Fuerteventura. In all the other islands monogamy was
maintained by law. There is a tribe in the Himalayas which
practises polyandry at the present day. The priests also
state that there were only three hundred fighting men left
in the island, it had been so devastated by pirates. The
MS translated by Glas classes these two islands together in
most of their habits and customs. It mentions that the
natives " were of a humane, social, and chearful disposition,
very fond of singing and dancing. They were very nimble,
and took great delight in leaping and jumping, which were
their principal diversions." If when quarrelling a man killed
his enemy, entering through the door of his house to do so,
he was not punished, but if he came upon him unawares,
the murderer was put to death by being carried to the sea-

PORTRAIT OF MESSIRE JEAN DE BETHENCOURT, KING OF THE CANARIES.

[*Page* 331.

shore, where his head was placed on a flat stone and his brains dashed out by another stone being dropped upon it. They, like the rest of the islanders, appear to have been splendid swimmers, and able to kill fish with sticks. They lived in stone houses, built without cement. They appear to have also had houses of worship, built in circular form and of the same material, in which they do not seem to have worshipped idols, but one God, to whom they offered libations of milk and butter, raising their hands heavenwards in supplication. Their dress was a cloak and hood of goat-skins and shoes of skins, with the hairy side outwards. They seem also to have had head-dresses, adorned with feathers, and in the case of the king with sea-shells. Goat's butter was used, as elsewhere, to cure wounds, and was put in earthen vessels and buried in the ground to preserve it. It was one of these jars we saw in the museum at Las Palmas. The dead were buried in caves, and goat-skins laid above and below them.

A little to our right as we ride along lies Aquila Tower, the castle of Rubicon, so often mentioned. The southern coast of this island is very beautiful, deeply indented as it is by little bays and sandy coves, bound by steep rocks. It is so charming, that one wishes to linger here. I do not wonder at the colonists from Normandy being satisfied with their new quarters, nor shall I pity Mr. B—— if he succeeds in establishing his fishery on this coast. The Punta de Papagayo runs into the sea beyond, and protecting the bay of that name, towards which we are now riding. Suddenly we come upon a steep descent, almost a precipice, near the edge of which, by a solitary hut, we dismount. The scene is one of exquisite beauty. Basaltic precipices are upon two sides, a silvery strand, backed by a cliff of sand, forming the third. The sea is deep blue, and upon its rippling surface, in the shelter of the bay, float white-plumaged sea-fowl and a boat. The sky above is blue; the sun is shining. Verily we have reached the Isles of the Blest.

Addressing a fisherman, who issues from the hut beside

which our dromedary kneels, we find he is the man who has received the order from Don Ruperto to take us across. It is almost necessary to order a boat by *forbud*, as the Norwegians say, if one do not desire to delay in crossing the Strait of Bocayna, otherwise the men may all be away fishing. The peasants usually pay one peseta for the journey from Papagayo to Corralejo when a boat is going there. A camel in these two westerly islands by the day, with its camellero, who provides it and himself with food, is two shillings, and the fare by schooner from Gran Tarajal to Las Palmas is four pesetas (three shillings and fourpence).

PAPAGAYO BAY.

There is a small trade done here in stone filters, the material for forming which is found a little distance off in the hills where they are cut, and brought here to be exported to the other islands.

It was 11.35 a.m. when we arrived, and 12.10 p.m. when we started for Fuerteventura, so we had a little time, which we devoted to photography. A couple of children, who had been playing on the strand below, suddenly perceived us, and in an incredibly short time scrambled in their bare feet up the cliff. Two women, also barefooted, belonging to the cottage, offered us seats inside, which we declined, preferring to remain outside to feast upon the view. The wind was blowing fiercely, so we had strong hopes of being carried rapidly across the narrow channel.

When ready to start, the men shouldered our baggage, and signing to us to follow, disappeared over the edge of the cliff. Hurrying after them, we found a narrow path descending partly in steps, and jumping and clambering, we arrived in a few minutes at the bottom on a firm, sandy beach. Here we were completely sheltered from the wind. A man carried me on board, a boy having previously divested himself of his clothing, a ragged shirt and short trousers, and swimming out to the boat, boarded and brought her near shore. The sail, a sort of lug, was immediately hoisted, and, by the aid of a few strokes of the oars, we got out to where a slight breeze rippled the calm blue waters, and where the gulls floated, regardless of our presence. Looking back as we glided out of the bay, we were enchanted with its beauty, as it nestled at the feet of the stern rocks on either side.

Unfortunate, depopulated, poverty-stricken, yet kindly Lanzarote! I do not know among all the seven an island for which I entertain more love. Is it because pity is akin to love?

> "Once more upon the waters! yet once more!
> And the waves bound beneath me as a steed
> That knows his rider. Welcome to their roar!
> Swift be their guidance, wheresoe'er it lead!"

Our crew consists of two old men and two boys besides the skipper, who sits with the tiller in his hand. He is dressed in a straw hat and linen smock and trousers, and has a rich brown beard and a fine face. All have open countenances, and are much superior to the fishing population of the other islands. The two other men wear hats that were once black and are now soiled, brown, and old; the boys are dressed similarly, save that they are barefooted, and their trousers are turned up to their knees.

Instead of encountering a small gale, as we expected, we found that the wind, which blew so fiercely a few hundred feet above the sea across Papagayo, was only a pleasant breeze on the surface of the water as we glided out of the bay and beyond the point. As we reached mid-channel, however, it failed us, or we got into calms, until near the island of Lobos, where the wind again filled our sails, and we sped merrily on into Corralejo. The sailing directions of Captain Glas for passing through this channel we thus found correct: "She" (a vessel) "must not stand to the northward, otherwise she will immediately lose it again" (a constant northerly wind), "but must stand towards Lobos, the nearer she approaches to which she will have the wind more large; and before she is two-thirds channel-over, she will have a steady wind at north or north-north-east." He goes on to say that there is a channel between Lobos and Fuerteventura, safe for those who know it.

Though calm and lovely to-day, these straits sometimes present anything but those serene features. " When there is a great westerly swell hereabouts, the sea breaks on the rocks at the north-west end of Lobos with such violence, that it is horrible to behold; and I may, without exaggeration, affirm that I have seen breakers there near sixty feet high. Was one of these to strike the strongest ship, she would be staved to pieces in a moment."

Lobos is an islet or rock, with low ground on either side of the centre height, where now there is a little green vegetation, but the greater part is sand. Shipwrecked mariners would find shelter now, for there is a lighthouse upon its northern extremity. It was 2 p.m. as we passed it, our expected half-hour's voyage being really one of nearly two and a half hours. While crossing we passed a couple of fishing boats, who exchanged "buenos tardes" with our crew.

Our boat was about twenty feet in length, broad in the beam, and stoutly built, and her crew were the most sailorlike men we came across. The proximity of the two islands is conducive to intercourse, and encourages a seafaring life. Our skipper, albeit unconscious of the existence of Glas, sailed by his directions, so we got a near view of Lobos, where the unfortunate Gadifer and his eleven companions were nearly starved to death. As we looked towards Fuerteventura we could see a number of rocks, like castles, which no doubt misled the first conquerors, who thought that the Majos, as the inhabitants of this island were called, had fortified dwellings.

Corralejo seems to be a collection of brown and yellow huts built on the sand. As objects become more distinct we see a camel, waiting for us no doubt.

CHAPTER XVI.

FUERTEVENTURA — CORRALEJO — OLIVA — BEEHIVE GRAIN STACKS—PUERTO CABRAS—MISMO.

I will fear you, O stars, nevermore.
I have felt it! Go on, while the world is asleep,
Golden islands, fast moored in God's infinite deep.
JEAN INGELOW.

Among no people are the relations between kindred more cordial, or between superior and dependant more frank and genial. In these respects there still remains, in the provincial life of Spain, much of the vaunted simplicity of the olden times.—WASHINGTON IRVING.

January 30th, Wednesday (continued).—The whole fishing population—not a great multitude, however—met us on the rocks as we dropped our sail and glided in. Among them we had noticed a man well dressed, and with a white umbrella, whom we thought could not belong to the cluster of huts called Corralejo. This turned out to be our next host, Don Victor Acosta, who had come all the way from Oliva to meet us, with two camels for us and our luggage, a truly hospitable welcome to Fuerteventura. Don Bernardo Calero, to whom we had a letter of introduction, was in bed ill, so handed us over to Don Victor's kind hospitality.

The good wives of the fishermen urged us to enter their houses and have some coffee. Poor souls, they would have given us the best they had, and scarcely a stitch upon their backs or a quarto in their pockets. We went into one house, or rather room, for the four walls contained but the

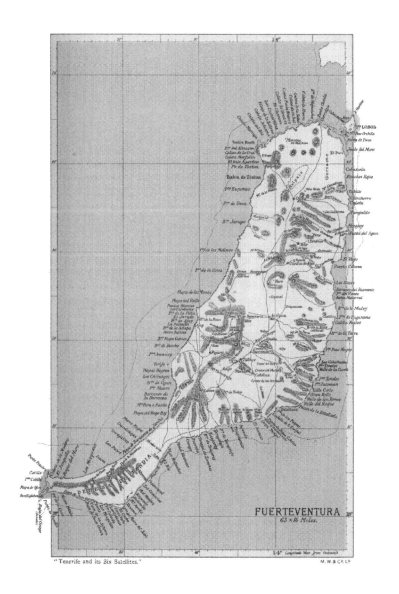

FUERTEVENTURA
63 × 16 Miles.

single apartment. Two low stretcher-beds, a few chairs, and one table formed the furniture. The floor was earthen and uneven, and the whole bespoke poverty of the necessaries of life, but not of the beauties, for through the open door sparkled the blue sea, as it lay like a lake, surrounded by the black rocks of Lobos, the mountains of Lanzarote, and the white strand of Fuerteventura. I had stooped to pick up a shell as I walked to the hut, and the woman who was with us eagerly asked did I like shells. As I answered in the affirmative, she sent off a girl, who brought in a basket of very pretty ones, picked up on the beach by the children, she said. Conch and cowries were the best, of which I was glad to have a few, the children being delighted with quartos in return.

Saying good-bye to our fine Conejero fisherman, who took the money bargained for cheerfully, and did not worry us with tiresome bickerings, we started at 2.20 p.m. in comfortable chairs on one camel, the luggage being on another. The chairs were padded, and covered with bright yellow leather. The baggage camel led the way, and we followed, a manservant walking in front, leading our dromedary by the usual two or three yards of halter, and our host, Don Victor, on a donkey by our side. The little feet of the donkey seemed to move very fast, while our camel, who was a particularly slow and stately individual, kindly condescended to place one foot before the other.

Behind Corralejo the sand extends for some distance, a little vegetation holding it together. Leaving the sand, we entered a curious district, consisting of clumps of rocks, or rather large volcanic stones, massed together and forming separate heaps. The black stones were partially covered with a grey lichen, and green vegetation of all kinds cropped up between them, giving them the appearance and beauty of rockeries. Our path, forced to turn and twist among these stony hillocks, helped the delusion as we wound slowly through this natural rockery. Beyond, towards Toston, and hidden among these hillocks, are the remains of some Majo dwellings. The ascent was gradual. On our right lay some volcanic hills and craters, the highest being Vahuhu, the caldera of which is large. The ground to our left and in front is entirely covered with greyish black stones, lichen-grown, and green with rama (?) bushes, which appear luxuriant and abundant. The view backwards is very pretty, almost beautiful, for the blue sea makes the most uninteresting landscape glorious. This is not uninteresting by any means. Far distant are the peaks of Lanzarote, the blue sea below and blue sky above vying with each other as to which should produce the most brilliant effect. The sea, however, calling in the accessories of fishing-boats and white sails, wins. The black, headlike rock of Lobos, with its long line of equally black rocks, running eastward, encircled in blue, and at our feet the white sand near Corralejo, add to the beauty of the scene.

For a couple of hours we ascended slowly and gradually, without meeting any living thing. Two dogs, which belonged to our host, scoured the stony land on either side of the road, in search of rabbits probably, but only succeeding in disturbing some distant flocks of goats, had to be recalled, and being chastised verbally, slunk behind, with drooping ears and tails. At last we met a boy on donkey-back, bound for Corralejo, and a little further on a couple of men and camels. All raised their hats civilly as we wished each other " buenos tardes." The roads here and in Lanzarote are broad, as broad as made roads, and it depends upon the nature of the ground what they are like. Some are smooth and stoneless, others are bare rocks or have points of lava sticking up between the soil, but they are never really bad roads, such as we encountered in the other islands. We reached Villa Verde at 5.30, all the country until then being one mass of stones. Herbage, however, grows plentifully among them, and large districts are enclosed with strongly built, high walls of loose stones, inside which the camels, donkeys, horses, goats, and sheep of the various owners feed. Our animals, seeing their companions in these enclosures, were much exercised in their minds, and the donkey especially gave vent to his unoiled hinges in a manner truly awful. Our host quaintly remarked, after we had enjoyed several repetitions of the braying, " Buenos pulmones ! " (" Good lungs ! "). The unusual appearance of a quantity of blue smoke against the clear sky made me ask what was astir. We found that there was a baking of bread going on for a fiesta on Saturday of the patron saint of the village, the Virgin of Candelaria. Bread is a luxury only for feast-days.

The people of this island, as well as Lanzarote, seem to be bright, cheerful, and witty. The appearance of the Majoreros, however, is different. They are tall, high-shouldered, and angular, with very large, liquid brown eyes. The women one notices more particularly than the men for their cheerfulness, which is sadly wanting in the other islands. The perpetual sighing out of " Si, Señor ! " is entirely absent here. Perhaps the air of Fuerteventura is good for digestion !

Villa Verde is a cluster of houses, or rather a slope on which are brown huts, with slanting roofs, chiefly of mud. It well deserves its name at present, for everything is young and green, even the ugly cochineal cactus. Stone walls divide the land into square fields, which in this village are planted chiefly with potatoes and the cochineal cactus. We reached the church at 5.45 p.m. It was rapidly getting dark, and beautiful as the silver crescent line of the young moon is, it does not give much light. The sticks for the photographic tripod slipped off the camel in front, luckily before it was quite dark. Everything put on a camel's back requires to be made very secure, or the severe jolting it gets rapidly loosens it. For human beings, however, the reverse is better. Any sort of riding is easier, less fatiguing, and safer when the body gives way to the motion of the animal.

The evening air was sensibly colder, and we found the thermometer at 62.6° F. (17° C.). It was quite dark, save for the brilliant stars, when we arrived in Oliva, and passing over what seemed to be a common, stopped at a long, low, one-storied house, at 6.20 p.m.

We had been told we should get nothing to eat in Fuerteventura. This was our supper, at 8 p.m.: fried eggs, mutton, fresh pork, excellent white, fresh goat's cheese, particularly good bread, fancy home-baked biscuits, and coffee. The meat was tender, and everything from Oliva except the wine, which was from Lanzarote. It being, however, more acid than our host liked, he had mixed it with champagne, an invention of his own which seemed rather odd, as the chief property of champagne is its effervescing quality. This wine was drunk at any interval after mixing, not immediately; therefore all the carbonic acid gas had gone off.

The comedor, and indeed the whole house, reminded us of an English country farm, if we can except the lack of fireplaces. The dining-room, a square room, with a window near the ceiling, was wainscoted, with large cupboards let into the wall, in which the best china was kept. Outside the window was a canvas blind on a frame to keep out the sun. This of course would be unnecessary in England, where the sun does not favour us with too much of his light. Our large and lofty rooms were immediately on the right as we entered the door. The windows were about five feet high from the floor, but window-seats and a place for the feet enabled one by climbing to see out. One window in the room was on the sunny side of the house, so was protected by venetian shutters outside glass windows, a thick linen blind and solid wooden shutters inside; all were closed and fastened. Coloured prints of the usual style adorned the walls. These pictures are universal in the islands, and generally represent the same scenes.

When first we came to the islands, the darkness of the rooms, amounting to gloom, was very depressing. After a time, however, we became only too glad to escape the glare, the flies, and mosquitos. Much, however, might be done among the wealthier classes, in Indian fashion, by means of straw mattings and curtains, to exclude everything except the air. It is also curious to note that—I suppose from using them so little—even the best houses have dirty windows. It is an absolute necessity of course with us in England to let in as much light as possible, and so we look to the cleanliness of our glass. The dining-rooms in houses here are generally entirely closed up by shutters and doors, and at the last moment, when dinner is served, the light is partially let in ; it is only by this means one can eat in peace, unmolested by flies.

At dinner we were placed near each other, Don Victor sitting further apart. Our hostess superintended the waiting of two servants. The old-fashioned English appearance of the room was further increased by our host lighting his after-dinner cigarette with flint and steel. When showing them some photographs after dinner, we were soon surrounded by three or four girls and a couple of men and boys who had been waiting outside the door in the patio, and now rushed in to look.

January 31*st, Thursday.*—There was a north-easterly wind this morning, fit to blow a house down. The temperature in our room, with the window open, at 8.30 a.m., was 62·6° F. (17° C.). The early morning air is always fresh and invigorating, so, throwing open the green wooden shutters and mounting to the window-seat, I looked out to enjoy the breeze and the scene. The first impression reminded one of many a village in Cambridgeshire. The house, long, straggling, one-storied, flat-roofed, with white walls and grass-green door and window-shutters, faces the north on one side of a large, common-like piece of ground. The opposite side, some 400 or 500 yards distant, is lined with a fringe of small houses, which, like the one we are in, are low, one-storied, and flat-roofed. The intervening ground is flat as a bowling-alley, the soil being reddish and clayey, scattered over with small stones. A few patches of green and an occasional yellow flower here and there alone enliven its red monotony. But if the flat roofs on a closer inspection had not dispelled the Cambridge-like aspect of

the view, the string of camels slowly wending their way across
the far end of the common would effectually have done so.   On
the left is the church, whose square, well-built stone tower is
more in harmony with the scene than is that of many churches
we have seen.   The chancel walls are whitewashed, and the
roof covering the three aisles is pointed and of greyish red tiles.
Forming a background to the church, a sharp-pointed, slender
volcanic mountain attracts attention.   Lying between it and
the church are farm-buildings, interspersed with the beehive-
like grain-stores.   Behind the houses on the opposite side of
the common, and on the right, the rough, broken-up appearance
of the ground and its dull grey-green colour show that a lava
stream has there found its course.   To the extreme right are

OLIVA CHURCH AND CAMEL CAUSEWAY.

two low, flattened peaks and several farm-buildings, the majority
of which have pointed and brilliantly red-tiled roofs.   Like
many a Cambridge landscape, the very peacefulness of the
scene, the quiet monotony of the flat distance, the dull, restful
colouring over all the compact details, make it more enjoyable
the more it is studied.   The sensation of enjoyment, however,
is undoubtedly heightened by the fresh, bracing feel of the
morning air.

We experienced the full force of the wind as we crossed the
common in front of the house to the church, whose tower we
ascended in order to get a view of the town.   It is hardly right
to call Oliva either a town or village.   There are scarcely two
houses together.   Large squares of cultivated land, enclosed
between high walls, divide the houses or farms from each other.

There is no street, nothing to mark a town. The church, with its plaza, where the people collect on feast-days, is the only general meeting-place. A flight of stone steps, each very high, leads to the unpainted door of the tower. A padlock fastens it, and we enter, stepping carefully to avoid the holes in the floor. We ascend the ladderlike stairs, wondering at each step if the bell-ringer or we are the heavier, and if the steps are accustomed to so much weight. The top story of all tries our nerves the most. The rafters are partially bare, and as one looks down to the floor beneath the planks have an unpleasant fashion of cracking under one's feet. No roof covers us; it was blown off, and the people have no money to put on another. Sheltering ourselves as well as we can from the fury of the wind, we see the plain of Oliva, spread like a map beneath. The church is in the middle of a flat, oval plain, about a mile and a half long by one broad, and is surrounded on all sides by hills and mountains. The plain is Oliva, and Oliva is the plain. Truly it is a village of magnificent distances. The main road runs on one side of the church, the common on the other. Our host's house lies on the other side, at one corner of this red, herbless tract, and a broad path of large stones joins the house and church. This path is necessary, as after rain the soil here becomes clayey and slippery, and when the plaza is flooded, it is not possible for the camels to walk upon it. At one place only are there any trees, at a spot sheltered from the wind by a high, perfectly shaped sugar-loaf cone. Some of the houses are flat-roofed, others tiled, and a good many huts are of stone, and roofed with straw and earth. Innumerable hives of grain cover the plain, each house has at least one or two near it, and the larger farms have a great many; twenty-eight we counted round our host's: how many more lie behind the building we cannot say. The green doors and windows, the whitewashed walls, and the plain, dark lava stone corners are all pleasing to the eye from their quaintness. The house is overawed by a large peak, which runs up, narrowing rapidly, to a very sharp top. The walls of the church tower are of honeycombed black lava, and two small bells occupy two of the niches in the west face. The three roofs of the church are beneath us, all of pipe-shaped red tiles. Curiously enough, the most northern has been thatched at its east end for several yards with flat, glazed tiles, red, yellow, bottle-green, and white. At one side the hills form a range, and at the other are in various peaks and cones. The situation is fine, but the strong wind, though healthy and invigorating, is too powerful,

CORN STACKS (PAJEROS), OLIVA, FUERTEVENTURA.

and clouds of dust or red earth raised by it cross the plain at one side. It is, in fact, the scourge in parts, though not so strong here as in Lanzarote. Oliva is 625 feet above the sea.

Don Victor kindly showed us over his house and farm-buildings. He has a gem for antiquaries in a coach about a hundred and twenty or a hundred and thirty years old, somewhat in the shape of a hansom on four wheels. The hind wheels are quite six feet in diameter. What it was ever brought here for is a mystery, as there is not a coach road in the island to this

day. Stables for horses and sheds for camels and donkeys, a
large cistern nine feet deep and nearly full of water, a flour mill
worked by a camel, all constitute comforts. A gate leads us into
a stack-yard. Here are thirty-nine stacks or beehives, not of
hay, but of grain. These hives are from twenty to thirty
feet high; they are made of straw, are circular in form, and
at the base six feet thick. Seeing a hole near the bottom
of one, just big enough to allow of entrance, I crept in, and
found a space of about four or five feet in diameter inside.
This hive was empty, the grain having been removed. These
stacks are called *pajeros*. They are so well and firmly built as
to last about sixty years. Each year the hole at the bottom is
filled in, and the top, or *corona*, is taken off, when the grain is put
inside, and a fresh crown put on again. The top is then roofed
with mud to keep out the rain. This flat, bald part at the top
makes the pajero not unlike a monk's head. The grain is
perfectly secure from rats or any harm, and may be left there
for two or three years. The outsides of the pajeros are brown,
and look as though plastered with mud, an appearance entirely
due to the action of the rain and wind.*

At breakfast we had two-year-old mutton that ate like lamb,
pork, and cold pancakes; at least, they were cold when we ate
them. They are never particular here about any of the food
being hot, and as often as not everything is put on the table
at once : eggs, meat, fish, omelet. The kind host and hostess
here, like those at Yaiza, insisted on our taking a large piece
of meat with us, for there would be none, they said, in Puerto
Cabras. It was ready cooked, and, with eggs, wine, and bread,
was put into our travelling basket. We were very glad of these
provisions later, as what they said was true enough : there was

---

* The only structures of a similar nature of which I have ever heard
occur in Persia. Dr. Wills, in "Land of the Lion and Sun," writes (p. 385),
"All about are curious conical buildings of mud, some ten and twelve
yards high. They have small terraces a few inches wide at top, others a
foot or two wide at bottom. These are the grain stores of the place, and
seem peculiar to Kūm and Kashan."

no meat in Puerto. At 10.30 a.m. we started for Puerto Cabras, in the same fashion in which we came yesterday, Don Victor most kindly coming with us again on his donkey. Leaving his house behind, we passed near an old, quaint grey building, two stories high, with small balconies to each of the upper windows and pointed, red-tiled roof. The house is said to be two hundred years old. We could scarcely breathe or speak while passing across the plain at the foot of the peak from the furious blast which greeted us. The dromedaries bent their swanlike necks to meet it, while their long hair blew apart. Through a culti-vated valley and round a green hillside we next rode. It is difficult to imagine all this verdure past and gone in a few months, not to return perhaps for years.

The dromedaries of these islands are always called camels —although they are considered by the inhabitants as drome-daries proper—probably through ignorance on the part of the peasants, as well doubtless because of the word itself being shorter and more easily pronounced. The two-humped camel is not to be found here. The dromedaries breed in both this island and Lanzarote, but the stock is constantly renewed from Africa, not, however, because of any imperfection in the breeding, but owing to the number being lessened in years of drought either through being sold or dying of hunger. All animals have to be thus renewed. The pastures of Fuerteventura are extensive after rain. Horses are brought from the mainland also, and after fattening in this island are shipped to Canaria and Tenerife. The horses from here are particularly valued for their strength, but they are usually ugly. The dromedaries are about two or three years old when imported, and are bought for five or six pounds. Their price in Fuerteventura depends upon and varies with the season. When the people are starving, and there is no food for man or beast, they are of course only too glad to sell the animals for anything. The dromedaries are very quiet, although less so just now than at any other season, owing to the green food." An ordinary rope halter is deemed quite sufficient to control them, a small stick and expostulations by word of mouth guiding them. They are seldom beaten, and I have never seen one ill-used. The stick is merely used to tap them on the neck to guide them from one side to the other. Frequently, however, the driver (camellero) will merely call to the animal as he walks a yard or two behind, and order him to go up or down as the inclination of the road may suggest. Our luggage-camel in this instance was called El Moro—he had come from Africa; the one we rode in contradistinction, being Majorero. So docile were they, that the halter was usually thrown across the necks of the animals we rode, and they walked gently onwards, picking their own way. There is a great difference in them, however, not in docility—they are all docile—but in sure-footedness, quickness, and motion. Many on the roughest road never make a false step, while others frequently stumble. The pace varies from two and a half to three and a half miles an hour, and whereas it is possible and comfortable to ride some whilst trotting, on others the motion is so violent, one is jolted off the seat several inches at each stride and dropped down again equally suddenly. Formerly, in the halcyon days of the cochineal, dromedaries were regularly trained for riding, the motion being then fast and easy. Now, however, they are taught to serve only as beasts of burden, and for this are trained to be sure-footed and to mount hills in zigzag fashion. It is certainly against their nature travelling on hilly ground. The soft, large pads of their feet cannot grip the earth, and they toil painfully upwards with short and laboured step. The load which on level ground they carry with ease becomes then a heavy burden. There is none of that putting the shoulder to the work, and with bent head facing the ascent, such as we are accustomed to in the horse tribe. The long, curved neck, with head laid back, so that nose and ears are horizontal, remains so, and the steps which before were a yard in length are reduced to half that distance.

The men on this island have a trick of getting on the dromedaries without stopping them, which I never saw done in Lanzarote. A crupper of two unjoined ropes or straps is on every camel. This can usually be reached just above the tail by stretching the arms upwards. A man seizes this with both hands, and putting his foot on the dromedary's hind-knee, hoists himself on its back, and thence gets astride the saddle.

Although, much to our surprise, we found the other five islands of the archipelago different in customs, habits, and scenery, we fully expected that these two would be very much alike, both from their contiguity, and from being always classed together by the inhabitants of the other islands. Not only, however, is the configuration of the ground different, but totally distinct words are used to express the same thing. Even in telling a camel to kneel, the Conejeros say, "Tutchi!" and the Majoreros "Fuchi!" The men in Fuerteventura are also different, being tall, square-shouldered, and angular. They are lively, however, like the Conejeros. They are said to be lazy. Of this I have had no means of judging, but I am inclined to think they are not more so than the other inhabitants of the archipelago. Their libellers belonged to other islands, and, knowing the animus among the islanders, but little faith can be put in what they say of one another. I was told by the engineer that during the work connected with laying the land part of the cable in Gran Canaria his best workers were Majoreros.

Our way is beguiled by the birds singing on either side of our path, undisturbed by the noiseless tread of the dromedaries. As not a tree is to be seen, they are perforce obliged to sit upon the ground, whence rise the clear, soft, liquid notes. Vainly do we scan the ground in all directions for the songster; the colour of the plumage mingles so well with that of the soil, that we can scarcely ever see him or her, for the female sings too. Her song is not the rapturous, long-sustained outburst of the male bird, but a few bars at a time are warbled, the song breaking off, to be taken up a few seconds later and pursued softly for some more bars. The birds, in these two islands especially, are always found near houses. Water, being scarce, is chiefly obtainable where man stores it, and the cisterns round the houses often afford the only watering places for animals for many miles. Hence, towards evening especially, the birds congregate in the neighbourhood, and I have frequently seen a flock of several hundred rise as we approached.

La Caldereta is a settlement of brown earth and stone houses, with earthen roofs, but little removed from huts. Near here we passed some palm trees despoiled of their plumes, which were being packed below on mules—preparations for the fiesta on Saturday.

Winding along a path on our left, in single file, comes a curious cavalcade towards us. A donkey leads the van—donkeys always do ; size goes for nothing : it is push that gains the day—next come two dromedaries, both laden on either side the hump with fresh green herbage ; both are halterless, and the food so temptingly close induces them to frequently stop, turning back their long necks to get a mouthful. Behind them trots a goat, its bell tinkling musically. This miscellaneous collection of animals is herded by a boy and girl, who, also in single file, bring up the rear. The donkeys supply the comic element ; they are so wise, or rather "knowing," that their movements are a perpetual source of amusement.

The ground here is yellowy-red and stony, with large flat or undulating tracts, so swept by the wind, that they remain uncultivated. Just now herbage covers the ground, not in our sense, however. It is seldom that grass springs up. The green pasturage that one hears so much of, and that is capable of feeding so many animals, is not what we know by that name at home. The herbage consists of separate plants of various kinds, much of it being three sorts of barilla. They grow between and among the stones, but every plant is distinct, and has usually a small space round it, so that the apparently even, grassy surface we are accustomed to in England is a thing unknown. We heard that Fuerteventura was looking "like an emerald in the ocean." It is plain that whoever said so had never seen *the* Emerald Isle, or such an idea could never have

been born.   Green herbage there is in Fuerteventura, but it has
to be looked for; a bird's-eye glance across the surface of the
country does not reveal a general mass of green, but the yellow-
ochre appearance predominates.   Here and there, where the
moisture is greater in depressions of the ground, the faint green
shade deepens into a real green.   But these oases are few and
far between.   Among the plants we noticed a lovely pale yellow
chrysanthemum (*Chrysanthemum coronarium*), and another flower
(*Malcomia litorea*), which also grew plentifully.

Crossing down and up the small barranco of Tinojae, in
whose low sides are some caves in which the ancient Majos
lived, we come to a large flat slope towards the sea.   This
plain is called El Rosa de Lagos.   When there is much rain,
the water covers it from the higher slopes above, until it looks
like a large river.   This fact has caused a curious change of
name to be perpetuated by the peasants, De Lagos being converted into Del Aguas.   It is very difficult throughout the archipelago to ascertain the correct names.   Many of the ancient
names remain; some are incorporated into Spanish, and others
are pure Spanish.   The present language being Spanish,
scholars are inclined to make the spelling of every word con-
form to that language.

Meeting a man driving a laden camel and riding a donkey,
we inquired for news of the schooner, and heard that it had not
yet arrived, probably, he said, owing to the calms.   The calms,
when we thought it was delayed by the wind!   Truly enough,
however, as we neared the sea level, we ceased to be blown
about, and we found not only was the sea calm, and not a breath
stirring the air, but that such had been the condition of the
weather all the morning.

Striking the shore at Laha Bay, formed of dark stones, we
followed the path along its wide curve.   The flat shore line was
only broken by one fisherman's cottage and a limekiln.   Quantities of small sponges lay on the beach, thrown up by the sea.
The heat was intense and stifling, the sea glared under the sun,
and our saddles and luggage almost scorched us if touched.

The thermometer rapidly registered 102·2° F. (39° C.) in the sun. We were glad after our hot ride along the sea to reach the shelter of Puerto Cabras, at 2.30 p.m.

Here our host led us to the house of Don Ramon Castaneyra, to whom we had a letter of introduction from our friend Don Gregorio Chil. Don Ramon was unfortunately ill in bed. The patient camels rising, we turned through the broad, deserted streets to a house where we were told we could find beds. Not being a regular fonda, great preparations were made for our entertainment. So great were the fears of the host and hostess that we should not be properly treated, especially in the matter of cooking, that they sent for a woman, who lived in the village, to cook for us, and who, having *once* been in the kitchen of the English hotel in Santa Cruz, was supposed to know all the wants of English people! Little did the good folk understand how we could live upon and eat anything. Being English, our peculiarities were put up with, and our tea made with boiling water. We found the little house so comfortable, that, upon the non-arrival of the northward-bound schooner, we stayed there two nights. Our good friend Don Victor, having arranged for our comfort in various ways, left us for his four hours' ride to his windy home.

Hearing that there was an Englishman in the village, the only one in the island of Fuerteventura, we went in search of him after dinner. We found the Englishman was a Scotchman! He tells us that times here are indeed sadly changed. There is no money and very little food. Rich and poor are alike in a half-starving condition. Three years have passed without a drop of rain, and for seven there has been only a chance shower now and then. The cattle consequently have died off or been sold, and so few are left, that there are none to spare for food. Even now, when the rain has come, the farmers have not sufficient grain to sow the land, nor money to purchase it elsewhere. This is doubly sad when one considers that the island is not by any means destitute of water, capital only being required to raise it to the surface. The beginning of this distress was caused by the absence of a market for the barilla. At the present moment this Scotchman has four warehouses of barilla, bought at three, four, and six shillings a quintal, and it is not now worth twenty cents. He owns seven of the best houses in the town, and although the rent is only three dollars (twelve shillings) a month, he cannot get it. The unfortunate people have not got that much. I asked him how the people lived ; he said he "really could not tell." Later I found that existence is spun out upon the seeds of the barilla, which are roasted and made into gofio, like grain. Although people could not actually be said to die of starvation, yet they assuredly did of insufficient nourishment.

Puerto Cabras is officially, but not really, the principal town of Fuerteventura. Several towns in the interior are larger and more important. It is, however, the only port, and hence its priority. The anchorage is not good, and the roadstead wide and open. The little village is built on the most hilly part of the shore, and so steep are its streets, that there is scarcely a house that has not a view of the sea. The streets are very broad, grass-grown, and deserted ; the houses are low, a few being two-storied, but are mostly in cottage style. They are neatly built. What vegetation there is being confined to the patios is consequently invisible, still further helping to give the dead appearance. A cannon-ball fired up a street would hurt no one. There is a humorous saying with regard to Lanzarote which might also be quoted of Fuerteventura—that it had been put in its Atlantic home as an experiment, and had failed! There is no doubt whatever that when Bethencourt invaded these islands they were fruitful and wooded in many parts. What has been may be again, and we much hope that when better known a little money will be expended upon growing trees and sinking wells. A few rocks run into the sea, immediately beneath the town. Round an angle of one a wall has been built, inside which a solitary cannon lies on the ground. We supposed this to be the fort. Walking northward over the rocks and past closed warehouses, we reached a little strand at whose further end we came upon the first signs of life. Here is a limekiln. Two men were engaged in lifting lime-stones into a small, roughly made cart, the solitary vehicle we had seen since landing, the dilapidated chariot at Oliva excepted. The only trade the island possesses is in limestone. Except in the Caldera of Palma, there is no limestone in any of the other islands. Fuerteventura is almost entirely formed of it, and as there is nothing else with which to freight the vessels on their return journey, it is cheaper even for Palma to get the stone from here than to draw it out of the Caldera. This may be readily understood, as the price of limestone brought to the edge of the sea is twopence-halfpenny for five hundred-weight. Burned, it is of course more expensive, coal having to be brought from England. It is then two shillings for the same quantity.

During the evening Don Secundino, a friend of Don Ramon's, called in his place, to offer his services and help us to obtain any information we might require. We are much gratified by the eagerness with which all aid our endeavours to obtain information, though very few have even the smallest idea of the sort of information we require.

February 1st, *Friday.*—As the boat is not yet in from Las Palmas, there is little use in our going southward. After touching here, the schooners go to Arrecife in Lanzarote, and staying there two days, return, calling at several ports before reaching Gran Tarajal, where we hope to embark. Usually the journey from Las Palmas to Arrecife is accomplished between Monday and Thursday, but everything depends on wind and weather.

I was again consulted about the dinner, and we succeeded in getting soup and meat out of Don Victor's present to us, which, with fresh fish and pancakes, made a by no means despicable meal. Puddings they never understand, so, in order to get even pancakes, I was obliged to ask for an omelet (*tortilla*) without anything in it, that is to say *minus* seasoning or flavouring of any sort. The cook came to me three or four times, anxiously inquiring about various matters, especially as to the order in which we would eat the food, and was greatly distressed and puzzled by our preferring fish before meat.

The correo came in at last, and we went down to see the cargo landed. The principal street of Puerto Cabras is wide and steep, and leads straight down to the water's edge, where there is a little piece of shingle suitable for landing boats. As we stood near the beach the scene up the hill behind us was curious. The wide, grass-grown street is bounded by low houses on either side. Tied to the handles of the doors at

STREET, PUERTO CABRAS, FUERTEVENTURA.

intervals, mostly on the shady side, are camels, standing or kneeling, interspersed with donkeys, the latter always comic when in juxtaposition to the stately dromedaries.

As we stood in the shade, leaning against a boat, waiting to see the patrón of the correo when he should come ashore, a man from a house near thoughtfully brought out two chairs for us to sit upon.

Much did we wonder what the cargo could be. It was not great, but varied—goats, calabashes, pottery, hides, long wiry grass for corn-sieves, barrels, a few boxes, and some goods enclosed in palm mats. I was surprised at first to see the goats, but remembered that they are still stocking the land after seven years of famine. The pottery consisted of the very commonest of water jars, and the hides—there being no animals to kill in Fuerteventura—were for shoes and sandals.

Our fonda is a curious, odd-shaped little house. The street door opens directly on a small yard; on the left is a room guiltless of windows, where we eat our meals; part of which is partitioned off for a shop. On the right a high wall encloses the yard from the street, the house being a corner one. Out of the yard rises a staircase, ending in a little wooden balcony, off which are two rooms. One of these is the sala, or drawing-room, the other an irregularly shaped room, the walls not running parallel, containing two small beds. Off each of these rooms are two others, one a bedroom and the other a writing-room, where the good man of the house, who is a tax-gatherer, does his business. He turned out of it for us, however, and placed table, paper, and ink at my disposal.

Don Secundino called for us about four or five in the evening, and we went for a walk to see a small farm or finca a short distance southward of the town. As we passed along the street the patrón of the schooner ran after Don Secundino, begging him to despatch the vessel first, as he wanted to get on to Arrecife; but he was told he must wait until his return in the evening. So the royal mail was kept waiting while we sauntered along the shore! Some other gentlemen joined us, and we had a pleasant walk in the cool of the evening, the ripple of the waves being the only disturbing sound. Two kinds of barilla, *Aizoon Canariense* and *Aizoon Hispanicum*, and another plant, the ordinary ice-plant, we trod beneath our feet. The two barillas formed the principal gofio during the past seven years. When the seeds are ready for pulling, they are placed in water, where they open; they are then dried and roasted, like other gofio. This is generally mixed with wheat or maize, as the nourishment from the seeds is very insufficient. Those who were so poor as to have been obliged to live on them entirely may be counted among the number who died of " insufficient nourishment."

The finca we came to see was merely a small, well-cultivated and irrigated farm. It is remarkable, no doubt, as it is the only one to be seen for miles, as far as the eye can reach—an oasis in the desert, a desert not of sand, but of yellow ochre, small stones, and good subsoil, lacking, however, that necessity under a burning sky, water. We returned by the upper part of the village through the plaza, here destitute of a single tree, past the plain, whitewashed church, and down the steep Calle Real.

The most remarkable feature of this the principal street of Puerto Cabras is the plentiful growth there of a plant of the tobacco genus, *Nicotiana glauca.* Between the rough cobble stones in the middle of the street, as well as under the shadow of the wall, it grew in quite a little forest, in defiance of all English ideas of street propriety, secure alike from the heavy tread of the camel—for that cynical animal carefully avoids it—and the molestation of the few passers-by. The plant had been cut down and uprooted ineffectually, so now it is allowed to run riot. No other vegetation of any kind, sort, or description besides this near relative of the common tobacco enlivens the hot, glaring monotony of Port Cabras thoroughfares. Until about 1867-69—I carefully obtained the date— the plant was unknown in the island. Then suddenly and almost simultaneously it appeared everywhere. As a peasant journeyed to a village at the other end of the island, he found it growing all along his route by the path-side. The villagers would ask him had he observed the same new plant growing at his home, and he would invariably answer, "Yes, the same." And so it came to pass that the singularity of the plant and the suddenness of its Fuerteventura advent—where no trees are to be seen, and scarcely any plants above a few inches in height, except round the houses in well-watered spots —led to the curiosity of the natives being aroused and to a regular fire of questions among themselves concerning it. Each had seen the *same* plant in some other part of the island, and hence in a short time became established its present native appellation of *mismo* (same). The plant is a native of Buenos

Aires, but it also grows on the neighbouring coast of Africa, whence birds or man may have brought it. In its native country it grows to a height of nine or ten feet. Here it is stunted, only attaining two or three feet of stem. Still it has taken kindly to Fuerteventura, and is growing and spreading rapidly. The harder and more stony the ground, the better it seems to thrive. It is not a pretty plant. The stem is thin and straggling, seldom, if ever, growing straight. The leaves are about the size of those of a Portugal laurel, but not of similar consistency, being soft. They are light greyish-green in colour, the backs being whity-grey, like those of an aspen. The blossom is funnel-shaped, and yellow in colour. Altogether it is an ugly, untidy plant. Being, however, the only green thing that survives without water, the Majoreros welcome it. Perhaps the inhabitants may be led to manufacture a variety of tobacco from its leaves. If such a use for *mismo* be discovered, so much the better for poverty-stricken Fuerteventura.

CHAPTER XVII.

CASILLAS DEL ANGEL—ANTIGUA—BETANCURIA— GRANITE GORGE—PAJARA.

There are two classes of people to whom life seems one long holiday, the very rich and the very poor, one because they need do nothing, the other because they have nothing to do. But there are none who understand the art of doing nothing and living upon nothing better than the poor classes of Spain. Climate does one half, and temperament the rest.—WASHINGTON IRVING.

The journey thither is easy and short, and comparatively uncostly; and as to the islands themselves, especially the Canary Islands, they have the most healthy climate of any, and contain no venomous animals, for during all the long time that Bethencourt and his company remained there, no one suffered from sickness, which surprised them greatly.—PIERRE BONTIER AND JEAN LE VERRIER.

February 2nd, Saturday.—We rose at half-past five, in order to get off during the cool of the morning. Another schooner, however, being in the offing, we decided to wait to speak to the patrón, as if it were the *Gaspar* we preferred returning to Canaria in it. Our camel was packed, and we were ready to mount at seven o'clock, when we at last saw the patrón come ashore, and found the schooner was really the *Gaspar*. We had spoken to the skipper before in Las Palmas, so he shook hands with us and greeted us warmly. We told him we should like to go back with him to Las Palmas if he could be in Gran Tarajal early enough, but that, in order to catch the English mail, we must take the first schooner that came. He promised to try and be there on Tuesday. Mounting our dromedary and waving a farewell, we started. I never heard his name, but he was a powerfully built man, with a fine, open face, and, we were told, was not extortionate, as the patrónes usually are.

Instead of to-day being broiling, like yesterday, it was quite cool and cloudy [61° F. (16° C.)]. We struck upwards towards the interior, past the small cemetery, built in 1871, and crossed the Enrique Prieto barranco, where we noticed quantities of mismo growing. Our camellero, Quiterio Gonzales by name, was a small, broad-set man, with a short neck, dark hair, and grey eyes, who proved a very pleasant fellow, talking away, and with such a clear pronunciation, that it was easy to understand him. He asked us if we were going to our "island" after leaving his. He was quite right, certainly, in calling England an island, but somehow it is a fact we frequently and generally lose sight of. Probably he had some vague idea it was about the size of Canaria or Tenerife. In any case, it seemed natural to him, as one islander speaking to another, to say, "su isla" ("your island"), rather than "Inglaterra" (England).

A flock of goats browsing attracted our attention, as the girl and boy who were herding were apparently making signs to us. They turned out to belong to our camellero. He hospitably urged us to have some milk, which, as we had just breakfasted, we declined. Kids, he said, are worth from one to four shillings.

Numberless canaries were singing around and about us as we gradually ascended towards the centre of the island.

We hoped we might have got a glimpse of Cape Juby, on the coast of Africa, from the higher parts of the island, but we are told that it is invisible. Fuerteventura can be seen from Cape Juby, owing to its being much higher than the mainland, which is low and flat. We recrossed the little barranco, remarkable for nothing save its amount of mismo.

Our dromedary was called Moreno (brown), a favourite name. It is also the Spanish for "a man of colour," or a negro. I asked the camellero if there were any Morenos (negroes) here. He said, "No, but many blacks. I am one"! The natives of these two islands are particularly smart and bright, though they may seem even more so to us by contrast with the Canarios, who are unpardonably stupid. It is amusing to hear the camel-drivers remonstrating with the camels—" Go on, or we shall be all day on the road;" "Get on, Moreno : we shall not arrive till night, and there is no moon;" "Mind your feet;" and various other expressions, uttered in a conciliatory or persuasive voice. The peculiar noises by which the animals are directed require to be heard to be understood. The usual urging-on sound is made by vibrating the tongue rapidly against the roof of the mouth whilst holding the breath. Another for the same purpose is that peculiar "cluck" like the drawing of a cork. The first of these sounds cut short just at the beginning of each vibration and repeated several times, like "Burr! burr! burr!" is used to tell the dromedary to go cautiously down a hill or bad bit of road. The dromedaries also make some very peculiar and disagreeable noises. One is a squeak, caused apparently by the grating of the teeth as the lower jaw is moved from left to right, which often goes on for half an hour, the squeak keeping time to the animal's stride. They have a curious power of, as it were, blowing up wind, which rumbles up and fills their tongues, puffing them out like bladders, while they hang six or eight inches out of the side of their mouths, like a dog's tongue. This noise they usually make upon catching sight of a comrade. It is wonderful how soon they will see another dromedary. Often have we scanned the horizon searching vainly for the animal that we knew, from the uncouth noises of ours, must be in sight.

We continued ascending over stony ground, and 500 feet above the sea reached a level plateau, crowned by a peaked mountain, Al Medio, the base spreading out and forming a Welsh hat. The solitudes were dedicated to crows, hoarser and lower of voice than those at home. Countless canary birds were singing their beautiful well-known song in the fresh, cool morning air. Our road, albeit a track, was fit to be a royal carriage drive, broad, level, and smooth.

The mountains on this island run principally east and west, tablelands lying between them, on which the towns and villages are built. These chains overlap each other, making a journey down the centre of the island devious. Our road lay between two chains of hills, Al Medio being the terminating point at one side and the Montaña de Tao at the other. At our feet as we strode softly along was a brilliant carpet of purple, white, yellow, and orange flowers ; whole patches of delicate creamy Marguerites, with golden centres, ravished us with their beauty ; and the short grey-green herbage toned down the colouring, making it " one harmonious whole." In a low-banked river-bed we were surprised to see in this thirsty land water trickling along. The Cabra river is, alas ! however, *amargo* (bitter). We realise how bitterly we might be disappointed, as many have been on a desert journey, when the sight of water has put joy into man and beast, and though hot and tired, the weary limbs, forgetting their languor, press towards the bright silvery streak, where the foremost bury their faces eagerly in the cooling stream, only to utter a cry and make a gesture of despair on finding it *amargo*. Tamarisk bushes lined the banks of the Rio de Cabra, and flitting in and among them were various kinds of small birds. Some are brown, something of the shape and build of our sparrows, but larger; others, also brown, have red beaks, and black on the wings. It is only, however, the green-and-yellow bird who sings that rapturous melody known to all the nations of the world.

We began to meet peasants as we got further across the plateau towards some houses. One man, driving a donkey in front of him, had on light blue-checked trousers and a dark, short blue jacket of cloth, with a stand-up collar. We walked up the barranco below the sloping-roofed mud huts of Teguate. A solitary palm adorns the hamlet. There are three wells, the water of which, though slightly mineral, is used. We met another man in Cambridge blue trousers, short Eton jacket, the collar turned down, and waistcoat of the same material. All the jackets are of the same cut, and the sky-blue trousers worn

by the majority are evidently fashionable.   Two round, roughly
cemented pillars are on one bank of the river, a cross being
erected on each.

The chain of mountains on the north side of the plain is
called El Cuchillo de Tetir, the narrow, knifelike appearance
of the ridge giving it its name.   The most westerly point is
called by some Montaña de Tao, by others the Fortelesa.   The
sides are much seamed, and the strata are in horizontal layers.
The houses of Teguate straggle on alongside the barranco
until near the larger and more important Casillas del Angel.
This village is scarcely discernible a short distance off.   The
low, one-storied houses are built either entirely of mud, or else
of loose stones plastered with mud, and as the surrounding earth
is used for the purpose, the distinction between the yellow
ground and the yellow walls of the houses and roofs is not by
any means clearly defined.

As we approached within a few hundred yards of the hamlet,
perched upon a wall was that bird of evil eye and ill omen, a
vulture.   Numberless are these scavengers, and undoubtedly
useful, in these islands.   This particular bird was very handsome.   The head was a deep orange, which shaded off to light
cream, relieved by black upon the wings.   He sat eyeing us,
and was, I think, about eighteen inches high.

The church of Casillas is not remarkable, save for its black
belfry, surmounted by little cupolas ; but as it is almost the
only building that can boast of any height in the village, it
courts publicity.

We had been given a letter of introduction to Don Francisco
Rugama Bethencourt, whose long, low house is on the outskirts
of the village.   We stopped to speak to Don Francisco for ten
minutes, but were obliged to refuse his urgent entreaties to
dismount and rest.   We might have done so had we known the
short distance before us, and had we also been aware that in
the mountain opposite was a cave containing a stone on which,
report says, are hieroglyphics.   The hour was 9.10 a.m., and
we were 650 feet above the sea, much the same height as Oliva,

but fortunately protected from the wind which scours that plain by the Cuchillo de Tetir. In the Peak of Fortelesa are many caves which were inhabited by the ancient Majos. One is still said to contain a stone table in preservation.

The priestly chroniclers say little of the people of Fuerteventura, whom they must have known so well. They speak, however, of running streams of water, on the banks of which "are large groves of trees called *tarhais* (probably breso). . . . The country is plentifully furnished with other trees. . . . The people of the country are not very numerous, but very tall, and difficult to take alive; and so formidable are they, that, if any one of them is taken by the Christians and turns upon them, they give him no quarter, but kill him forthwith. They have villages in great number, and they live more closely together than is the custom with the inhabitants of the island of Lanzerote." They lived on meat dried without salt, which the priests preferred to "any that is prepared in France." They also ate tallow, and had cheeses "which are superlatively good." The ease with which wells might be made struck the conquerors as it did us later. "The inhabitants are of a resolute character, very firm in their religion, and they have temples, in which they offer their sacrifices," which would seem to have been simply libations of milk and offerings of butter. Glas's MS states that the people of Fuerteventura were dressed in "jackets made of sheepskins, the sleeves short and reaching no farther than their elbows. They wore also short breeches, that left the knees bare, and short hose or stockings, that reached little higher than the calf of the leg." Two women, a mother and daughter, called Tibiatin and Tamonante, appear to have acted as peacemakers among the chiefs when disputes arose. They also are said to have foretold future events and prophesied the arrival of the Europeans, a story similar to that in other islands. At any rate, they appear to have materially assisted the invaders by their prognostications, notwithstanding which the worthy Galineo attributes their wisdom to their holding "a correspondence with the devil."

There were said to have been four thousand fighting men in the island when Bethencourt went there, under two kings, and it was divided in two by a wall, a king reigning over each half.

The information concerning the customs and habits of all the former inhabitants is vague and unsatisfactory. Somewhat has been done by later Spanish writers in gathering up information and in describing what evidences still remain of the habits and lives of this interesting people. But it is not *savants* alone who can unearth this subject in their libraries. It requires a *savant* who is a traveller to live for years in the islands, to ramble in their most out-of-the-way recesses, exploring, examining, and excavating, to really attempt to unravel the mystery which yet hangs over this ancient people. No doubt, could the hieroglyphics that have been discovered on stones be deciphered, we should have a partial solution of what, after all that is known and conjectured, is still an unknown history.

As we strode majestically out of the town, ourselves much higher than the houses, we passed a row of little terra-cotta mud cabins that, save in colour, might have been in the Emerald Isle. The analogy was carried out still further by a pot and cat, both black, on either side of the doorway. A number of small yellow butterflies, lazy fliers, fluttered along our road. The path here is wide, of reddish soil, that in a less dry climate might degenerate into clay, but here is rich and loamy. No walls, except in a few places, bound the road. Sometimes the land is cultivated to the edge, in other places barren, not because the soil is unproductive, but by reason of the poverty of the people and the lack of hands to till and water to irrigate.

We met a great number of people dressed in their best, for this is a saint's day, bright, cheerful women, notwithstanding the scarcity of food. Three passed us walking rapidly. One of them, an elderly woman, who wore a white mantilla, with a black hat surmounting it, asked our camellero a string of questions concerning us. "Are these people from Puerto Cabras?" "Si, Señora," said our man. "Are they going to Antigua?" "Si, Señora." "Have they come from Lanzarote?" "Si,

Señora." " Are they going to Canaria ?" " Si, Señora." As
we were both walking rapidly away from each other, each question was fired off the moment " Si, Señora," was answered, but
had to be repeated louder than the preceding one. With
smiling face she asked, and equally good-humouredly was
answered. The manner of asking reminded me of nothing so
much as a repeating rifle, shot after shot being fired.

Our path led up and over a low dip in a range of limestone
formation. As we reached the summit, a large, plain-like valley,
bounded by mountains, the whole a bright terra-cotta colour, lay
spread before us. Our road, cut out of the firm red soil, wound
round the side of the hill towards Hampuientas. The wayside
was literally strewn with flowers. The three kinds of barilla, wild
mignonette, and Palma Christi toned down the brilliant Roman
purple, poppy-red, and every shade, from deep orange to pale
yellow, of the numberless flowers known and unknown.* A
shower of rain made umbrellas a necessity. I doubt not we
shall be remembered by the Majoreros as bringers of good luck
and happy portents of a year of plenty.

We had walked thus far on foot, but wishing for some
luncheon, we remounted. Our lunch we kept in a basket upon
the animal's hump, so of course it was utterly impossible to
reach it until he knelt. One always feels unwilling to bring
him to his knees unnecessarily, he protests and grumbles so
much at the operation, so we thought it better to mount and eat
on dromedary-back.

Hampuientas is a small village, with nothing to distinguish
it from Casillas, not even the tower of its church, except that it
is smaller. The black belfry may be seen any day on the
outside of a box of German bricks, wanting only in a little more
ink to make the likeness perfect. The high-road or path winds
through the outskirts of the village. The houses, guiltless of
windows and with closed doors, betrayed no signs of containing
inhabitants. We made no sound as our dromedary noiselessly

* Amongst others *Reseda lutea, Papaver hybridum, Vicia sativa,
Anagallis arvensis, Erucastrum Canariense.*

placed his soft pads upon the red soil.   Awed by the stillness,
we spoke not.   We felt as though fleeing silently and swiftly
from an unseen foe.   The habitations of men surrounded us, but
no sign of life was present.   Just as we were leaving the sleeping hamlet, two shock-headed urchins, a boy and girl, half naked,
appeared from behind a wall.   They neither spoke nor moved,
but, with eyes and mouths wide open, watched us out of sight.

Beyond Hampuientas lies Llanos, where some pottery is
made.

Our ideas of Fuerteventura are rapidly undergoing a great
and surprising change.   Instead of that island being a vast
sandy desert, as we had been led to expect, we find it almost
entirely composed of good soil, lacking only irrigation.   The
gently undulating slopes are favourable to a thorough system of
irrigation, while the water has only to be dug for to be obtained.
The American company which was started to raise water in
Lanzarote was very ill advised as to the geological formation of
the two islands.   One might as readily expect to find milk as
water in the volcanic Lanzarote, whereas it needs no geologist
to tell us that limestone and water are close neighbours.

Our road is a gentle descent towards Antigua, which lies
hidden in a depression below, scarcely worth the name of
valley.   All around, as far as the eye can see, is the rich ochre
soil, virgin land lying fallow.   Not a tree is visible.   Our vision
is bounded by a range of hills crossing the island from east to
west on the southern side of the plain.   Seamed and lined are
its slopes with deep holes, such as one makes by resting one's
hand upon a feather-bed.   The resemblance that first struck me
on seeing it was to the "crow's-feet" and wrinkles on the faces
of some of the old hags one sees.   The blue sky and bright
sunshine only served to bring out the lines.   The women we
meet, as well as the men, differ in appearance from those of the
other islands.   They generally wear small black shawls over their
heads.   Their faces are round and well coloured; the features
are plain, but the bright, kind expression gives them a beauty
that is often lacking in the sister islands.

A few windmills, standing on the brow of something, betray the presence of a town. Wherever in Fuerteventura a windmill is to be seen, a town or hamlet is certain to be at hand. A few more camel-paces, and we sight the waving palm trees of Antigua. This village is said to be the same size as Oliva, but it looks much larger, as the houses are clustered together and not scattered in the magnificent distances of Oliva. The road into the village, or rather to the church, which always seems the only centre of the towns, is on a slope. At either side of it in the ditches were holes leading into the fields, so that every drop of water might run into them, and not be wasted upon the road. Our curiosity was very much aroused by seeing a deep hole dug at one side of the road; it looked suspiciously gravelike in shape, and we thought we were about to view a corpse. Craning our necks eagerly as far as we dared over the edge of the camel, we got a glimpse of the contents, and were considerably amused and relieved to find that it was only a funeral of aloes ! Looking around, we then saw a man on a neighbouring farm cutting the long-shaped leaves. They are put into the ground, because when half rotten it is much easier to beat and extract the fibre.

We arrived at 11.30 a.m. at the church, and found we were 860 feet above the sea level. Don Marcos Ferryillo's house is a long, low building, like an English cottage without the roses and columbine. The old priest himself came out to welcome us, and brought us into his sala. Don Marcos is the head priest (*arcipreste*) of the island, where he has lived all his life. It was exceedingly difficult to hold a conversation with him, owing in the first place to his speaking so rapidly that it was almost impossible to catch what he said, and also to his being used so long to living alone, buried in a small village in a semi-depopulated island, that the poor man seemed dried up both in his tongue and ideas.

We had breakfast soon after our arrival. To us it was more like lunch, being after twelve o'clock, and owing to the nature of the food, which consisted of eggs, fish, cheese, and honey, all excellent. The good priest apologised for the absence of meat, a luxury they were seldom able to procure. The chain of mountains, with the church in the foreground, was the view from the window of the priest's sala. This room was apparently given up to our use, as Don Marcos knocked at the door when entering. At one end of the room, which was one-storied and long in shape, was another room, more like a recess, being destitute of any light save that from the sala. Two doorways showed two beds inside, one opposite each, but

VIEW FROM PRIEST'S HOUSE, ANTIGUA.

neither curtains nor doors separated the bedroom from the sitting-room. Seeing two doorways, we expected to find two recesses, but the beds were foot to foot, undivided.

After breakfast we set out for a walk to explore the neighbourhood and see anything that was to be seen. Don Marcos assured us there was absolutely nothing, but we found much of interest. Antigua strikes one forcibly as being an oasis in the desert, not because the surrounding country is barren, but because a depression, that might or might not be a river-bed if there were rain, runs through the hamlet, making it green. Here wells innumerable, with water-wheels

attached, have been sunk, and the rich soil, only scratched by
the wooden ploughs, yields, by means of plentiful irrigation,
three crops every year. Standing on a slight elevation on the
northern side of the river-bed, the scene before us is strikingly
Eastern. Near each wheel—and we counted ten or fifteen—
is a cistern, in which the water from the well is stored. Palms
of all kinds dot the valley, which has scarcely any other trees.
Ploughing in the rich red soil were dromedaries, whilst numbers
of small birds circled round the cisterns and gave out their
sweet songs perched on stones or walls. The water is
slightly what is called *salino*, or mineral, which does not prevent its being used for every purpose. It is drawn from the
wells in a primitive manner. Two cogged wheels, fitting each
other at right angles, are turned by means of a pole, attached
to a dromedary who walks round blindfolded. Near the
larger and lower wheel is placed a box or tub. An endless
ladder of ropes, the steps formed of tin or wooden boxes,
moves up and over the tub at the top, emptying its contents
into it in succession, somewhat as mud-dredgers bring up their
contents. A trough conducts the water thence into the cistern.
As the water is high or low in the well, the ladder is lengthened
or shortened.

We continued our walk, winding in and out among the
fields and along the cisterns, now passing below a gigantic
palm and anon frightening a flock of birds from the tanks.
Poor little songsters, only here, near man, can they get water,
and taking advantage of their necessity, man entraps them in the
evening with torch and cages. Dinner of soup, tinned meat, and
fowl in the puchero, fritters of sliced potatoes, and ground rice
or something of that sort, needed not the apologies that Don
Marcos insisted on making. He asked us if we would have
supper, and although we said only a cup of tea, he had meat
and eggs prepared for us. Canarians have an idea English
people are always eating; we certainly have meals more
frequently, but if we have, we do not eat so much at each.
It was 59° F. (15° C.) at 6 p.m. in the house.

February 3rd, Sunday.—Hundreds of people went to mass this morning, the whole of the population, one would think. The women were dressed chiefly in coloured print dresses and white mantillas ; a few wore black.   The men were in short dark blue or black jackets and light blue cotton trousers, the colour in various stages of being washed out.   Those that had on new ones were readily distinguishable a long distance off, the colour was such a brilliant sky-blue.   The church, although of fair size, was inadequate for the worshippers, and many knelt at the open door and for some distance on the steps outside.   Service over, the people trooped off to their homes

ANTIGUA CHURCH, FUERTEVENTURA.

for breakfast.   Here was a group of rosy-cheeked and dark-eyed maidens, laughing together, and there some elderly women, discussing matronly matters ; the men, as usual, kept apart, save where some ancient Joan guided the faltering footsteps of her still more ancient Darby.   Happy-looking peasants all, and although poorer and used to greater hardships than those on the neighbouring islands, not so lined and withered as their more "hard-fisted" compatriots.

The weather at eight o'clock this morning [59° F. (15° C.)], reminded one of a summer day in England when everyone is trying to imagine that it is summer, and each secretly wishing for a good blaze upon the desolate hearth.   A strong breeze was blowing yesterday, and to-day there are skiffs of rain, the wind still rioting in the palm leaves and displaying the sturdy ankles of the country girls.

Unwilling to trespass further on our host's hospitality, we procured a camel, and determined to move on to Betancuria, only a ride of an hour or two across the hill. Don Marcos looked upon it as rather foolish our riding by way of Betancuria to Tiscamanita when we could so readily reach there by continuing down the valley southwards, having no hill to climb. Fortunately we adhered to our original intention, or we should have lost the finest bit of scenery north of Jandia, and mention of which had never been made to us. Leaving some alms for the poor, we bade farewell, and mounted a camel once more. Pillows and quilts were brought us for seats, but we had sufficient rugs to make ourselves comfortable without injuring the priest's property.

The road, on the lower part of which was the cemetery, led over a hill of limestone in the range which crosses the island to the south of Antigua. The ascent is not really steep, but is sufficiently so to be trying to the "ship of the desert." The wind blew colder and colder as we ascended, and we were fain to don our ulsters and wrap our rugs around us. There is no shelter upon a camel, and to have one's legs dangling in mid-air is a particularly cold position, but then camels were not intended for cold climates or weather. At the top of the pass, which we reached at 11.40 a.m. (2,000 feet), we found the thermometer registered 51·8° F. (11° C.). Cold is comparative. In the sunny south, in the land of the olive and the fig, where the palm waves her slender leaves in the breeze, where the mighty river and trickling streamlet are unknown, where the blue sky reflects the bluer sea, and the yellow soil, destitute of softening green turf, glares into the very eyeballs, here, in this land of golden sunlight and royal blue, one does not expect only 52° F. on a hill of 2,000 feet. We dismounted in order to enjoy the country behind and before us at leisure, and to admire a view which is said to be the finest the island possesses, both in extent and beauty. Not always, however, do its natives know the best points of a country.

Northward we have first a general impression of redness, shading to ochre, and sometimes almost white, where the limestone creeps out, in the colour of the treeless tract before us. At our feet lies the fertile depression—I can scarce call it a valley—of Antigua. Low mountains bound the horizon in all directions, with vast rolling level plains between. The mountains are rounded, the hills are rounded, nothing abrupt or bold catches the attention, but all is softened off, edges smoothed, the line where the plain ends and the hill begins being undiscernible. A county such as this in England would be reckoned mountainous; in Las Islas Canarias it is called flat. The sea to right and left bounds our vision, and reminds us of the narrowness of the island, although the longest in the archipelago. Turning directly round and facing southwards, the view changes in style, though not in colour. Immediately beneath us lies the little town of Betancuria, the ancient capital of the island, nestling in a hollow beneath the shelter of overhanging hills. The houses clustered at the foot have never clambered up the sides, and generally the Betancuria of to-day suggests no alterations from the Santa Maria de Betancuria founded by Bethencourt, and which contains the second church built in the archipelago. The view is circumscribed, as the Villa is entirely and closely surrounded by steep, low hills, amid which it lies embosomed. Northward the scene is extensive, southward minute. A few fruit trees and fewer palms, such as one always finds around the habitations of man, take from the barren appearance.

Our dromedary has been patiently kneeling all this time on the summit, the camellero keeping him supplied with fresh green herbage, a weed, beloved of camels, growing abundantly on the top of the ridge. It is nothing but a ridge, there being barely the length of the camel of level ground. The road downwards to Betancuria winds round the hillside, cut out of the rich soil, and follows the undulations of the surface.

All the way down we speculated as to which of the few fair-sized houses our introduction was addressed. There is a delightful uncertainty in thus moving from village to village, not knowing where our heads may rest at night, or whether we shall get aught to eat, or whether our hosts will be gentle or

HALT ON THE HILL BETWEEN ANTIGUA AND BETANCURIA.

simple. That our welcome will be at least courteous, possibly warm, and certainly hospitable, we have no doubt. For one contingency we were not prepared, and it was that which awaited us—the absence of our host. Reaching Betancuria, we stopped our camel at a long, low, whitewashed house, the residence of Don Rafael Mota. One of the womenfolk of the establishment opened a venetian shutter, and resting her arms on the window-sill, surveyed us. We learned from her that Don Rafael was attending the festivities in Oliva. A somewhat tardy and hesitating invitation to us to "stay there if we pleased" we declined with thanks.

The men are always warmer in their invitations than the women, which may be accounted for in two ways. Upon the latter falls the trouble of providing for the newly arrived travellers, and owing, I should think, to the want of education on the part of the women, the advantage of conversation with people from other countries is not appreciated, and the trouble alone is thought of. The men, on the other hand, are so accustomed to be waited upon, that the extra trouble for the women of providing and attending upon wayfarers is a thought which never crosses their minds. They are generally thoughtful, self-educated men, anxious for the welfare of their island, and particularly desirous that we should be pleased with it and its inhabitants. I speak of course of the small shopkeeper and farmer class. A Spanish gentleman is the most perfect gentleman in the civilised world, only to be equalled by that *rara avis* an educated Spanish lady. It is a curious and noteworthy fact that there is nothing in the language to correspond to *caballero* (gentleman), *mujer* (woman) being used for all classes. As long as a girl is a maiden she is somebody, but once married, she sinks to a *mujer*, and as such stays at home and is the household drudge. Although staying in many houses of all classes of the community, we never, save in two or three notable instances, had any conversation with the women. They waited upon us, made us comfortable and welcome, but, except in the houses of those of gentle blood, never sat at table with us. This seemed to me the more remarkable inasmuch as I, being a woman, did not expect them to shun my society, but they always left the entire conversation to the men. Often I tried to win them to talk, and could only succeed in doing so by stating facts about myself personally. They were pardonably curious, and much interested in details of a private nature. Frequently there would be a tertulla, at which none but men would be present. I fancy I must have been looked upon as something between a man and a woman! It is so unusual for their women to travel and ride about, to read and talk to men, much less to write, that at last I used to feel I must be very unwomanly. Once or twice we never even caught a glimpse of the women-folk until retiring for the night. Fairy hands prepared our rooms, and fairylike our table was spread, the agents remaining invisible, so much so indeed that we did not hear their voices.

We walked to the bottom of the little village and up the other side to the church, which was kindly opened for us. It is an ancient edifice, and being built about the same time as the conquest, is about therefore four hundred and fifty years old. There are curious paintings in the vestry of events in the life of Christ. One picture of large size, filling a wall, is emblematical, wildly so. It represents a barge full of people, out of whose mouths come scrolls with sentences written upon them. Unfortunately the light colour of the scrolls destroys the smallest pretence at art the picture might possess. The port-holes show the mouths of cannons, out of which flash the seven sacraments of the Church of Rome. No doubt the picture is a pious record of Christianity brought to the Canary Islands by Spanish vessels, the cannons pouring out with shot and shell the seven sacraments. I fear the cannons in the portholes are an anachronism, the artist forgetting the date of the invasion, for cannons were fired from the decks long after they were first used on ships in the fourteenth century. The ceiling of the sacristy is of rather a rich Moorish pattern, coloured in gold and red. The reredos and altars are all highly painted. The floor is composed of unequally sized stones, placed in a framework of wood. The ceiling of the church is of wood, the beams carved, with stars upon them.

The Villa de Betancuria is a quaint little town, all up and downhill, for there is no level bottom to the valley. The trees are chiefly orange and fig, and in their vicinity one sees the inevitable well and cistern.

After consultation with our camellero, we found him willing

to take us on to Pajara, if there were time. All the answer
however, we could elicit from the two or three people we
encountered in the Villa as to the distance was, "It takes a
day." As it was then about twelve o'clock, we doubted if we
should have enough daylight, but knowing by our map that the
distance could not be very great, we determined to set out.
Our man had never been this road, so did not know the way
nor how long it took. However, supposing we should find
people to ask, we started. We never have had regular guides

BETANCURIA.

in these islands except for the Peak, they were only peasants
who happened to know the paths. A path led us through a
break in the hills into a narrow, winding valley. Sometimes we
rode along its side, and sometimes descended into the river-bed
at the bottom. Tamarisk bushes were the only trees of any
kind, but the soil on the sloping sides was good, sheltered from
wind and cultivated. We were really quite surprised as we
wound onwards by the sudden and unexpected sight of this
pretty winding gorge. The variety of the road, which sometimes lay high and again low, even in the river-bed, with a hut
or two at intervals above us, was charming. A bend would

perhaps bring a stately palm in sight, forming a pretty picture, and make us greatly enjoy our ride. Whether the valley was really pretty, or whether it was the contrast with the large, flat plains to the north of the island which magnified its beauty, I feel scarcely capable of saying. A little stream ran for a short distance along the river-bed, but being too precious to lose, dams were made of clay, forming troughs, to collect it for the animals. They resembled the dams children make in a stream in England, the liliputian character of the rivulet demanding reservoirs of a similar size, although not made by little hands. Several times the water appeared in the river-bed, trickled along for a few yards, and again disappeared. When this occurred, we found our path led up and above the barranco, as camels do not like walking near or over water. Our animal did not object much. He was, in fact, the gentlest beast of any sort I have ever ridden, and as a camel was particularly easy, sure-footed, and fast in motion.

At 2 p.m. we came to Rio de Las Palmas, and found we were 1,150 feet above the sea, at a new little church. A quantity of palms clustered along the valley and between the houses, which extend for some distance, showed that the name was not a misnomer. The hills on either side widen out, and on the left bank become higher and precipitous. Down a groove in the cliff quite a respectable stream was running. Taro, farvero, olive, and other trees and even a few flowers decorate the valley, and give a pleasant look to the rambling village of poor mud huts. Not one large or even moderately sized house did we see. The little church stands alone, save for two huts, upon rising ground, upon the left bank of the river. Above, also on the left bank, about a kilometre from the Villa, are a few vestiges of the castle of Val Tarajal, in which Gadifer shut himself up when he and Bethencourt were falling out over his reward. Here also Bethencourt came on his return from Spain, and presented the church with gifts, a child being baptised in his honour ; and here he stayed while arranging the affairs of his new conquest. Truly he chose the most lovely spot in the whole island for his residence. Asking the way from two men seated outside their houses, we descended into the river-bed, and crossed to the palms and main part of the village, some distance from the church. The mud roofs and walls of the houses, the green vegetation up the mountain sides, the fine grey granite rocks along the river-bed, the whole crowned by the old and picturesque church built on a bend of the river, an ancient weather-beaten cross standing some twenty or thirty yards from its western door, formed a picture that in any land would be pretty, and that here was simply delightful. Here, for the first time in the last of the seven islands, we encountered granite, or rather sienite. The hills are formed of it in quantities to last any number of years' quarrying.

It was to this spot that Gadifer made his expedition to Fuerteventura in search of the natives. Landing on a part of the island near Lanzarote, he and thirty-five companions walked until they came to the "Vien de Palmes," where they found "a fountain, by which they rested a while, and then began to climb a high mountain, whence they could overlook a great part of the country." Twenty-one of the Spaniards struck, however, and refused to go further, so Gadifer and the rest only reached the summit. Here, taking six of the men, he descended to the sea to try and find a harbour, and returning up stream, met his companions again "at the entrance to the Palm Grove, which is wonderfully difficult of access, and is only two stones'-throw in length and two or three lances broad. They found it necessary to take off their shoes to pass over the slabs of marble, which were so smooth and slippery, that they could only cross them on hands and feet, and even those who were behind had to hold the ends of their lances for the foremost to push their feet against, and they, when safely over, in their turn pulled the hindmost after them. Beyond, the valley was lovely and unbroken, and very pleasant; it was shaded by about eight hundred palm trees, in groups of a hundred and twenty-six, with streams

running between them; they were more than twenty fathoms
high, like the masts of a ship, and were so green and leafy,
and full of fruit, that they were a goodly sight to behold.
There they dined in the shade on the turf, near the running
brooks, and rested a while, for they were very weary." Ichabod!
the glory has departed, for but few palms are now left. Still
very beautiful is the Valley of Palms. It would have been
well had the chronicle ended here, so that this peaceful record
should not leave a sad memory behind. Resuming their
journey, the invaders climbed the hillside, sending forward
three scouts, who encountered some Majos, whom they put to
flight, capturing some women in a cavern, "one of whom had
a little child at the breast, which she strangled, it is supposed
from fear of its crying." It is said that after this they
encountered some fifty natives, who held them in check until
their wives and children had escaped, when they fled to the
mountains. Here Gadifer tried to pursue them, but night fell,
and proved so dark, that they were unable to see each other,
so returned to the vessel, with four women as captives.

Leaving the village and its groups of inhabitants all outside
their doors, enjoying the pleasant freshness of the winter air
and the bright sun, we descended to the river, and crossed
quite a bubbling stream, broad enough to require one stepping-
stone in the middle. Masses of granite, festooned with green
verdure, grassy banks, and fresh-looking trees, made one long
to linger, as did Gadifer and his companions, drinking in their
sweetness. Crossing the stream, we ascended a steep path
over granite rocks, the road lying some distance above the
river-bed, where there is, alas! now no water; man has stepped
in, made aqueducts, and carried off all the precious fluid. Consequently the land all along is very fertile, the utility increased
but the beauty diminished. Although Sunday, the more elderly
of the village folk were sitting on the ground at their doors,
making palm mats and brushes. In this remote quarter little
disturbs the even monotony of their lives. Without books and
education, the day would pass slowly were not the hands

occupied.   As we wish them good-day in passing, all lift their hats civilly and respectfully

Descending again, we walk along the bottom of the river-bed, masses of beautiful grey granite on either side of us.   As we come once more to water, the path rises, until we find ourselves entering a magnificent granite gorge.   Across the entrance, where the river is hemmed in by two blocks of granite, a wall, many feet thick, was built, thus forming a reservoir.   This year, however, owing to the unusual rain, the weight of water was too great, and the masonry gave way, the breach letting us see the barrier's thickness.   Our path wound along the right bank a considerable distance above the river.   Above us was a sloping block of granite, massive and grey, while the other side of the narrow gorge was bounded by a mountain of granite.   The Pass of Las Peñitas, unknown and unappreciated, in a remote corner of a despised island, is one of the finest bits of scenery in the archipelago.   The very fact of its being granite gives it a magnificence that even basalt never reaches.   Unexpectedly we came upon the pass, a breath of its existence never having reached us, except through the MSS of the conquerors, which, however, are exceedingly vague as to locality.   We had asked a native of the island, who was supposed to have travelled all over it, what there was to see, and his answer was, " Nothing, absolutely nothing."   By chance we directed our steps first to Betancuria and then to Pajara, instead of going direct to Tiscamanita from Antigua, as we were urged to do by many. An hour and a half would have taken us to Tiscamanita from Antigua, but we preferred seeing more of the island by going the other route.   Being obstinate English folk, we were given in to and pityingly allowed our own way.   The result in this instance was satisfactory.

The path, hewn and built with difficulty half-way up the steep slope of granite, is about three feet wide, and one or two wider places are formed where a camel can stand to allow of another passing.   Three feet of path is of course not nearly wide enough for a laden camel, which requires six feet, but owing to the granite wall on the right being a slope, there was sufficient room for us to pass, with careful watching and making the animal walk close to the edge of the precipice, over which I sat complacently, dangling my feet. A curve in the path brought into sight a tiny house, built on a ledge beneath us, close to a waterfall. It is a little chapel, dedicated to the "Virgin of the Little Rocks." The legend connected with this place states that the Virgin having here appeared to a worthy friar, he lived in a cave close to so sacred a spot until his death. Hence the name of the hermitage or chapel now erected is Cueva de las Peñitas (Cave of the Little Rocks). Viera throws much doubt upon the apparition, and is inclined to think that the Spaniards settled in Fuerteventura were not content at the absence of miraculous appearances in their island when the Virgin had been seen elsewhere, so manufactured an apparition. It answers its purpose, however, by drawing attention to the island, two pilgrimages being yearly made to the place. It seems a suitable spot for a hermitage, and, at any rate, adds to the beauty of the scene.

Whilst the stream descended in huge leaps down perpendicular granite towards the valley, which here turns westward, we descended by a steep path, winding between blocks of granite. We preferred dismounting, for, wonderfully surefooted as was our gentle camel, the path seemed almost an impossibility to such an animal, and was indeed fit neither for man nor beast. Frequently he had not a large enough space for his cushioned foot, and our luggage suffered from many a knock, now on this side and now on that. The valley from Betancuria is narrow, ending in this magnificent gorge, which forms a sort of division between the two cultivated winding valleys, sparsely inhabited, but plentifully sprinkled with stately palms. The valley we now enter is different in appearance, being lower and wider, the granite ceasing and the limestone reappearing. Here fortunately two men were ploughing with a yoke of oxen, or we should have been rather at a loss to know the path. The water in the river-bed had been conducted away by aqueducts again, so we walked down it for a time, and then struck westward over a broad, billowy hill of limestone. In the valleys between the waves we twice encountered walls built across to form reservoirs, but both broken by the unusual rain. About 4 p.m. we came to another valley and riverbed, a village, studded with palms, winding along its banks. Our camellero did not know it, and as we were quite ignorant of the next turn, we proceeded to inquire the route. Seeing a little house, our man jumped the loose wall dividing us from it, and knocked at the door. All attempts to gain admittance or see anyone proved fruitless, however. Whilst wondering which could be the road, two women, driving a laden mule, came in sight, and told us that the way to Pajara lay up the barranco. They also informed us that the unknown village was called Masca. It was then 4.15 p.m., and we wondered much if we should be able to reach our shelter before nightfall. We asked the women how far it was to Pajara, although perfectly aware it was useless to do so. Peasants have no idea of distance or time. We were frequently reminded of Biblical language when told it was " a day's journey " to a place.

Our poor camel was getting a little lame, and was going very slowly. Fortunately for it, the owner was lame also, a permanent infirmity, so did not urge it on, but it made us the more anxious to reach our destination. A few houses came in sight, but they turned out to be deserted, the empty cistern and neglected cactus fields imparting a particularly melancholy aspect to the place. Another little cottage further on was quite a contrast, its low roof and surrounding walls being thronged with tiny kids, chiefly black-and-white, and some pure white, which seem to be the prevailing colours here. At last we neared a settlement of mud houses, and wondered which way to turn among the labyrinth of walled-in paths. Meeting a man, he volunteered to show us the way to Don Pedro Brito's house. The peasants here are exceedingly civil and courteous, with no trace of the surliness and stupidity one frequently meets in Canaria.

We arrived at Don Pedro's house at 5.30. Our camel knelt

with less grumbling than usual, being tired, poor thing, and we gladly scrambled off, being rather stiff with so much sitting. After some delay and much knocking at the closed door in the yard of Don Pedro's house, a shrill voice screeched rather than asked, "Quien?" ("Who is there?"). We asked the unknown to open the door. She wished to know what we wanted, and, after much persuasion on our part and that of our camellero, she opened the door about four inches, looked out, said she did not understand our letter, that Don Pedro was not at home, and slammed the door. The vision that appeared to us during the two seconds in which the door was open was of a wizened, filthily dirty old hag. Here we were in a pretty plight. The

CHURCH AT PAJARA, FUERTEVENTURA.

sun was rapidly sinking—and sunset in these latitudes means night—a tired camel, laden with our luggage, crouching in the street, and ourselves tired and hungry, our hearts going down with the sun, standing helplessly outside a closed door. In vain we asked a crowd of about a dozen men if there were no room in the whole village of Pajara we could have; we could do without beds if there were only a room in which we might rest. No, there was none. At last one respectable-looking man stepped forward and said that if we would like to sit down and rest in his brother the cura's room until Don Pedro returned we were welcome. So we gladly followed him to the upper part of the village, beyond the church (880 feet). Here, entering a little house, he opened a door, uttered a few words of explanation to someone inside, and ushered us into the presence of the village priest.   He rose as we entered from a table where he had been quietly reading some book of devotion, and made us welcome, opening the shutters to let in the waning light, and handing us chairs.   A few words explained our position.

The cura was a young man, almost a youth, with thoughtful grey eyes and a simple, earnest expression that spoke volumes for his purity of thought, word, and action.   A small stretcher-bed, two old tables, on which stood his meagre library of theological works, a little washstand, and a few chairs formed the furniture. The room was boarded, the walls whitewashed, and the roof of open laths.   He and his brother pressed us to have somewhat to eat, but, fearful of trespassing too much upon their hospitality, we said we would wait until the return of Don Pedro. This they considered such an uncertain event, that they insisted on our eating something.   Eggs were proposed, with many apologies for scanty fare.   However, we declined the eggs, as it is really impossible to live upon them morning, noon, and night, and asked, knowing well they would have it, for gofio. They were so delighted to think we could eat and really liked gofio, that it would have been worth while to have refused the daintiest dishes to have seen their faces.   An excellent supper of fried bread, gofio, cheese, and good, well-tasting tea of the native theine shrub we thoroughly enjoyed.

Previously, at six o'clock, whilst talking to the young priest, the bell for vespers rang out, when he rose, saying it was the custom of the place to repeat some prayers at that hour, and would we join him ?   We thanked him, declining, as the form of words was unknown to us.   It was only another pleasing trait in his character, the simplicity and conscientiousness with which the whole action was performed.   Leaving us at our supper, he went to the church, and returning later, we had some interesting conversation with him upon the island and its inhabitants.

He says the emigration during the past seven years of famine has kept the country in such a desolate condition, the farms are only half cultivated.   One farm he mentioned has one

hundred and eighty hectareas, of which only eighty are cultivated. This is merely an instance of the condition everywhere.
We had passed many deserted houses and much uncultivated
land, bearing out the truth of what he said.

Notwithstanding the intense poverty of the people, the truly
paternal Government of Spain abated not one jot or tittle of
the heavy taxes. A representation was even made to the
home Government of the starving condition of the inhabitants
by the people of Canaria and Lanzarote, and the humane,
generous, and noble answer returned by the Fatherland was
that if the petitioners made up the deficit, they would forgive
poverty-stricken Fuerteventura to the extent of laying the
burden upon the other already overtaxed islands. Words
cannot convey the scorn one feels for such an executive. The
money, too, instead of being used even for public works to aid
the unfortunate people, all goes to support the broken finances
of the Peninsula, leaving Fuerteventura guiltless of a single
road. In this of course it is not alone, Gomera and Hierro
sharing a like fate.

CHAPTER XVIII.

TISCAMANITA—ENGLISH REVERSES IN FUERTEVEN-TURA—GRAN TARAJAL—GRAN CANARIA.

> Rolling among the furrows of the unquiet,
> Unconsecrate, unfriendly, dreadful sea.
>
> Jean Ingelow.
>
> And some, who seemed but ill to brook
> That sluggish calm, with many a look
> To the slack sail impatient cast,
> As loose it flagged around the mast.
>
> Moore.

February 4th, Monday.—Last night, with true hospitality, the priest would not allow us to await the uncertain return of Don Pedro, but turned out of his room for us. Another canvas stretcher was procured from somewhere, and we gladly went to rest. Unfortunately, if there be a flea anywhere in my neighbourhood, it is sure to settle upon me, so during the early part of the night I divided my time between dozing, lighting matches, and catching my enemies. I have become quite an adept in this latter art, proving the truth of the saying that "practice makes perfect." It must not be thought from this that we were in a dirty house. On the contrary, our sheets were spotlessly clean. But this little animal seems to exist in the very ground—it certainly does in sand—and it is almost impossible to escape him. One's only chance of relief is to live in the higher parts of the islands, where the cold is the best preventive. I do not say, however, that an English house here, kept clean in every corner, would not be free from pulgas.

As soon as we appeared this morning Don Pedro Brito called. He had come last night, but we were in bed, and from early morning he was waiting to tender many apologies for his absence and his servant's churlishness, about which he seemed much distressed. As we had not sent any message to him, of course he did not expect us. He very kindly asked us to stay that day with him, and we being obliged to refuse, he sent his camel and servant to take us to Tiscamanita, although up to the last he urged us to remain. We would gladly have done so but for the fear of missing the schooner at Gran Tarajal. The servant was an excellent fellow, as are all the peasants here. He told us several times over how vexed Don Pedro was with his woman-servant. Evidently, from the way he laughed over it, the old woman is a well-known character.

Half an hour or less after leaving Pajara — we started at 9.30—we passed through Toto. This village seems a part of Pajara, and is very small, containing only one good house, which belongs to Don Pedro Brito, and in which his sister is living; he wished us to stay there for breakfast, Spanish fashion, but we had broken our fast in English style before setting out. Much land about here was going to waste, the untidy cactus covering good soil. One valley contained well-cultivated land, lying in terraces. Sluices between the fields or terraces allowed of the water being passed on from one to the other. We could see it trickling down the higher hills or mountains forming the chain, or *cordillera*, which, like a backbone, runs along the southerly part of the island. It was this chain which we crossed from Antigua to Betancuria, and which we were about to recross between Toto and Tiscamanita. Quantities of birds were singing around. They perched on the roadside a yard from our camel, and looked at us fearlessly with their bright black eyes. One saucy fellow, I remember particularly, never attempted to move until the camellero flicked at him with his whip. The water in Pajara, as in many other parts of the island, is slightly mineral. This to those unaccustomed to it is not pleasant, although drinkable. An Englishman who had resided in Gran Tarajal some years told me that he liked it so much after a time, that on his return to Gran Canaria he disliked the ordinary pure, tasteless water. It is perhaps bearable cold, but when used for making tea or coffee, those drinks become almost nauseous.

"Fuchi!" the word used to make the dromedaries kneel, said to be of African origin, was introduced doubtless with the animal.

The country about here consists of steep, undulating hills, guiltless of trees. We have met with few ferns either in this island or Lanzarote, save in the dripstones, the filters of the Canary Islands. To-day was cloudy, very little sun, like a dull day in England, and the temperature 57·2° F. (14° C.). As we reached the summit of the hill over which we had to pass between Pajara and Tiscamanita, we found the height to be 1,510 feet. A bright little yellow butterfly was disporting himself on the sheltered side of the hill. Near this an old woman caught us up, thin, active, and wiry physically. The activity extended itself to her mind and tongue, for she never ceased talking from the time she joined our caravan until we arrived in Tiscamanita. Vainly we tried to fall behind—we had dismounted on the summit for a walk—she thought it her duty to be in the rear, and it cost us much manœuvring to avoid her chatter. When one has been talking all the morning, and will probably have to talk all the evening, with the constrained attention necessary when speaking in a language not so familiar as one's native tongue, it is a rest to get among the solitudes of nature, and not be obliged to utter a word, either English or Spanish.

A short and rapid descent brought us to a small barranco, down which, as usual, the road ran, and, after winding in and out of the stone walls dividing the farms, we at last arrived at Don Marcial Velasquez's house. He had received our letter sent from Antigua, and was ready to welcome us. We were much interested in a map and raised plan of the island which he had made himself from personal observation while travelling, while shelves filled with books betrayed the literary tastes of Don Marcial and his brothers.

Taking the camera with us, we started for a walk to get a general idea of Tiscamanita and its surroundings. The straggling village of this name is situated on a large plain, sloping southwards towards Gran Tarajal. The plain is surrounded, though not in an unbroken chain, by low mountains. These hills are sometimes conical, and between their abrupt sides one catches a glimpse of the blue waters of the surrounding Atlantic. A few small and old craters are around, almost the only volcanoes in the island, but the general aspect of the mountains is that of rugged ridges, extending in short, broken chains, with a background of blue sea.

The Montaña de la Torre, to the north of the plain, is an unmistakable crater. At its foot runs, or ran, an ancient lava stream, now lichen-covered and green, harmless and peaceful enough, but a witness to a force once terrible and relentless, creeping slowly, but surely and pitilessly, down the hillside and over the sloping plain, until its hideous blackness, like the darkness of death, was mercifully engulfed in the depths of the Atlantic.

Here, as in the rest of this island, the depressions or valleys are the oases in the desert. A bird's-eye view gives the impression that the plain beneath is one vast, level surface, with strips of green verdure here and there. Experience teaches, however, that those strips of green are not on a level with the surrounding land, but depressions where the moisture lies more readily, and where the water filling the wells sunk at the bottom of the valleys affords means for irrigation.

Nature generally provides compensation for her own deficiencies. So here the rich red soil is covered with a hand's depth of black cinders, which keeps the moisture in the ground hidden from the penetrating rays of the sun.

After dinner, at three, we were actually kept in the house by the rain. Fancy the intense excitement to a child who had never seen rain before, as those under seven years of age cannot have ! Even the grown folk seem to suspend all work, and stand at the door looking at the refreshing drops as they fall upon the thirsty land. Just before sunset it cleared, and we took a stroll amid the twisting lanes, bound on either side by loose stone walls instead of banks or hedges. The rapidly increasing gloom warned us to return, as, with no moonlight, it was not easy to avoid stumbling upon the rough paths, paved in parts with whole sheets of rock outcrop. Once, as we turned a corner, we were nearly walked over by a couple of camels. Their cushioned pads make no noise, and in the gloaming it was difficult, well-nigh impossible, to distinguish their dull, dust-coloured hair from the walls and roads of the same colour. I quite jumped when I found myself immediately beneath the uplifted head and cynical eyes of a noiseless dromedary.

Supper consisted of a national dish prepared expressly for us by Don Marcial's orders. *Frangollo* is coarsely ground wheat, boiled with rice in water, and eaten with hot milk. The general appearance is that of porridge well boiled, but thick and stiff. It is exceedingly good and palatable, at any rate to those accustomed to porridge, and to us it was particularly grateful, after the everlasting bread and eggs. Our real enjoyment of this national dish gave evident pleasure to our worthy host, who is a true patriot.

After much conversation upon matters political, personal, historical, and geographical, we were escorted to our sleeping apartments by Don Marcial's mother, a sweet, placid woman, and his sister, a beautiful young girl, who in a year or two would eclipse all the belles and set London in a furore over a face like Fra Angelica's. I fell asleep in a room scented with rose leaves, and haunted by gazelle-like eyes, the bloom of a peach, and a mouth fit to drive a man crazy.

February 5th, Tuesday.—After breakfast we started in search of a good place from whence to take a view of the town. From a neighbouring undulation we could see the yellow houses, with the crater of Gayria, whose mouth is but little broken, in the background. The volcanic mountains near the sea look blue and clear against the sky, shadows from passing clouds flitting across them.

In the little valley beneath is one of the numerous water-wheels over a well, a couple of camels standing patiently ready for any work they may be put to, and various are the labours of the camel in this island. A man who is directing their

WATERWHEEL, TISCAMANITA, FUERTEVENTURA.

labours is dressed in most picturesque attire, for it is one mass of patches from top to bottom, and over his shoulder he carries one of the hoes used as spades. Behind us a few houses and palm trees denote where Tuineje lies beneath a red rounded hill. The presence of towns here is first indicated by the waving plumes of the palm in the distance; later one discovers the low, one-storied houses, built of the same stone as the neighbouring country affords, and thus scarcely discernible against the hillsides or on the undulating ground.

Three kinds of stone are found and used in this island,—
granite, both red and grey, the stones for filters, and limestone;
so there is no reason why Fuerteventura should be the poorest
island of the group, with such internal resources.   Land capable
of growing wheat or barley is sold at the most for three
hundred and seventy-five pesetas a hectarea, but there is plenty
much cheaper.   Numerous small yellow butterflies lazily hover
around us as we walk across the stony ground towards the
church.   Here the villagers, chiefly women, are gathered waiting for mass, this being a saint's day.   They wear white
mantillas, and have pleasant, though not pretty, faces.

At 11 a.m. we started for Gran Tarajal, where we expect to
meet our schooner.   We had only been some fifteen minutes on
our journey when we saw, through a dip in the hills seaward, a
vessel getting into the port.   Trying to hasten with a camel is
useless.   He goes his own pace, in this instance a very quick
one, as we trotted quite five or more miles an hour, if such
his swinging strides can be called.   However, the patrónes
of these schooners are never in a hurry, so we had small doubt
we should be in plenty of time.   Half an hour's riding brought
us close to Tuineje, whose limestone houses and mud roofs we
left on our right beneath the red dome of Montaña Tamaceite.
Tuineje is of interest to us English, as it was here, or rather at
Tamaceite, our compatriots were routed, and nearly all killed by
the Spaniards, in October, 1740.   An English privateer landed
a considerable number of men at Las Playas who marched here,
where they were attacked by the natives with clubs and stones,
and most of them killed, a few prisoners who were taken being sent
to Tenerife.   This occurred on the 13th, and on the 29th of the
same month some other privateers, landing at the same place,
marched inland too, and, curiously enough, to the same spot.
The islanders, enraged at being again disturbed, drew up a line
of camels to defend themselves, and butchered every one, giving
no quarter.   No doubt then, as now, the deserted appearance of
the coast led the English to believe the island uninhabited,
whereas all the towns are in the interior.

As we got further south towards Tarajal the vast extent of country that we had seen lying between the limestone and craters, and which looked like a plain, turned out to be un-dulating limestone hills, with good surface soil, but, alas ! only a deserted wild met our view. Now, owing to the recent heavy rains, green herbs are scattered in patches across the yellowy-red surface.

Between Tuineje and Gran Tarajal one house alone broke the monotony. Catalina Garcia seems as though built and planted on purpose to show what might be made of the soil. It is like an oasis in the desert, but the desert is an unnecessary one. A barranco winds here between the low hills, and where most sheltered a house has been built and the soil cultivated. Not only are there palm trees, but also olives, their dark green foliage contrasting well with the rich, loamy red soil. The bare whity-grey stems of numerous fig trees show that figs may be had later on, while below, following closely the turns of the river-bed, are numerous tamarisks, in various autumnal shades, and mismo shrubs.

Dark clouds have been hanging over Canaria all morning, and on looking back, we see it is raining in Tiscamanita. It has been blowing fiercely in our faces since we started, and it is not long until the rain comes too. When it rains in Fuerteventura, it does so in earnest. It has to make up for lost time. In England there is no hurry; the clouds can let the water out of their cistern gently. But here it rained not for three years, so who can be surprised that it came like an avalanche at the last ? A short, very short, time, I know, sufficed to wet our cavalcade thoroughly. The anomaly of sitting upon a camel in a storm of rain, to say nothing of the addition of the modern and Western umbrella, was ever present to our minds. The boy perched on the hump between us was soaked to the skin, another lad vainly sought shelter as he walked on the leeward side of the camel, while Don Marcial and his donkey bravely bore the brunt of the pitiless storm. Half-way or thereabouts is a hill in the road which is called the Half-way Hill, which we reached at 12.15 p.m., and where the boy on the camel dismounted to let the other up.

Eastward of this at a little distance is the Corral de los Asnos, where fifteen hundred donkeys were killed in 1590. When brought to the island first, they increased so rapidly, running wild upon the mountains, that they destroyed the grain. Use and pleasure were combined, and a hunt organised in honour of the captain-general who was in the island at the time settling some disputes.

The hillock led to a small ridge of limestone, on either side of which was a barranco so called, but really only streamlet-beds which have water trickling down them. That of La Mata lies on the left, and that of Tuineje on the right. Near Gran Tarajal these streams, joining, have, from the force of water when there is rain, made a wide river-bed. The hills close in on either hand, and from one side to the other stretch in tolerable quantities tamarisk and mismo bushes. Sand has gathered, and helped to plant them more firmly, so that laughingly the Majoreros call this their forest. Glas says a sort of wild pine called *tarrahala,* used for fuel for ships, grew here. Hence no doubt the name of the bay.

Gran Tarajal appears a much more formidable place when described than when seen. A bay, neither very deep nor wide, with bluffs at either end of a dark brown strand, forms the port. The fishing village consists of some dozen or two of houses at the western side of the bay, clumped in two parallel lines at right angles to the sea.

It is still blowing hard, and speaking to the captain of the *Santiago,* whom we see in the street, we find he has postponed his departure till the morning. So here we are, without a place in which to sleep. Our host, however, Don Marcial, foreseeing the possibility of our being delayed here, brought with him the key of a room which he has in the village for his own use. We were only too thankful to put a roof between us and the pelting rain. Our next thought was of provisions. Though one may not live to eat, still it is very necessary to eat to live. The

room we were in was reached by a flight of stone steps from a
yard, the rest of the house being occupied by fisherfolk. Now,
of all the people in all the islands, the fishing population is
always the poorest—and dirtiest. When this is remembered, it
will not be wondered at with what feelings of relief we found
we were to have a room all to ourselves, without other human
beings, and consequently other animals. The room was some
eighteen or twenty feet square; two windows, a door, and a
cupboard faced each other respectively in the four walls; the
ceiling was plastered and whitewashed between the pine beams,
leaving the logs half uncovered; and the floor was cemented in
the usual way in this island, where limestone is so plentiful
and wood so scarce. Half a dozen plain deal chairs, two
tables, upon the largest of which was a narrow straw mattress,
covered by a palm matting, and a piece of matting on the floor
completed the furniture,—nothing superfluous, but to us,
under the present circumstances, all-sufficient. My basket and
portmanteau supplied us with bread and sardines, a sort of
stop-gap until we could get something better, or at any rate
more substantial. Don Marcial induced one of the girls from
below to come up and brush the floor. Four others accompanied
her, and tumbled over each other into the room, half shy, half
wild, and stood giggling whilst the elder one scratched the floor
with a palm brush. They were induced, with some persuasion,
to leave, in order to prepare some food for us.

From our window the view was rather pleasing. The sea in
all its moods is a never-ceasing picture. The house lies at right
angles to the water, in front of us stretches the brown, slightly
curved strand, ending in an abrupt cliff of moderate height,
while breaking the monotony of its basaltic face, presenting an
almost straight and perpendicular line to the sea, is a heap of
rocks, shattered and worn, lying at its base. The *Santiago* rolls
helplessly, straining and tugging at her anchor, while the breakers
thunder on the shore. Inland the green tamarisk bushes give
colouring to the picture.

About five o'clock the dinner arrived, and we seated ourselves at an ancient card-table, guiltless of a cloth. Two large and oval red earthenware dishes, the one with small peeled potatoes and the other with dried fish, comprised the repast. Stuck upright in the potatoes were two iron spoons, our dinner-service, with the addition of an old *Times* and our pocket-knives. As we were unwilling, however, to eat the scales of the fish, we had to take to our fingers. I must confess that I would have preferred the potatoes served in their skins. It prevents any doubt as to the cleanliness of the peeling operations. We proposed having some coffee after our meal. The girl stood aghast, for where could coffee be procured ? We had the coffee ; how to make it was the difficulty. Cups of course we did not expect, but thought we might have a bowl each. The village was searched, and at last a solitary red one was found. We begged for a little water to wash our hands, which was willingly supplied, with the remark that they had no towel. That and the soap, however, we produced from our invaluable portmanteau. We sadly missed our canteen, but not expecting to live in the tent, owing to the uncertain weather, we had not brought it.

As there was nothing to do but wait patiently for the gale to abate, I did some writing. Before dinner we had lit two or three candles, also from the portmanteau, and to the people the extravagance of using more than one seemed great. Their bewilderment was still further increased by my writing, the art of reading, to say nothing of writing, being almost unknown. Open-eyed and mouthed, leaning over each other's shoulders on tiptoe, barefooted, and with rough, uncombed hair, they stood. The three half-candles stuck on a coffee tin and table by their own grease, and throwing us into relief as we sat at the table, two boys in the dim shadow on a window-seat, finishing the fish and potatoes, wet rugs spread on chairs, open portmanteaus, and the shy group of sea-maidens form a curious picture. The stillness in the room is profound for some minutes, while the thunder of the surf outside alone forms the music to my pen. All our accessories are new to these half-dressed children of nature, and their merry laughter and noisy chatter cease at a few of the simplest products of civilisation. Do they wonder of what I write? They little think it is of themselves.

We retired to our table and mattress early, and slept peacefully until about two o'clock, when we were wakened by a stone thrown at the shutters which alone formed the window. Opening them we saw a sailor below, who asked if we were going to Canaria, for they were about to start. Groaning, we packed, and groping down the steps, left without being able to say good-bye to our kind host, who had waited to see us off. Two or three of the sailors shouldered our luggage, and turning the corner of a house, passed out of sight as we stopped to turn the key in the door. Quickly following as well as we could in the dark, they were nowhere to be seen. A flood of light from an open doorway revealed, however, one house where the people were awake. We went in, and found the sailors there, and the patrón settling his accounts, for the house was a shop, kept in the most primitive style by a man and woman. The house was one long room. At the back, along its length, was a roughly fitting shelf, and on it, in hopeless confusion, lay an assortment of articles, tins and baskets; a few feet in front of the shelf, a row of boxes, varied in size and appearance, formed the counter. Sitting on one of these was the patrón, entering the expenditure, with evident difficulty, in a small note-book. The men had been sleeping here and buying food, for which he was paying. A coarse linen bag constituted the purse, tied with cord. Just as he had concluded his writing and had tied the bag up carefully—how one is again reminded of Biblical language: "keeping the bag"—he remembered four quartos owing for something else, so the untying and writing in the book had to be gone through again. Once more all was put away, when one of the men remembered three quartos more, so the process was repeated, until I thought we should never get off.

When anything unpleasant has to be got through, it is better to do it at once. We knew the passage to Canaria would be disagreeable from former experience in correos, so the sooner over the better. However, we were much amused by the scene before us as we sat on the counter of boxes, the owners of the shop and the patrón scarcely able among them to count two and two, the rough sailors, barelegged, standing near the door, the confusedly arranged room, dimly lighted by two small lamps, whilst the patrón, with knitted brows and cramped fingers, essayed to settle his accounts ; outside —pitch darkness and the roll of the surf.

A few seconds' tramping over sand brought us to the boat, into which our luggage and ourselves were carried. It took some minutes to pass the surf, during which a sailor hung on to the stern, keeping her head to the waves. My heart sank as I was lifted over the bulwarks into the schooner, and disappeared in my shoes as I descended into the hole denominated first cabin, at 2.15 a.m.

February 6th, Wednesday.—It is difficult for anyone to realise who has not experienced it the perfect agony of discomfort one endures in these schooners. There is no deck room, so that even when well one is unable to be on deck. The cabin of the *Santiago* was about twelve feet by six feet, and surrounded by bunks that for discomfort beat those of other schooners. We were allotted one which was called double for both. We measured it. It was three feet wide, and so low, that whoever lay inside could not pass out without the other rising first. A sail was fortunately stowed there, so we were not quite lying on the boards. There were ten berths in the cabin, which had been painted white, but dirty finger-marks and black smudges had long ago lost it all claim to that cleanly colour. The floor was brushed every morning with a palm brush, and bits of straw, cigarette ends, and other dirt swept under the three steps leading to the deck, where they lay unmolested.

Our companions added to our misery, for it was only by such forced intercourse we could see how really dirty people are capable of being. Opposite, in the corresponding bunk, was a woman of about thirty-five or forty. Her person was excessively dirty, and her habits worse. The inside of the bunk, its walls, floor, or any corner within reach served for a spittoon. A box lay outside her berth, and on this she laid her head, employing her leisure time, when she was not ill and groaning, in catching the live stock therein preserved and executing them with her thumb-nail on the lid of the chest. At right angles with us was a young fellow, who smoked continually. Besides these, the sailors, or at least the head men amongst them, slept in the spare berths, and used the cabin as a dressing-room. In the evening, or when becalmed, they all sat in it, and all smoked, and expectorated, and talked, and laughed day and night. One of them was evidently a good story-teller, and entertained the rest by graphic, supernatural, and detailed accounts originated in his brain. I was amused at first by the recital, but after a time the atmosphere overcame the preoccupation of my mind, and I felt as if I were sinking, a sort of desperate feeling coming over me, as if I must struggle out of the place or shriek. By this time the air must have been very impure. There were eleven or twelve of us in the cabin, all the men smoking, the dim lamp suspended in the middle adding its quota of odour to the general smells of the place. Sorry as I was to interrupt the story, I was really obliged—or we should have been suffocated— to ask them to open the trapdoor above. They acceded readily. But is it not incredible that they were able themselves to endure such an amount of bad air?

When morning broke, we were close to Jandia and its isthmus of dune sand, like the Isleta, instead of being near Canaria. The sand hillocks are higher here, and the mountains of Jandia are higher than those of the Isleta. All day the sails flapped, and the boom groaned wearily as it swayed from side to side, while we endeavoured to make our way round the promontory.

February 7th, Thursday.—About two o'clock in the morning a breeze sprang up, which carried us along swiftly; hope revived that we should reach Las Palmas for breakfast, as we could see its snow-covered cumbres, and with a horrid satisfaction be-gotten of starvation, the mind no longer controlled by the will,

but subject to the pressing needs of the body, we gloated helplessly over various forms of food. Doubtless if we had asked for
it the men would have shared their gofio and salt fish with us.
It was not the food we minded, but the manner of eating and the
surroundings. We could not make up our minds to eat out of
the same dish with a number of dirty men, and to use the same,
or half-washed, spoons. We knew the only other crockery of
any sort they had besides their own large dishes was a small
white bowl from which the filthy woman opposite had been
drinking, and rather than use it I could have starved another
day. Besides, every hour we expected to reach Las Palmas,
so, though by no means dainty, and much experienced in roughing it, we decided to wait. Breakfast-hour passed, and merged
into lunch, and it was four o'clock before the breeze came.
When the morning passed without wind, we knew we should
have none until about 4 p.m. The clock had scarcely struck
that hour, when the boom ceased its moaning, the vessel heeled
over and steadied, and my ears were greeted by the pleasant
swish of the ripples against the ship's side as we glided through
the water. Gladly we left the *Santiago*, and at 5 p.m. landed
on the mole. It is scarcely necessary to say that we hurried to
the Fonda Europa, thinking only of material wants after an
absolute fast of forty-six hours.

CHAPTER XIX.

LAS PALMAS—SANTA CRUZ—MADEIRA—PLYMOUTH.

> Hail, thou, my native soil, thou blessed plot,
> Whose equal all the world affordeth not!
> Show me who can so many crystal rills,
> Such wood-ground, pastures, quarries, wealthy mines,
> Such rocks, in whom the diamond fairly shines;
> And if the earth can show the like again,
> Yet will she fail in her sea-ruling men.
> Time never can produce men to o'ertake
> The fames of Grenville, Davies, Gilbert, Drake,
> Or worthy Hawkins, or of thousands more,
> That by their power made the Devonian shore
> Mock the proud Tagus, for whose richest spoil
> The boasting Spaniard left the Indian soil
> Bankrupt of store, knowing it would quit cost
> By winning this, though all the rest were lost.
>
> W. BROWNE.

February 8th, Friday.—We have failed in our intention of catching the homeward-bound boat, which was punctual this week, so has come and gone. It is just as well, perhaps. A few days' recruiting will do us no harm. We were the more content when we saw, on our way to spend the evening with Mr. and Mrs. Miller, a large ring round the moon, which is generally considered indicative of a storm.

February 9th, Saturday.—We visited the isthmus once more this afternoon, and wandered along the shore of the Puerto past Santa Catalina. We vainly endeavoured to enter the bathing-house near here, which is situated on the edge of the sea. The mineral baths of Santa Catalina are said to be very excellent. There are many mineral waters in the island, and some more powerful than these, which have the advantage, however, of being within a short distance of Las Palmas, and easy of access.

The tide was out to-day, and we were rewarded by our searches in the numerous and deep pools that abound by finding many of the beautiful objects of the sea: anemones, red and green, to which one pays a poor compliment by comparing them to shot silk, cowries of all kinds and sizes, and quantities of hermit crabs, walking about in their borrowed houses. The rocks were simply alive with these little hermits. How much more beautiful all things belonging to the sea look seen through its clear depths than when taken out of their native element and placed high and dry upon the inhospitable land.

When posting some letters this morning at the post-office, a man on a mule stopped opposite with a letter in his hand, and looked inquiringly at us. We offered to post it for him, as he was mounted. The stamp was in the *middle* of the envelope, and the address was written all round it. He said it was the first letter he had ever written. " Was this the post-office," he asked, " and would the letter be all right if dropped into that hole in the wall ?" Our assurances in the affirmative were received doubtfully, I fear, for the good man saw his precious epistle disappear with misgiving written upon his countenance.

February 10*th, Sunday.*—Don Gregorio Chil came in this morning to see me, and was quite content with the effect of Lanzarote air upon his patient, notwithstanding the scarcity of meat and food generally on our homeward way.

We went up and through some steep and narrow byeways this afternoon to the signal-station on the bluff overlooking the town. The odours in the contracted and stone-paved streets were unbearable, and we were relieved to find ourselves above them. From this elevation there is a fine view up the Barranco Guiniguada. We found the signal-station a comfortable little

house, containing flags for the signalling, also a bell, which
hung outside. Regular places are worn upon the wall around
the bare spot of ground enclosed on the crest of the hill, where
the signalman methodically places his telescope to cover certain
points on the horizon. This individual was very glad to see us,
and showed us all his belongings. He was an old man, with
keen, bright blue eyes, worthy of a Norseman.

The cable has brought us most unwelcome news to-day,
which everyone secretly hopes may not be true, or rather no
one will believe is true without further confirmation : that
Baker Pasha is defeated and Chinese Gordon captured.
Apropos of warlike news and conversation this evening, there
is a story of the days of Palmerston that is more like the
spirit of England than to-day's unhappy news. An English
vessel was sent to Buenos Aires, and went ashore in the river,
where, stuck firmly, she was surrounded by a regiment of
cavalry and captured, the only instance on record when a
ship has been taken by mounted soldiers ! The flag taken out
of her was put in the cathedral of Buenos Aires. Some time
later the Brazilians, being hard up, offered the flag to England
for ten thousand pounds, to which Lord Palmerston replied
that we were " much obliged, but that when we wanted it we
should come and take it " !

February 11*th, Monday.*—We have had a large box made of
Canary pine, and tin-lined, to carry our heavy luggage and
curiosities direct to England, and to fill up the top we went out
in search of palm mats. A little shop, or rather room, fitted
with various-sized mats, on the right bank of the Guiniguada,
supplied our wants. These palm mats are very pretty and
durable. They are used in the poorest house, so are of
course cheap ; in fact, nearly every peasant makes them for
himself. It is on them that the household sit or recline while
eating their meals, chairs being seldom or never used. They
are also said to be good as preservatives against insects of all
kinds. We then wandered along the town to the mole, over

which and the rocks and blocks of concrete we found a magnificent sea dashing. Next we paid a visit to the isthmus, our favourite resort. When we returned to the hotel, we found a boy had been there with a letter for us, and, instead of leaving it, had waited in the patio from one o'clock until our return at sunset. What patience ! or was it indolence ?

February 12th, Tuesday.—Hearing there are two steamers in, we dress hurriedly, and commence packing, only to be informed a little later that neither of them is ours. John's dark tent being packed up, we went out to the cable hut, which is windowless, for him to change his plates there, once more, and for the last time, as we thought, visiting our beloved Isleta, for to-morrow is the day the steamer is due. Mr. and Mrs. James Miller kindly asked us to spend what we supposed was our last night in the Canary Islands with them, which we gladly did.

February 13th, Wednesday.—Another false alarm of a vessel in this morning again. Fearing to leave the vicinity of the town during the morning, we visited an old English resident,* who was anxious to show us how well and cheaply pineapples could be grown under glass in these islands. He gave us much information upon the cost of living. The rent of a four-roomed house, the rooms of fair size, in a good part of the town half up the hill, the keep of one person, a servant, and a boy, living well and including wine, is twenty-seven and a half dollars a month, or five pounds ten shillings. The boy, a lad of about thirteen or fourteen, gets his food and clothes and one shilling and sixpence a month wages. Thus, the pines costing little for labour, the boy doing all under directions, the cost of production is reduced to a mere nothing. The great objection to foreign pines in England is that they have not the flavour of the English hothouse fruit. This is obviated by growing the fruit under glass in this climate, where, there being

* Since dead.

six or eight hours of sunshine against two or three in England, and artificial heat totally unnecessary, only a little care in opening and shutting the windows being required, the expense is very small indeed. The object in Mr. H—— devoting so much time and attention to the subject is a patriotic desire to increase the prosperity of his adopted islands, which he loves even better than the island of his birth. He hoped, by practically demonstrating the ease with which innumerable pineapples can be produced at trifling cost and sold at an enormous profit, although then half the price of English hothouse pineapples, to encourage an industry to which the eyes of the Canarios have not yet been opened.

February 14th, Thursday.—Mounting to the azotea as soon as dressed, we eagerly scanned first the offing, then the horizon, for a vessel, but none was in sight. Staying in the town all morning, on chance of the vessel coming in, we thought we might venture to the isthmus in the afternoon. If a vessel be not in here in time to load and get on to Santa Cruz before night, she generally does not start until late in the evening, so as to reach Tenerife in the early morning. We felt that this must surely be our last day, so tea this evening with our cable friends was quite a melancholy affair. One becomes so intimate with one's fellow-countrymen abroad, that those who might be acquaintances at home become friends when isolated by different nationality from those among whom they live.

February 15th, Friday.—A lovely morning, the sky cloudless, and the atmosphere calm, greeted what proved to be our last day of sojourn in Gran Canaria. We had a false alarm, however, for we saw a steamer coming which we thought was ours; it proved to be only a collier, but the *Volta* soon came. Packing and saying good-bye, and kindly seen off by Mr. W——, we left at 6 p.m. We had gone down to the mole at four, hearing we should be on board at five o'clock, but the boat to the

steamer did not leave until two hours later.   There was a
high swell and surf, and we had to wait behind the corner of
the pier, so as to get round it safely when a smaller wave than
usual should roll in.   The oars ready, we waited until the word
was given, and then the men pulled rapidly round the head of
the pier, a few more strokes taking us out of all danger of a
ducking.   The *Volta* rolled a little as she lay at anchor.   She
is a small boat, with very poor accommodation; there is no
ladies' cabin and no stewardess, so fortunately there were only
two of us womenfolk on board.   Getting up half-steam, we
started, and went slowly towards and round the Isleta, of which
we hoped to obtain a good view, but just as we neared it the
dinner-bell rang, and the pangs of hunger called us imperatively
to the saloon.

February 16th, Saturday.—We arrived in Santa Cruz at 7.30.
It is not of course a twelve hours' journey by steam, taking
really only about five hours.   But, as I said before, it is useless
getting into any of these ports except in daylight.   The
landing is considered too bad to be made in the dark; at
any rate, the Canarios won't attempt it, or perhaps it is the
health officers, who object to being disturbed during the small
hours.

I was amused at finding the steward on the *Volta* knew
only Tenerife of all the islands.   In fact, I think he believed
that this with Canaria formed the group.   His impressions
of the archipelago were consequently those commonly current,
and comprised one word—barren.

Mr. Hamilton came on board, also Camacho, and we
returned to shore with them, and breakfasted at the hotel.
When we entered the bay of Santa Cruz, after our visit to the
more easterly islands, it struck us as being very charming,
and the town prettily situated and picturesque after the better-
built but ugly, flat-roofed dwellings in Las Palmas.   It was
like returning to an old friend to tread once more the streets
of the capital.   We received a cold and wet welcome, for the

rain came down in torrents, and made no attempt at clearing.
We called at Messrs. Hamilton's for letters, and were able
to say good-bye to Mrs. Edwards, who has returned to Santa
Cruz for the winter. Very dreary the rain made us feel,
but it fortunately stopped later, and we·got on board dry,
and saw the last of the Canary Islands amid sunshine. As
we passed the Punta de Anaga, where a semaphore station has
been established, we got the full force of a strong breeze
that was blowing, and I took to my berth after luncheon, at
3 p.m., and stayed there until we reached Madeira. The
run to that island from Santa Cruz ought to occupy some
twenty-two hours, but it was exactly double that time before
we reached Funchal.

February 17*th, Sunday.*—It was so rough to-day, that I
remained in my berth, but was able to eat. John succeeded
in securing all his meals in the saloon except one. The others
on board had become more or less seasoned by having come
from the west coast of Africa, so ate in peace.

February 18*th, Monday.*—We arrived at 6.30 a.m. in the
roadstead of Funchal. The morning was fine, and the wind
was fortunately not blowing into the bay, so there was no
heavy surf upon the beach. The snow lay upon the mountains. Very beautiful, everyone agrees, is Funchal from the
sea. Houses rise up the steep mountain side, trees and
gardens, luxuriantly filled, dividing them from each other, the
tiled roofs peeping out from between, while gorges and
barrancos, all green with the winter rains, lie between the
hills and mountains. Boats came out immediately from the
beach, containing all sorts of baskets, and in a few minutes
the decks were covered by the far-famed basket-ware of
Madeira, the equally well-known Madeira work being piled in
great bundles in the chairs. The manager of Myles's Hotel,
Reid, took us under his wing, metaphorically tucking us

under his arm, not allowing us to look after our belongings or ourselves, and taking an amount of care of our limbs in descending into the boat to which they were totally unaccustomed. We felt that we surely must be invalids, though we looked sunburnt and in rude health.

The spirit of invalidism broods over Madeira. This is felt at once on landing, ay even before, for the hotel manager, who comes off to the steamer, asks, in the softest accents, what luggage you have, with the object of saving you all trouble and anxiety. When once he has received the inventory of your packages, you have nothing to do. He tells you when the boat is at the companion, sits beside you in the stern after carefully handing you down, and warns you not to move when approaching the shore until the boat has been drawn up. A yoke of oxen are ready, and directly the boat reaches the beach she is turned stern on, and a man rushes down and attaches the rope to the end of the pole between the beasts, who are pricked up, and haul the boat high and dry upon the beach. The manager jumps out, and helps you to get out. Chairs were provided on landing, so that we might rest after the fatigue of a few minutes' row in a softly cushioned boat over a calm sea! We, declining the offer of resting or driving to the hotel, follow the manager, and see a little of the bother and red-tapeism imposed upon visitors. Luckily he takes all the trouble upon his shoulders. Invalids could not stand the worry. A payment for each package, even an umbrella or hand-bag, a scrupulously minute inspection of everything, and we are at length allowed to proceed on our way. Everyone, even the porters and 'longshoremen, speak in quiet and hushed tones in Funchal, and the painfully subdued manners and voices of the natives are further increased by their noiseless tread on the stone pavements, for they wear a sort of canvas slipper. The quiet and careful attentions of everybody and the comforts which meet one at every turn, though ludicrous to us as strong travellers, have also their intensely sad side, and one which prevails above any other.

We tread noiselessly over the thick carpets in the hotel; noiselessly we are conducted to our rooms, where, with a sigh of relief, we feel we may at last draw a deep breath and raise our voices above a whisper. As, however, we investigate our comfortable apartment, we are horrified to see large ventilators above the door, which communicate directly with the corridors, so, with a groan, notwithstanding this admirable sanitary arrangement, we subdue our voices once more to the Madeira whisper.

Breakfast was in *table-d'hôte* style, long tables running down the room. The guests almost took away our appetites, for nearly all, with but few exceptions, were branded with the signs of that remorseless enemy and fatal malady. It is a terrible sight,—young and old, men and women, all, all slowly but surely hastening to their end, some so ill that they ought to be in their bedrooms, but, with that reluctance peculiar to phthisis, they refuse to give in, and crawl to table, where they try one dish after another, wondering that none seems to suit their palates. Perhaps the forced cheerfulness of the parent, or sister, or child who accompanies the doomed one thus into exile is a more pitiable sight than the struggle of the unfortunate sufferer against his fate. The stern repression of all betrayal of anxiety, the endeavour to lead the conversation from the painful subject of health, the cheerful and sometimes playful suggestion of different food to be tried to tempt the appetite, which will never be fresh and healthy again, are nearly as sad as the faces of the sufferers. What a fearfully morbid interest all display in their health! Do what one will—and the few healthy ones struggle hard— the conversation goes round in the same narrow circle. " What was the temperature in your room last night ? " " 67° F." " Ah, that was too high. You should not let it get above 66° ; you see the corridors," etc., etc. " Take this wine away, and bring me my mixture. I shall take that to-day." " How bad the weather is, such an unusually wet season ! It does not suit me. I was comparing it with past seasons, and find," etc.

"Ah, poor Mr. A——! He has left the table. How ill he looks to-day!" "How lucky we have been this year—no death in the house, while all the other hotels have had some!" "What sort of a night had you? I thought I heard you coughing a great deal," and so on, meal after meal. The waiters have endless patience, born no doubt of pity as well as tips, and as they move noiselessly, change the plates and tempt the appetites with everything the tables contain. The peculiar wants of each individual are carefully remembered and never omitted again at any meal. The food is excellent, and most of it suitable for invalids, who nevertheless grumble, of course, and are soothed and pacified by waiters and manager as one would soothe a fractious and sickly child. The strongest only are at table. What scenes of suffering lie behind the chamber doors we know not, but, as a rule, the invalids move about until almost the last.

We have a letter of introduction to the well-known firm of Messrs. Blandy, which we deliver after breakfast, are duly initiated into the mysteries of Portuguese money, are introduced to the public reading-room, and have all interrogations courteously answered. The reading-rooms are supplied with telescopes, with which the incoming mails can be seen and the names of the steamers lying in the offing read; but few people seemed to frequent them, though the rooms were luxuriously furnished. Both ladies and gentlemen are admitted. We next walked some distance to the residence of the English chaplain, Mr. Addison, who kindly gave us a set of observations of temperature made by himself during January and February, taken each day at 8 a.m. As these exactly correspond with similar observations made for us in Orotava and Las Palmas, it may be instructive to summarise them all here. It must be noted, however, that Mr. Addison's house, where the temperatures were taken, is at a considerable elevation above the sea, and that therefore the temperatures are probably cooler than if taken at the sea level at Funchal.

The following tables give a comparison of temperatures at

Madeira, Orotava, and Las Palmas during January and February, 1884, taken in each place at 8 a.m. :—

		Highest in January.		Lowest in January.		Greatest Variation in January.
		F.	C.	F.	C.	F.
Funchal	... ...	72·0	(22·3)	48·0	(8·9)	24·0
Orotava	... ...	78·8	(26·0)	52·7	(11·5)	26·1
Las Palmas ...	...	73·0	(22·8)	52·0	(11·2)	21·0

		Highest in February.		Lowest in February.		Greatest Variation in February.
		F.	C.	F.	C.	F.
Funchal	... ...	74·0	(23·4)	44·0	(8·9)	30·0
Orotava	... ...	74·3	(23·5)	49·1	(9·5)	25·2
Las Palmas ...	...	75·0	(23·9)	47·0	(8·4)	28·0

We encountered many hammocks suspended on the shoulders of their two bearers, who trotted gently and noiselessly over the stone pavements. Inside reclined, amid cushions and warm wraps, some unfortunate. The other means of locomotion are by sledges, drawn by oxen, and riding on horses. There are a few carriages, but the noise they make in driving over the cobbles must be distracting to their occupants. I think one of the most disappointing things about Funchal is the paved streets. They are very tiring to walk upon, and noisy when horses are used.

The prison is in mid-town, and the prisoners enjoy looking out and conversing with the passers-by from behind their bars. Food is handed in to them also, either by their friends or for which they pay. The shops are very fair, and one can obtain most English requisites at not too extortionate prices. The basket goods are particularly cheap, less than half the price that they are in England.

There is a piano in the drawing-room of the hotel, above which is affixed a notice to the effect that, owing to the number of invalids in the house, it is requested that it will not be played

upon after 10 p.m., another reminder of the pervading atmosphere.

February 19th, Tuesday.—After calling for our letters at the
post-office, we walked up the steep hill behind the town by a
barranco, and came upon a level road going half-way round the
hillside.   This and the slopes above and below are thickly
dotted with houses, surrounded by gardens—quintas.   There is
an unmistakably English look about the arrangements, which
suggests their being permanently tenanted by our countrymen.
We were searching for the road to the church at the top of
the mountain—the Monte—which can be seen from Funchal,
and from which the famous sleigh ride is taken by strangers,
when a gentleman, English of course, in a hammock, kindly
directed us, for it is useless asking the natives in Spanish,
Portuguese alone being understood here.   Sleighs and their
attendants were waiting on the way up, and we bargained with
one to bring us down from the top.   Half-way, however, we
obtained oxen to take us the rest of the road, for the walk was
hot, lying between high walls and upon the everlasting pavement, besides being very steep.   The church, up to which steps
lead, is situated amid the pleasant shade of trees, whence there
is a fine view of Funchal.

Leaving the oxen, we re-entered the double sleigh. Two men
were on either side behind, each holding a rope, with which
they guided the sleigh.   The drag is put on by a man placing
his foot on the runner behind and pulling back with the other
on the ground.   A piece of oiled rag is occasionally placed in
front of the runners, which are allowed to slip over it, the man
picking it up again behind.   As the pace increased, it was
difficult to believe that an accident was not inevitable.   As we
dashed down between the high walls over the stone road, turning round corners that looked unturnable, and threading the
narrow lanes, a collision with the walls, which we could touch
with our hands, a lurch too much, or an obstruction in our path
seemed sufficient to jerk us out of our low seats and throw us

on the pavement with crushing force. However, we consoled ourselves with the reflection that accidents are rare, though we scarcely breathed for the ten minutes during which we flew down a distance that had taken an hour and a half to climb.

The natives of this island are not nearly so pleasant to work with and speak to as the Canarios. There is a fixed melancholy in their faces. In appearance they are, as a rule, small, with square shoulders and short necks, but are very strong. The heavy duty upon all articles imported and exported, besides the internal taxes, render the Madeirese, notwithstanding their thrifty and hard-working habits, very poor. The predilection of English people for Madeira has been traded upon by the Portuguese Government, and tax after tax has been imposed with the view of extorting money from the "rich visitors." The English of course suffer, but the natives suffer more in proportion. Before a basket of any sort is taken on board the steamers which touch here, the number and price of each are carefully taken by the custom-house officials.

The landing of strangers, as I before mentioned, is subject to so many duties, that I scarcely remember all. If it were not for the hotel managers, the process is so long, and the duties so numerous, that no one would attempt it. The Canary Islands have a great advantage here, for they are free ports, where there is none of that tiresome tumbling about of one's bonnets and laces that is so trying to the temper as well as the finery.

During the evening we played whist with some visitors, a game which seemed more suited to the silence of the place than the piano in the corner.

February 20th, Wednesday.—We arranged last night to ride to the Gran Corral, one of the sights of Madeira, so at 8.50 a.m. our horses came round. My Canary riding-habit being much the worse for wear after all its hard work there, I thought I had better take one of the linen skirts provided by the hotel for visitors. My old grey flannel would have been much pleasanter, for the smooth, shining brown linen slides about the saddle, and renders one's seat very uncomfortable. Our horses were good, quiet cobs, and we could have ridden fast on them but for the disagreeable roads. The noise the horses' hoofs made going along the road was so great, that, although riding beside each other, it was impossible to shout even a sentence that could be heard. By gesture alone could we draw attention to anything. As in the Canaries, the horsekeepers ran on foot. One man, who started before us, carried a lunch-basket sent by the hotel manager, for, living *en pension* as one does, luncheon is always provided for any excursion. Some miles from Funchal we at last got off the stones. What a relief it was! It was like leaving a room of noisy machinery that has been dinning in one's ears for hours. These paved lanes extend for a long way past the town. Sitting on the horses, we could generally see over the walls on either hand, but to foot-passengers they must be as uninteresting as the much-praised Devonshire lanes, in whose depths one is buried for miles, a state bearable only when flowers deck the hedges. Glad were we to leave these stone lanes and get on a pleasant earth path, shaded by fine trees.

We passed a few small villages and valleys, and wound round a hillside, until we came suddenly upon the Gran Corral, lying beneath us. This gorge is deep and narrow. Above rise perpendicular cliffs, which on the side at which we stand are broken and sloping in one part, thus allowing of a descent being possible. The river in the depths below winds in curves, and a few houses nestle between. It was 11.20 when we reached our destination. Dismounting, we walked out upon a sort of bluff, which ran like a knife out into the gorge, and from whence we had a splendid view all around. The gorge is magnificent in size and proportions, and well worth a comfortable ride to see. It is well known by description, Madeira's beauties having been exhausted by innumerable pens. Luncheon proved a welcome, and to us a luxurious, meal, accustomed as we were to starve from morning until evening. The houses of the peasants have curious square thatched roofs.

Once mounted, and knowing now our way back to the town, we cantered away from our horse-keepers, arriving at the hotel at 3.15 p.m. The view as one enters the town from its southern side is very pretty, the islets giving a charming break to the sea line. There is little or no bay at Funchal, and the beach where one lands is of shelving pebbles.

February 21*st, Thursday.*—The Union steamship *Trojan* is expected in to-day, so we must not leave the neighbourhood of the town, as the stay the steamers make is frequently very limited. We revisited the library, made some purchases in the wickerwork native to the place, and took a walk in and around the town, going half-way up the hill in order to enjoy the pleasurable excitement of the ride down. We went to bed in peace, however, the steamer not being in yet.

Lying on the writing-table in the bedroom, we found a visitor's book, in which we were requested to write. Turning over the leaves, we came across an interesting entry, the signatures of the Princes of Wales on their way out from home when in the *Bacchante*. It is dated "H.M.S. *Bacchante*, November 28th, 1879," and beneath is signed,

> " EDWARD,
> GEORGE,"

the writing of the former name being well formed and of the latter boyish. The Princes reached Madeira on the evening of November 21st, but owing to the rough sea, a landing could not be made until the 24th, when some of the officers went ashore by the Loo rock, it not being possible to do so on the beach, because of the surf. The next day they had to weigh anchor and run for shelter at 5 p.m. to the other side of the island, passing the San Lorenzo light to the northward. They were able to get back to Funchal on the 27th, and on the 28th the Princes went ashore for a few hours, upon which occasion no doubt they signed the book in Myles's Hotel, where the officers had stayed.

February 22nd, Friday.—We were awakened at 6 a.m., and told that the *Trojan* was in and would leave in half an hour. As the captains of these vessels are very independent, and will wait for no one, we had a regular hurry to get off in time. When starting, we found some things we had bought and paid for had not arrived, so we were obliged to knock up the shopkeepers to get them. Then most of our luggage we had left in the custom-house to avoid having to open it, and the officials there were not yet out of bed, so Reid had some trouble to get the baggage out. However, we got off safely and easily, the sea being perfectly calm, a fortunate state of affairs for us.

The scene on board and around the *Trojan* was " confusion worse confounded." The vessel was closely surrounded by boats, filled with all sorts of men and boys, jabbering Portuguese and broken English, who clambered up the sides, hanging on to nothing apparently, their bare toes almost prehensile. The deck was strewn fore and aft with wicker chairs, tables, and baskets, in and on which were thrown quantities of beautiful embroidery. Besides selling these wares, a number of boys were trying to induce the passengers who leaned over the bulwarks to throw money into the water for them, for which they dived, catching it before it sank a few yards beneath the surface. These urchins, when not thus employed, sat shivering in their boats, the morning air being chilly. They were little more than children. Some dived under the ship, but none went really completely beneath her keel; they sneaked round astern. It was exactly eight o'clock when the ship weighed anchor and the deck was cleared, so we need not have hurried ourselves to get on board by 6.30 a.m.

As we steamed northwards we passed a long neck of low and pointed hills and rocks, along the summits of which bridges are thrown to connect the lighthouse and telegraph station on the point with the main island. The Desertas, three large islets, lie on our right. They are uninhabited, save by a few fisherfolk, who resort there for turtles. It is said that a rabbit, which had littered on board a sailing vessel on its way to the Indies, was put ashore on the largest island, where they increased so rapidly, that now the island is unfit for use. They are low and barren-looking, quite opposite in character to Madeira, which derived its name from *madera* (wood), owing to the forests in which it abounded.

As we left the shelter of the islands we encountered a swell, which, though uncomfortable, did not prevent us appearing at table. We were surprised to find that tinned butter was in use, fresh butter having just run short. One would have thought that in the Union Company's boats fresh butter and vegetables would have been taken in at Madeira, where they could easily be procured. It was not pleasant for us, who arrived at the end of the voyage, getting the worst of the food, which contrasted very unfavourably with that of the Atlantic liners. The run from the Cape is of course three times the length of that to America, but the price of the passage from Madeira to Plymouth being twelve guineas, one has a right to expect first-rate food when there is the opportunity to procure it.

Those who have experienced what it is to drop on board a homeward-bound steamer when near the end of her journey must know the uncomfortable feeling that the late arrivals have. The cliques on board are all arranged; the habits of those who have been living together for weeks previously are known to each other; friends and acquaintances have settled down. It is too late in the voyage for it to be worth while to make new friends. That feeling which pervades everyone, when starting on a long voyage, of perils to be encountered together, and which makes one look around to "take stock" of one's new companions, is entirely absent near the end of a voyage, when habit has rendered one accustomed to the new conditions. Home or a new land is in everyone's thoughts, and it is too much trouble to even look at new faces. The captain and officers exchange, as in duty bound, a few civil words, but they too are thinking of home. The new-comers have no share in the jokes and allusions that have amused the passengers in the past, and it is too much trouble to enter into elaborate explanations. Former experience of our own feelings taught us what the passengers on the *Trojan* felt towards those who joined the good ship at Madeira. We smilingly acquiesced in our fate, and indeed we had so much to occupy our own thoughts, that there was little room left for " talkee-talkee "!

February 24th, Sunday.—Service was held at eleven this morning, also at eight in the evening. The crew were marshalled on deck, as is usual on large ships. Why people should be more religious in proportion to the tonnage of a vessel is a puzzling question. Nevertheless, our tonnage being 4,000 tons, we were religious in proportion, and crew and passengers attended service twice.

February 25th, Monday.—There was much less roll last night than the two previous days; in fact, it was calm. We are thankful that our outward-bound adventures in the Bay of Biscay are not to be repeated.

February 26th, Tuesday.—The pilot boarded us this morning at 6 a.m., and we reached Plymouth at 8 a.m., exactly four days to a minute since we weighed anchor at Madeira. At 10.15 we went ashore, and passed the customs easily. The day was a typical English one. Dull sky; atmosphere heavy and full of moisture, which threatened occasionally to descend in rain; not even a gleam of that perpetual sunshine that we left behind us but a few days previously,—such was England in February. Yet it was home. Very mixed were our feelings in thinking of the beautiful lands we had left, and which, under the influences of an ever-advancing civilisation, we shall scarcely find in the same condition when next we visit them.

Whatever may be the future advances of these wealthy islands—and that they will advance in material prosperity, and that quickly, is nearly certain, for they possess such vast latent resources—we shall always rather remember them as we first found them : rough, wild, beautiful ; toilsome to see, but happy to remember ; peopled with quiet, contented, peace-loving, honest, and hospitable inhabitants, who pleasantly pass their days in the enjoyment of the good things so abundantly provided by nature, and beguile the starry nights with the song, the dance, and the tinkling of the guitar. We shall always recall the islands as they appeared to us—truly Happy Isles, the nearest approach to an Earthly Paradise of which a Morris could sing or a Tadema paint.

> " My land of the sun,
> Am I not true ?   Have I not done
> . All things for thine, for thee alone,
> O sun-land, sea-land, thou mine own ?
> From other loves and other lands,
> As true, perhaps, as strong of hands,
> Have I not turned to thee and thine,
> O sun-land of the palm and pine,
> .And sung thy scenes, surpassing skies,
> Till Europe lifted up her face
> And marvelled at thy matchless grace,
> With eager and inquiring eyes ?
> Be my reward some little place
> To pitch my tent, some tree and vine
> Where I may sit above the sea,
> And drink the sun as drinking wine,
> . And dream, or sing some songs of thee."

FINIS.

APPENDIX I.

ITINERARY AND EXPENSES CONNECTED WITH THE TOUR.

In the following Tables it must be distinctly understood that each item is for TWO *persons.*

The PESETA *is taken in the Tables as the equivalent of exactly* 10*d.*

	Hotel and Food in Camp.		Travelling.		
			£	s.	d.
London to Havre (first class), *viâ* Southampton			... 2	15	0
,, ,, excess on luggage...			... 0	10	6
			£3	5	6

	Fr.	Cnt.	Fr.	Cnt.
Custom-house dues at Havre			4	0
Custom-house porters at Havre			6	0
Carriage to *Parana* and station			2	40
Breakfast at Hotel Bordeaux, Havre	5	50		
Havre to Rouen (first class)			22	0
Hotel d'Albion (one night)	22	15		
Boat down the Seine from Rouen to Havre			16	20
Dinner on board	9	0		
Hotel Bordeaux, Havre	5	80		
Carriage to *Parana*, 2 fr. 30 c. ; porter, 40 c.			2	70
	42	45	53	30

(£3 19s. 9½d.)

	Hotel and Food in Camp.	Travelling.
		£ s. d.
Passage to Tenerife from Havre by Chargeurs Réunis steamship *Parana* (gratuities to stewards, wine, etc., extra)	...	24 0 0
Going ashore at Santa Cruz (after sunset)	...	0 10 0
		£24 10 0

London to Tenerife ... ...   Total **£31 15s. 3½d.**

TENERIFE.

	£ s. d.
Hotel Marina at Santa Cruz (evening of Sept. 5th to morning of 7th)	1 6 8
	£1 6 8

	Pese-tas.	Centi-mos.	Pese-tas.	Centi-mos.
Carriage from Santa Cruz to Laguna	...	...	10	0
Fonda at Laguna (two days)	15	0	...	
Carriage from Laguna to Puerto de Orotava	...	...	25	0
Luggage from Santa Cruz to Puerto de Orotava in a cart...	...	...	10	0
Fonda at Icod de Los Vinos (one night)	10	0	...	
To see Guanche cave at Icod de los Vinos	...	...	2	0
Wine at Tanque	0	80	...	
Two fowls, five eggs, and charcoal at Santiago ...	5	0	...	
Washing hands in street	0	35	...	
Higos pigos (prickly pears) on road...	0	10	...	
Cooking of dinner and the dinner, grapes, pears, and wine	5	0	...	
Policeman at Guia to keep boys from tent	...	...	1	0
Wine, 1 p. ; eggs, bread, and milk, 1 p. (Guia) ...	2	0	...	
Wine, eggs, bread, and charcoal	4	0	...	
Guide from Guia to Villa Flor	...	...	6	0
Milk, 35 c. ; fowls, 2 p. 80 c. ; and dinner (Villa Flor)	5	0	...	
Eggs, 35 c. ; coffee, 1 p. 60 c. ; sugar, 55 c. ...	2	50	...	
Eggs and sugar, 60 c. ; ink, 10 c. ; candles, 50 c. ...	1	20	...	
Cord, 5 c. ; basket, 45 c. ; fruit, 1 p. ; bread, 70 c.	2	20	...	
Guide from Chasna to Peak and back to Guia (with mule and water-barrels)	...	...	22	50
Dinner at Guia, 3 p. 60 c. ; eggs, bread, etc., 1 c. ...	4	60	...	
Milk, 35 c. ; bread, 20 c. ; dinner, 2 p. 45 c. ...	3	0	...	
Potatoes, vegetables, and wood, 1 p. 57 c. ; fish, 35 c.	1	92	...	
Mule to the port of Guia	...	...	2	0
Water, 5 c. ; washing, 1 p. 20 c. ... , ...	1	20	...	
One yard of linen (to carry gofio in), 90 c.; three tin plates, 90 c.	1	80	...	
Carried forward	65	67	78	50

	Hotel and Food in Camp.		Travelling.	
	Pese-tas.	Centi-mos.	Pese-tas.	Centi-mos.
Brought forward	65	67	... 78	50
Candles, 90 c. ; milk, 10 c. ; bread, 25 c. ; eggs, 25 c.	1	50	...	
Oil and bottle, 10 c.; wine, 2 p. 10 c.; sugar, 60 c. ; bottle, 5 c.	2	85	...	
Vegetables, 40 c.; milk, 15 c.; coffee, 1 p.... ...	1	55	...	
Large tin, 1 p. 40 c.; small tin, 35 c.	1	75	...	
Honey, 1 p. 25 c. ; wine, 2 p. 10 c. ; potatoes, 50 c.	3	85	...	
Fowl, 90 c.; bread, 25 c.; sweets and vegetables, 20 c.	1	35	...	
Spoon, 35 c. ; half-yard of muslin for coffee bags, 45 c.	0	80	...	
Milk, 5 c.; oil, 40 c.; pepsicums, 30 c.; salt, 5 c. ...	0	80	...	
Box (to carry used photographic plates), 35 c. ; pens, 5 c.	0	40	...	
Gratuity, 1 p. ; milk, 20 c. ; pan, 60 c. and 45 c. ; laundry, 70 c.	2	95	...	
Two mules from Guia to the port	...	...	4	0
Fish, 25 c. ; fowl, 1 p.; wine, 2 p. 5 c.; rice, 50 c.	3	70	...	
Six eggs, 30 c. ; bread, 10 c. ; milk, 10 c. ; fish, 35 c.	0	85	...	
Two horses and men for nine days at 6 p. 25 c.	...	...	112	50
Horse and man for eight days at 6 p. 25 c.	...	...	50	0
Lorenzo as *practico* for the ascent of Peak	...	...	20	0
	73	12	220	0

(£14 14s. 2¼d.)

	Pese-tas.	Centi-mos.
Schooner from Guia to Gomera and thence to Hierro (three days' delay), return to Gomera (four days' delay), and landing at Puerto de Orotava, occupied 14 days, and when on board we had food ...	150	0
	150	0

(£6 5s. 0d.)

HIERRO.

	Pese-tas.	Centi-mos.	Pese-tas.	Centi-mos.
Luggage on mule to Valverde from the schooner	...	...	1	25
Eggs and bread (Valverde)	1	75	...	
Honey, 90 c.; milk, 70 c.; wood, etc., 10 c. (Sabinosa)	1	70	...	
Three horses and men for two days	...	...	45	0
Cheese, 45 c. ; wine, 50 c.	0	95	...	
Luggage to port of Valverde	...	...	1	25
	4	40	47	50

(£2 3s. 3d.)

GOMERA.

	Hotel and Food.		Travelling.	
	Pese-tas.	Centi-mos.	Pese-tas.	Centi-mos.
Luggage from port to fonda at San Sebastian	...	...	0	45
Three men from San Sebastian to Hermigua (two horses supplied by friend)	...	...	8	50
Gratuity to servants	1	60	...	
Two men from Hermigua to Valle Hermoso	...	...	4	0
Fodder for horses	...	...	0	50
Two men from Valle Hermoso to San Sebastian, 5 p. and 6 p. ...	...	...	11	0
Three days, at 4 p. per day, at fonda, laundry, and Lorenzo	37	50	...	
Luggage to boat, 50 c. ; luggage ashore, 1 p.	...	...	1	50
Lorenzo's food, 5 p. 50 c. ; Lorenzo, 17 days at 5 p., 85 p. (£3 10s. 10d.).	...	...	80	0
	39	10	114	95

(£6 8s. 4½d.)

PALMA.

	Pese-tas.	Centi-mos.	Pese-tas.	Centi-mos.
Boat from Puerto de Orotava to *Matanzas*	...	...	10	0
On the *Matanzas* from Tenerife to Palma	...	...	*Nil.*	
Luggage from *Matanzas* to Santa Cruz de la Palma ...	...	...	1	50
Crupper for saddle	...	...	4	0
Bread, 5 c. ; breakfast at fonda, 3 p. 75 c.	3	80	...	
Man with mule, 50 c., 1 p. 25 c., 1 p. (gratuities) ...	...	...	2	75
Guide across Pico de Muchachos	...	...	7	50
Man carrying camera at Las Sauces	...	...	0	50
Three mules and two men, four days at 5 p.	...	...	60	0
Fonda at La Ciudad, five days at 3 p. 75 c.... ...	37	50	...	
Baskets, 1 p. 20 c. ; sponge cakes, 35 c.	1	55	...	
Luggage from fonda to boat, 1 p. ; boat to steamer, 2 p. ...	...	...	3	0
	42	85	89	25

(£5 10s. 1d.)

	Pese-tas.	Centi-mos.	Pese-tas.	Centi-mos.
Steamer (Forwood Brothers) from Palma to Orotava Lemonade, 1 p. 80 c. ; breakfast, 3 p. 60 c.... ...	5	40	50	0
(we did not pay for this)	...	...		
Coming ashore at Puerto from steamer	...	...	4	0
Luggage to fonda from boat	...	...	1	0
	5	40	55	0

(£2 10s. 4d.)

TENERIFE (OROTAVA).						Hotel and Food.			Travelling.	
						Pese-tas.	Centi-mos.		Pese-tas.	Centi-mos.
Boy in Villa carrying camera, 50 c. and 25 c.	...		...	...	...		...	...	0	75
One horse and two donkeys from Puerto to Villa	...			...	...		...	...	3	60
Boy to Puerto with message ...	...	...	...	...	...		...	...	0	60
Two horses from Villa to Puerto	...	...	...	...	...		...	...	2	80
Fonda at Villa (one day)	...	...	...	...	...	10	0	...		
Horse to Rambla and Icod Alto	...	...	...	...	...		...	...	7	20
Luncheon at Icod Alto	...	...	...	...	1	50	...		
Hotel at Puerto	...	...	...	...	...	137	0	...		
Luggage (50 c.) and gratuities	...	...	...	...	4	0	...		
Laundry at Puerto	...	...	...	...	...	5	5	...		
						157	55		14	95

(£7 3s. 9d.)

						Pese-tas.	Centi-mos.		Pese-tas.	Centi-mos.
Coach from Puerto de Orotava to Tacoronte	...	...				...	...		6	50
Gratuities, 1 p. 50 c. ; boy, 10 c.	...	...	...			1	60	...		
Coach from a short distance on road into Laguna (one person)						...	...		0	60
Fonda Comimela, Laguna, two days, 3 p. ...		...				12	0	...		
Carriage from Laguna to Santa Cruz	...	...	...			...	...		3	60
Hotel at Santa Cruz (morning of Nov. 2nd to night of 5th)	...	...	...	...	...	74	0	...		
Gratuities	...	...	..	...	...	3	50	...		
						91	10		10	70

(£4 4s. 10d.)

						Pese-tas.	Centi-mos.
Steamer from Santa Cruz to Las Palmas, Gran Canaria (Spanish)					...	44	0
Going on board and luggage ...	...	...	...	...	...	11	0
Landing at La Luz, Las Palmas, and drive to Fonda Europa	...			...		12	50
						67	50

(£2 16s. 3d.)

GRAN CANARIA.

	Hotel and Food.		Travelling.	
	Pesetas.	Centimos.	Pesetas.	Centimos.
Carriage to La Luz			2	80
Biscuits	1	60		
Coach to Arucas, 3 p. and 50 c.			3	50
Breakfast at Arucas	4	0		
Two horses to Guia from Arucas			10	0
Hotel in Guia (one day)	10	0		
Three horses from Guia to Agaete			12	0
Mule and horse to El Valle (Agaete)			3	75
Mule from Agaete to Aldea			6	25
Donkey from Aldea to Tejeda			5	0
Wine at Artenara, 50 c.; to see chapel, 50 c. ...	1	0		
Man with horses from Aldea to Tejeda			7	0
Woman at whose house we stayed at Tejeda ...	4	0		
Horse to Teror, 3 p. 75 c.; mule, 2 p. 50 c.			6	25
Food in Teror, 10 p.; wine, 20 c.	10	20		
Two horses to Osorio			2	50
Three horses to Tamaraceite			7	50
Coach to Las Palmas			2	50
Carriage from Las Palmas to San Mateo			15	0
Fonda at San Mateo	8	0		
Two horses to San Bartolemé			12	50
Two mules from San Bartolemé to Aguimes			7	50
Fonda at Aguimes	7	0		
Two mules from Aguimes to Telde			5	0
Coach from Telde to Las Palmas			2	0
Six days' board at Fonda Europa, 7 p. 50 c. ...	90	0		
	135	80	111	5
Carriage to Bandama and back			20	0
Carriage to Isleta and back			1	50
Pound of tea	5	0		
Marmalade (in one-pound pots)	1	0		
Coach to Isleta			1	50
Tin of Mackenzie's Albert biscuits	8	75		
Thirty-nine days' board at Fonda Europa (to Dec. 31st)	487	50		
Breakfast and dinner at Firgas	10	0		
Laundry from Nov. 6th to Dec. 31st	8	0		
Horse and its food for a day to Firgas and back			15	50
Horse to Doramas			15	0
Coach to Telde and back			4	0
Twenty-two days' board at Fonda Europa	275	0		
	931	5	166	5

(£56 3s. 0½d.)

	Hotel and Food.		Travelling.	
--	Pese-tas.	Centi-mos.	Pese-tas.	Centi-mos.
By steamship *Vérité* from Las Palmas to Arrecife, Lanzarote	...	...	60	
Luggage to wharf	...	...	2	0
Tea on *Vérité*	3	0	...	
Luggage to fonda in Arrecife	...	...	1	25
	3	0	63	25

(£2 15s. 2½d.)

LANZAROTE.	Pese-tas.	Centi-mos.	Pese-tas.	Centi-mos.
Guide to Cueva de los Verdes	...	...	1	90
Breakfast and dinner at Haria	7	50	...	
Camel for three days at 5 p.	...	...	15	0
Fonda in Arrecife	24	0	...	
Camel with luggage to Yaiza...	...	...	5	0
Two donkeys, horse, and camel during two days	...	...	7	0
Camel, 1 p. ; boat to Corralejo, 7 p. 50 c.	...	...	8	50
	31	50	37	40

(£2 17s. 5d.)

FUERTEVENTURA.	Pese-tas.	Centi-mos.	Pese-tas.	Centi-mos.
Puerto Cabras fonda	12	50	...	
Camel from Puerto Cabras to Antigua	...	...	4	0
Camel from Antigua to Pajara by Betancuria	...	...	3	65
Camel from Pajara to Tiscamanita	...	...	1	25
Bread	0	25	...	
Schooner from Gran Tarajal to Las Palmas (fare is 8 p.) ...	...	...	10	0
	12	75	18	90

(£1 6s. 4d.)

GRAN CANARIA.	Pese-tas.	Centi-mos.	Pese-tas.	Centi-mos.
Fonda Europa, Las Palmas	100	0	...	
Luggage, 1 p. 30 c. ; boat to steamer, 4 p. 60 c.	...	...	5	90
	100	0	5	90
Breakfast at Camacho's Hotel in Santa Cruz (Tenerife)	6	60	...	
	106	60	5	90

(£4 13s. 9d.)

GRAN CANARIA TO LONDON, *viâ* MADEIRA.	Hotel and Food.			Travelling.		
	£	s.	d.	£	s.	d
Steamship *Volta* from Canaria to Madeira	...	...	...	9	0	0
Myles's Hotel at Madeira	5	19	8	...		
Steamship *Trojan* (Union Line) from Madeira to Plymouth ...	...			25	4	0
Train to London	...			2	5	0
	£5	19	8	£36	9	0

(**£42 8s. 8d.**)

CONCISE SUMMARY OF THE FOREGOING TABLES.

	£	s.	d.
London, *viâ* Havre, to Santa Cruz de Tenerife	31	15	3½
Tenerife until we left for Gomera	14	14	2⅛
Schooner to visit Gomera and Hierro	6	5	0
Hierro	2	3	3
Gomera (including £3 12s. 5d. to Lorenzo)	6	8	4½
Palma	5	10	1
Steamer, etc., from Palma to Tenerife	2	10	4
Orotava (Tenerife)	7	3	9.
From Orotava until we left Santa Cruz	4	4	10
Steamer from Santa Cruz to Las Palmas, etc.	2	16	3
Canaria	56	3	0½
Steamer, etc., from Canaria to Lanzarote	2	15	2½
Lanzarote	2	17	5
Fuerteventura	1	6	.4
Canaria and Tenerife	4	13	9
Steamer from Canaria to Madeira	9	0	0
Madeira	5	19	8
Steamer from Madeira to Plymouth	25	4	0
Train to London	2	5	0
	£188	4	1⅕

APPENDIX II.

*Average temperatures at Las Palmas, Gran Canaria, from January 1 to December 18, 1884.**

| | 8 A.M. | | 8 P.M. | | Average difference between wet and dry bulbs. | | | |
| | | | | | 8 A.M. | | 8 P.M. | |
	F.	C.	F.	C.	F.	C.	F.	C.
January ...	61·48	(16·38)			3·9	(2·17)		
February ...	59·0	(15·0)			4·17	(2·31)		
March ...	61·83	(16·57)	62·40	(16·8)	4·48	(2·49)	3·67	(2·03)
April	66·23	(19·17)	63·26	(17·36)	5·6	(3·1)	5·23	(3·9)
May	65·83	(18·79)	64·48	(18·04)	5·77	(3·20)	5·70	(3·17)
June	69·26	(20·7)	68·63	(20·35)	6·30	(3·5)	5·56	(3·09)
July	73·16	(22·86)	73·58	(23·1)	5·0	(2·7)	4·48	(2·49)
August ...	75·64	(24·24)	75·74	(24·3)	4·58	(2·55)	4·0	(2·3)
September ...	74·60	(23·7)	74·70	(23·72)	6·30	(3·5)	5·50	(3·05)
October ...	70·70	(21·5)	70·87	(21·59)	5·19	(2·88)	5·51	(3·06)
November ...	67·16	(19·54)	67·2	(19·6)	4·06	(2·25)	4·2	(2·4)
December ...	64·88	(18·27)	64·7	(18·17)	5·05	(2·80)	5·17	(2·88)

Extremes of temperature at Las Palmas, Gran Canaria, from January 1 to December 18, 1884.

| | Highest. | | Lowest. | | Lowest. | | | |
| | | | | | 8 A.M. | | 8 P.M. | |
	F.	C.	F.	C.	F.	C.	F.	C.
January	73·0	(22·8)	52·0	(11·2)	56·0	(13·4)		
February	75·0	(23·9)	47·0	(8·4)	53·0	(11·9)		
March	75·0	(23·9)	51·0	(10·6)	57·0	(13·9)	54·0	(12·3)
April	79·0	(26·2)	55·0	(12·8)	61·0	(16·2)	59·0	(15·0)
May	76·0	(24·5)	56·0	(13·4)	61·0	(16·2)	63·0	(17·3)
June	77·0	(25·0)	59·0	(15·0)	66·0	(18·9)	66·0	(18·9)
July	81·0	(27·3)	65·0	(18·4)	71·0	(21·7)	71·0	(21·7)
August	83·0	(28·4)	71·0	(21·7)	74·0	(23·4)	74·0	(23·4)
September ...	85·0	(29·5)	70·0	(21·2)	73·0	(22·8)	72·0	(22·3)
October	78·0	(25·6)	65·0	(18·4)	67·0	(19·5)	67·0	(19·5)
November ...	77·0	(25·0)	62·0	(16·7)	64·0	(17·8)	59·0	(15·0)
December ...	74·0	(23·4)	57·0	(13·9)	63·0	(17·3)	62·0	(16·7)

* Observations specially made for me by A. H. Béchervaise, Esq.

Average temperatures at Puerto de Orotava from November 1, 1883, to May 11, 1884. *

	8 A.M.		2 P.M.		9 P.M.		Mean.		Mean of Max. and Min.		Mean of Max.		Mean of Min.		Mean diff.	
	F.	C.	F.	C.	F.	C.	F.	C.	F.	C.	F.	C.	F.	C.	F.	C.
November ...	65·3	(18·5)	71·42	(21·9)	64·22	(17·9)	66·92	(19·4)	66·38	(19·1)	71·96	(22·2)	60·8	(16·0)	43·16	(6·2)
December ...	61·52	(16·4)	68·0	(20·0)	61·7	(16·5)	63·86	(17·7)	64·22	(17·9)	69·98	(21·1)	58·28	(14·6)	43·7	(6·5)
January ...	61·52	(16·4)	68·54	(20·3)	61·7	(16·5)	64·24	(17·8)	64·24	(17·8)	71·06	(21·7)	57·02	(13·9)	46·02	(7·8)
February ...	59·18	(15·1)	64·94	(18·3)	58·28	(14·6)	60·8	(16·0)	60·26	(15·7)	66·92	(19·4)	53·78	(12·1)	45·14	(7·3)
March ...	61·7	(16·5)	66·33	(19·1)	59·72	(15·4)	62·6	(17·0)	61·32	(16·3)	68·0	(20·0)	54·86	(12·7)	45·14	(7·3)
April... ...	65·3	(18·5)	69·44	(20·8)	62·24	(16·8)	65·66	(18·7)	64·94	(18·3)	71·6	(22·0)	58·28	(14·6)	45·32	(7·4)
May 1—11 ...	64·58	(18·1)	66·74	(19·3)	62·06	(16·7)	64·4	(18·0)	65·3	(18·5)	68·0	(20·0)	59·36	(15·2)	38·64	(4·8)
Nov.—April	62·42	(16·9)	68·18	(20·1)	61·32	(16·3)	63·86	(17·7)	63·5	(17·5)	69·98	(21·1)	57·2	(14·0)	44·78	(7·1)

* Observations by Dr. Hjalmar Öhrvall, of Upsala.

Extremes of temperature at Puerto de Orotava from November 1, 1883, to May 11, 1884.*

	Highest.		Lowest.		Lowest at 8 A.M.		Lowest at 9 P.M.	
	F.	C.	F.	C.	F.	C.	F.	C.
November ...	78·8	(26·0)	56·3	(13·5)	59·9	(15·5)	58·28	(14·6)
December ...	79·7	(26·5)	48·2	(9·0)	53·6	(12·0)	53·42	(11·9)
January ...	78·8	(26·0)	52·7	(11·5)	54·14	(12·3)	57·2	(14·0)
February ...	74·3	(23·5)	49·1	(9·5)	52·88	(11·6)	51·8	(11·0)
March	72·5	(22·5)	51·8	(11·0)	56·3	(13·5)	52·12	(13·4)
April	76·1	(24·5)	53·6	(12·0)	59·9	(15·5)	57·38	(14·1)
May 1—11 ...	70·7	(21·5)	56·3	(13·5)	60·44	(15·8)	60·44	(15·8)

Temperature of Sea at end of Mole, Puerto de Orotava, at 12 noon.*

	1884.		1885.			1884.		1885.	
	F.	C.	F.	C.		F.	C.	F.	C.
January 1	67·1	(19·5)	66·92	(19·4)	May 1 ...	64·94	(18·3)	65·3	(18·5)
February 1	65·3	(18·5)	65·12	(18·4)	June 1 ...	66·2	(19·0)	67·28	(19·6)
March 1 ...	64·4	(18·0)	64·58	(18·1)	July 1 ...	68·36	(20·2)		
April 1 ...	65·3	(18·5)	64·4	(18·0)					

Average relative and absolute humidity at Puerto de Orotava and Madeira from November 1, 1883, to May 1, 1884.*

	PUERTO DE OROTAVA.			FUNCHAL.	
	Percentage Saturation.	Aqueous Tension.		Percentage Saturation.	Aqueous Tension.
	%	mm.		%	mm.
November ...	67·3	11·2	November ...		
December ...	63·2	9·5	December ...	72	10·5
January ...	61·5	9·3	January ...	70	9·7
February ...	68·6	9·1	February ...	73	9·7
March ...	66·9	9·3	March ...	73	10·3
April ...	62·1	9·9	April ...	70	10·9
Nov.—April ...	64·9	9·7	Nov.—April ...	72	10·3

* Observations by Dr. Hjalmar Öhrvall, of Upsala.

APPENDIX III.

Number of vessels which entered ports in the Canary Islands during 1882.

THESE RESUMÉS ARE FROM STATISTICS SPECIALLY PREPARED FOR US FROM THE REGISTER AT THE OFFICIAL OFFICES.

STEAMERS.

	Santa Cruz de Tenerife.	Las Palmas.	Puerto de Orotava.
British	176	136	15
French	120	38	...
Spanish	67	60	...
German	21	...	...
American	4	...	...
Portuguese	2	...	...
Italian	1	...	...
Argentine	1	...	...
Prussian	...	1	...

SAILING VESSELS.

	Tenerife.		Las Palmas.	Santa Cruz de la Palma.*	San Sebastian de Gomera.
	Santa Cruz.	Puerto de Orotava			
British	19	2	12	45	...
French	23	...	...	20	...
Spanish	51	323	953†	273	140
German	9	...	2	14	...
American	17	...	5	15	...
Portuguese	6	...	3	...	...
Italian	3	3	1	...	...
Argentine	...	...	...	...	...
Russian	1	...	...	...	...
Norwegian	4	...	4	...	...
Danish	1	...	1	...	...
Austrian	2	...	...	...	...

* Some of these are steamers, but the returns given us do not say how many.
† 799 of these were coasting schooners, and 100 fishing schooners owned by Gran Canarians.

Gross tonnage of vessels entering the ports in 1882.

Santa Cruz de Tenerife ...	...	...	...	627,750
Las Palmas	...	...	...	508,074
Puerto de Orotava (Tenerife) ...	...	...	...	29,599
San Sebastian de Gomera	...	...	...	6,088

Santa Cruz de Tenerife.—Vessels entering the port.

			Steamers.	Sailing Vessels.	Coasters.	Total.
1880 ...	...	...	335	127	905	1,367
1881 ...	...	...	349	131	935	1,415
1882 ...	...	...	392	136	961	1,489
1883 ...	...	...	448	128	908	1,484

APPENDIX IV.

Journals of Tenerife.

Name.	Politics.	When issued.	Price monthly.
El Memorandum ..	Republican	6 times per month	5 Reales = 1s.
La Opinion ...	Monarchical	,, ,,	4 ,, = 10d.
La Democracia ...	Republican	,, ,,	4 ,, = 10d.
Las Noticias	Monarchical	,, ,,	4 ,, = 10d.
Las Novedades ...	Republican	,, ,,	4 ,, = 10d.
El Diario de Avisos...	Daily news	Daily issue	4 ,, = 10d.
La Caridad	Spiritualist	4 times per month	2½ ,, = 6d.
La Salud	Medical	Twice per month	5 ,, = 1s.
La Iniciation ...	Local interests	6 times per month	4 ,, = 10d.

Journals of Gran Canaria.

Name.	Politics.	When issued.	Price monthly.
La Correspondencia de Canarias	Liberal	Every 5 days	5 Reales = 1s.
La Localidad	Conservative	,, ,,	4 ,, = 10d.
El Pueblo	Republican	,, ,,	4 ,, = 10d.
Revista de Las Palmas ...	Clerical	Weekly	4 ,, = 10d.
El Cronista	Conservative	Every 5 days	5 ,, = 1s.
El Siglo XIX.	Liberal	Twice a week	5 ,, = 1s.
El Liberal	Liberal	,, ,,	5 ,, = 1s.
El Museo Canario	Scientific	Fortnightly	8 ,, = 1s. 8d.
El Comercio	Commercial	,,	3 ,, = 7½d.
Boletin Eclesiastico	Clerical official gazette from the Bishop.		

APPENDIX V.

RECIPES.

TORTILLA DE JAMON (VOL. I., PAGE 288).

Chop up a little ham, and slice or chop some potatoes into small pieces, frying them until sufficiently cooked. Then pour in either eggs plainly prepared, as for an omelet or batter, and allow the whole to set. Take out and serve on a hot dish without rolling.

PUCHERO AND SOPA DE ARROZ (VOL. I., PAGE 186).

Half fill a large saucepan with cold water, and into it throw three or four large onions and a fowl, and let the whole boil. Then take another saucepan of cold water, into which throw some rice, and let it boil for a little. Next add to the fowl and onions about a dessert-spoonful of sweet ground capsicums (*pimiénto dulce*), a little whole pepper, a little garlic, and some tomatos. Pour most of the liquor from this after it has boiled for a little into the saucepan containing the rice, which now allow to burst fully. Add more water to the fowl, and also put peeled potatoes and large pieces of calabash, and if liked apples, pears, and cabbage, in with the fowl. The soup when served is thick and red in colour, owing to the pimientos and tomatos. The fowl and vegetables form the puchero. Sometimes a piece of meat, or pork, or fish is used instead of a fowl, or if there be none of these things, the vegetables alone are boiled together and called *puchero blanco*.

MILK TOAST (a Madeira recipe).

Cut a thick piece of bread, and toast it quickly, cutting off the crust. Butter it and put in a soup plate, pouring over it cold milk, after which place it in the oven for fifteen minutes.

AGUA SEDATIVA.

Dissolve in a pint of water ½ oz. of sea-salt; then filter. Add 1 oz. of ammonia and a little over ¼ oz. of spirits of camphor. Shake before using.

> APPLICATION : *Headache and sore throat*—bandages dipped in the above placed round the part affected. *Fever*—bandages round the wrist. *Indigestion*—rub in over the stomach. *Colds*—rub into back and chest. *Rheumatism*—rub into part affected.

APPENDIX VI.

MALAGUEÑA DEL "PAIS."

Allegretto moderato.

PIANO.

[See Vol. I., page 246.

This form of the Malagueña, which is peculiar to the Canary Islands, was kindly procured for me by Mr. Belchervaise from the Bandmaster of Santa Cruz de Tenerife.

APPENDIX VII.

(VOL. II., PAGES 53, 55, 61 ; 216, 221.)

ANALYSES OF THE MINERAL WATERS OF AGAETE AND FIRGAS, GRAN CANARIA.

I have examined in collaboration with Professor J. Alfred Wanklyn, M.R.C.S., two waters brought by Mrs. Stone from the Canary Islands.

I. AGAETE.

This water issues from the spring hot, and surcharged with carbonic acid gas. The sample had been imperfectly corked, and most of the free carbonic acid gas had accordingly escaped. The carbonic acid gas was therefore not determined. The quantity of water was not sufficient for an exhaustive analysis. The following appears to be its composition :—

	Grains per gallon.
Silica	8·0
Iron (ferrous) carbonate	10·0
Lime (calcium) carbonate	3·0
Magnesium carbonate	33·5
Sodium sulphate	2·5
Sodium chloride	4·5

The taste is strongly saline, and is not agreeable. It would be more palatable in its natural aerated condition.

II. FIRGAS.

The analysis of this water yields the following results :—

	Grains per gallon.
Lime (calcium) carbonate	12·6
Magnesium carbonate	11·7
Sodium carbonate...	1·5
Sodium sulphate	1·2
Sodium chloride	5·0

The water is highly carbonated, and would possess a pleasant and brisk effervescence when bottled at the spring. The sample submitted contained 110·1 grains per gallon of free and loosely combined carbonic acid.

Examined as to its organic purity by the ammonia process, this water yields—

Parts per million.

Free ammonia	0·28
Albuminoid ammonia	0·02

This indicates extreme purity.

Its taste is highly saline, which is perhaps remarkable, considering the comparatively small quantity of mineral salts that it contains. This special feature is probably due to the *proportion* which the magnesium salts bear to the alkaline salts. The following table will indicate this comparison :—

	Firgas.	Vichy.	Ems.	Apollinaris.
Magnesium carbonate	11·7	11·0	7·0	25·0
Alkaline carbonates and sulphates	2·7	242·0	87·0	87·0

The water is rather of the Apollinaris character, but probably less lowering to the system.

As a table water it is one of the most unique and valuable in existence.

PELHAM R. OGLE, M.A., F.C.S.

LONDON, *September* 21st, 1887.

APPENDIX VIII.

The following letter appeared in the *Times* of January 4th,. 1884:—

"THE GUANCHES, CANARY ISLANDS.

"To the Editor of the 'Times.'

"Sir,—During the last few months I have been travelling through these islands, and have been delighted by the magnificent scenery, which has made nearly each day a surprise and a gratification. Enjoying a healthier, drier, and more bracing climate than Madeira, they require only to be known to be much resorted to by the English. As an instance that they are virtually undiscovered by our nation, I may mention the fact of the head priest on the exquisite island of Hierro telling me that I was the first Englishman who had been there in modern times. Certainly Tenerife has its yearly handful of tourists to the world-famed Peak, Palma its annual individuals who visit the Caldera, and the town of Las Palmas now and then receives casual and passing strangers bound for far-distant lands, but, with these trifling exceptions, no English visit the Fortunate Islands. In the near future it is very probable, for several reasons, that this charming archipelago will be as much resorted to as it is now singularly neglected. But my object in writing to you is not to attempt lauding what nature has so lavishly endowed, but to ask you, for the sake of the present and future generations, to raise your far-reaching voice in the endeavour to stay a spoliation which, if continued, will be for ever regretted. The gentle and noble Guanches—that extinct race which formerly inhabited these islands—have left behind them several records of their existence. Two are particularly worthy of note: the cemetery at Agaete and that on the Isleta in Gran Canaria. These have the common features of the graves, being upon the roughest of volcanic ground, and each grave covered by a carefully constructed pile of loose lava stones. That at Agaete, from being in a part of the island at present approached by the worst of bad mule-tracks, has escaped the hand of the spoiler. But the Guanche burial-ground on the Isleta, being only three miles from the town of Las Palmas, has been terribly mutilated. There is a great demand for Guanche skulls, and consequently nearly every pile of stones here has been dilapidated, and the contents of the grave stolen. The last visit I paid to this interesting spot was a few days ago, when I found two urchins squatting by a half-ruined pile amusing themselves by grinding up the whitened and powdery femurs of a gigantic Guanche. A few more years will suffice to level the remaining piles, to dissipate the bones, and to wipe this record of a bygone race from the face of the earth. When the carriage road to Agaete is completed, as it will be in a few months, we cannot hope that the other cemetery will escape. Now why cannot the Spanish Government resolutely forbid this wilful destruction of monuments which really belong to no race or nation ? Half-measures will not do. A firm hand, stringent precautions, and carefully enacted penalties are the only measures to meet the urgent needs of the case. A word from King Alfonso would effect much out here. He is young, generous, and his education will enable him to appreciate the importance of the subject. He is deeply beloved, and his wishes would almost be as good as laws. There is unfortunately no international Sir John Lubbock, but King Alfonso can in this instance make a name which may perhaps be thought more of by posterity than those of many of his warrior predecessors. I would also, Sir, speak of the magnificent painted Guanche cave at Galdar, and other interesting monuments scattered over these islands, but I should only have to relate the same sad tale and take up more of your space.

"Yours obediently,

"J. HARRIS STONE.

"LAS PALMAS, GRAN CANARIA,
"*December* 23*rd*."

INDEX.

PLANTS—continued:—

Juniperus Phœnicea, i. 227.
Malcomia litorea, ii. 309, 352.
Maruta cotula, i. 249.
Micromeria lasiophylla, i. 218.
Mirabilis salappa, i. 329.
Nicotiana glauca, ii. 358, 361, 396
Ononis variegata, ii. 208.
Oreodom regia, i. 73.
Papaver hybridum, ii. 367.
Phytolacca decandra, i. 228.
Pinus Canariensis, i. 73.
Plocama pendula, ii. 178—181.
Polypodium vulgare, ii. 86.
Portulaca oleracea, i. 184.
Ranunculus spicatus, ii. 291.
Reseda lutea, ii. 367.
Reseda scoparia, i. 183.
Rhytispernum arvense, ii. 309.
Ricinus communis, i. 183.
Romulex bulbocodium, ii. 290.
Rumex lunarin, i. 204.
Ruta pinocala, i. 315.
Salix Canariensis, i. 329.
Salvia Bronsonetti, ii. 281.
Satureia montana, i. 232.
Schozzogine argentea, i. 225.
Selaginella denticulata, i. 274.
Sida rhombifolia, i. 255; ii. 50.
Silybum marianum, ii. 281.
Sonchus leptocephalus, i. 212.
Spergularia media, i. 435; ii. 281.
Teline congesta, ii. 72.
Vicia sativa, ii. 367.
Vinca major, ii. 224.
Plaza de Santiago, i. 240.
Pliny, i. 1.
Population, i. 368.
Postigo, i. 23, 402.
Potatoes, i. 209, 233, 235, 262; ii. 77, 91, 247.
Pottery, ii. 158.
Prickly pears, i. 30, 35, 102, 314.
Princes, young, of Wales, i. 380, 411; ii. 417.
Puchero, i. 39, 119, 170, 186.
Puerto Cabras, ii. 347, 353—360.

Printed by Hazell, Watson, & Viney, Ld., London and Aylesbury.

MILLER & CO.

(Late THOMAS MILLER & SONS),

𝕭ankers and 𝕲eneral 𝕸erchants,

LAS PALMAS,

GRAND CANARY.

The Oldest Established English House in the Island.

Telegraphic Address—" MILLER, LASPALMAS."

FOREIGN MONEY CHANGED.

BANK-NOTES, BILLS, AND CHEQUES CASHED.

BILLS GRANTED ON LONDON, PARIS, MADRID, ETC.

AGENTS FOR THE FOLLOWING ENGLISH AND FOREIGN BANKS :—

LONDON AND WESTMINSTER BANK.
NATIONAL BANK OF SCOTLAND, Ld.
UNION BANK OF SPAIN AND ENGLAND, Ld.
LONDON AND RIVER PLATE BANK, Ld.
AMERICAN EXCHANGE IN EUROPE.

London Agents, SWANSTON & CO., Laurence Pountney Hill, E.C., who can furnish full particulars as to the Canaries.

STEAM COAL DEPÔT,
Harbour and Port of Refuge,
LAS PALMAS, GRAND CANARY.

FOR STEAMERS TRADING WITH AFRICA, AUSTRALIA, SOUTH AMERICA, ETC.

MILLER & CO,
(LATE THOMAS MILLER & SONS).

Telegraphic Address: "MILLER, LASPALMAS."

Steamship Agents, Bankers, and Merchants.

FIRST-CLASS WELSH STEAM COALS
Always in Stock, for supply with immediate despatch.

Coaling Agents in London—
HULL, BLYTH & CO., 1, FENCHURCH AVENUE, E.C.

SUBMARINE TELEGRAPHIC AGENCY.

CANARY TOBACCO AND CIGARS.
MILLER & CO.
(LATE THOMAS MILLER & SONS),

Manufacturers of Cigars,

BRAND "LA INDUSTRIA,"

LAS PALMAS, GRAND CANARY.

Telegraphic Address: "MILLER, LASPALMAS."

LARGE ASSORTMENT. EXTENSIVE STOCK.
MODERATE PRICES.

These Cigars can be delivered, Duty Paid, in any part of the United Kingdom.

NORWAY IN JUNE.

By OLIVIA M. STONE.

Crown 8vo, Cloth, Gold and Black. Second Edition. Price 7s. 6d.

*** *With Illustrations (from Photographs taken during the tour), accompanied by a Sketch-Map, a Table of Expenses, and a List of Articles indispensable to the Traveller in Norway.*

The "SPECTATOR" says:

"The intending tourist in Norway will find it most useful. It will guide without dictating to him, and suggest without bothering him. The minutest instructions as to the means, routes, and expenses of travelling, outfit, time, and regulations are set down in plain and intelligible form. To the stay-at-home traveller its interest is equally great; for it gives him a thorough knowledge of a country which has generally been treated either too scientifically for the general reader's taste, or too much in the summer-playground style. The concluding chapters, in which the author treats of the institutions of the country, of education, agriculture, peasant-proprietorship, and especially of the advantages offered by Norway to immigrants from Great Britain, are of serious and vivid interest. A very interesting chapter is devoted to the Viking ship."

MARCUS WARD & CO., Ld.,
LONDON, BELFAST, AND NEW YORK.